D0266635

# THE PENGUIN GIANT TRIVIA MASTERMIND QUIZ BOOK

# THE PENGUIN GIANT TRIVIA MASTERMIND QUIZ BOOK

TREASURE PRESS

First published in Great Britain by Penguin Books Ltd in six separate volumes under the series title: *Utterly Trivial Knowledge,* and individually entitled *The Arts and Entertainment Game, The Pure Trivia Game, The Sports Game, The Music Game, The Politics Game,* and *The Business Game*

First published in Great Britain in 1986 by Penguin Books Ltd as a one-volume edition under the title *Total Trivia*

This one-volume edition published in 1987 by
Treasure Press, Michelin House, 81 Fulham Road, London SW3 6RB

Reprinted 1988



ISBN 1 85051 247 7

Printed in Austria

# Contents

# Part 1
# The Arts and Entertainment Quiz

Jonathan Philips

# Introduction to The Arts and Entertainment Quiz

General knowledge has long been one of the staples of twentieth-century entertainment and, combined with a competitive quiz element, has always proved irresistible. The galaxy of game-shows on television which require at least the basic ability to answer a question correctly, the 'open sesame' to a hoard of cash and more or less desirable consumer durables, is telling witness to this. On a more genteel level, the success of *University Challenge*, *Twenty Questions* and *Mastermind* shows that we are fascinated not only by the excitement of people returning home the richer for music-centres and Sheraton-dining-suites-for-twelve, but also by one person proving 'cleverer' than another. The glory of being right is enough, equally for the contestant and the millions watching or listening, and a glowing sensation burns in the breast of all. By answering correctly the questions in this section, the same glow can be yours, again and again. Should I, by some almost inconceivable failure in my system of double cross-referencing, have got the answer wrong, you can glow with indignation, at no extra charge. Should you not know the answer, you can look it up, ask yourself the question in a week and get it right.

In this section are 1,368 questions, in 228 separate quizzes. Each quiz is divided into six categories:

1. **Films**
2. **Stage**
3. **Literature**
4. **Fine Arts**
5. **Decorative Arts, Architecture, Fashion**
6. **Broadcasting**

The six categories represented here inevitably overlap. Many **Stage** questions could equally well appear under **Literature**, and the distinctions between categories 4 and 5 have always been fluid.

The deeply trivial aspect of this section and, indeed, of all the sections in this book, is that for the purpose of self-congratulation all subjects are of equal value. It is just as satisfying to identify Sonja Henie as it is to name the discoverers of DNA. Indeed, I would not be surprised if some people would not actually prefer to know the height of Little Richard rather than that of Mount Everest, or the circumference of Chubby Checker rather than that of the Earth.

Though the concept of a quiz book *is* trivial, it is difficult and arguably boring to sustain this triviality in questions on subjects which are basically far from lightweight and which lend themselves less readily to flippancy than others. Some of the questions may therefore seem too serious. Essentially, however, it must be admitted that any question which can be answered in one word or sentence tends to be trivial, though it may also be obscure. Category 6, **Broadcasting**, is obviously the most suitable for this type of treatment. As it is concerned closely with people or 'personalities' rather than ideas, things or even, surprisingly, visual stimulation, and as it is available to a huge audience at the same time, it creates instant shared points of reference for millions. Overnight, programmes give rise to catchphrases and clichés which may be given further exposure by other programmes – parodies in comedy shows, for example. Broadcasting values are far from immutable and the public is fickle, today's *succes fou* becoming tomorow's joke and, if lucky, the day after tomorrow's affectionate memory; but half-submerged recollections are ideal targets for unintellectual quizzes.

As a tip to answering the questions, it might be helpful to know that here they are often set like crossword-puzzle clues, the question itself containing a pointer to the answer; for example, a seemingly innocent phrase, if put within inverted commas, might give you the title of a television programme. Such childish ruses have pleased me no end and will, I hope, give you a limited degree of amusement.

Jonathan Philips

# 1

1. Who was the Million-dollar Mermaid?
2. Which circus musical has Michael Crawford made his own?
3. What was the origin of Samuel Langhorne Clemens's pen-name, Mark Twain?
4. Who painted 'The Morning Walk'?
5. What is a kilim?
6. Who was the Galloping Gourmet?

# 77

1. Who played the role of Isadora on film in 1968?
2. Which farce used a make of aircraft as its title?
3. Which famous gardener wrote *The Edwardians*?
4. Which painter's name means Hulking Tom?
5. Where would you find tatami?
6. Who played Elaine Stritch's butler?

# 153

1. *Nanook of the North* depicts the life of which race?
2. Which ballet by Stravinsky is based on music by Tchaikovsky?
3. What is the name of Ngaio Marsh's detective?
4. Who painted the death of Marat in his bath?
5. What is a tazza?
6. Who played Mr and Mrs Huggett in *Meet the Huggetts*?

# 1

1. Esther Williams.
2. *Barnum*.
3. It was a river-boat cry for deep water.
4. Thomas Gainsborough.
5. A Middle-Eastern woven rug.
6. Graham Kerr.

# 77

1. Vanessa Redgrave.
2. *Boeing-Boeing*.
3. Vita Sackville-West.
4. Masaccio's.
5. On the floor of a Japanese house (it is straw matting).
6. Donald Sinden.

# 153

1. The Eskimo.
2. *The Fairy's Kiss*.
3. Inspector Alleyn.
4. Jacques-Louis David.
5. A stemmed bowl or cup.
6. Jack Warner and Kathleen Harrison.

## 2

1. Who was the Oomph Girl?
2. Where did *Lock Up Your Daughters* run to packed houses?
3. Who was the great Cham of literature?
4. Which artist has a whole museum dedicated to his work in Haarlem?
5. Who designed the colonnade of St Peter's, Rome?
6. What claimed to make you a little lovelier each day?

## 78

1. What was Jacques Tati's job in *Jour de fête*?
2. In which opera does a man suddenly grow breasts?
3. Which famous character was created by Edgar Rice Burroughs?
4. Which famous art collection was started by the Marquess of Hertford?
5. Who was the founder of the Art Nouveau School of Nancy?
6. Who, having enjoyed *The Good Life*, went *Solo*?

## 154

1. Who played Violette Szabo in *Carve Her Name with Pride*?
2. Who was the leading light of the Group Theatre in London between the wars?
3. Which English novelist is less well known as the Hon. Mrs Peter Rodd?
4. Who championed Constable in Paris?
5. What were Vile and Cobb?
6. Who is the presenter of *Weekend World*?

## 2

1. Ann Sheridan.
2. The Mermaid Theatre.
3. Samuel Johnson.
4. Frans Hals.
5. Gianlorenzo Bernini.
6. Fabulous pink Camay (soap).

## 78

1. Delivering letters: he was a postman.
2. *Les Mamelles de Tirésias*, by Francis Poulenc.
3. Tarzan.
4. The Wallace Collection.
5. Émile Gallé.
6. Felicity Kendal.

## 154

1. Virginia McKenna.
2. Rupert Doone.
3. Nancy Mitford.
4. Eugène Delacroix.
5. Eighteenth-century cabinet-makers.
6. Brian Walden.

# 3

1. Who played the title role in *The Outlaw Josey Wales*?
2. The hero of whose light operetta is the Red Shadow?
3. Which French writer was exiled to the Channel Islands?
4. In painting, what is represented on St Veronica's handkerchief?
5. Which public figure popularized the Gannex raincoat?
6. Which sinister castle was under Bernard Hepton's authority?

# 79

1. In which film did Basil Rathbone make his first appearance as Sherlock Holmes?
2. Which Diaghilev ballet starred the Dolly Sisters?
3. Who wrote a volume of poems entitled *Ariel*?
4. Which eighteenth-century French politician gave his name to a black cut-out or painting?
5. Which Scottish cabinet-maker's greatest success was in Philadelphia?
6. Who was Batman's side-kick?

# 155

1. Which film by Lindsay Anderson concerns unrest at a boys' public school?
2. Who were the five husbands of music-hall star Denise Orme's four daughters?
3. Who was the Muse of lyric poetry?
4. What was Basil Hallward's most famous picture?
5. What is slip?
6. Whose secretary was Della Street?

## 3

1. Clint Eastwood.
2. Sigmund Romberg's.
3. Victor Hugo.
4. The face of Christ.
5. Harold Wilson.
6. Colditz.

## 79

1. *The Hound of the Baskervilles* (1939).
2. *Le Dieu bleu.*
3. Sylvia Plath.
4. Étienne de Silhouette.
5. Duncan Phyfe's.
6. Robin.

## 155

1. *If . . .*
2. Lord Cadogan (Primrose), the Duke of Bedford (Lydia), Lord Ebury (Denise), and Loel Guinness and Prince Aly Khan (Joan).
3. Euterpe.
4. *The Picture of Dorian Gray.*
5. A diluted coating of clay.
6. Perry Mason's.

## 4

1. Who played the heroine in the 1943 version of *Jane Eyre*?
2. Who created the role of Countess Rosmarin Ostenburg in Christopher Fry's *The Dark Is Light Enough*?
3. Who wrote *Le Grand Meaulnes*?
4. Who painted 'Bonjour, Monsieur Courbet'?
5. Who designed the Piccadilly Hotel?
6. Which periodical had Carmen Silvera on its staff?

## 80

1. What age was Sidney Greenstreet when he made his first film?
2. Who wrote the play *Le Mariage de Figaro*?
3. Who wrote *The Republic*?
4. Who were the two leading Symbolist painters in France?
5. What is the most famous building designed by Buschetto?
6. Which family was composed of Ben, Bebe, Barbara and Richard?

## 156

1. Which film is credited with killing the career of silent star John Gilbert because of the timbre of his voice?
2. Who created the role of Judith Bliss in *Hay Fever*?
3. Who invented the character of Maudie Littlehampton?
4. Who was the painter sister of Virginia Woolf?
5. What shape is an oeil-de-bœuf window?
6. Who played Endora in *Bewitched*?

# 4

1. Joan Fontaine.
2. Dame Edith Evans.
3. Alain-Fournier.
4. Gustave Courbet.
5. Richard Norman Shaw.
6. *Compact*.

# 80

1. Sixty-one.
2. Pierre-Augustin de Beaumarchais.
3. Plato.
4. Gustave Moreau and Odilon Redon.
5. The Leaning Tower of Pisa.
6. The Lyon family, in *Life with the Lyons*.

# 156

1. *His Glorious Night*.
2. Dame Marie Tempest.
3. Osbert Lancaster.
4. Vanessa Bell.
5. Round or oval.
6. Agnes Moorehead.

## 5

1. Who was the star of *Pépé le Moko* (1936)?
2. At the première of which musical work did some of the performers sit behind a screen shouting through megaphones?
3. Which fairy-tale character let her hair down?
4. Which French poet and writer invented the term 'Surrealism'?
5. Who designed St Pancras Station?
6. Which were the too-good-to-hurry mints?

## 81

1. Who was the star of *Jailhouse Rock*?
2. Who played the headmaster in the original production of *40 Years On*?
3. Who wrote *J'Accuse*?
4. Who was famous for painting people in industrial surroundings in northern England?
5. What do many tesserae make?
6. Which cowboy hero was played by Hugh O'Brien?

## 157

1. Of which two actresses was King Kong enamoured?
2. In which operetta by Gilbert and Sullivan does the judge marry the plaintiff?
3. Whose nickname was The Beast?
4. In which city is Leonardo's 'Last Supper' to be found?
5. Who created Strawberry Hill?
6. Which man of the law was played by Brian Reece?

## 5

1. Jean Gabin.
2. *Façade*, by William Walton and Edith Sitwell.
3. Rapunzel.
4. Guillaume Apollinaire.
5. Sir George Gilbert Scott.
6. Murraymints.

## 81

1. Elvis Presley.
2. Sir John Gielgud.
3. Émile Zola.
4. L. S. Lowry.
5. A mosaic.
6. Wyatt Earp.

## 157

1. Fay Wray and Jessica Lange.
2. *Trial by Jury*.
3. Aleister Crowley's.
4. Milan.
5. Horace Walpole.
6. P.C. 49.

# 6

1. Which famous Hollywood director and star made a home movie with Edwina and Louis Mountbatten?
2. The staging of which ballet requires live birds?
3. Who wrote *South Riding*?
4. Who painted a series of pictures of water-lilies at his home at Giverny?
5. What did Johann Friedrich Böttger first produce in Europe in the eighteenth century?
6. Who got his *Marriage Lines* and enjoyed *The Good Life*?

# 82

1. Of which film was 'Colonel Bogey' the theme tune?
2. Which opera concerns a misunderstanding over smoking?
3. Who wrote a series of comic novels about life in the village of Tilling?
4. Which painter became notorious for faking the work of Samuel Palmer?
5. Which style was described by Aldous Huxley as 'a mixture of greenhouse and hospital ward furnished in the style of a dentist's operating chamber'?
6. Who starred in the title role of the *Topper* series?

# 158

1. Who directed the 1931 version of *M*?
2. Who first played the title role in Shaw's *St Joan*?
3. Who wrote *My Dog Tulip*?
4. Which painter was the scenic director at Covent Garden under Garrick and Sheridan?
5. The entrances to what in Paris were designed by the architect Hector Guimard?
6. In which year was the first television broadcast made from Alexandra Palace: 1928, 1932, 1936 or 1942?

# 6

1. Charles Chaplin.
2. *Les Deux Pigeons*.
3. Winifred Holtby.
4. Claude Monet.
5. Hard-paste porcelain.
6. Richard Briers.

# 82

1. *The Bridge on the River Kwai*.
2. *Il Segreto di Susanna*, by Ermanno Wolf-Ferrari.
3. E. F. Benson.
4. Tom Keating.
5. Art Deco.
6. Leo G. Carroll.

# 158

1. Fritz Lang.
2. Sybil Thorndike.
3. J. R. Ackerley.
4. Philippe de Loutherbourg.
5. The Art Nouveau metro stations.
6. 1936.

## 7

1. What was *The One That Got Away* (1957)?
2. Who was the first music-hall star to be knighted?
3. What was the name of Fleur Forsyte's house?
4. About which of his purchases did American art-collector Henry Huntingdon complain that it wasn't blue enough?
5. Who created the New Look?
6. Of which radio show was 'The Dreaded Batter-pudding Hurler of Bexhill-on-Sea' a typical example?

## 83

1. Who was the unlikely male lead in the film version of Ivor Novello's *King's Rhapsody*?
2. What word-less spectacle was produced by Max Reinhardt at the Great Hall, Olympia, in 1911, with music by Engelbert Humperdinck?
3. Who swept fair Ellen off her feet (and on to his horse)?
4. Of which group of people did J. B. Priestley write, 'They stand for violence and neurotic unreason. They are truly decadent'?
5. What did the Aztecs describe as 'the excrement of the Gods'?
6. What sort of birds were Polly James and Nerys Hughes?

## 159

1. Which singing star successfully switched to a dramatic role in *The Country Girl*?
2. Who created both plays and buildings?
3. Who wrote *Nostromo*?
4. Who illustrated the 1931 edition of Balzac's *Le Chef-d'œuvre inconnu*?
5. Who designed Horseguards Parade?
6. Who was *My Hero*?

# 7

1. An escaped German prisoner-of-war.
2. Harry Lauder.
3. Robin Hill.
4. Gainsborough's 'Blue Boy'.
5. Christian Dior.
6. *The Goon Show*.

# 83

1. Errol Flynn.
2. *The Miracle*.
3. Lochinvar.
4. The Surrealists.
5. Gold.
6. Liver Birds.

# 159

1. Bing Crosby.
2. Sir John Vanbrugh.
3. Joseph Conrad.
4. Pablo Picasso.
5. William Kent.
6. Robert Cummings.

# 8

1. Who was the It Girl?
2. What were the names of King Lear's three daughters?
3. Which poet immortalized the character of Joan Hunter Dunn?
4. Who painted the portrait of the Duke of Urbino later used to advertise lager?
5. What was a sudatorium?
6. Of which primate group was Micky Dolenz a member?

# 84

1. Name four actresses who have portrayed Catherine the Great of Russia in films.
2. Who first played the role of Sari in *Bitter Sweet* on Broadway?
3. Who said he 'quickly grew up after hearing someone suggest Edith Sitwell was a bad poet'?
4. Which painter was the son of Suzanne Valadon?
5. Who designed the Franconian church of Vierzehnheiligen?
6. What helped you keep that schoolgirl complexion?

# 160

1. Who played Little Lord Fauntleroy in the 1921 version of the film?
2. What was Lady Bracknell's favourite sandwich filling?
3. Who wrote *The Secret Garden*?
4. Who has written a sequence of novels which takes its title from a painting by Poussin?
5. Who designed the 'Wassily' chair?
6. Which inspector was played by Rupert Davies?

# 8

1. Clara Bow.
2. Cordelia, Goneril and Regan.
3. John Betjeman.
4. Piero della Francesca.
5. The sweating room in a Roman bath.
6. The Monkees.

# 84

1. Elisabeth Bergner, Tallulah Bankhead, Marlene Dietrich, Jeanne Moreau and Bette Davis.
2. Evelyn Laye.
3. Thom Gunn.
4. Maurice Utrillo.
5. Johann Balthasar Neumann.
6. Palmolive soap.

# 160

1. Mary Pickford.
2. Cucumber.
3. Frances Hodgson Burnett.
4. Anthony Powell (*A Dance to the Music of Time*).
5. Marcel Breuer.
6. Maigret.

## 9

1. Which singing film-star was reputed to be descended from the Incas?
2. Who was the first British singer to top the American Hit Parade?
3. Who wrote *One Hundred and One Dalmatians*?
4. What was the Ashcan School?
5. Who designed the Aviary at Regent's Park Zoo?
6. Who played the title role in the series *The Scarlet Pimpernel*?

## 85

1. Who directed *On the Waterfront*?
2. Who wrote *The Beaux' Stratagem*?
3. Who wrote *Peyton Place*?
4. Which sculptor drew a series of underground scenes during the Second World War?
5. Who designed the staircase at 12, rue de Turin, Brussels?
6. Who played the title role in *Adam Adamant*?

## 161

1. In which film is there a credit for an 'anxious tunnel person'?
2. Who wrote *A Flea in Her Ear*?
3. Who wrote 'Sohrab and Rustum'?
4. Who was the first English portrait-painter to seek his fortune in India?
5. Who designed the lions in Trafalgar Square?
6. Who had the greenest fingers on television?

# 9

1. Yma Sumac.
2. Vera Lynn.
3. Dodie Smith.
4. A group of early-twentieth-century American 'realist' painters.
5. Lord Snowdon.
6. Marius Goring.

# 85

1. Elia Kazan.
2. George Farquhar.
3. Grace Metalious.
4. Henry Moore.
5. Victor Horta.
6. Gerald Harper.

# 161

1. *Jaws 3.*
2. Georges Feydeau.
3. Matthew Arnold.
4. Tilly Kettle.
5. Sir Edwin Landseer.
6. Percy Thrower.

## 10

1. Who played the 1936 Sweeney Todd?
2. Name three operas by Verdi inspired by Shakespeare.
3. Who is said to be the model for Mrs Stitch in Evelyn Waugh's *Scoop*?
4. What are the *Très Riches Heures* of the Duc de Berry?
5. Who designed Lorenzo de Medici's tomb?
6. Who wrote and presented *The Ascent of Man*?

## 86

1. The cast of which film included Benny Hill, Rossano Brazzi and Noël Coward?
2. Which famous band-leader was married to a Sarawaki princess?
3. Who wrote *Lorna Doone*?
4. Which artist was commissioned by Madame du Barry to paint the 'Progress of Love'?
5. What is the name of the small compartmentalized boxes used by the Japanese instead of pockets?
6. Which of Charlie's Angels was married to the Bionic Man?

## 162

1. Who was Luis Buñuel's collaborator in *Un Chien andalou*?
2. Who wrote the plays *Antigone* and *Electra*?
3. Who wrote about the land of Beulah?
4. Who painted 'The Avenue at Middelharnis'?
5. Where is Cleopatra's Needle?
6. On which show would you regularly have seen Vivian Vance and William Frawley?

## 10

1. Tod Slaughter.
2. *Otello*, *Macbeth* and *Falstaff*.
3. Lady Diana Cooper.
4. An illuminated Book of Hours showing the Labours of the Months.
5. Michelangelo.
6. Dr J. Bronowski.

## 86

1. *The Italian Job*.
2. Harry Roy.
3. R. D. Blackmore.
4. Jean-Honoré Fragonard.
5. Inro.
6. Farrah Fawcett-Majors.

## 162

1. Salvador Dali.
2. Sophocles.
3. John Bunyan, in *The Pilgrim's Progress*.
4. Meindert Hobbema.
5. On the Thames Embankment.
6. *I Love Lucy*.

# 11

1. Which 1968 film charted the progress of the SS *Batavia Queen* in 1883?
2. Which leading British stage personality was responsible for the screenplay of the first Tarzan film?
3. By what name was author Cyril McNeile better known?
4. Which famous artist did wall-paintings for the Logge of the Vatican?
5. Who designed the stained glass for the baptistery of Coventry Cathedral?
6. Who did a trick with a shop window during the introduction to his show each week?

# 87

1. Who was the 'Boop-de-doop' girl?
2. To star with which famous husband-and-wife team did Noël Coward write *Design for Living*?
3. Which American poet was indicted as a Fascist and spent several years in a lunatic asylum?
4. Which painter is said to have been able to draw a perfect circle free-hand?
5. Who is credited with the invention of the mobile as an art form?
6. Who was the 'I' in *Hugh and I*?

# 163

1. Which film was described by Alexander Walker as 'Camille with bullshit'?
2. Who wrote the play *Hernani*?
3. How does Captain Hook die?
4. Which are the three primary colours?
5. In which city would you find the 'Salute' church?
6. Who played Queen Elizabeth I in the series about her life?

## 11

1. *Krakatoa, East of Java.*
2. Ivor Novello.
3. Sapper.
4. Raphael.
5. John Piper.
6. Harry Worth.

## 87

1. Helen Kane.
2. Lynn Fontanne and Alfred Lunt.
3. Ezra Pound.
4. Giotto.
5. Alexander Calder.
6. Terry Scott.

## 163

1. *Love Story.*
2. Victor Hugo.
3. He is eaten by a crocodile.
4. Red, blue and yellow.
5. Venice.
6. Glenda Jackson.

## 12

1. Which film starred Jack Benny, Buster Keaton, Joan Crawford, John Gilbert, Norma Shearer, Laurel and Hardy and Marie Dressler?
2. Who wrote *The Children's Hour*?
3. Who wrote *Sons and Lovers*?
4. Which painter gave his name to a shade of hair?
5. Which Thamesside suburb was famous for its tapestry factory?
6. Whose experiences in Ireland were portrayed by Peter Bowles?

## 88

1. Who played the Angel of Death in *Orphée*?
2. Who was the leading impresario in London in the 1920s?
3. Who created the character of Father Brown?
4. Did Lord Duveen sell Gainsborough's 'Blue Boy' for $220,000, $420,000, or $620,000?
5. From which century does the earliest extant knotted carpet date?
6. In which series did the character Benson first appear?

## 164

1. Who starred in the title role of the *Rocky* films?
2. At which ballet première was there an uproar over a scarf?
3. Who wrote the *Faerie Queene*?
4. Which American painter was married to the photographer Alfred Stieglitz?
5. In which city is the treasury known as the Green Vault?
6. Who tried to *Raise a Laugh*?

## 12

1. *Hollywood Revue of 1929*.
2. Lillian Hellman.
3. D. H. Lawrence.
4. Titian.
5. Mortlake.
6. An Irish R.M.'s.

## 88

1. Maria Casarès.
2. C. B. Cochran.
3. G. K. Chesterton.
4. $620,000.
5. The fifth century BC.
6. *Soap*.

## 164

1. Sylvester Stallone.
2. *L'Après-midi d'un faune*.
3. Edmund Spenser.
4. Georgia O'Keeffe.
5. Dresden.
6. Ted Ray.

## 13

1. Which film by Federico Fellini starred Giulietta Masina, Valentina Cortese and Sylvia Koscina?
2. Which famous actor was responsible for the words of 'Rule Britannia'?
3. Who wrote *The Loom of Youth*?
4. Where is the Hermitage Museum?
5. Which is the most famous group of dolmens in England?
6. Who was *My Dear Secretary*?

## 89

1. Who is the wife of Mel Brooks?
2. Who, historically, was the first actor/manager?
3. Who wrote *Some Tame Gazelle*?
4. Which painter is associated with Cookham?
5. In which city is there an art school designed by Charles Rennie Mackintosh?
6. Who played Reginald Perrin?

## 165

1. Who played the Elephant Man in the film?
2. *I Am a Camera* and *Cabaret* are based on the stories of which writer?
3. When was the magazine *Picture Post* founded?
4. Who first put a moustache on the 'Mona Lisa'?
5. Who said, 'A house is a machine for living'?
6. Who played George Burns's wife both on and off screen?

## 13

1. *Juliet of the Spirits*.
2. David Garrick.
3. Alec Waugh.
4. Leningrad.
5. Stonehenge.
6. Ann Sothern.

## 89

1. Anne Bancroft.
2. Thespis.
3. Barbara Pym.
4. Stanley Spencer.
5. Glasgow.
6. Leonard Rossiter.

## 165

1. John Hurt.
2. Christopher Isherwood.
3. 1938.
4. Marcel Duchamp.
5. Le Corbusier.
6. Gracie Allen.

## 14

1. Why did Max Fleischer stop making *Betty Boop* in 1935?
2. How do the performers get around in *Starlight Express*?
3. Who wrote *Homage to Catalonia*?
4. Who painted 'King Cophetua and the Beggar-maid'?
5. Who designed the Petit Trianon, Versailles?
6. Who was the resident antiques expert on *Going for a Song*?

## 90

1. Who looked for Mr Goodbar?
2. Who wrote *The Browning Version*?
3. Which seventeenth-century woman was possibly the first to earn her living as a writer?
4. Which nineteenth-century French painter was famous for depicting life at fashionable seaside resorts?
5. Who designed the palace of Caserta and its Great Cascade, outside Naples?
6. Which is the local of *Coronation Street* fame?

## 166

1. What was Baby in *Bringing Up Baby*?
2. What name is shared by the witch in *La Sylphide* and Dame Edna Everage's best friend?
3. Who wrote 'How They Brought the Good News from Ghent to Aix'?
4. Who painted 'Just what is it that makes Today's Homes so different, so appealing?'?
5. Which building did the columns of the National Gallery once grace?
6. Who was the dumb blonde of *Rowan and Martin's Laugh-in*?

# 14

1. The cartoon character was accused of immorality by the Hays Office.
2. On roller-skates.
3. George Orwell.
4. Sir Edward Burne-Jones.
5. Ange-Jacques Gabriel.
6. Arthur Negus.

# 90

1. Diane Keaton.
2. Terence Rattigan.
3. Aphra Behn.
4. Eugène Boudin.
5. Luigi Vanvitelli.
6. The Rover's Return.

# 166

1. A leopard.
2. Madge.
3. Robert Browning.
4. Richard Hamilton.
5. Carlton House.
6. Goldie Hawn.

## 15

1. Which film was based on J. B. Priestley's *Benighted*?
2. Who wrote an opera about a famous Philistine hair-cut?
3. Who invented the character of Adrian Mole?
4. Who painted 'The Awakening Conscience'?
5. For whom was the Red House built by Philip Webb?
6. Which is the colourful arts programme on Radio 4?

## 91

1. Who played the missionary Gladys Aylward in *The Inn of the Sixth Happiness*?
2. Who wrote *The Second Mrs Tanqueray*?
3. What was the *nom de plume* of J. B. Morton?
4. Which painter is known for his racing and ballet pictures?
5. What is the name for the carved toggles, usually in ivory or wood, once worn by the Japanese?
6. Who was in charge of the motor pool under Colonel Hall?

## 167

1. Which actress was carried off by Rudolph Valentino in *The Sheik*?
2. Which Ibsen play is concerned with a social disease?
3. Which headmaster ran Tom Brown's school?
4. Which French photographer captured the seamy side of Paris in the 1920s?
5. Where would you have found René Lalique's 'Spirit of the Wind'?
6. Which programme's opening cry was 'Wakey wakey'?

## 15

1. *The Old Dark House* (1932).
2. Camille Saint-Saëns (*Samson et Dalila*).
3. Sue Townsend.
4. William Holman Hunt.
5. William Morris.
6. *Kaleidoscope*.

## 91

1. Ingrid Bergman.
2. Arthur Wing Pinero.
3. Beachcomber.
4. Edgar Degas.
5. Netsuke.
6. Sergeant (Ernest) Bilko.

## 167

1. Agnes Ayres.
2. *Ghosts*.
3. Dr Thomas Arnold.
4. Brassaï.
5. On a car (it was a mascot made from glass).
6. *Billy Cotton's Band Show*.

## 16

1. What was the occupation of the leading character in *One Night of Love* (1934)?
2. Who played the piano with the Savoy Orpheans?
3. What was the name of the evil Chinaman created by Sax Rohmer?
4. Who drew 'The man who . . .' cartoons?
5. With which glass-maker would you associate 'favrile' glass?
6. Who played Rumpole of the Bailey?

## 92

1. Who was the star of *I'm No Angel*?
2. Who said, 'I must get out of these wet clothes and into a dry Martini'?
3. Who created the character of Margot Metroland?
4. Who painted 'American Gothic'?
5. Who sculpted the 'Burghers of Calais'?
6. Who played Miss Jones in *Rising Damp*?

## 168

1. Who directed *Once Upon a Time in the West*?
2. On whose play was Donizetti's opera *Maria Stuarda* based?
3. What was the name of Max Beerbohm's Oxford heroine?
4. Who is the only painter to have become a peer of the realm?
5. What is a piano nobile?
6. Who played Edward VII in the series based on his life?

## 16

1. Opera-singing.
2. Carrol Gibbons.
3. Fu Manchu.
4. H. M. Bateman.
5. Louis Tiffany.
6. Leo McKern.

## 92

1. Mae West.
2. Alexander Woollcott.
3. Evelyn Waugh.
4. Grant Wood.
5. Auguste Rodin.
6. Frances de la Tour.

## 168

1. Sergio Leone.
2. Friedrich Schiller's.
3. Zuleika Dobson.
4. Lord Leighton.
5. The principal floor of an Italian palazzo.
6. Timothy West.

## 17

1. In which film did the song 'Springtime for Hitler' appear?
2. Which French film-star played Lady Macbeth on stage opposite Sir Alec Guinness?
3. How many diamond clips did Anne of Austria give the Duke of Buckingham?
4. Who painted 'Bolton Abbey in the Olden Time'?
5. What is an arras?
6. Whose was the face never seen in the British *Candid Camera*?

## 93

1. Who were the adolescent stars of Zeffirelli's 1968 film version of *Romeo and Juliet*?
2. To which poet was actress Jill Balcon married?
3. Who wrote *How Green Was My Valley*?
4. What is the name of the female slaves much painted by Ingres?
5. From which country does Arita porcelain come?
6. What was the profession of Amos and Andy?

## 169

1. Who played the Salvation Army heroine in Gabriel Pascal's film version of *Major Barbara*?
2. Who wrote the song 'La Mer'?
3. Who wrote 'The Ugly Duckling'?
4. What is a 'Kit-Cat' portrait?
5. Which sculptor executed thirteen versions of the theme 'Bird in Space'?
6. Who was the star of *Dragnet*?

# 17

1. Mel Brooks's *The Producers*.
2. Simone Signoret.
3. Twelve.
4. Sir Edwin Landseer.
5. A tapestry.
6. Jonathan Routh's.

# 93

1. Leonard Whiting and Olivia Hussey.
2. Cecil Day Lewis.
3. Richard Llewellyn.
4. Odalisques.
5. Japan.
6. Driving taxis.

# 169

1. Wendy Hiller.
2. Charles Trenet.
3. Hans Christian Andersen.
4. A portrait measuring 36 inches by 28 inches, showing the head, shoulders and one hand.
5. Constantin Brancusi.
6. Jack Webb.

## 18

1. In *Monsieur Hulot's Holiday*, Jacques Tati awarded himself one word of dialogue. What was it?
2. Under what name was Javanese dancer Marguerite Zelle better known?
3. Who wrote *Under Milk Wood*?
4. Which painter was married to Antonio Zucchi?
5. What is a gazebo?
6. Who played the title role in the play *Mrs Palfrey at the Claremont*?

## 94

1. Who choreographed the 1935 film version of *A Midsummer Night's Dream*?
2. Who wrote the libretto for *Otello* and composed *Mefistofele*?
3. What were used as mallets in the Red Queen's croquet match?
4. Whose portrait by Sargent typifies the foreigner's idea of the 'Milord anglais'?
5. Who designed the Upper Belvedere Palace, Vienna?
6. What did Eileen Fowler enjoin us to do?

## 170

1. Who played the title role in *The Barefoot Contessa*?
2. Which musical comedy contains 'Slaughter on Tenth Avenue'?
3. Which novel starts, '"Take my camel, dear," said my Aunt Dot'?
4. Who painted 'The Death of Wolfe'?
5. Who designed Chiswick House?
6. Whose friend was Boo-boo?

# 18

1. 'Hulot.'
2. Mata Hari.
3. Dylan Thomas.
4. Angelica Kauffmann.
5. A small tower or summer-house with a view.
6. Celia Johnson.

# 94

1. Bronislawa Nijinska.
2. Arrigo Boito.
3. Flamingoes.
4. Lord Ribblesdale's.
5. Lukas von Hildebrandt.
6. Keep fit.

# 170

1. Ava Gardner.
2. *On Your Toes*.
3. *The Towers of Trebizond*, by Rose Macaulay.
4. Benjamin West.
5. Lord Burlington.
6. Yogi Bear's.

## 19

1. How many parts did Alec Guinness play in *Kind Hearts and Coronets*?
2. Which opera ends with a black page removing a handkerchief from the stage?
3. What name did Portia assume when impersonating a lawyer?
4. Who designed the Guinness toucan?
5. For which emperor is the 'Empire' style named?
6. What was the name of Mr Turnip's friend in *Whirligig*?

## 95

1. Who played the male lead in the 1953 version of *Hobson's Choice*?
2. Who wrote the play *Medea*?
3. Who called her memoirs *Unshackled*?
4. Which Jesuit priest was court painter to the Emperor Qianlong?
5. What animal stands on the entrance-gate screen to Syon House?
6. Which programme has been presented by both Peter West and Terry Wogan?

## 171

1. Who made *Flesh*?
2. Which French composer of operettas was director of the Royal Opera House, Covent Garden?
3. Which family lived at 'The Laurels', Holloway?
4. Which painter was the first President of the Royal Academy?
5. In which ancient city is the Treasury of Atreus?
6. Whose opening gambit was, 'Hello my darlings'?

# 19

1. Eight.
2. Richard Strauss's *Der Rosenkavalier*.
3. Balthazar.
4. John Gilroy.
5. Napoleon.
6. Humphrey Lestocq.

# 95

1. Charles Laughton.
2. Euripides.
3. Christabel Pankhurst.
4. Castiglione.
5. A lion.
6. *Come Dancing*.

# 171

1. Andy Warhol.
2. André Messager.
3. The Pooters.
4. Sir Joshua Reynolds.
5. Mycenae.
6. Charlie Drake's.

Q



## 20

1. Who directed Maria Callas in her only non-singing film appearance?
2. Who created the role of Amanda in *Private Lives*?
3. Who wrote *Five Children and It*?
4. Whose most famous painting is of a farm vehicle?
5. Which building contains the tomb of Shah Jahan?
6. What sort of young men were James Bolam and Rodney Bewes?

## 96

1. Which inventor was played by Michael Redgrave in the film *Dam Busters*?
2. Which prima donna played the heroine in a production of *Dido and Aeneas* in Sir Bernard Miles's back garden?
3. Who wrote *The Adventure of the Beryl Coronet*?
4. Who painted 'La Grande Jatte'?
5. Who was the sculptor of the famous 'Discobolus'?
6. Who played the headmaster in *Whacko*?

## 172

1. Which 1971 detective thriller starred Jane Fonda and Donald Sutherland?
2. Who made the joint jump?
3. In the alphabet of which language do J, K, W, X and Y not exist?
4. Who painted 'The Garden of Worldly Delights'?
5. What is a campanile?
6. Why is the Berceuse from Fauré's *Dolly Suite* so familiar?

# 20

1. Pier Paolo Pasolini, in *Medea*.
2. Gertrude Lawrence.
3. E. Nesbit.
4. Constable's ('The Hay Wain').
5. The Taj Mahal.
6. Likely Lads.

# 96

1. Dr Barnes Wallis.
2. Kirsten Flagstad.
3. Sir Arthur Conan Doyle.
4. Georges Seurat.
5. Myron.
6. Jimmy Edwards.

# 172

1. *Klute*.
2. Fats Waller.
3. Italian.
4. Hieronymus Bosch.
5. A bell-tower.
6. It was the signature tune to *Listen with Mother*.

# 21

1. What was the cause of Rudolph Valentino's death?
2. By what name is Beethoven's operatic heroine Leonora better known?
3. What was the name of E. W. Hornung's jewel thief?
4. Who was famous for his *Birds of America*?
5. What landmark in Rome was sculpted by Nicola Salvi?
6. Who tried to persuade people to 'Have a go'?

# 97

1. Who played the leading role in *A Man Called Horse*?
2. Which playwright created the character of Sir Epicure Mammon?
3. Who was the chatelaine of Garsington Manor?
4. Which nineteenth-century French painter was a count?
5. What is Jørn Utzon's most famous building?
6. What is the name of the female dance group who appeared regularly on *Top of the Pops*?

# 173

1. Who played Luke Skywalker in *Star Wars*?
2. Which Leonard Bernstein musical was based on a story by Voltaire?
3. Which Jane Austen character liked 'an egg boiled very soft' for breakfast?
4. Which artist was famous for his nonsense rhymes?
5. Where is the Gloriette?
6. Who played Lily Langtry in the series based on her life?

# 21

1. Peritonitis.
2. Fidelio.
3. Raffles.
4. John James Audubon.
5. The Trevi Fountain.
6. Wilfred Pickles.

# 97

1. Richard Harris.
2. Ben Jonson.
3. Lady Ottoline Morrell.
4. Henri de Toulouse-Lautrec.
5. The Sydney Opera House.
6. Pan's People.

# 173

1. Mark Hamill.
2. *Candide*.
3. Mr Woodhouse.
4. Edward Lear.
5. Schönbrunn Palace, in Austria.
6. Francesca Annis.

## 22

1. Which 1956 film caused riots in cinemas all over the world?
2. Who wrote *The Caucasian Chalk Circle*?
3. Who is credited with writing the first English novel?
4. Name one of two seventeenth-century Dutch painters particularly known for their cows.
5. Of which architect were the following lines written: 'Lie heavy on him Earth, for he / Laid many a heavy load on thee'?
6. What made you feel better when you wished you hadn't eaten the whole thing?

## 98

1. In 1976 Ingmar Bergman was arrested by two plainclothes policemen. What was the charge?
2. Which musical-comedy star is Larry Hagman's mother?
3. Which writer had an omelette named after him?
4. Who painted the series of portraits known as the 'Windsor Beauties'?
5. Who designed a hat in the shape of a shoe?
6. Which two things did every castaway have on Roy Plomley's desert island?

## 174

1. Who played the female lead in *Born Yesterday*?
2. Who is George in *An Afternoon with George in the Park*?
3. What was Bram Stoker's most famous creation?
4. Whose work-boots were painted by Sir William Nicholson?
5. Who designed Marie-Antoinette's frocks?
6. To which militia did Corporal Jones and Captain Mainwaring belong?

# 22

1. *Rock Around the Clock*.
2. Bertolt Brecht.
3. Samuel Richardson.
4. Albert Cuyp or Paulus Potter.
5. Sir John Vanbrugh.
6. Alka Seltzer.

# 98

1. Income-tax fraud.
2. Mary Martin.
3. Arnold Bennett.
4. Sir Peter Lely.
5. Elsa Schiaparelli.
6. The Bible and the Complete Works of Shakespeare.

# 174

1. Judy Holliday.
2. Georges Seurat.
3. Dracula.
4. Gertrude Jekyll's.
5. Rose Bertin.
6. The Home Guard in *Dad's Army*.

## 23

1. Why did Veronica Lake pose a threat to the Allies in the Second World War?
2. On which play was the Rodgers and Hart musical *The Boys from Syracuse* based?
3. Who wrote *A Severed Head*?
4. Which Swiss artist was described by Horace Walpole as 'Shockingly mad, madder than ever, quite mad'?
5. Who decorated the night-club The Golden Calf?
6. For what organization did Ilya Kuryakin work?

## 99

1. Why did Hedy Lamarr cause a scandal in *Ecstasy*?
2. Who wrote *Home and Beauty*?
3. Who was Greenmantle?
4. Which Italian portrait-painter was the favourite of Englishmen on the Grand Tour?
5. Who was the first director of the Gobelins factory?
6. Who had a friend called 'Spotty' Muldoon?

## 175

1. Who were the vintage stars of *On Golden Pond*?
2. Who was the first theatrical knight?
3. Who wrote *Les Mouches*?
4. Which opera opens with Marcello working at his painting 'The Passage of the Red Sea'?
5. For producing what was Bernard Leach famous?
6. Who recently played the nanny in a series of her own devising?

## 23

1. Her much-imitated hairstyle was said to cause accidents to female munitions workers.
2. *The Comedy of Errors* by William Shakespeare.
3. Iris Murdoch.
4. Henry Fuseli.
5. Wyndham Lewis.
6. U.N.C.L.E.

## 99

1. She appeared nude.
2. W. Somerset Maugham.
3. A prophet in John Buchan's novel of the same name.
4. Pompeo Batoni.
5. Charles Lebrun.
6. Peter Cook as Wisty.

## 175

1. Henry Fonda and Katharine Hepburn.
2. Sir Henry Irving.
3. Jean-Paul Sartre.
4. *La Bohème*, by Giacomo Puccini.
5. Pottery.
6. Wendy Craig.

## 24

1. Which Swedish director launched Greta Garbo?
2. Who wrote *Journey's End*?
3. Why did the widow of the poet Scarron become famous?
4. Who was the girl-bride of the painter G. F. Watts?
5. Which Finn bent wood to good effect?
6. How did Richard Baker first become known in broadcasting?

## 100

1. Who was famous for directing epic films with casts of thousands?
2. Who wrote *Becket*?
3. Who wrote 'The Lady of Shalott'?
4. Which painter inspired Granados to compose a set of piano pieces?
5. Which early-nineteenth-century arbiter of taste stated that the colour green should *never* be used in interior decoration?
6. Who played Jeeves in the television series?

## 176

1. Which part was played by Jackie Coogan in 1931 and Mickey Rooney in 1939?
2. Beyond what were Jonathan Miller, Peter Cook, Alan Bennett and Dudley Moore?
3. Who wrote *It*?
4. Which artist was commissioned to paint Anne of Cleves by her future husband?
5. In which city does the collection of Elias Ashmole form the basis for a museum?
6. Which two actresses have played J. R.'s mother in the series *Dallas*?

## 24

1. Mauritz Stiller.
2. R. C. Sherriff.
3. As Madame de Maintenon, she became the last mistress, and possibly wife, of Louis XIV.
4. Ellen Terry.
5. Hugo Alvar Henrik Aalto.
6. Reading the news.

## 100

1. Cecil B. de Mille.
2. Jean Anouilh.
3. Alfred, Lord Tennyson.
4. Goya ('Goyescas').
5. Thomas Hope.
6. Dennis Price.

## 176

1. Huckleberry Finn.
2. The Fringe.
3. Elinor Glyn.
4. Hans Holbein.
5. Oxford.
6. Barbara Bel Geddes and Donna Reed.

## 25

1. Name four films which starred Spencer Tracy and Katharine Hepburn.
2. Who wrote *Steaming*?
3. As what were Mrs Vesey, Mrs Montagu and Mrs Carter better known?
4. What was Anthony Blunt's position in the Royal Household?
5. Where are the Spanish Steps?
6. Who played the title role in the television series *The Prisoner*?

## 101

1. Who directed *The Go-Between*?
2. Who founded the Old Vic company?
3. Which writer claimed that his story of 'Puss in Boots' was first told to him by his infant daughter?
4. Who painted Anna Thomson Dodge as Madame de Pompadour?
5. Who was the architect/engineer of the Suez Canal?
6. Who narrated the *Civilization* series on television?

## 177

1. Which Hollywood star had something to wear named after her?
2. Of whom did Oscar Wilde say, 'He hasn't an enemy in the world and none of his friends like him'?
3. Who wrote *A Town Like Alice*?
4. Who was the leader of the Camden Town Group?
5. Who produced Red Books of designs for his clients?
6. Which animal was brought to life by Annette Mills?

# A



## 25

1. *Adam's Rib*, *Pat and Mike*, *Guess Who's Coming to Dinner*, *Woman of the Year*, *Desk Set*, *State of the Union*, *The Sea of Grass*, *Without Love* and *Keeper of the Flame* all starred this famous couple.
2. Nell Dunn.
3. As three of the original 'Blue Stockings'.
4. Surveyor of the Queen's Pictures.
5. Rome.
6. Patrick McGoohan.

## 101

1. Joseph Losey.
2. Lilian Baylis.
3. Charles Perrault.
4. Sir Gerald Kelly.
5. Ferdinand de Lesseps.
6. Kenneth Clark.

## 177

1. Mae West.
2. George Bernard Shaw.
3. Nevil Shute.
4. Walter Sickert.
5. Humphry Repton.
6. Muffin the Mule.

## 26

1. Who was famous for his aerial views of chorus girls?
2. Which Italian family designed the most fantastic baroque stage sets in the first half of the eighteenth century?
3. Which author wrote of the Pleydell family?
4. Which leader of the modern movement was commissioned to decorate the Four Seasons restaurant in New York?
5. Which 1950s fashion model married Baron von Thyssen?
6. Who played Harry Lime in the television series *The Third Man*?

## 102

1. Who was the leading exponent of the Nouvelle Vague in French films?
2. Who wrote the music and lyrics for *Oklahoma*?
3. Which writer is married to the director of the National Gallery?
4. Who painted a picture of Dr Tulp giving a lesson?
5. In what style did Horace Walpole build his house, Strawberry Hill?
6. Who was the first Doctor Who?

## 178

1. Who played Darcy in the 1940 film version of *Pride and Prejudice*?
2. By what name is Lesley Hornby better known?
3. Who wrote *The Birthday Party*?
4. Whose paintings were described as 'Oodles of Goddesses/ Without any bodices'?
5. As what is Sir Alfred Gilbert's memorial to Lord Shaftesbury better known?
6. Who is the question-master of *University Challenge*?

## 26

1. Busby Berkeley.
2. The Bibiena family.
3. Dornford Yates.
4. Mark Rothko.
5. Fiona Campbell-Walter.
6. Michael Rennie.

## 102

1. Jean-Luc Godard.
2. Richard Rodgers and Oscar Hammerstein.
3. Brigid Brophy.
4. Rembrandt van Rijn.
5. Gothic Revival.
6. William Hartnell.

## 178

1. Laurence Olivier.
2. Twiggy.
3. Harold Pinter.
4. Sir Peter Paul Rubens's.
5. Eros.
6. Bamber Gascoigne.

## 27

1. Who played the Matron in the film *If . . .*?
2. Who wrote *Our Town*?
3. Which poet was reported to have 'died of wounds' on his twenty-first birthday in 1916 but was in fact alive?
4. Who painted the murals in the restaurant of the Tate Gallery?
5. From which town did Colbert import the lacemakers to start the factory at Alençon in 1675?
6. Who was the squeaky-voiced star of *Yakety-Yak*?

## 103

1. Who directed *Les Enfants du Paradis*?
2. Who was 'one of the ruins that Cromwell knocked about a bit"?
3. Who wrote *The Shape of Things to Come*?
4. Which artist sketched Marie-Antoinette going to her execution in a tumbril?
5. Who designed a house called 'Falling Water' for the Kaufmann family?
6. Who introduces *The South Bank Show*?

## 179

1. Who was "The Look"?
2. Who wrote *Dr Faustus*?
3. Who was a member of a ghastly crew?
4. Who published the *Hundred Views of Mount Fuji*?
5. Which classical sculpture was considered by Pliny to be 'of all paintings and sculptures the most worthy of admiration"?
6. Who was Mr Bellamy's cook?

# 27

1. Mona Washbourne.
2. Thornton Wilder.
3. Robert Graves.
4. Rex Whistler.
5. Venice.
6. Theresa Burton.

# 103

1. Marcel Carné.
2. Marie Lloyd.
3. H. G. Wells.
4. Jacques-Louis David.
5. Frank Lloyd Wright.
6. Melvyn Bragg.

# 179

1. Lauren Bacall.
2. Christopher Marlowe.
3. The Ancient Mariner.
4. Hokusai.
5. The Laocoön.
6. Mrs Bridges.

## 28

1. Which song was featured in Hitchcock's 1956 version of *The Man Who Knew Too Much*?
2. Of which actress did Max Beerbohm write: 'In this, as in every other part, she behaved like a guardian angel half asleep at her post over humanity'?
3. Whose dusky lady may well have been a gentleman?
4. Who painted the European statesmen and sovereigns in the Waterloo Chamber of Windsor Castle?
5. Who designed the National Theatre?
6. Which two actors have played Robin Hood in television series?

## 104

1. Which actor won an Academy Award for his part in *The Philadelphia Story*?
2. Who wrote *A Voyage Round My Father*?
3. Who wrote *Pippa Passes*?
4. Which painter murdered his father and spent the remainder of his life in an asylum?
5. Who sculpted a statue of Mercury shown supported on one foot on wind blown from a cherub's mouth?
6. Which tea-time entertainer later ran a motel?

## 180

1. Who played the title role in *Beverly Hills Cop*?
2. Name two of the three Merry Wives of Windsor.
3. Which romantic novelist married two men called McCorquodale?
4. Which painter was a customs official?
5. What was the year of the Great Exhibition in London?
6. Who was the host of *Double Your Money*?

# 28

1. 'Que Sera Sera'.
2. Eleanora Duse.
3. William Shakespeare's (the Dark Lady of the Sonnets).
4. Sir Thomas Lawrence.
5. Sir Denys Lasdun.
6. Richard Greene and Michael Praed.

# 104

1. James Stewart.
2. John Mortimer.
3. Robert Browning.
4. Richard Dadd.
5. Giambologna.
6. Noele Gordon.

# 180

1. Eddie Murphy.
2. The three were Mistress Quickly, Mistress Alice Ford and Mistress Meg Page.
3. Barbara Cartland.
4. Henri 'Douanier' Rousseau.
5. 1851.
6. Hughie Green.

## 29

1. Who played the title role in *Mr Moto*?
2. Of which actor did James Agate write in 1944: 'He can summon up all the expressions there are except the tragic one, the lack of which, in a tragic actor, must be a shortcoming'?
3. Who was the poetess Carmen Sylva in everyday life?
4. Who invented Rayonism?
5. What technique did André-Charles Boulle make famous?
6. Which actress was described by her television husband as a 'Silly Old Moo'?

## 105

1. Which Hollywood film-star successfully sued Graham Greene for libel?
2. The Portsmouth bum-boat woman Mrs Cripps was better known as who?
3. Who wrote *Of Mice and Men*?
4. What is the term for under-painting showing through in a picture?
5. Who designed the Teatro Olimpico at Vicenza?
6. What were the names of the flower-pot men?

## 181

1. The film *Ninotchka* was made into which musical?
2. Which play by Tom Stoppard deals with the fate of two minor Shakespearian characters?
3. Why is *Edwin Drood* unique amongst Dickens's novels?
4. Which artist is associated with thinly sliced raw beef?
5. What was the name of the famous Russian family of jewellers of Huguenot extraction working from the mid nineteenth century until the Revolution?
6. Which programme ended with the words 'Carry on London'?

## 29

1. Peter Lorre.
2. Donald Wolfit.
3. Queen Elizabeth of Romania.
4. Mikhail Larionov.
5. Inlay of metal (usually brass) and wood or tortoiseshell.
6. Dandy Nicholls.

## 105

1. Shirley Temple.
2. Little Buttercup in *H.M.S. Pinafore.*
3. John Steinbeck.
4. Pentimento.
5. Andrea Palladio.
6. Bill and Ben.

## 181

1. *Silk Stockings.*
2. *Rosencrantz and Guildenstern Are Dead.*
3. It is unfinished.
4. Carpaccio.
5. Fabergé.
6. *In Town Tonight.*

## 30

1. 'Greer Garson in furs' was used to describe which particular screen personality?
2. Who wrote *A Day in the Death of Joe Egg*?
3. Who wrote *The Water-Babies*?
4. What subject did Louis Wain primarily paint?
5. Who was responsible for the G-plan furniture of the 1950s?
6. Who played Mrs Basil Fawlty in *Fawlty Towers*?

## 106

1. In which film did a group of four men kill themselves by over-eating?
2. Which English lord's grandmother was Dame Nellie Melba?
3. What was the name of the forest in *As You Like It*?
4. Which Pre-Raphaelite painting, one of several versions, hangs in St Paul's Cathedral?
5. Which was the first metal used by man?
6. Who played the title role in the television series *Callan*?

## 182

1. Who sported a mink bikini in Venice?
2. Who killed Ophelia's father?
3. Who wrote in bed in a cork-lined room?
4. Which Swiss pastellist worked for a time at the Austrian Imperial Court?
5. Who designed Westminster Cathedral?
6. Who played the title role in *Edna, the Inebriate Woman*?

## 30

1. Lassie.
2. Peter Nichols.
3. Charles Kingsley.
4. Cats.
5. Donald Gomme.
6. Prunella Scales.

## 106

1. *La Grande Bouffe*.
2. Lord Vestey.
3. Arden.
4. Holman Hunt's 'The Light of the World'.
5. Copper.
6. Edward Woodward.

## 182

1. Diana Dors.
2. Hamlet.
3. Marcel Proust.
4. Jean-Étienne Liotard.
5. J. F. Bentley.
6. Patricia Hayes.

## 31

1. Which kingdom was attacked by the Blue Meanies?
2. To which troupe did 'Monsewer' Eddie Gray belong?
3. Who wrote the novel *Hadrian VII*?
4. Which twentieth-century patron of the arts set up a museum in Venice?
5. What was the date of the Paris Decorative Arts Exhibition?
6. Who created 'The Radio Ham' and 'The Blood Donor'?

## 107

1. Which silent-screen star made a comeback in *Sunset Boulevard*?
2. Who founded the Moscow Arts Theatre?
3. Who owned the Empress of Blandings?
4. Who was accused of 'throwing a pot of paint in the public's face'?
5. Who wrote in 1928: 'It is our supreme object to have a head looking like a wet football on a neck as thin as a governess's hatpin'?
6. Who were the two leading lights of *Much Binding in the Marsh*?

## 183

1. In which film did Clark Gable perform a tap routine?
2. What caused the 'Old Price Riots' in 1809?
3. What is the *nom de plume* of writer J. I. M. Stewart?
4. Which Sienese artist painted the 'Rucellai Madonna'?
5. Who designed a room based on Mae West's face, the lips formed from a red satin sofa?
6. Who was the female presenter on *Ready, Steady, Go*?

# A

## 31

1. Pepperland, in *Yellow Submarine*.
2. The Crazy Gang.
3. 'Baron' Corvo.
4. Peggy Guggenheim.
5. 1925.
6. Tony Hancock.

## 107

1. Gloria Swanson.
2. Konstantin Stanislavsky.
3. Lord Emsworth.
4. James Abbott McNeill Whistler.
5. Cecil Beaton.
6. Kenneth Horne and Richard Murdoch.

## 183

1. *Idiot's Delight*.
2. A rise in seat-prices at Covent Garden.
3. Michael Innes.
4. Duccio.
5. Man Ray.
6. Cathy McGowan.

## 32

1. Who said of Bette Davis, 'I could have tweaked every hair out of her moustache'?
2. Which comedian famous for his loud suits and dirty jokes was known as the Cheekie Chappie?
3. Who wrote the story 'The Canterville Ghost'?
4. Who painted 'Derby Day' and 'Ramsgate Sands'?
5. What is a Nonesuch chest?
6. Who played Dr Kildare in the television series of the same name?

## 108

1. The atom bomb dropped on Bikini carried a pin-up picture of an American 'Love Goddess'. Who?
2. Who played Madame Arcati in the original production of Noël Coward's *Blithe Spirit*?
3. Who considered how his light was spent?
4. Which painter shares his name with a cocktail?
5. What was the date of the first tunnel under the Thames?
6. Which star of *Minder* used to lurk around St Trinian's?

## 184

1. Who was 'the man in the white suit'?
2. What are the three dramatic unities?
3. Where did Kubla Khan decree a stately pleasure-dome?
4. Which painter contracted a fever in pursuit of a dead whale?
5. The tower of whose Gothic house fell down twice?
6. Which television series originally starred Ronnie Barker and Richard Beckinsale?

## 32

1. Tallulah Bankhead.
2. Max Miller.
3. Oscar Wilde.
4. William Powell Frith.
5. A late-sixteenth-century or early-seventeenth-century chest, probably from the Baltic area, decorated in marquetry with fantastic architecture.
6. Richard Chamberlain.

## 108

1. Rita Hayworth.
2. Margaret Rutherford.
3. John Milton.
4. Bellini.
5. It was started in 1826.
6. George Cole.

## 184

1. Alec Guinness.
2. Action, time and place.
3. Xanadu.
4. Albrecht Dürer.
5. William Beckford's.
6. *Porridge.*

# 33

1. Which composer's life was dramatized on film in *A Song to Remember*?
2. Which actress continued to work after losing a leg?
3. Who was described by his mistress as 'mad, bad and dangerous to know'?
4. Who designed the backdrops for the Diaghilev ballets *Le Train bleu* and *Parade*?
5. Which style was named after a character who symbolized the German bourgeoisie in an early-nineteenth-century book by Ludwig Eichrodt?
6. Who played Patrick Wymark's wife in *The Power Game*?

# 109

1. In which film did Lauren Bacall and Humphrey Bogart first star together?
2. How did Vesta Tilley and Hetty King dress on stage?
3. When threatened with exposure in the courtesan Harriette Wilson's autobiography, who replied: 'Publish, and be damned'?
4. Who was the photographer of the Crimean War?
5. At which craft did Penelope, Ulysses' wife, seem awfully slow?
6. What was Radio 4's previous name?

# 185

1. Who danced the carioca in Rio de Janeiro?
2. Who wrote *A Month in the Country*?
3. In which novel by Dickens does the Artful Dodger appear?
4. What are 'Las Meninas' in Velazquez's painting of that name?
5. Which two architects were involved with the design of the Houses of Parliament, Westminster?
6. Who was the original female presenter of *Blue Peter*?

## 33

1. Frédéric Chopin's.
2. Sarah Bernhardt.
3. George, Lord Byron.
4. Pablo Picasso.
5. The Biedermeier style.
6. Barbara Murray.

## 109

1. *To Have and Have Not*.
2. In men's clothes.
3. The first Duke of Wellington.
4. Roger Fenton.
5. Weaving.
6. The Home Service.

## 185

1. Fred Astaire and Ginger Rogers.
2. Ivan Turgenev.
3. *Oliver Twist*.
4. Maids of honour.
5. C. Barry and A. W. N. Pugin.
6. Valerie Singleton.

## 34

1. Name four people who have played James Bond on film.
2. Whose valet was Leporello?
3. What was the assembly point of Chaucer's Canterbury pilgrims?
4. Who painted 'The Monarch of the Glen'?
5. In which city would you find Michelangelo's 'David'?
6. Who wrote the books on which the series *The Jewel in the Crown* was based?

## 110

1. Who, in 1932, was a fugitive from a chain-gang?
2. Who wrote *Who's Afraid of Virginia Woolf*?
3. Who wrote *The Return of the Native*?
4. Which painter depicted the triumphal progress of Marie de Médicis?
5. Who arranged for the building of Port Sunlight?
6. In which series was Caroline Blakiston married to Timothy West?

## 186

1. Who proved she could play the trumpet in the film *Genevieve*?
2. Who wrote *The Passing of the Third Floor Back*?
3. As what were Georgina, Ann, Julian, Dick and their dog better known?
4. Which painter was born at Pontormo, near Empoli, in Italy?
5. Who designed the Viceroy's House in New Delhi?
6. What relation was J. R. Ewing to the person who shot and tried to kill him?

## 34

1. Sean Connery, Roger Moore, George Lazenby and David Niven.
2. Don Giovanni's.
3. The Tabard Inn, Southwark.
4. Sir Edwin Landseer.
5. Florence.
6. Paul Scott.

## 110

1. Paul Muni.
2. Edward Albee.
3. Thomas Hardy.
4. Sir Peter Paul Rubens.
5. Lord Leverhulme.
6. *Brass*.

## 186

1. Kay Kendall.
2. Jerome K. Jerome.
3. The Famous Five.
4. Jacopo Pontormo.
5. Sir Edwin Lutyens.
6. Brother-in-law.

## 35

1. Which two veteran dancers appeared in *The Bandwagon*?
2. Who wrote *The Duchess of Malfi*?
3. Which novel starts, 'It was the afternoon of my eighty-first birthday, and I was in bed with my catamite . . .'?
4. What is the term for the 'objective' movement which sprang up in reaction to Expressionism in Germany in the early 1920s?
5. Who pioneered the all-white look in interior decoration?
6. Who played the captain of the pirate ship in *The Buccaneers*?

## 111

1. Which actress was painted gold in *Goldfinger*?
2. Who wrote *Waiting for Godot*?
3. What was the name of the Scarlet Pimpernel?
4. Who was the poet/painter of *Songs of Innocence and Experience*?
5. Who sculpted the 'Colleoni' in Venice?
6. What was Leonard Nimoy's most prominent feature?

## 187

1. Who played Mrs Miniver?
2. Who wrote the music for *Oliver*?
3. What was H. H. Munro's pseudonym?
4. Which seventeenth-century French painter was much admired by J. M. W. Turner?
5. Who sculpted the tombs of Henry VII and Elizabeth of York in Westminster Abbey?
6. Who found it 'Nice to see you, to see you nice'?

## 35

1. Jack Buchanan and Fred Astaire.
2. John Webster.
3. *Earthly Powers*.
4. Neue Sachlichkeit.
5. Syrie Maugham.
6. Robert Shaw.

## 111

1. Shirley Eaton.
2. Samuel Beckett.
3. Sir Percy Blakeney.
4. William Blake.
5. Verrocchio.
6. His ears (as Mr Spock in *Star Trek*).

## 187

1. Greer Garson.
2. Lionel Bart.
3. Saki.
4. Claude Lorrain.
5. Torrigiano.
6. Bruce Forsyth.

## 36

1. Which actress played the star who broke her leg in Ken Russell's *The Boyfriend*?
2. Who wrote *Death of a Salesman*?
3. Under what name did Teodor Korzeniowski write novels?
4. Which sculptor was married to the painter Ben Nicholson?
5. What is 'famille rose'?
6. Which sign meant happy motoring?

## 112

1. Who played Ruth Etting in *Love Me or Leave Me* (1955)?
2. What is Caruso reputed to have once pressed into Melba's hand while singing 'Your Tiny Hand is Frozen'?
3. Who wrote novels about life at court in the kingdom of Ruritania?
4. Which contemporary artist has designed sets for *The Rake's Progress*, *The Magic Flute* and *Parade*?
5. A statue of which composer stood at the centre of Vauxhall Gardens?
6. Who loved Lucy?

## 188

1. Who were known as the 'Iron Butterfly' and the 'Singing Capon'?
2. Who wrote *On Approval*?
3. The hero of which novel is Edgar, Master of Ravenswood?
4. Which painter wrote *Lives of the Artists*?
5. Which is 'the rose-red city half as old as time'?
6. Whose friend was Tonto?

## 36

1. Glenda Jackson.
2. Arthur Miller.
3. Joseph Conrad.
4. Barbara Hepworth.
5. Chinese porcelain decorated primarily in pink.
6. Esso.

## 112

1. Doris Day.
2. A hot sausage.
3. Anthony Hope.
4. David Hockney.
5. Handel.
6. Ricky Ricardo, played by Desi Arnaz.

## 188

1. Jeanette Macdonald and Nelson Eddy.
2. Frederick Lonsdale.
3. *The Bride of Lammermoor*, by Sir Walter Scott.
4. Giorgio Vasari.
5. Petra.
6. The Lone Ranger's.

## 37

1. Who directed *It's a Wonderful Life*?
2. Which Australian entertainer described Stratford-on-Avon as 'the place where Shakespeare wrote his shows'?
3. Whom did Noël Coward satirize as Hernia Whittlebot?
4. What is William Grant shown doing in Gilbert Stuart's portrait of him?
5. Who designed the National Gallery?
6. Which family's oldest son was John-boy?

## 113

1. Which child star became an ambassadress?
2. Who was the 'Monarch of Mirth'?
3. What was the cause of the most serious row between Noddy and Big Ears?
4. Which school of painting grew up around the Forest of Fontainebleau in the 1830s?
5. Which city in Spain would you go to in order to visit the Alhambra Palace?
6. Which mother and daughter ran The Swan?

## 189

1. In which cult 1950s science-fiction classic does Sam Peckinpah make a minor appearance as a meter reader?
2. Which star was Robert Morley's mother-in-law?
3. Which novel has been nicknamed 'The Gropes of Roth'?
4. Who painted a picture of Louise O'Murphy's bottom?
5. Which colour did Elsa Schiaparelli invent?
6. Who changed from beloved 'Auntie Vi' into a harridan in a hairnet?

## 37

1. Frank Capra.
2. Dame Edna Everage, alias Barry Humphries.
3. Edith Sitwell.
4. Skating.
5. William Wilkins.
6. The Waltons'.

## 113

1. Shirley Temple.
2. George Robey.
3. The colour of Noddy's curtains.
4. The Barbizon School.
5. Granada.
6. Margaret and Julia Lockwood.

## 189

1. *Invasion of the Bodysnatchers.*
2. Gladys Cooper.
3. *Portnoy's Complaint.*
4. François Boucher.
5. Shocking pink.
6. Violet Carson.

## 38

1. Who played Vincent van Gogh in the film *Lust for Life*?
2. Who were the two Hermiones famous for appearing in revue?
3. Who carries Sindbad the Sailor out of the Valley of Diamonds?
4. Who painted the frescoes at the Residenz in Würzburg?
5. For what was Grinling Gibbons famous?
6. Who played Lady Marchmont in the series *Brideshead Revisited*?

## 114

1. Which actress played the part of *His Girl Friday*?
2. Of which two actresses appearing in *Pelléas et Mélisande* by Maeterlinck did one critic write that both ladies were old enough to know better?
3. In which novel is Sergeant Cuff the investigating detective?
4. Who paints the American flag?
5. Who sculpted the 'Rima' in Hyde Park?
6. Name the two radio stars who played Dame Celia Molestrangler and Rambling Sid Rumpo.

## 190

1. What is to be found outside Grauman's Chinese Theatre?
2. Who wrote *The Royal Hunt of the Sun*?
3. On the title-page of which book is one enjoined to 'Study to be Quiet'?
4. What is a tondo?
5. Which contemporary London fashion figure has had shops named 'World's End' and 'Nostalgia of Mud'?
6. In which television film about a notorious figure did Coral Browne play herself?

## 38

1. Kirk Douglas.
2. Gingold and Baddeley.
3. The Roc, a mythical gigantic bird.
4. Giambattista Tiepolo.
5. Elaborate wood-carving.
6. Claire Bloom.

## 114

1. Rosalind Russell.
2. Sarah Bernhardt and Mrs Patrick Campbell.
3. *The Moonstone*, by Wilkie Collins.
4. Jasper Johns.
5. Sir Jacob Epstein.
6. Betty Marsden and Kenneth Williams (in *Round the Horne*).

## 190

1. The hand-prints of film-stars.
2. Peter Shaffer.
3. *The Compleat Angler*, by Izaak Walton.
4. A round painting (or relief sculpture).
5. Vivienne Westwood.
6. *An Englishman Abroad*.

# Q

## 39

1. Who played the title role in *Hercules Unchained*?
2. On which play was the film *Boom* based?
3. Who wrote the story of Giselle?
4. A painting by which artist has been stolen from the Dulwich Picture Gallery three times?
5. What is an Adlerhumpen?
6. What was *Panorama*'s most famous April Fool joke?

## 115

1. Who were the original 'United Artists'?
2. Which work was described by Samuel Pepys as 'the most insipid, ridiculous play that ever I saw in my life'?
3. Who was described by Virginia Woolf as 'a greasy undergraduate scratching his pimples'?
4. Who slashes his canvases?
5. Who received the O.B.E. for services to fashion in 1966?
6. Which stargazer plays the xylophone?

## 191

1. Who was 'the minx in mink with a yen for men'?
2. By what name is Miriam Ramberg better known?
3. Who created the heroine Cigarette?
4. Which artist painted a portrait of Louis XIV with his son, grandson and great-grandson, later Louis XV?
5. Which greenish-grey stoneware, imported into Europe from China, was named after a character in *L'Astrée* by Honoré d'Urfé?
6. Robertson Hare, Derek Nimmo and Mervyn Johns co-starred in which comedy series?

## 39

1. Steve Reeves.
2. *The Milk Train Doesn't Stop Here Any More*, by Tennessee Williams.
3. Théophile Gautier.
4. Rembrandt van Rijn.
5. A kind of German drinking glass, sometimes lidded, and decorated with coloured enamels.
6. 'The Spaghetti Harvest'.

## 115

1. Charlie Chaplin, D. W. Griffith, Mary Pickford and Douglas Fairbanks.
2. *A Midsummer Night's Dream*, by William Shakespeare.
3. James Joyce.
4. Fontana.
5. Mary Quant.
6. Patrick Moore.

## 191

1. Ginger Rogers in *Lady in the Dark*.
2. Marie Rambert.
3. Ouida.
4. Nicolas de Largillière.
5. Celadon.
6. *All Gas and Gaiters*.

## 40

1. Who were the two stars of *Spring in Park Lane* and *Maytime in Mayfair*?
2. Which female singing star launched her career in a sauna bath?
3. Under what name was Madame Dudevant better known?
4. Who painted 'The Scream'?
5. Which dynasty is earliest, Sung, T'ang, Ming or Ch'ing?
6. What came down the line right on time?

## 116

1. What was the name of Nick and Norah Charles's dog?
2. Who starred in the musical version of H. G. Wells's *Kipps*?
3. Who lived at Dingley Dell?
4. Whom did Robert Hughes describe as a 'heifer on steroids'?
5. Why was the Savonnerie carpet factory so called?
6. Which television personality was briefly deprived of his knighthood by Mrs Thatcher?

## 192

1. Which play inspired Kurosawa's *Throne of Blood*?
2. Which long-running musical was originally written to fill a three-week slot at the Bristol Old Vic?
3. Who wrote *La Peste*?
4. Who paid for Zoffany to travel to Florence to study?
5. Who claimed that his house at 9 Melbury Road, London, looked like 'a model residence of the fifteenth century'?
6. Who was manipulated by Bruff?

# 40

1. Anna Neagle and Michael Wilding.
2. Bette Midler.
3. George Sand.
4. Edvard Munch.
5. T'ang.
6. *The 6.5 Special*.

# 116

1. Asta.
2. Tommy Steele.
3. Mr Wardle, in *The Pickwick Papers*.
4. Adrian Schnabels.
5. It was set up in an abandoned soap factory (the French for soap is *savon*).
6. Sir Robin Day.

# 192

1. *Macbeth*.
2. *Salad Days*.
3. Albert Camus.
4. King George III.
5. William Burges.
6. Archie Andrews.

## 41

1. Who played the star in the 1972 *Lady Sings the Blues*?
2. Which playwright died on stage in one of his own plays?
3. Who created the private detective Philip Marlowe?
4. Which two brothers painted the Ghent altarpiece?
5. Which nineteenth-century monarch built a copy, never completed, of Versailles?
6. Which TV personality was married to Peter Dimmock?

## 117

1. A quotation from Walt Whitman was used by Olive Higgins Prouty as the title for a book later made into a film with Bette Davis. What is the title?
2. Shakespeare's Globe Theatre burned down during the performance of which play?
3. Who wrote about life in the town of Cranford?
4. Who painted the tapestry cartoons of the triumph of Caesar now at Hampton Court?
5. To where did the Vincennes porcelain factory move in 1756?
6. Who played the title role in *Boyd Q.C.*?

## 193

1. Which part was played by Lon Chaney in 1923 and Charles Laughton in 1939?
2. Which eighteenth-century woman of fashion was discovered behind a screen?
3. Which town links John Fowles's *French Lieutenant's Woman* and Jane Austen's *Persuasion*?
4. Which painter is associated with Mont-Ste-Victoire?
5. Whose tomb in St Paul's has the inscription in Latin, 'If you seek his monument, look around'?
6. Whose side-kick was Pancho?

# 41

1. Diana Ross.
2. Molière.
3. Raymond Chandler.
4. Jan and Hubert van Eyck.
5. Ludwig II of Bavaria.
6. Polly Elwes.

# 117

1. *Now Voyager*.
2. *Henry VIII*.
3. Mrs Gaskell.
4. Andrea Mantegna.
5. Sèvres.
6. Michael Denison.

# 193

1. The title role in *The Hunchback of Notre Dame*.
2. Lady Teazle.
3. Lyme Regis.
4. Paul Cézanne.
5. Sir Christopher Wren's.
6. The Cisco Kid's.

## 42

1. What happens to the bullion stolen in *The Lavender Hill Mob*?
2. Who played Fagin in *Oliver* on stage and on film?
3. In which books does Dr Prunesquallor feature?
4. Which Greek classical artist painted such lifelike grapes that the birds tried to eat them?
5. Where is the Whispering Gallery?
6. Who kept the law in Dock Green?

## 118

1. Which was the last Marx Brothers film?
2. Which stage designer had an affair with Isadora Duncan?
3. Who created the character of Gustav von Aschenbach?
4. Who painted the Isenheim altarpiece?
5. Who designed the statue of Peter Pan in Kensington Gardens?
6. Who played Miss Marple in the series based on the Agatha Christie novels?

## 194

1. Who played Jungle Jim on many occasions?
2. Who founded the Shakespeare Festival at Stratford, Ontario?
3. Who was the Man in the Iron Mask?
4. Of which still-life painter did Diderot say, 'His brush has on it the actual substance of objects'?
5. In which town is the Bauhaus?
6. Who played Old Jolyon in *The Forsyte Saga*?

# A

## 42

1. It is melted into souvenirs of the Eiffel Tower.
2. Ron Moody.
3. The Gormenghast books by Mervyn Peake.
4. Apelles.
5. St Paul's Cathedral.
6. P.C. Dixon.

## 118

1. *Love Happy* (1949).
2. Edward Gordon Craig.
3. Thomas Mann.
4. Matthias Grünewald.
5. Sir Bertram Mackennal.
6. Joan Hickson.

## 194

1. Johnny Weissmuller.
2. Sir Tyrone Guthrie.
3. Louis XIV's twin brother.
4. Jean-Baptiste-Siméon Chardin.
5. Dessau, in Germany.
6. Kenneth More.

## 43

1. Who made the German film of the 1936 Olympic Games?
2. Who was romantically pursued by Harlequin?
3. Which fictional detective was famous for his 'little grey cells'?
4. Who was Floria Tosca's favourite painter?
5. In which city would you find the Madeleine?
6. At the end of which weekly show did the performers wave goodbye whilst slowly revolving?

## 119

1. Who played Hercule Poirot in the 1974 version of *Murder on the Orient Express*?
2. Which was the only theatre to remain open during the whole of the Second World War?
3. Who wrote *A Journal of the Plague Year*?
4. Who was the 'little chicken' of the seventeenth-century art world?
5. Which artist designed the furniture for Marie-Antoinette's dairy at Rambouillet?
6. Which former regular performer on *That's Life* was a revue star?

## 195

1. Name two of the three female stars of *How to Marry a Millionaire*.
2. Who wrote *Uncle Vanya*?
3. What nationality was Gertrude Stein?
4. Who is famous for Action Painting?
5. What was a Sloppy Joe?
6. Who were the writers of *Porridge*?

## 43

1. Leni Riefenstahl.
2. Columbine.
3. Hercule Poirot.
4. Mario Cavaradossi.
5. Paris.
6. *Sunday Night at the London Palladium*.

## 119

1. Albert Finney.
2. The Windmill ('We never closed').
3. Daniel Defoe.
4. Poussin.
5. Hubert Robert.
6. Cyril Fletcher.

## 195

1. The three were Lauren Bacall, Betty Grable and Marilyn Monroe.
2. Anton Chekhov.
3. American.
4. Jackson Pollock.
5. A kind of loose jumper.
6. Dick Clement and Ian la Frenais.

## 44

1. Who performed in her underwear in *Our Dancing Daughters*?
2. On whose life was the musical *Call Me Madam* based?
3. Who was the heir to the Dukedom of Omnium?
4. Why was Jacopo Robusti nicknamed Il Tintoretto?
5. What process did George Richards Elkington invent in the mid nineteenth century?
6. Who played Henry VIII in the series about his life?

## 120

1. By what name was the Countess Dombski better known?
2. Who lost a handkerchief embroidered with a strawberry, which eventually led to her death?
3. Which man of the church wrote a fantastic travelogue?
4. Which artist was nicknamed 'Velvet'?
5. Who never finished the cathedral of the Sagrada Familia in Barcelona?
6. To whom is Desmond Wilcox married?

## 196

1. Who played the title role in *American Gigolo*?
2. Who was the young star of the play *Another Country*?
3. Who wrote *South Wind*?
4. Which photographer liked to capture his subjects jumping in the air?
5. Which British architect co-designed the Beaubourg in Paris?
6. Who talked about his 'Mom' and appeared with his brother George?

## 44

1. Joan Crawford.
2. Perle Mesta's.
3. Plantagenet Palliser.
4. Because his father was a dyer by trade.
5. Silver electroplate.
6. Keith Michell.

## 120

1. Pola Negri.
2. Desdemona.
3. Dean Swift (*Gulliver's Travels*).
4. Jan Bruegel.
5. Antonio Gaudí.
6. Esther Rantzen.

## 196

1. Richard Gere.
2. Rupert Everett.
3. Norman Douglas.
4. Richard Avedon.
5. Richard Rogers.
6. Liberace.

## 45

1. What was Peter Sellers in *Only Two Can Play*?
2. What was the name of Mistress Quickly's tavern in *Henry IV* and *Henry V*?
3. What colour according to Homer were the ships of Thisbe?
4. Which early Renaissance artist has given his name to a word-game?
5. Which French architect gave his name to a style of roof?
6. Who had 'Discoveries'?

## 121

1. Which bride of Frankenstein was in reality married to Charles Laughton?
2. The heroine of which opera is killed by Jack the Ripper?
3. Who wrote *The Amazing Quest of Mr Ernest Bliss*?
4. Who paints everything upside down?
5. In which city would you find the Blue Mosque?
6. Which major film-star worked under travel-boss Gil Favor in *Rawhide*?

## 197

1. Who was a male war bride?
2. On which play was the musical *Kiss Me Kate* based?
3. Who wrote *Prancing Nigger*?
4. Who painted 'Venus, Cupid, Time and Folly'?
5. Who pulled down the Palace of Nonsuch to sell for scrap?
6. What is the first Brazilian soap opera to appear on British television?

## 45

1. A librarian.
2. The Boar's Head.
3. Black.
4. Botticelli.
5. François Mansart.
6. Carroll Leavis.

## 121

1. Elsa Lanchester.
2. *Lulu*, by Alban Berg.
3. E. Phillips Oppenheim.
4. George Baselitz.
5. Istanbul.
6. Clint Eastwood.

## 197

1. Cary Grant.
2. *The Taming of the Shrew*, by William Shakespeare.
3. Ronald Firbank.
4. Agnolo Bronzino.
5. The Duchess of Portsmouth.
6. *I Saura*.

## 46

1. Who directed *The Seventh Seal*?
2. Who were known as 'The Royal Family of Broadway'?
3. Who owned Winnie-the-Pooh?
4. Who painted 'A Tiny Tale of a Tiny Dwarf'?
5. Of what type of building is the Tacoma Building in Chicago usually thought to be the first?
6. Who played the Baron's assistant?

## 122

1. Who directed *Padre Padrone*?
2. Of which work did H. G. Wells write, 'the play is unquestionably very poor'?
3. In which series of books is the Mrs Joyful prize for rafia-work awarded?
4. Which artist has wrapped a coastline?
5. In which city would you find the Baths of Caracalla?
6. Who shot at and tried to kill Bobby Ewing?

## 198

1. Who was the bumbling star of *Oh, Mr Porter*?
2. Who immortalized the role of Mazeppa in the nineteenth century?
3. Who saw the Piper at the Gates of Dawn?
4. Who painted 'The Last of England'?
5. For which sculptor did Van Dyck paint a triple portrait of Charles I?
6. Who played the Larkins?

## 46

1. Ingmar Bergman.
2. The Barrymores.
3. Christopher Robin.
4. Paul Klee.
5. The skyscraper.
6. Sue Lloyd.

## 122

1. Paolo and Vittorio Taviani.
2. *An Ideal Husband* by Oscar Wilde.
3. The Molesworth books by Geoffrey Willans and Ronald Searle.
4. Christo.
5. Rome.
6. Katherine Wentworth.

## 198

1. Will Hay.
2. Adah Isaacs Menken.
3. Mole and Rat in *The Wind in the Willows*.
4. Ford Madox Brown.
5. Gianlorenzo Bernini.
6. Peggy Mount and David Kossoff.

## 47

1. Who directed the 1950 version of *La Ronde*?
2. Which ballet dancer was married to John Maynard Keynes?
3. Who wrote the novel *A Room with a View*?
4. Which Australian painter has designed sets for Covent Garden including *Samson and Delilah*?
5. In which city would you find the Frick Collection?
6. Whose television wife was played by June Laverick?

## 123

1. What did the men do in *One Hundred Men and a Girl* (1937)?
2. Who had fairies at the bottom of her garden?
3. Who wrote *Journey to the Centre of the Earth*?
4. Which painting was stolen from the National Gallery in London and discovered in a railway station?
5. To which king was Jean-Henri Riesener appointed ébéniste?
6. Who was the star of the *Wells Fargo* series?

## 199

1. Who played the Indian princess in *Around the World in Eighty Days*?
2. Who were the two stars of *Share My Lettuce* in the late 1950s?
3. Who wrote *Gigi*?
4. Which draughtsman created 'The Impending Gleam'?
5. Which English architect did the French Rothschilds choose to design their country house in the mid nineteenth century?
6. What game was played by Michael Medwin, Alfie Bass, Bernard Bresslaw and Bill Fraser?

# 47

1. Max Ophüls.
2. Lydia Lopokova.
3. E. M. Forster.
4. Sir Sidney Nolan.
5. New York.
6. Dicky Henderson's.

# 123

1. They were an orchestra.
2. Bea Lillie.
3. Jules Verne.
4. Goya's portrait of the Duke of Wellington.
5. Louis XVI.
6. Dale Robertson.

# 199

1. Shirley Maclaine.
2. Maggie Smith and Kenneth Williams.
3. Colette.
4. Glen Baxter.
5. Sir Joseph Paxton.
6. *The Army Game*.

## 48

1. Who played Sergeant Troy in the film *Far from the Madding Crowd*?
2. For which dancers was the ballet *Marguerite and Armand* created?
3. Who wrote, 'He fell in love with himself at first sight and it is a passion to which he has always remained faithful'?
4. Who wrote the Futurist Manifesto?
5. Who laid out the gardens at Versailles?
6. Who made Joyce Grenfell, Robin Ray and Bernard Levin 'face the music'?

## 124

1. Which film revolves around a lottery ticket sent to the cleaners?
2. Who wrote the story on which the ballet *The Nutcracker* is based?
3. In which decade did the periodical *Punch* first appear?
4. Who painted 'Les Parapluies'?
5. Who sculpted Prince Albert on top of his memorial?
6. Which magician was Basil Brush's first co-star?

## 200

1. What is the name of Françoise Dorléac's sister, who starred with her in *Les Demoiselles de Rochefort*?
2. Which European kingdom inspired Lehar to write *The Merry Widow*?
3. Who were Stalky and Co.?
4. On which painter did Somerset Maugham base *The Moon and Sixpence*?
5. To what type of furnishing did Lorenzo Lotto give his name?
6. Which couple showed us underwater life?

# 48

1. Terence Stamp.
2. Margot Fonteyn and Rudolph Nureyev.
3. Anthony Powell.
4. Filippo Marinetti.
5. André Le Nôtre.
6. Joseph Cooper.

# 124

1. René Clair's *Le Million*.
2. E. T. A. Hoffmann.
3. 1840s (1841).
4. Auguste Renoir.
5. John Foley.
6. David Nixon.

# 200

1. Catherine Deneuve.
2. Montenegro.
3. Schoolboy creations of Rudyard Kipling.
4. Paul Gauguin.
5. Carpets.
6. Hans and Lotte Hass.

## 49

1. Who played Miss Havisham in the David Lean version of *Great Expectations*?
2. Which operetta by Gilbert and Sullivan contains 'A Latin word, a Greek remark and one that's French'?
3. What is Margaret Mitchell's claim to fame?
4. Which Vorticist wrote *The Apes of God*?
5. Who designed and made the sculpture for Cardinal Mazarin's tomb?
6. Which toxophilites live at Ambridge?

## 125

1. Who was the tap-dancing male lead in *Footlight Parade*?
2. How does Rosalinde disguise herself at Prince Orlofsky's ball?
3. In which collection of poems and tales does 'The Jackdaw of Rheims' appear?
4. Which artist is famous for portraying the saucier side of Plymouth life?
5. Which was reputedly the first steel-framed building in London?
6. Which television star was married to Janet Brown?

## 201

1. Who were the two famous Hollywood gossip columnists of the 1930s?
2. Who was 'putting on the agony, putting on the style'?
3. Which authoress was married to the head of Reuters?
4. Which pioneer of photography lived at Lacock Abbey?
5. Who sculpted the 'Gates of Paradise' for the Baptistery in Florence?
6. What was the name of the resident band in *Oh Boy!*?

# 49

1. Martita Hunt.
2. *Iolanthe.*
3. She wrote *Gone with the Wind.*
4. Wyndham Lewis.
5. Antoine Coysevox.
6. The Archers.

# 125

1. James Cagney.
2. As a masked Hungarian countess.
3. *The Ingoldsby Legends.*
4. Beryl Cook.
5. The Ritz Hotel.
6. Peter Butterworth.

# 201

1. Louella Parsons and Hedda Hopper.
2. Lonnie Donegan.
3. Enid Bagnold.
4. William Fox Talbot.
5. Lorenzo Ghiberti.
6. Lord Rockingham's Eleven.

## 50

1. *Here Comes Mr Jordan* was remade as which 1978 film starring Warren Beatty?
2. Who created the role of the Firebird?
3. Who wrote 'Rip Van Winkle'?
4. Who painted the 'Adoration of the Magi' which recently achieved a record price?
5. Who designed the costumes for the Diaghilev ballet *Le Train bleu*?
6. Who starred in *The Goodies*?

## 126

1. Which star was Olivia de Havilland's sister?
2. Which revue star was described as 'a cross between a boxing kangaroo, a piece of chewing gum and a racing cyclist'?
3. Who wrote *The G-String Murders*?
4. What is scumbling?
5. Where is Diocletian's Palace?
6. Which former presenter of *Crackerjack* now thinks the price is right?

## 202

1. Who played the two reporters in *High Society*?
2. What use was made of the Royal Opera House, Covent Garden, during the Second World War?
3. Who wrote *Schindler's Ark*?
4. Who invented the term 'Post-Impressionism'?
5. Why was the small chamber-pot produced in the eighteenth century named after Louis Bourdaloue?
6. Who were the three female leads in *Rock Follies*?

## 50

1. *Heaven Can Wait.*
2. Tamara Karsavina.
3. Washington Irving.
4. Andrea Mantegna.
5. Coco Chanel.
6. Bill Oddie, Graeme Garden, Tim Brooke-Taylor.

## 126

1. Joan Fontaine.
2. Josephine Baker.
3. Gypsy Rose Lee.
4. Differently coloured layers of paint forming an uneven effect.
5. Spalato (Split, Yugoslavia).
6. Leslie Crowther.

## 202

1. Frank Sinatra and Celeste Holm.
2. It was turned into a dance hall.
3. Thomas Keneally.
4. Roger Fry.
5. He was a Jesuit preacher, famous for the length of his sermons.
6. Rula Lenska, Julie Covington and Charlotte Cornwell.

## 51

1. Who was the Mexican Spitfire?
2. How many times did Maria Callas play Carmen on stage?
3. Who wrote *Gentlemen Prefer Blondes*?
4. Where would you go to see 'The Laughing Cavalier'?
5. Who designed the Adelphi in London?
6. What was Radio 2's previous name?

## 127

1. Who played Sam in *Casablanca*?
2. For which opera was Molière's *Le Bourgeois Gentilhomme* the inspiration?
3. Who said, 'You can lead a whore to culture but you can't make her think'?
4. In which museum would you find the 'Mona Lisa'?
5. Whose Paris house is now the Travellers' Club?
6. Whose greeting was, 'Hallo, playmates'?

## 203

1. Which is Claudette Colbert's favourite profile?
2. Who sucks where the bee sucks?
3. Who wrote a poem to his coy mistress?
4. Who portrayed 'Marriage à la Mode'?
5. Who sculpted the Pietà in St Peter's, Rome?
6. Who was the bearded television cook?

# 51

1. Lupe Velez.
2. Never.
3. Anita Loos.
4. The Wallace Collection.
5. Robert Adam.
6. The Light Programme.

# 127

1. Dooley Wilson.
2. *Ariadne auf Naxos*, by Richard Strauss.
3. Dorothy Parker.
4. The Louvre, Paris.
5. The courtesan La Paiva's.
6. Arthur Askey's.

# 203

1. The left.
2. Ariel.
3. Andrew Marvell.
4. William Hogarth.
5. Michelangelo.
6. Philip Harbin.

## 52

1. In which film did Mickey Mouse make his first appearance?
2. Who wrote *Juno and the Paycock*?
3. Who illustrated *The Tailor of Gloucester*?
4. Who painted a picture of a train emerging from a fireplace?
5. Which architect designed himself a grand house in Mantua in the 1540s?
6. Who played Gert and Daisy?

## 128

1. Who was the orchestra leader in *Orchestra Wives* (1942)?
2. Who played Rosalind in the 1967 National Theatre production of *As You Like It*?
3. Whose hero is Ripley?
4. Which French painter was supervisor of the Gobelins factory from 1755 until 1770?
5. For whom did Oscar de la Renta design a special collection?
6. How did Khachaturian's Adagio from *Spartacus* become known to millions?

## 204

1. Who was married to both Charles Chaplin and Erich Maria Remarque?
2. Of what were six characters in search in a Luigi Pirandello play?
3. Whose smile made all the world gay?
4. Who illustrated the 1894 edition of Oscar Wilde's *Salome*?
5. Who designed the Mansion House?
6. Which television personality was married to Dora Bryan?

# 52

1. *Steamboat Willie*.
2. Sean O'Casey.
3. Beatrix Potter.
4. René Magritte.
5. Giulio Romano.
6. Elsie and Doris Waters.

# 128

1. Glenn Miller.
2. Ronald Pickup.
3. Patricia Highsmith's.
4. François Boucher.
5. Barbie Doll.
6. It was the signature tune to *The Onedin Line*.

# 204

1. Paulette Goddard.
2. An author.
3. Belinda's, in Pope's *The Rape of the Lock*.
4. Aubrey Beardsley.
5. George Dance.
6. Pete Murray.

## 53

1. Which film-musical star was married to Al Jolson?
2. Which role characterized the Angry Young Man?
3. Who wrote *The American Dream*?
4. Which eighteenth-century English artist had a film company named after him?
5. Which house was presented to the Duke of Wellington by a grateful nation?
6. Who went from *Beat the Clock* to *The Generation Game*?

## 129

1. Which historical character have Dame Flora Robson and Bette Davis both portrayed more than once?
2. Which famously mean comedian never got older than thirty-nine?
3. Whose shoulder was branded with a fleur-de-lys?
4. Which Venetian painter found that the light on the Thames reminded him of his native city?
5. Why was bone china so called?
6. What product made you wonder where the yellow went?

## 205

1. Which director was famous for making an appearance in his own films?
2. Which Swedish palace has an intact eighteenth-century theatre?
3. Who was the 'Sage of Weimar'?
4. Who painted Van Gogh painting sunflowers?
5. In which city would you find the Belvedere Palace?
6. Who was the head-boy of Greyfriars?

## 53

1. Ruby Keeler.
2. Jimmy Porter's in *Look Back in Anger*.
3. Theodore Dreiser.
4. Gainsborough.
5. Stratfield Saye.
6. Bruce Forsyth.

## 129

1. Queen Elizabeth I.
2. Jack Benny.
3. Milady de Winter's.
4. Canaletto.
5. One of the ingredients was bone ash.
6. Pepsodent toothpaste.

## 205

1. Alfred Hitchcock.
2. Drottningholm.
3. Goethe.
4. Paul Gauguin.
5. Vienna.
6. Harry Wharton.

## 54

1. Name Elizabeth Taylor's husbands in order.
2. Who wrote *The Odd Couple*?
3. Who wrote *The Name of the Rose*?
4. Which painter's frequent model was Dorelia?
5. Who was Christian Dior's successor at the House of Dior?
6. Which cowboy had a horse called Topper?

## 130

1. Who played the title role in *Morgan – A Suitable Case for Treatment*?
2. Who wrote *Lorenzaccio*?
3. Who wrote the Hornblower novels?
4. Which painter decorated the auditorium ceiling of the Paris opera house?
5. For what was Clarice Cliff famous?
6. Which antipodean zithered her way to stardom?

## 206

1. What did the films *It Came from Outer Space*, *Kiss Me Kate*, *The Creature from the Black Lagoon* and *Dial M for Murder* have in common?
2. Who was the Lord High Executioner in *The Mikado*?
3. Who was the heroine of Edith Wharton's *The House of Mirth*?
4. Which Cretan artist became a naturalized Spaniard?
5. Where is the Palace of Queluz?
6. Which singing star of fifties films now plays a leading role in a popular soap opera?

# 54

1. a) Conrad Hilton, b) Michael Wilding, c) Mike Todd, d) Eddie Fisher, e) Richard Burton, f) Richard Burton, g) John Warner.
2. Neil Simon.
3. Umberto Eco.
4. Augustus John's.
5. Yves St Laurent.
6. William Boyd as Hopalong Cassidy.

# 130

1. David Warner.
2. Alfred de Musset.
3. C. S. Forester.
4. Marc Chagall.
5. Brightly coloured Art Deco china.
6. Shirley Abicair.

# 206

1 They were made (although not always shown) in 3-D.
2. Ko-ko.
3. Lily Bart.
4. El Greco.
5. Portugal.
6. Howard Keel.

## 55

1. Who played Rita Tushingham's uncle in *Dr Zhivago*?
2. What was the title of John Osborne's play about the life of Colonel Redl?
3. Who wrote about the Lost Boys?
4. Who described J. M. W. Turner's paintings as 'airy visions, painted with tinted steam'?
5. Who paid £30,000 for an incomplete set of marbles?
6. How did Lady Marjorie Bellamy die?

## 131

1. Who was the male star of *8½*?
2. What did Miss Otis regret?
3. Who wrote *The Cloister and the Hearth*?
4. Louis Daguerre was a pioneer in which field?
5. Which nineteenth-century archaeologist decked his wife in the jewels of Helen of Troy?
6. Who played the title role in the television series *The Fugitive*?

## 207

1. Who provides the devil's voice in *The Exorcist*?
2. Who wrote the play *The Cenci*?
3. Who created the character of Fielding Gray?
4. Who painted 'Experiment with an Air Pump'?
5. Which sculptor/goldsmith's most famous extant work is a salt-cellar?
6. Which presenter of two-way *Family Favourites* is married to Cliff Michelmore?

# 55

1. Alec Guinness.
2. *A Patriot for Me*.
3. J. M. Barrie.
4. John Constable.
5. Lord Elgin.
6. She drowned in the *Titanic* disaster.

# 131

1. Marcello Mastroianni.
2. That she was unable to lunch.
3. Charles Reade.
4. Photography.
5. Heinrich Schliemann.
6. David Janssen.

# 207

1. Mercedes McCambridge.
2. Percy Bysshe Shelley.
3. Simon Raven.
4. Joseph Wright of Derby.
5. Benvenuto Cellini's.
6. Jean Metcalfe.

## 56

1. Which film by Sergei Eisenstein contains a famous coronation sequence?
2. Who wrote *Rookery Nook*?
3. Where was there something nasty in the woodshed?
4. Which painting in the National Gallery in London was slashed by a suffragette?
5. Whose bronze statue of David originally stood in the courtyard of the Palazzo Medici in Florence?
6. What was Hesicos?

## 132

1. Who played the title role in *The Graduate*?
2. Who wrote *The Playboy of the Western World*?
3. Which poet was killed by an insect bite?
4. What is grisaille?
5. In which city did the four horses of St Mark's stand before going to Venice?
6. Which singer was married to Joan Collins?

## 208

1. In 1940, Tyrone Power played Diego de Vega, better known as . . .?
2. Which operatic heroine throws herself into an avalanche?
3. Who was the Laird of Abbotsford?
4. The death of which poet was depicted by Arthur Hughes?
5. Of what is the Portland vase made?
6. Who played Lord Peter Wimsey in a television series?

# 56

1. *Ivan the Terrible.*
2. Ben Travers.
3. *Cold Comfort Farm*, by Stella Gibbons.
4. Velazquez's 'Rokeby Venus'.
5. Donatello's.
6. A fictitious planet in a television series.

# 132

1. Dustin Hoffman.
2. J. M. Synge.
3. Rupert Brooke.
4. A method of painting in tones of grey.
5. Constantinople.
6. Anthony Newley.

# 208

1. Zorro.
2. Alfredo Catalani's 'La Wally'.
3. Sir Walter Scott.
4. Chatterton.
5. Glass.
6. Ian Carmichael.

# 57

1. Who designed the costumes for *Gone with the Wind*?
2. Who created the role of Eliza Doolittle in the musical *My Fair Lady* on the London stage?
3. What is the other name of Victoria Holt and Philippa Carr?
4. Which painting by Picasso is associated with a famous bridge?
5. Who designed the Anglican cathedral in Liverpool?
6. Who was the general manager of the British Broadcasting Company?

# 133

1. As which literary sisters did Hollywood cast Ida Lupino, Olivia de Havilland and Nancy Wilson?
2. Who wrote *Jumpers*?
3. Who was the housekeeper at Manderley?
4. Who painted a portrait of whom, subsequently destroyed by Lady Churchill?
5. To whom was Jean Bérain court designer?
6. Which television character was immortalized by Richard Hearne?

# 209

1. Who directed *The Dance of the Vampires*?
2. What was the previous profession of the Emperor Justinian's wife, Theodora?
3. Which English novelist lived in Henry James's former house on the south-east coast?
4. Who painted 'Bubbles'?
5. Why did the Empress Eugénie favour the crinoline?
6. Whose assistant in the kitchen wore a monocle?

## 57

1. Walter Plunkett.
2. Julie Andrews.
3. Jean Plaidy.
4. 'Les Demoiselles d'Avignon'.
5. Giles Gilbert Scott.
6. John Reith.

## 133

1. Emily, Charlotte and Anne Brontë.
2. Tom Stoppard.
3. Mrs Danvers.
4. Graham Sutherland of Sir Winston Churchill.
5. Louis XIV.
6. Mr Pastry.

## 209

1. Roman Polanski.
2. Acting or mime-playing.
3. E. F. Benson.
4. Sir John Everett Millais.
5. She was trying to boost the Lyons silk industry.
6. Fanny Craddock's.

# 58

1. Who was Juliet to Leslie Howard's Romeo on film in 1936?
2. Which critic wrote in 1819 of the all-woman play *Belles Without Beaux*, 'We do not want to encourage these Amazonian vanities'?
3. Who wrote under the pseudonym 'Q'?
4. To which school of painters did 'Old Crome' belong?
5. Which character in a Dickens novel gave her name to a hat?
6. Who played Inspector Barlow in *Z Cars* and *Softly, Softly*?

# 134

1. Which child star played in *Paper Moon*?
2. Whom did Bertrand Russell describe as 'more bounder than genius'?
3. Who wrote *The Seven Pillars of Wisdom*?
4. Which nineteenth-century painter's mistress was Mrs Newton?
5. Who designed Centre Point?
6. Who played the sergeant-major in the series *It Ain't Half Hot Mum*?

# 210

1. Who thanked Shirley Ross for the memory?
2. Who wrote the masque *Comus*?
3. To which bird did Keats write a poem?
4. Who painted Gilles?
5. Which nineteenth-century hostess gave her name to a piece of furniture?
6. Who was the host of *Zoo-time*?

# 58

1. Norma Shearer.
2. Charles Lamb.
3. Sir Arthur Quiller-Couch.
4. The Norwich School.
5. Dolly Varden.
6. Stratford Johns.

# 134

1. Tatum O'Neal.
2. George Bernard Shaw.
3. T. E. Lawrence.
4. James Tissot's.
5. Richard Seifert.
6. Windsor Davies.

# 210

1. Bob Hope.
2. John Milton.
3. A nightingale.
4. Antoine Watteau.
5. Madame Récamier.
6. Dr Desmond Morris.

## 59

1. Who was the star of *Love at First Bite*?
2. Who founded the Method school of acting?
3. Who wrote, 'A woman with fair opportunities and without a positive hump, may marry whom she likes'?
4. Who turned invisible ink into a collage?
5. Which Flemish dwarf was famous for his plasterwork?
6. Which ward was ministered to by Charles Tingwell and Frederick Bartman?

## 135

1. Which Hollywood star played Anna Karenina twice?
2. Which film-star had a walk-on part in an Oxford Playhouse production in 1966?
3. Who was the man of La Mancha?
4. Who were the Beggarstaff Brothers?
5. Which Scotsman was Catherine of Russia's favourite architect?
6. Whose girlfriend was Luby-Loo?

## 211

1. Who was the Brazilian Bombshell?
2. Which Russian prima ballerina took the starring role in a revival of *On Your Toes*?
3. Who wrote *Vathek*?
4. Who founded the Kelmscott Press?
5. What is a caryatid?
6. Who was the *Tonight* reporter who spoke with a strong Scots brogue?

## 59

1. George Hamilton.
2. Lee Strasberg.
3. William Thackeray.
4. Kurt Schwitters.
5. François Cuvilliés.
6. Emergency Ward 10.

## 135

1. Greta Garbo.
2. Elizabeth Taylor.
3. Don Quixote.
4. William Nicholson and James Pryde.
5. Charles Cameron.
6. Andy Pandy's.

## 211

1. Carmen Miranda.
2. Natalia Makarova.
3. William Beckford.
4. William Morris.
5. A support in the form of a female figure.
6. Fyffe Robertson.

## 60

1. Which film-star couldn't help it?
2. Who was the Israeli star of *Fiddler on the Roof*?
3. Which second-century bard was 'resurrected' by James Macpherson in the mid eighteenth century?
4. What did Ruskin find so disturbing in his wife?
5. What is a polonaise, apart from a dance?
6. Who played Joan in *I Married Joan*?

## 136

1. Which Hitchcock film featured James Stewart with a broken leg?
2. Who wrote *Long Day's Journey Into Night*?
3. Name three people who might have been in the Hons' cupboard with Nancy Mitford.
4. Who decorated the Panthéon in Paris with the 'Life of Sainte Geneviève'?
5. Which mistress of Louis XIV gave her name to a head-dress?
6. Which cartoon couple lived in a cave?

## 212

1. Which film concerns a mutiny and massacre in Odessa?
2. Which actor was the brother of Sarah Siddons?
3. Who killed Guy of Gisborne?
4. What do the letters P.R.B. stand for?
5. Who was 'The Shrimp'?
6. Who was the first person to *Do It Yourself*?

## 60

1. Jayne Mansfield.
2. Topol.
3. Ossian.
4. Pubic hair.
5. A type of carpet.
6. Joan Davies.

## 136

1. *Rear Window.*
2. Eugene O'Neill.
3. Unity, Diana, Pamela, Jessica, Deborah and Tom.
4. Pierre Puvis de Chavannes.
5. Mademoiselle de Fontanges.
6. Fred and Wilma Flintstone.

## 212

1. *Battleship Potemkin.*
2. John Philip Kemble.
3. Robin Hood.
4. The Pre-Raphaelite Brotherhood.
5. Jean Shrimpton.
6. Barrie Bucknell.

## 61

1. Which film is credited with the origin of the phrase 'Not tonight, Josephine'?
2. The 'Haughty, Gallant, Gay Lothario' appears in which seventeenth-century play?
3. Who wrote *She*?
4. Which two painters were the leading proponents of the style known as Intimisme?
5. An Imperial Chinese dragon has how many claws?
6. Why is the Mall roadway red in colour?

## 137

1. Who directed *Ordinary People*?
2. What was the name of Nana Mouskouri's backing group?
3. Who established the Académie française?
4. What was considered scandalous about Manet's 'Déjeuner sur l'herbe'?
5. Who sculpted the figure of Nelson in Trafalgar Square?
6. Which famous detective was played by Bruce Seton?

## 213

1. Which photographer was the model for the main character in Antonioni's film *Blow-Up*?
2. Who staged *Oh What a Lovely War*?
3. Which art historian won the Booker Prize in 1984?
4. At the end of his life, who was Ruskin's favourite painter?
5. Who designed the Cenotaph?
6. Who were always *On Safari*?

# 61

1. *I Cover the Waterfront.*
2. *The Fair Penitent* by Nicholas Rowe.
3. H. Rider Haggard.
4. Pierre Bonnard and Édouard Vuillard.
5. Five.
6. It was changed to this colour in 1953 for the televising of Elizabeth II's coronation.

# 137

1. Robert Redford.
2. The Athenians.
3. Cardinal Richelieu.
4. The lady has no clothes on.
5. Edward Hodges Baily.
6. Fabian of the Yard.

# 213

1. David Bailey.
2. Joan Littlewood.
3. Anita Brookner.
4. Kate Greenaway.
5. Sir Edwin Lutyens.
6. Armand and Michaela Denis.

## 62

1. Who played the leading role in *Hud*?
2. What is the name of the Prince's servant/companion in the pantomime *Cinderella*?
3. What kind of animal was Shere Khan?
4. Which artist was the author of 'The Analysis of Beauty'?
5. For what was a canopic vase used?
6. Who immortalized the part of Mrs Slocombe of Grace Brothers department store?

## 138

1. Which film starred Vivien Leigh, Lotte Lenya, Warren Beatty and Coral Browne?
2. What is the name of the laundress in the pantomime *Aladdin*?
3. Who wrote *Pantagruel*?
4. What flaming moment was captured by J. M. W. Turner?
5. Who designed Monticello, Virginia?
6. What was Champion?

## 214

1. Which two cousins both starred and danced in films opposite Fred Astaire?
2. What precedes performances at the Comédie Française?
3. Who wrote *Nightmare Abbey* and *Headlong Hall*?
4. Who painted Mrs Siddons as the Tragic Muse?
5. Which silversmith had a famous ride?
6. Name three of the four actresses who played John Steed's companion in *The Avengers*.

## 62

1. Paul Newman.
2. Dandini.
3. A tiger.
4. William Hogarth.
5. Holding the entrails of embalmed bodies in Ancient Egypt.
6. Mollie Sugden.

## 138

1. *The Roman Spring of Mrs Stone* (1961).
2. The Widow Twankey.
3. François Rabelais.
4. The burning of the Houses of Parliament.
5. Thomas Jefferson.
6. The Wonder Horse.

## 214

1. Ginger Rogers and Rita Hayworth.
2. Three knocks on the floor.
3. T. L. Peacock.
4. Sir Joshua Reynolds.
5. Paul Revere.
6. The four were Honor Blackman, Diana Rigg, Linda Thorson and Joanna Lumley.

## 63

1. Who were the two stars of *The Paleface* (1948)?
2. What did Miss Prism think she had put in her handbag?
3. What is the name of Dorothy Sayers's sleuth?
4. Who painted 'The Night Watch'?
5. What is an aquamanile?
6. Which panel game regularly taxed the wits of Isobel Barnett, Nancy Spain, Barbara Kelly, Bernard Braden and Gilbert Harding?

## 139

1. Which film-star was Mia Farrow's mother?
2. Who wroteathe lyrics for the musical *West Side Story*?
3. Than what had Earth not anything to show more fair?
4. Who had an 'Apparition of a Face and Fruit-dish on a Beach'?
5. Who designed Somerset House?
6. Who painted the adventures of Willoughby all over the wall?

## 215

1. Which star wore the Red Shoes?
2. Who wrote *Saved*?
3. Which writer was the lover of Una, Lady Troubridge?
4. To which family do Camille, Lucien and Orovida belong?
5. What was a Macaroni?
6. Which comedy series starred Miriam Karlin, Peter Jones and Esmé Cannon?

## 63

1. Bob Hope and Jane Russell.
2. A three-volume novel of her own composition.
3. Lord Peter Wimsey.
4. Rembrandt van Rijn.
5. A medieval ewer, often in the form of an animal, for washing the hands at the table.
6. *What's My Line?*

## 139

1. Maureen O'Sullivan.
2. Stephen Sondheim.
3. A view of London in the early morning from Westminster Bridge.
4. Salvador Dali.
5. Sir William Chambers.
6. Rolf Harris.

## 215

1. Moira Shearer.
2. Edward Bond.
3. Radcliffe Hall.
4. The Pissarro family.
5. An eighteenth-century dandy.
6. *The Rag Trade.*

## 64

1. Which Spencer Tracy film was concerned with the theory of evolution?
2. What was Prospero before he became a magician?
3. Who wrote *Les Fleurs du mal*?
4. What is the colour of the Gainsborough boy at Waddesdon?
5. For which queen did Inigo Jones design a house at Greenwich?
6. Who played Eric Sykes's 'twin' sister?

## 140

1. Who are the three stars who have played Sadie Thompson on screen?
2. Who wrote the comedies *Knights*, *Wasps*, *Birds*, *Clouds* and *Frogs*?
3. Who wrote the story 'The Letter'?
4. Who wrote about the Larkin family of End Street?
5. In which city did Charles III found the Buen Retiro porcelain factory in 1759?
6. Who was the host of *Take Your Pick*?

## 216

1. Which Blue Angel later had a successful singing career on stage and in cabaret?
2. Who was the scandalous star of *The Little Show* in New York between the wars?
3. Who wrote *The Woman in White*?
4. Why is the Jeu de Paume museum in Paris so called?
5. For producing what were the Biller and Drentwett families of Augsburg famous?
6. Who created the role of Jason King?

# A

## 64

1. *Inherit the Wind.*
2. A duke.
3. Charles Baudelaire.
4. Pink.
5. Anne of Denmark.
6. Hattie Jacques.

## 140

1. Joan Crawford, Gloria Swanson and Rita Hayworth.
2. Aristophanes.
3. W. Somerset Maugham.
4. H. E. Bates.
5. Madrid.
6. Michael Miles.

## 216

1. Marlene Dietrich.
2. Libby Hollman.
3. Wilkie Collins.
4. Because the building was the former royal tennis-courts.
5. Finely worked silver objects.
6. Peter Wyngarde.

## 65

1. Which two stars of *The Misfits* died within a year of its completion?
2. Who made the cachucha the rage in the 1840s?
3. Who wrote *Whisky Galore*?
4. Who painted twin portraits of his patroness dressed and undressed?
5. What is a buskin?
6. Where do the Wombles live?

## 141

1. Name two of the three actors who have played Richard Hannay in *The Thirty-Nine Steps*.
2. How does the Duke of Clarence die in *Richard III*?
3. Who created the character of Frankenstein?
4. Who was the most famous pupil of Perugino?
5. Who carved 'Prospero and Ariel' on Broadcasting House?
6. Which former newsreader showed that she could shake a leg?

## 217

1. Who played Leslie Caron's grandmother in *Gigi*?
2. Who wrote *Le Cid*?
3. Who wrote *The Sword in the Stone*?
4. Who was court painter to Philip IV of Spain?
5. What was the 'Skylon'?
6. At which address would you have regularly found Roger Smith, Ed Byrne and Efrem Zimbalist Jr?

## 65

1. Marilyn Monroe and Clark Gable.
2. Fanny Elssler.
3. Compton Mackenzie.
4. Francisco de Goya y Lucientes.
5. A kind of boot worn by a classical actor.
6. Wimbledon Common.

## 141

1. Robert Donat, Kenneth More and Robert Powell.
2. He drowns in a butt of malmsey wine.
3. Mary Shelley.
4. Raphael.
5. Eric Gill.
6. Angela Rippon.

## 217

1. Hermione Gingold.
2. Pierre Corneille.
3. T. H. White.
4. Diego Velazquez.
5. A sculptural symbolic structure created for the Festival of Britain.
6. 77 Sunset Strip.

## 66

1. Who directed *The Damned*?
2. What is the stage name of Peggy Hookham?
3. Who was David Copperfield's nurse?
4. Who painted Monet painting in his boat?
5. Who designed the old Bank of England?
6. Who showed us what things would be like in *Tomorrow's World*?

## 142

1. Name two of the three actors who played the sailors in *On the Town*.
2. What was the profession of Jane Avril?
3. Which poet was in love with Fanny Brawne?
4. Who painted 'Whaam'?
5. Who designed the trousseau for the Duchess of Windsor?
6. Who was the presenter of *Checkpoint*?

## 218

1. To whom did Judy Garland sing 'You made me love you'?
2. The playwright Gordon Daviot had another *nom de plume*. What was it?
3. Which lexicographer wrote *Rasselas*?
4. Which artist was famous for drawing ingenious joke contraptions?
5. Who designed the Paris opera house?
6. Who was the star of *Harbour Patrol*?

## 66

1. Luchino Visconti.
2. Margot Fonteyn.
3. Peggotty.
4. Édouard Manet.
5. Sir John Soane.
6. Raymond Baxter.

## 142

1. The three were Frank Sinatra, Gene Kelly and Jules Munshin.
2. She was a singer and can-can dancer.
3. John Keats.
4. Roy Lichtenstein.
5. Mainbocher.
6. Roger Cook.

## 218

1. Clark Gable.
2. Josephine Tey.
3. Samuel Johnson.
4. W. Heath Robinson.
5. Charles Garnier.
6. Wendell Corey.

## 67

1. Which actress played the lady who vanished in Alfred Hitchcock's 1938 film?
2. Who were the two stars of *Vivat! Vivat Regina!*?
3. Which novel by Flaubert is set in North Africa?
4. Who was the most important member of the Fauves?
5. Where would you find the late Gothic style called Manueline?
6. To which family did Uncle Fester belong?

## 143

1. Which film was nicknamed 'Elizabeth and her German Garden'?
2. Who was the poet who wrote the libretti for Richard Strauss's *Der Rosenkavalier* and *Elektra*?
3. Who came down like a wolf on the fold?
4. Which painting was inspired by a cannibalistic sea voyage?
5. Who supplied the furniture for the Khedive's palace in Istanbul in 1900?
6. Who founded the television company Desilu?

## 219

1. Who played the title role in *That Hamilton Woman*?
2. Which royal mistress ended up as a side-show attraction at a circus?
3. What were the heroines of Angela Brazil's novels?
4. Who painted 'The Isle of the Dead'?
5. Who popularized tartan in England in the nineteenth century?
6. Who was Cowboy Hank's sworn enemy?

## 67

1. Dame May Whitty.
2. Eileen Atkins and Sarah Miles.
3. *Salammbô.*
4. Henri Matisse.
5. In Portugal.
6. The Addams family.

## 143

1. Paul Czinner's 1936 version of *As You Like It* with Elisabeth Bergner as Rosalind.
2. Hugo von Hofmannsthal.
3. The Assyrian.
4. Théodore Géricault's 'Raft of the Medusa'.
5. Carlo Bugatti.
6. Desi Arnaz and Lucille Ball.

## 219

1. Vivien Leigh.
2. Lola Montez.
3. Schoolgirls.
4. Arnold Böcklin.
5. Prince Albert.
6. Mexican Pete.

## 68

1. In Hitchcock's *Psycho* what was Norman Bates's hobby?
2. On which story did Verdi base his opera *La Traviata*?
3. Name three of Lytton Strachey's eminent Victorians.
4. A painting by which artist was recently found in a Butlin's holiday camp and sold for a record price?
5. Whose mother had herself portrayed after a classical sculpture of Agrippina?
6. Who was the original presenter of *Panorama*?

## 144

1. What was the Titfield Thunderbolt?
2. Who staged a series of farces at the Whitehall Theatre?
3. Who wrote *Cautionary Tales*?
4. Which sixteenth/seventeenth-century Italian painter is reputed to have remained a lifelong virgin?
5. In which city did Charles III found the Capodimonte porcelain factory in 1743?
6. What was 'my friend Flicka'?

## 220

1. Which art historian's descendant played the heroine in Stanley Kubrick's *Barry Lyndon*?
2. Who wrote *Phèdre*?
3. Who wrote *The Little White Doves of Love* and *Men Are Wonderful*?
4. Who painted a dual hamburger?
5. What is amber?
6. Whose catchphrase was, 'Ooh, you are awful!'?

## 68

1. Stuffing birds.
2. *La Dame aux camélias* by Alexandre Dumas.
3. Florence Nightingale, Thomas Arnold, General Gordon, Cardinal Manning.
4. William Dyce.
5. Napoleon's.
6. Richard Dimbleby.

## 144

1. A train.
2. Brian Rix.
3. Hilaire Belloc.
4. Guido Reni.
5. Naples.
6. A horse.

## 220

1. Bernard Berenson's.
2. Jean Racine.
3. Barbara Cartland.
4. Claes Oldenburg.
5. A yellowish translucent fossil resin.
6. Dick Emery's.

# Q

## 69

1. Who was the male lead in *Bolero* and *Rumba*?
2. Who was Nancy Spungen's boyfriend?
3. Which eighteenth-century author wrote a famous parody of Richardson's *Pamela*?
4. Which painter was Sir James Thornhill's son-in-law?
5. To which movement did Vladimir Tatlin and Naum Gabo belong?
6. Who hosted *Juke-Box Jury*?

## 145

1. Who directed *Rebecca*?
2. Which city is the setting for *Romeo and Juliet*?
3. Who wrote *For Whom the Bell Tolls*?
4. Who were Rossetti's three main models?
5. What was Lancelot Brown's nickname?
6. Who, having been one of Robin Hood's merry men, headed a ministry?

## 221

1. 'Garbo talks' announced her first sound role. What was it?
2. Who were the 'wilis'?
3. Which Sicilian nobleman wrote *Il gattopardo*?
4. Who painted a mural in the Rockefeller Center, New York, which included a portrait of Lenin?
5. In which city did Caspar Lehmann first produce cut glass in the late sixteenth century?
6. Which character's son was played by Harry H. Corbett?

## 69

1. George Raft.
2. Rock-star Sid Vicious.
3. Henry Fielding (*Shamela*).
4. William Hogarth.
5. Constructivism.
6. David Jacobs.

## 145

1. Alfred Hitchcock.
2. Verona.
3. Ernest Hemingway.
4. Elizabeth Siddal, Jane Burden/Morris, Fanny Cornforth.
5. Capability.
6. Paul Eddington.

## 221

1. *Anna Christie*.
2. Ghosts of jilted brides in the ballet *Giselle*.
3. Giuseppe di Lampedusa.
4. Diego Rivera.
5. Prague.
6. Steptoe's.

# 70

1. Who played Mr Micawber in the 1935 film version of *David Copperfield*?
2. Who created the female lead role in *Who's Afraid of Virginia Woolf?*
3. Who coveted Naboth's vineyard?
4. By what name is the painter Giovanni Antonio Bazzi better known?
5. What is an andiron?
6. What did TW3 stand for in the early sixties?

# 146

1. The book *Pentimento* by Lillian Hellman gave rise to which film in 1977?
2. Who hailed from Brazil, where the nuts come from?
3. Who is reputed to have proposed the toast, 'Let us drink to the queer old Dean'?
4. For whose equestrian portrait was Stubbs's 'Whistlejacket' originally intended?
5. Which dress designer also had an interior decorating salon called 'Martine' after one of his daughters?
6. With whom did people come *Face to Face*?

# 222

1. Who played Professor Higgins in the 1938 film version of *Pygmalion*?
2. Who was described by Kenneth Tynan as 'the glass eye in the forehead of English acting'?
3. Who wrote a novel about Jane Eyre's predecessor, the first Mrs Rochester?
4. Who painted three battle pictures for the Medici?
5. What is the architect B. Lubetkin's most visited structure?
6. Whose tricks never went right?

## 70

1. W. C. Fields.
2. Uta Hagen.
3. King David.
4. Il Sodoma.
5. A fire-dog.
6. *That Was The Week That Was*.

## 146

1. *Julia*.
2. Charley's Aunt.
3. Rev. W. A. Spooner.
4. George III's.
5. Paul Poiret.
6. John Freeman.

## 222

1. Leslie Howard.
2. Sir Ralph Richardson.
3. Jean Rhys.
4. Paolo Uccello.
5. The Penguin Pool at Regent's Park Zoo.
6. Tommy Cooper's.

## 71

1. Which was reputedly the first film with an all-black cast?
2. Which country first developed a theatrical tradition?
3. Who wrote *The Fountainhead*?
4. Who produced a famous lithograph of Aristide Bruant?
5. What is japanning?
6. Who played the blonde night-club singer in *The Roaring Twenties*?

## 147

1. Who played the Irish nurse in the film version of Joe Orton's *Loot*?
2. What was Cyrano de Bergerac's most noticeable feature?
3. Who wrote "The Battle Hymn of the Republic"?
4. Who were the two most famous miniature painters of Elizabethan England?
5. For which other structure is the designer of the Statue of Liberty well known?
6. Who introduced *Animal Magic*?

## 223

1. 'Nobody's perfect' is the last line of which classic comedy?
2. Who wrote *Noises Off*?
3. Who wrote the story 'The Three Fat Women of Antibes'?
4. With which branch of portraiture would you associate Julia Margaret Cameron?
5. Which Italian was Empress Elizabeth of Russia's favourite architect?
6. Who played George IV in the series about the king's life?

# 71

1. *Cabin in the Sky*.
2. Greece.
3. Ayn Rand.
4. Henri de Toulouse-Lautrec.
5. A type of European lacquer-work.
6. Dorothy Provine.

# 147

1. Lee Remick.
2. His nose.
3. Julia Ward Howe.
4. Nicholas Hilliard and Isaac Oliver.
5. The Eiffel Tower.
6. Johnny Morris.

# 223

1. *Some Like It Hot*.
2. Michael Frayn.
3. W. Somerset Maugham.
4. Photographic.
5. Bartolomeo Rastrelli.
6. Peter Egan.

# 72

1. What does not appear in *The Women* that has appeared in virtually every other Hollywood film?
2. Who wrote the words and music for 'Let's Do It'?
3. Who wrote *Casanova's Chinese Restaurant*?
4. Whose portrait of the Princess of Wales was slashed soon after going on public view?
5. Who commissioned Westmacott's statue of Achilles at Hyde Park Corner?
6. Who used to tell us what the prizes were on *Take Your Pick*?

# 148

1. Who was the first *My Man Godfrey*?
2. Who wrote *The Queen Mother*?
3. Who wrote *Our Man in Havana*?
4. Which mid-nineteenth-century portrait-painter found great favour both with Queen Victoria and Empress Eugénie?
5. What is stumpwork?
6. Who was the star of *Highway Patrol*?

# 224

1. Who directed *Apocalypse Now*?
2. Who wrote *Gaslight*?
3. In which street did Robert Browning's future wife live?
4. Who was reputedly the teacher of Giotto?
5. What is a baldachin?
6. Who played the landlady in *Man About the House*?

## 72

1. A man.
2. Cole Porter.
3. Anthony Powell.
4. Bryan Organ's.
5. The 'Grateful Women of England'.
6. Bob Danvers-Walker.

## 148

1. William Powell.
2. Algernon Swinburne.
3. Graham Greene.
4. Franz Xaver Winterhalter.
5. Raised needlework.
6. Broderick Crawford.

## 224

1. Francis Ford Coppola.
2. Patrick Hamilton.
3. Wimpole Street.
4. Cimabue.
5. A canopy.
6. Yootha Joyce.

## 73

1. Who directed *Fahrenheit 451*?
2. Who was the producer of *Cowardy Custard*?
3. Who wrote *Pale Fire*?
4. Which Austrian Expressionist painter is known for his erotically charged work?
5. What is Opus Anglicanum?
6. Who was the loquacious compère of *The Good Old Days*?

## 149

1. Who directed the 1980 *Lili Marleen*?
2. Who wrote *The Front Page*?
3. Who was the headmaster of Dotheboys Hall?
4. Who founded the Pittura Metafisica movement in 1917?
5. What is the term used in England for Jugendstil and Stile Liberty?
6. Who played the title role in *Father, Dear Father*?

## 225

1. Who directed *E.T.*?
2. Who wrote *A Taste of Honey*?
3. Which of Pushkin's characters shot Lensky?
4. Who, together with Pablo Picasso, was one of the first exponents of Cubism?
5. Who restored the Warwick vase?
6. Who stops weeks and calls bluffs?

## 73

1. François Truffaut.
2. Wendy Toye.
3. Vladimir Nabokov.
4. Egon Schiele.
5. Medieval English ecclesiastical embroidery, used for vestments.
6. Leonard Sachs.

## 149

1. Rainer Werner Fassbinder.
2. Ben Hecht.
3. Mr Wackford Squeers.
4. Giorgio de Chirico.
5. Art Nouveau.
6. Patrick Cargill.

## 225

1. Steven Spielberg.
2. Shelagh Delaney.
3. Eugene Onegin.
4. Georges Braque.
5. Giambattista Piranesi.
6. Robert Robinson.

# 74

1. Which two French actresses have starred as the mistress of Crown Prince Rudolf in *Mayerling*?
2. Who wrote the musical *Perchance to Dream*?
3. Who wrote *The Snow Goose*?
4. With which group of intellectuals were the Omega Workshops associated?
5. Where might you find the initials BVRB or RVLC?
6. Where does Captain Peacock work?

# 150

1. Who played the title role in *The Millionairess*?
2. Which is 'the Scottish play'?
3. Of which Jane Austen novel is Anne Elliot the heroine?
4. Who illustrated the 'Shell Book' and the 'Hundred Screamers'?
5. What colour is cinnabar lacquer?
6. What lifts and separates?

# 226

1. Which Proust characters were played on film by Jeremy Irons and Ornella Muti?
2. Which musical by Frank Loesser concerns the fate of a Salvation Army lass?
3. Chaucer's Wife of Bath had had how many husbands?
4. Which Scottish artist was appointed official painter to George III?
5. What were Paul de Lamerie and Paul Storr?
6. Who played Handel in John Osborne's *God Rot Tunbridge Wells*?

# 74

1. Danielle Darrieux and Catherine Deneuve.
2. Ivor Novello.
3. Paul Gallico.
4. The Bloomsbury Group.
5. On a piece of French eighteenth-century furniture.
6. At Grace Brothers department store.

# 150

1. Sophia Loren.
2. *Macbeth.*
3. *Persuasion.*
4. Utamaro.
5. Red.
6. A Playtex 'Cross Your Heart' bra.

# 226

1. Charles Swann and Odette de Crécy.
2. *Guys and Dolls.*
3. Five.
4. Allan Ramsay.
5. Silversmiths.
6. Trevor Howard.

## 75

1. Who starred as the Sicilian nobleman in *The Leopard*?
2. What was the profession of Adrienne Lecouvreur?
3. In which sequence of novels would you read about Mrs Proudie and Archdeacon Grantly?
4. On whose painting is Manet's 'The Balcony' based?
5. What does pinchbeck try to imitate?
6. Which former newsreader now introduces *The Saturday Six O'Clock Show*?

## 151

1. Which pioneer of the cinema showed comical landings on the moon?
2. Which professor of mathematics wrote 'The Masochism Tango'?
3. Who wrote *Fanny Hill*?
4. Who is the most famous painter and sculptor of the old American West?
5. Which English ex-serviceman became a leading Paris couturier?
6. The advertisement for what ends with the words 'Vorsprung durch Technik'?

## 227

1. Who were the 'two little girls from Little Rock'?
2. Which two actors alternated in the role of Othello and Iago on the London stage in 1956?
3. Of which novel is Dorothea Casaubon the heroine?
4. Who was the British-born French Impressionist?
5. With which medium would you associate the name of Johann Joachim Kändler?
6. Which former radio disc-jockey is now known for his outrageous comedy shows?

# 75

1. Burt Lancaster.
2. Acting.
3. Anthony Trollope's Barsetshire chronicles.
4. Goya's.
5. Gold.
6. Michael Aspel.

# 151

1. Georges Méliès.
2. Tom Lehrer.
3. John Cleland.
4. Frederic Remington.
5. Captain Edward Molyneux.
6. Audi motor-cars.

# 227

1. Marilyn Monroe and Jane Russell.
2. John Neville and Richard Burton.
3. George Eliot's *Middlemarch*.
4. Alfred Sisley.
5. Porcelain (at Meissen).
6. Kenny Everett.

## 76

1. Who directed and produced *The Private Life of Henry VIII*?
2. Who wrote the play *Entertaining Mr Sloane*?
3. Who wrote *Lettres de mon moulin*?
4. Which movement was parodied by W. S. Gilbert in 'Patience'?
5. Which two famous interior designers of the French Empire period were buried in the same tomb?
6. Where did the Jumblies sleep?

## 152

1. Who directed and designed the version of *La Traviata* starring Teresa Stratas and Placido Domingo?
2. Who founded the Royal Court Theatre and wrote *The Voysey Inheritance*?
3. Who was given a tour of the infernal regions by Virgil?
4. Which painter was imprisoned for caricaturing King Louis-Philippe?
5. Which Florentine Renaissance sculptor is especially associated with glazed ceramic sculptures?
6. Which television series depicts life in a holiday camp?

## 228

1. Who played Bluebeard's eighth wife?
2. Which musical celebrated the Age of Aquarius?
3. A novel by which American-born writer was made into the Hollywood film *The Heiress*?
4. Who painted 'The Birth of Venus' and 'Primavera'?
5. Which Czech artist produced work in many media epitomizing the spirit of continental Art Nouveau?
6. Than what sort of ice-lolly could there be nothing nicer?

# 76

1. Sir Alexander Korda.
2. Joe Orton.
3. Alphonse Daudet.
4. The 'Aesthetic' movement of the 1880s.
5. Charles Percier and Pierre-François-Léonard Fontaine.
6. On the ceiling.

# 152

1. Franco Zeffirelli.
2. H. Granville-Barker.
3. Dante.
4. Honoré Daumier.
5. Luca della Robbia.
6. *Hi-de-hi.*

# 228

1. Claudette Colbert.
2. *Hair*.
3. Henry James (*Washington Square*).
4. Sandro Botticelli.
5. Alphonse Mucha.
6. A Pendleton's Twicer.

# Part 2
# The Pure Trivia Quiz

Edited by Margaret Hickey

with

Bruce Alexander
Roxy Beaujolais
Anne Beech
Faye Carney
Andrew Kennedy
Giles MacDonogh
Lesley Venn
Martin Venn

# Introduction to The Pure Trivia Quiz

When I was twelve, a music teacher started reading to us from a book about Wagner. He had, we were told, a huge Newfoundland dog. 'But you needn't remember that,' said the teacher. Needless to say, that was the only thing I *have* remembered – in fact it has stayed with me ever since, and I shall undoubtedly carry it with me to the grave.

The question is Why? Is it the rebel in all of us which refuses to hearken to reason and be bound by matters of weight and import? Do certain facts, like fish hooks, have barbs attached to them? Or is it that we have never lost the child's delight in all that is wider, faster, richer and larger than our own lives – but not larger than life itself? Whatever the answer, a good store of trivial knowledge is not to be sniffed at.

This particular section contains real gold-plated trivia – the categories into which they have been divided are as follows:

1. **People.** Who would have thought that Evelyn Waugh presented Marie Stopes with a bunch of yellow mimosa after one of her meetings? (And what is the significance of yellow mimosa?) Or that ex-President Gerald Ford was actually born Leslie King?
2. **Nostalgia.** Some of our readers will remember as far back as Queen Victoria, but we have confined our 'Do you remember?'s to the past forty years or so – from the days when we were all worrying about which twin had the Toni and shielding our eyes from the glare of Kathy Kirby's lips to more recent phenomena, such as those windscreen stickers that declared to the world that Dave and Tracy were indissoluble for at least as long as the adhesive lasted.
3. **Food and Drink.** You might have thought it was the Beatles who conceived the idea that you are what you eat, but Brillat-Savarin got there before them. Eating and drinking are the (literally) vital concern of us all, although few of us care quite so passionately as that French master cook who declared, 'Dessert without cheese is like a beautiful woman with only one eye.'
4. **Deep Trivia.** This category encompasses all the trivia which is so ephemeral as to defy categorization. You may have

known that George Washington was proud of his (wooden) set of false teeth, but I'll bet a pound to a penny you didn't know he soaked them overnight in port.

5. **Living Creatures.** From the bedbug, which can live for up to two years without food (so none of us should be complacent), to the elephant, which spends twenty-three out of twenty-four hours seaching for and then eating its food, this category provides a rich repository of trivial knowledge.

6. **Leisure.** Most of us work on the chain gang from Monday to Friday, so it is only at the weekend that we get a chance to *really* slave – digging the garden, decorating the house and thinking up ways of staunching the infinite floods of boredom that children seem able to generate. There are some occasions when leisure means hobbies, treats and travel, too, and this category presents the facets of life as seen during our spare time. If no one has ever explained the facets of life to you, we will. Do you, for instance, know where to find a Royal Sovereign in bed with a Hampshire Maid? You'll find the answer here!

Enjoy yourselves. I hope you don't learn anything *too* useful from this section, but if you do, don't be alarmed – there is every chance it won't stick.

Margaret Hickey

# 1

1. Which Old Etonian had the greatest difficulty in dealing cards?
2. What ran out of kippers and steam on 30 April 1972?
3. In which country do they serve chicken in a chocolate sauce?
4. Cockneys should be born within the sound of Bow Bells. Where are they?
5. What is the colouring of a Palomino horse?
6. Who would talk about his hobby in terms of squeakers, YBs and OBs?

# 77

1. Karl Frahm changed his name to avoid arrest by the Gestapo. By what name do we know him today?
2. Why did Victor become a matter of public concern in 1977?
3. What was introduced in the 1970s by the chairman of the English Country Cheese Council?
4. What broke out in Barcelona in 1493 following Columbus's return from the New World?
5. The fur of which animal makes the lightest, yet warmest, coat?
6. Habutai, tussah and georgette are all types of what?

# 153

1. Who wrote, 'After us, the deluge'?
2. When did the Cannes Film Festival first begin?
3. What is mock turtle soup made of?
4. What are Napier's bones?
5. What is a badger's home called?
6. What started to brighten our weekends on 4 February 1962?

# 1

1. Captain Hook. (J. M. Barrie, the author of *Peter Pan*, is at pains to point out where the pirate was educated.)
2. The *Brighton Belle*, the Brighton to Victoria train, which made its last journey then.
3. Mexico.
4. In the church of St Mary-le-Bow in Cheapside, not in Bow.
5. It is cream-coloured, with a light mane and tail.
6. A pigeon-fancier. (A squeaker is a chick or young bird still squeaking; a YB is a young bird; and an OB is an old bird.)

# 77

1. Willy Brandt.
2. He was a giraffe that collapsed and eventually died at a Winchester zoo.
3. The ploughman's lunch. The food (bread, cheese and pickled onions) is traditional, but the phrase was coined as an advertising slogan.
4. Syphilis.
5. The mink.
6. Silk.

# 153

1. Madame de Pompadour.
2. In 1947.
3. Sheep's head and spices.
4. John Napier's logarithm tables.
5. A set.
6. The first *Sunday Times* colour supplement appeared.

## 2

1. Who met the maidservant Hannah Cullwick in 1854 and finally married her in 1873?
2. When did the last London tram go to the Great Scrapyard in the Sky?
3. Which fish is the principal ingredient of *quenelles de brochet*?
4. In an astrological birth chart, what is the ascendant?
5. What kinds of creature are archy and mehitabel?
6. In the grounds of which Yorkshire 'castle' do you find Vanbrugh's Temple of the Four Winds and Hawksmoor's Mausoleum?

## 78

1. John Paul II is the first non-Italian pope since which century?
2. Where did Marlon Brando get 'a one-way ticket to Palookaville'?
3. What is *hotchi-witchi*?
4. ETA seeks the liberation of . . . what?
5. Napoleon's horse was seized by the British as a prize of war. Where is its skeleton to be found?
6. When was the first Chelsea Flower Show?

## 154

1. Which arm and which eye did Nelson lose in service?
2. Who was worried about Jim?
3. With what is *sole véronique* garnished?
4. From which country do cars bearing the letters RCH come?
5. What was the name of Dorothy's little dog in *The Wizard of Oz*?
6. Where in England would you find a reproduction of part of George Washington's flower garden in Mount Vernon?

# 2

1. Arthur Munby, poet and socialite.
2. In 1952.
3. Pike.
4. The sign coming over the horizon at the time of someone's birth.
5. Archy is a cockroach and mehitabel an alley cat in Don Marquis's *archy's life of mehitabel.* (For a correct answer, both must be right.)
6. Castle Howard.

# 78

1. The fifteenth century. (Adrian VI was born in Utrecht in 1459.)
2. In *On the Waterfront.*
3. The Romany name for hedgehog. Gipsies bake it in clay, and when the hog is cooked the case is broken off, bringing with it prickles and skin.
4. The Basque homelands in Spain.
5. The National Army Museum, London.
6. In 1913.

# 154

1. The right in both cases.
2. Mrs Dale in *Mrs Dale's Diary.*
3. White grapes.
4. Chile.
5. Toto.
6. The American Museum, Claverton Manor, near Bath.

## 3

1. In Italy, in 1981, the world's largest-ever fine for an individual was imposed on this man. Who is he?
2. Who was the first Doctor Who?
3. What is the difference between York ham and that of Bradenham, Westphalia, Parma and Bayonne?
4. Why did the Jarrow March take place?
5. In cold conditions many animals go into hibernation. What is the opposite process (inactivity during hot, dry conditions) known as?
6. What was the traditional way of propelling a narrowboat through a long tunnel?

## 79

1. Who is believed to have had a vocabulary of 32,000 words?
2. Who took more than three steps to heaven in 1960?
3. What is measured on the Gay–Lussac scale?
4. How did the jeep get its name?
5. What is the opposite of a bird's-eye view?
6. According to Bram Stoker, to which popular holiday resort did Count Dracula float ashore in his coffin?

## 155

1. Who was the first Poet Laureate?
2. Who composed the score for the 1960s film *Shaft*?
3. *Gefiltefisch* is a Jewish speciality. Which fish is used?
4. Who developed a vaccine against polio?
5. What is the name of the mysterious ape-man reportedly sighted in North America?
6. What does British law require pedal cyclists to have on them every time they take to the road?

## 3

1. Carlo Ponti, husband of Sophia Loren.
2. William Hartnell.
3. York ham is cooked; the rest are cured raw.
4. It was organized in 1936 to protest against severe unemployment.
5. Aestivation.
6. Two 'leggers' lay on their backs on a board placed across the boat and 'walked' crabwise along the walls. (Their boot marks are still visible in some places.)

## 79

1. William Shakespeare.
2. Eddie Cochrane, killed while touring Britain.
3. Alcoholic strength: 100° is pure alcohol.
4. It is a General-Purpose Vehicle – hence GP.
5. A worm's-eye view.
6. The Yorkshire town of Whitby.

## 155

1. John Dryden, in 1668.
2. Isaac Hayes.
3. Carp.
4. Jonas Salk, in 1952.
5. Bigfoot.
6. An 'audible warning of approach' – even the human voice fits the bill.

# 4

1. Which scholar and philosopher always wore a padded cap to disguise the fact that his head was tiny?
2. Which London landmark closed down in July 1975?
3. Which soup do millions of Japanese have for breakfast?
4. By what name was the Earl of Beaconsfield better known?
5. Which animal runs faster uphill than downhill?
6. At a Burns Night supper, an essential ingredient is the reading aloud of Burns's 'Address to a . . .' what?

# 80

1. What were President Brezhnev's two first names?
2. What was 1977's 'sale of the century'?
3. What is Gravelly Hill interchange better known as?
4. When was the first Last Night of the Proms?
5. In Adam Mars-Jones's short story, a Royal Personage contracts hydrophobia after being bitten by . . . what?
6. Why do pensioners in the Republic of Ireland spend so much of their leisure time travelling?

# 156

1. Who was the first woman MP?
2. What slogans did Stokeley Carmichael popularize in the 1960s?
3. What is the name for the Mexican dish consisting of a beef, onion and tomato mixture rolled up in *tortillas* and baked with chillies?
4. Who died when a passing eagle, having mistaken his bald head for a stone, dropped a tortoise on to it?
5. A large number (17,000) of these were dropped into enemy-occupied territory to assist in the war effort during the Second World War. What were they?
6. What are many workers at Grimethorpe Colliery famous for doing in their spare time?

# 4

1. Erasmus.
2. The Biba department store in Kensington High Street.
3. *Miso* soup, made with vegetables, seaweed and *miso* soybean purée.
4. Disraeli.
5. A hare – because of its long back legs.
6. A haggis.

# 80

1. Leonid Ilyich.
2. The disposal of Lord Rosebery's house and contents at Mentmore.
3. Spaghetti Junction.
4. In 1895.
5. A rabid corgi.
6. Because they travel free on the buses and trains.

# 156

1. Constance, Countess Markiewicz, elected in 1918 for St Patrick's, Dublin. Nancy Astor was the first to take her seat.
2. 'Black power' and 'Power to the people'.
3. *Enchiladas*.
4. Aeschylus.
5. Carrier pigeons.
6. Playing in a brass band.

# 5

1. Of which American President did Jane Wyman say, 'Ask him the time and he'll tell you how the watch was made'?
2. With what material did Paco Rabanne become closely associated in the mid-1960s?
3. What would you expect to be served in Whitstable, Belon, Ostend or Colchester?
4. Between which cities does the Trans-Siberian railway run?
5. What is the normal position of birds' eggs in a nest?
6. Name three French ports at the end of cross-Channel ferry routes.

# 81

1. Of whom did Lord Mountbatten say, 'You've no idea what it costs to keep that old man in poverty'?
2. Who was Twiggy's early mentor?
3. What is known by the Falkland Islanders as '365'?
4. For what feat is the Blue Riband awarded?
5. Which bird is the national emblem of New Zealand?
6. What does SLR stand for?

# 157

1. Which producer said, 'For me cinema is not a slice of life, but a piece of cake'?
2. Who created E. L. Wisty?
3. What is *pisco*?
4. Which light tool may surgeons use in place of a heavy scalpel?
5. Night hawk, dor hawk, fern owl, moth owl, lich fowl, flying toad, goat sucker and puckeridge are all names for which bird?
6. Which National Trust property had the most visitors in 1984?

## 5

1. Ronald Reagan. (She was his first wife.)
2. Plastic – he used it as chain mail for clothing and exotic jewellery.
3. Oysters. (All are famed for their oyster beds.)
4. Moscow and Vladivostok (57,224 miles).
5. Sharp end pointing inwards.
6. Dunkirk, Calais, Boulogne, Dieppe, le Havre, Cherbourg, Roscoff.

## 81

1. Mahatma Gandhi.
2. Justin de Villeneuve.
3. Lamb, because it is eaten every day of the year.
4. The fastest Atlantic crossing by liner.
5. The kiwi.
6. Single-lens reflex – a type of camera.

## 157

1. Alfred Hitchcock.
2. Peter Cook.
3. A clear grape spirit, produced principally in Peru.
4. A laser beam.
5. The nightjar.
6. Fountains Abbey and Studley Royal, North Yorkshire (210,000 visitors).

# 6

1. Which title did Tony Benn renounce?
2. What was the name of those once fashionable, ultra-wide ties, usually with a psychedelic pattern?
3. What is a 'brown turkey'?
4. In what did George Washington soak his wooden false teeth to give them flavour?
5. How old was Red Rum when he won the Grand National for the last time?
6. Which Prime Minister got the raspberry?

# 82

1. Whose invention, made of bicycle parts, cocoa tins, lenses, sealing wax and string, was first successfully demonstrated on 26 January 1926?
2. Who sang a song called 'Dominique' in the early 1960s?
3. What were Tom Ewell and Marilyn Monroe drinking, while eating crisps, in *The Seven-Year Itch*?
4. In 1985 what had the following in common: Big Ben, the Parthenon, the Statue of Liberty and the Kremlin?
5. Who wrote the *Carnival of Animals*?
6. Where can you see Lord Elgin's marbles?

# 158

1. Which famous English writer was named by his parents after a lake in Staffordshire?
2. Which hollow plastic tube was a craze in the late 1950s?
3. Auguste Escoffier was chef at which London hotels?
4. In 1845 Captain Washington dressed his crew in blue-and-white striped jackets. What was the name of the ship?
5. Who was the mischievous hero of the Uncle Remus tales?
6. In which country are dominoes most commonly believed to have originated?

## 6

1. Lord Stansgate.
2. Kipper ties.
3. A fig tree.
4. Port.
5. Twelve years old.
6. Lloyd George.

## 82

1. John Logie Baird's – it was his 'televisor' or television.
2. The Singing Nun.
3. Champagne.
4. They were all hidden by scaffolding and canvas while repairs were carried out.
5. Camille Saint-Saëns.
6. In the British Museum.

## 158

1. Rudyard Kipling.
2. The hula hoop.
3. First the Savoy, then the Carlton.
4. HMS *Blazer*, from which the garment got its name.
5. Brer Rabbit.
6. China.

# 7

1. Who is said to have cracked his head on a rock in the sea near Tenby and then to have emerged a brilliant artist?
2. What was the name of the character played by Clint Eastwood in the TV series *Rawhide*?
3. Russet, Cobb, Winter Pearmain, Cox's Orange, Worcester, Mirabelle: which is the odd one out?
4. Apart from the voters of his own state, who returned Walter Mondale in the 1984 US presidential election?
5. What is strange about the body hair of a three-toed sloth?
6. On what would you find a leech, a foot and a luff?

# 83

1. Who was the English-speaking Japanese radio propagandist who broadcast during the Second World War?
2. Whose boomerang wouldn't come back?
3. Pennyroyal was once used to drive away fleas. What is it?
4. What was the name of the yacht in which Sir Francis Chichester sailed single-handed around the world?
5. Where, in Britain, would you not expect to see a Camberwell Beauty butterfly?
6. Which beginner would use a cavaletto?

# 159

1. Archibald Ormsby-Gore was whose much mended teddy bear?
2. Who awarded what to the Beatles in 1964?
3. The choke is the inedible part of what plant?
4. The supporters of which non-sportsman made their mark at Headingley in 1975?
5. Which animal chased thousands of Scots families from their homes?
6. Which English cathedral has the tallest spire?

# 7

1. Augustus John.
2. Rowdy Yates.
3. Mirabelle is a species of plum; the rest are apples.
4. The people of Washington, DC.
5. It grows in the opposite direction to that of other animals to let the rain drain away when it is upside-down.
6. On a sail. (The leech is the rear edge, the foot is the bottom edge and the luff is the front edge.)

# 83

1. Tokyo Rose.
2. Charlie Drake's.
3. A variety of mint.
4. *Gipsy Moth IV*.
5. Anywhere on the west coast. It is seen mostly in summer and autumn on the east coast.
6. A show jumper – it is a simple practice fence.

# 159

1. John Betjeman's.
2. The Queen awarded them the MBE.
3. The artichoke.
4. George Davis. They dug up the pitch to protest his innocence.
5. The sheep – in the Highland Clearances.
6. Salisbury Cathedral – 404 feet.

# 8

1. Who had a group of islands and a snack named after him and kept his mistress at Admiralty House?
2. If you asked for a Fry's Five Boys in the 1950s, what would you be buying?
3. What is *remuage*?
4. Which order of monks is known as the Greyfriars?
5. For how long can a dolphin stay under water?
6. In Scotland, 7 October – 14 March is the close season for which fish?

# 84

1. Who took a pipe of tobacco, before going to the scaffold, 'to settle his spirits'?
2. Who sang the improbably named 'Gilly Gilly Ossenfeffer Katzenellen Bogan by the Sea' in 1954?
3. What would you expect of a dish cooked *à la sultane*?
4. What is joined-up handwriting more formally called?
5. Which fish, thought to be extinct for 70 million years, was recognized by scientists in 1938?
6. In ballooning, what are the two popular forms of inflation?

# 160

1. Which son of a Carnaby Street trader became a great poet and artist?
2. Which American character actor was known as the 'Man of a Thousand Faces'?
3. What are *dim sum*?
4. What is Holy Island also known as?
5. Which animal gives it name to a Strauss operetta?
6. How many players are there in a bicycle polo team?

# 8

1. John Montagu, Earl of Sandwich.
2. A bar of chocolate.
3. The step in the making of champagne in which the bottles are placed on their ends and shaken, causing the sediment to collect on the cork.
4. The Franciscans.
5. Two or three minutes only. A dolphin will die if kept under water for five minutes.
6. Trout.

# 84

1. Sir Walter Raleigh.
2. Max Bygraves.
3. That it was finished off with pistachio nuts or pistachio butter.
4. Cursive script.
5. The coelacanth. (One was caught off the coast of Madagascar.)
6. Hydrogen and hot air.

# 160

1. William Blake.
2. Lon Chaney.
3. Small Chinese pastries or boiled dough filled with various ingredients.
4. Lindisfarne.
5. The bat (*Die Fledermaus*).
6. Six, one of whom is a reserve.

## 9

1. Who did Hitler say, when speaking of the First World War, was 'the man who won the war'?
2. Who made his reputation at Gerde's Folk City coffee bar in Greenwich Village?
3. What is mock goose?
4. Professor T. Huxley coined this term in 1869 to express a third position in the debate about the existence of God. What is it?
5. People often remarked on the likeness between Hogarth and Trump, his dog. What kind of dog was Trump?
6. What is the meaning of the Persian or Turkish word *tuliban*, from which our word 'tulip' is derived?

## 85

1. How did a Lyons's work turn Swallows into Jaguars?
2. Who was 'the Man in Black'?
3. What name do we give to a castrated cockbird?
4. Which name did Lord Beaverbrook give in 1941 to the workers in the Research Department of the Air Ministry?
5. Tolstoy's horse recently appeared on Broadway and in London. Explain.
6. What is the function of a *cache-pot*?

## 161

1. After whom was Piaf called Edith?
2. In 1957 Colin Chapman designed a new British sports car with a glass-fibre body. What was it?
3. What is the carapace (outer shell) of a nutmeg?
4. Which slang word for lavatory paper has come to mean useless information?
5. What was the name of the Lone Ranger's horse?
6. Which flower appears on the crest of the Borough of Saffron Walden?

# 9

1. David Lloyd George.
2. Bob Dylan.
3. It is bullock's heart, stuffed with forcemeat, which, when roasted, has a texture and taste similar to that of goose.
4. Agnosticism.
5. A pug.
6. Turban.

# 85

1. Sir William Lyons started the Swallow Sidecar Company, which eventually made Jaguar cars.
2. Valentine Dyall.
3. A capon. The birds grow large and fat.
4. 'The backroom boys'.
5. Tolstoy's *Strider*, the story of a horse, was made into a musical.
6. It covers a plastic or terracotta flower pot.

# 161

1. Nurse Edith Cavell.
2. The Lotus Elite.
3. Mace – a useful spice with port, particularly used in *terrines*.
4. Bumf.
5. Silver (as in 'Hi-ho Silver!').
6. The crocus.

# 10

1. What have Margaret Kempson and Margaret Roberts in common?
2. Which sort of art made Bridget Riley famous in the 1960s?
3. Blue Vinny is native to which English county?
4. Up to which London hotel do cars drive on the right?
5. Which poet took his pet lobster for a walk on the end of a ribbon through the streets of Paris?
6. How much would you have to pay for a monopoly on the railways at Monopoly?

# 86

1. Who was the bareback-riding wife of Leofric, Earl of Chester?
2. In 1941 a much pilloried panel show began on BBC radio. What was it?
3. What is beeswing?
4. What is an American Indian baby known as?
5. Which Goodie watches birds?
6. What is the most common cause of fungus disease in a greenhouse?

# 162

1. Who worked on a Volga steamboat and as a railway guard before becoming a full-time writer?
2. Which French fashion designer introduced the New Look?
3. Which two ingredients give the Greek soup *avgolemono* its name?
4. What do Haifa and Hackney have in common?
5. Which creature did Grinling Gibbons include in his carvings by way of a signature?
6. The first dahlias were introduced to Europe in 1789. Where did they come from?

# 10

1. They both married Denis Thatcher.
2. Op Art.
3. It is an increasingly rare cheese from Dorset.
4. The Savoy. (Savoy Street, leading up to the Savoy, reverses the usual rule of the road.)
5. Gérard de Nerval.
6. £800.

# 86

1. Lady Godiva.
2. *The Brains Trust.*
3. It is the second crust that forms on very old port.
4. A papoose.
5. Bill Oddie – he is a keen ornithologist.
6. Bad ventilation.

# 162

1. Maxim Gorky (Alexei Maximovich Peshkov).
2. Christian Dior.
3. Eggs and lemons.
4. They are twin towns.
5. A mouse.
6. Mexico. The Spanish *conquistadores* discovered them being cultivated by the Mexicans 400 years ago.

## 11

1. In 1917 Stravinsky was detained by Italian border guards on suspicion of smuggling out of Germany a plan of fortifications. What was it really?
2. When was the first Pirelli calendar issued?
3. What colour is young Cognac?
4. What was the message that appeared on the wall on the night of Belshazzar's feast?
5. Of which sex is a worker honey bee?
6. What is Up-Helly-Aa?

## 87

1. Which playwright learned from Mozart 'to say important things in a conversational way'?
2. Who hosted *Double Your Money* on television?
3. What is *feijoada*?
4. Count Emil Jellinek, Austro-Hungarian consul at Nice, had a daughter after whom he named his new car. What was her name?
5. The prolonged and toughened bone of the upper jaw of *Xiphias gladius* is more commonly known as what?
6. Which game was invented by Charles Darrow of Philadelphia and first sold in 1935?

## 163

1. How did Samuel Langhorne Clemens protect his pseudonym?
2. How did James Rado and Gerome Ragni shoot to fame in the 1960s?
3. Where does the name 'Spam' come from?
4. What was the first motor car produced by the Ford Motor Company?
5. Which creatures travel in groups called 'pods'?
6. Which popular tropical fish would light up your tank?

## 11

1. His portrait by Picasso.
2. In 1964.
3. Clear. (The barrel and/or caramel imparts the colour normally associated with the spirit.)
4. *Mene, mene, tekel upharsin* ('Thou art weighed in the balance and found wanting').
5. Female.
6. The annual Shetland Fire Festival.

## 87

1. George Bernard Shaw.
2. Hughie Green.
3. It is a Portuguese dish of beans and pork.
4. Mercedes.
5. The 'sword' of the swordfish.
6. Monopoly.

## 163

1. He registered it as a trade mark (Mark Twain).
2. They wrote the musical *Hair*.
3. It is SPiced hAM.
4. The Model A, in 1903. It cost $830.
5. Killer whales.
6. A neon.

## 12

1. Which famous composer had an equally talented sister who played all Bach's forty-eight preludes and fugues from memory at the age of thirteen?
2. When it was introduced in Macmillan's Budget Harold Wilson called it 'a squalid raffle'. What was it?
3. Which fruit is best eaten as it starts to decay?
4. Joseph Gayetty introduced this in 1857 as a preventative against piles. What is it?
5. In which Shakespeare play does a dog appear on stage?
6. What was the name given to the first Hybrid Tea rose, produced in 1867?

## 88

1. Who built the *Great Western*, the *Great Eastern* and the *Great Britain*?
2. When was Margaret Thatcher first elected Member for Finchley?
3. What is pisciculture?
4. Baby Fae and Goober hit the headlines in 1984. Why?
5. What was the name of Gene Autry's horse?
6. Where would you find a Royal Sovereign in bed with a Hampshire Maid?

## 164

1. Who was the first king to be styled formally with a number after his name?
2. They last came out in 1958. Who were they?
3. *Quetsch eau-de-vie* is made from which fruit?
4. On the night ITV began broadcasting, BBC Radio killed off someone. Who?
5. Who announced that his master was the Marquis de Carabas?
6. What is a parterre?

## 12

1. Felix Mendelssohn. His sister's name was Fanny.
2. The sale of Premium Bonds.
3. The mulberry.
4. Lavatory paper.
5. *The Two Gentlemen of Verona*. The dog is called Crab.
6. La France.

## 88

1. Isambard Kingdom Brunel. (They are all steamships.)
2. In 1959.
3. The rearing of fish by artificial means.
4. Fifteen-day-old Baby Fae received the heart of Goober, a baboon.
5. Champion (as in 'Champion, the Wonder Horse').
6. In a strawberry bed.

## 164

1. Henry VIII.
2. Debutantes.
3. Alsatian plums.
4. Grace Archer.
5. Puss-in-Boots.
6. Any level garden area containing ornamental flower beds.

## 13

1. To which clan did Rob Roy belong?
2. What was the name of the hero in *Dragnet*?
3. What are devils on horseback?
4. What is a *felucca*?
5. Which animal reputedly started the Great Chicago Fire in 1871?
6. What are the four suits in a Tarot pack?

## 89

1. What have Winston Churchill, Albert Camus, Salvatore Quasimodo and William Golding in common?
2. Who was our Redskin Chum in the *Beano*?
3. What do you understand by *animelles*?
4. In which year was the 999 emergency call first introduced in the London area?
5. What was unusual about the children's nurse in *Peter Pan*?
6. Crewel, chenille and beading are all types of what?

## 165

1. Which saint, who rediscovered a forgotten spring, served as a nurse in the Franco-Prussian War?
2. Which motor car first rolled off the Nuffield production line in 1948?
3. Which biscuit is named after the unifier of Italy?
4. What is the unit of currency in China?
5. Which are the two animals in the Bible that talk?
6. Which game did Edward VII (when still Prince of Wales) introduce to England?

## 13

1. MacGregor.
2. Joe Friday.
3. Prunes wrapped in bacon.
4. A distinctive Egyptian sailing boat, seen on the Nile.
5. Mrs O'Leary's cow, which kicked over a lantern.
6. Cups, swords, money (pentacles) and batons (wands).

## 89

1. They were all awarded the Nobel Prize for Literature (in 1953, 1957, 1959 and 1984 respectively).
2. Little Plum.
3. The culinary term for testicles.
4. In 1937.
5. It was Nana, a huge St Bernard dog.
6. Embroidery needles.

## 165

1. Bernadette of Lourdes (1844–89).
2. The Morris Minor.
3. Garibaldi.
4. The *yuan*.
5. The serpent in the Garden of Eden and Balaam's ass.
6. Baccarat.

# 14

1. Whose novel sold over 200,000 in a matter of days in 1963?
2. The Anzus Pact was agreed in 1952. What is it?
3. Who was chef to Talleyrand, the Prince Regent in England, Tsar Alexander and Baron de Rothschild, and founder of *la Grande Cuisine*?
4. Farmer Green of Wiltshire is said to have taken away some of these stones for his own use. Which?
5. What does the name 'orang utan' mean?
6. How long does the average fours match at bowls last?

# 90

1. Whose famous speech did the *Chicago Times* describe as 'silly, flat and dish-watery'?
2. Who was Dwight Eisenhower's vice-president?
3. Name the Indian film star who has a BBC cookery programme.
4. Captain Briggs, his family and crew failed to arrive in 1868. What was their ship?
5. What is the only food of the giant panda?
6. What is the nationality of the inventor of the Rubik Cube?

# 166

1. What were the first names of Scott of the Antarctic?
2. Who saw Reds under the bed in the 1950s?
3. What makes a Pink Gin pink?
4. How big is the image on the retina of the human eye?
5. To which creature did four of the *Eight Feet in the Andes* belong?
6. What are protected by druggets in Britain's stately homes?

## 14

1. D. H. Lawrence's (*Lady Chatterley's Lover*).
2. A treaty signed by Australia, New Zealand and the USA.
3. Carême.
4. Stones from the Ring of Avebury.
5. 'Old man of the woods'.
6. Three and a half hours.

## 90

1. Abraham Lincoln's Gettysburg Address.
2. Richard Nixon.
3. Madhur Jaffrey.
4. The *Marie Celeste*.
5. Bamboo shoots.
6. Professor Erno Rubik is Hungarian.

## 166

1. Robert Falcon.
2. Senator Joseph McCarthy.
3. Angostura bitters.
4. Two centimetres (just over three-quarters of an inch) across.
5. Juana, the mule. The other four belonged to Dervla Murphy and her daughter.
6. Carpets. (Druggets are loosely woven protective mats.)

## 15

1. Whose car had the numberplate PET 1?
2. What is snoek?
3. What does hydromel become when fermented?
4. One inch of rain is equivalent to what depth of snow?
5. What is the Alpine mastiff more popularly called?
6. At which game did Steve McQueen try to beat Edward G. Robinson in *The Cincinatti Kid*?

## 91

1. Who is said to have written a prose tale of Abyssinia in a week to pay for his mother's funeral expenses?
2. Which athletic family together won four gold medals at the Helsinki Olympic Games?
3. Who said 'A dessert without cheese is like a beautiful woman with one eye'?
4. Which wedding anniversary is represented by a pearl?
5. What was the name of Dick Turpin's horse?
6. What is the maximum number of coins a spoof player may hold in his hand at one time?

## 167

1. To whom did Evelyn Waugh once give a bouquet of yellow mimosa when she spoke on birth control?
2. Which theatre staged *Look Back in Anger* in 1956?
3. What is the name of the traditional Good Friday dish from the Languedoc?
4. At the last count, how many *de facto* countries were there in the world?
5. Which animal was involved in the twelfth of Hercules' labours?
6. What is a hooked rug?

# 15

1. Petula Clark's.
2. A fish resembling the barracuda. The Ministry of Food tried to persuade doubtful British housewives to buy it in 1947–8, when stocks of other fish were severely rationed.
3. Mead.
4. One foot.
5. The St Bernard.
6. Stud poker.

# 91

1. Samuel Johnson. (The title of the tale is *Rasselas*.)
2. The Zatopecs.
3. Anthelme Brillat-Savarin (1755–1826), a French gastronome.
4. The thirtieth.
5. Black Bess.
6. Three.

# 167

1. Marie Stopes.
2. The Royal Court.
3. *Brandade de morue* (salt cod cooked and whipped with olive oil).
4. One hundred and sixty-five.
5. Cerberus, the watchdog of Hades.
6. One made of rags or coarse wool pulled through a canvas backing.

# 16

1. Who renounced his divinity in 1946?
2. Who partnered Pearl Carr in the popular singing duo of the 1950s and 1960s?
3. Where was Pimm's first drunk?
4. What is the name of the fairy woman who attends the scene of a death?
5. What do starlings do when a bird of prey approaches?
6. What is a pergola?

# 92

1. Which son of a Hungarian rabbi escaped?
2. Name Mary Quant's husband.
3. What is the difference between green and black olives?
4. Which London police station has a white, not a blue, lamp above its door?
5. How many nuts can a chipmunk hold in its mouth?
6. What do foxgloves, delphiniums, laburnums and daffodils have in common?

# 168

1. Which composer became totally deaf ten years before his death and died in an asylum?
2. What is the name of Dennis the Menace's dog?
3. What is *gravad lax*?
4. What, in nautical terms, is a Turk's head?
5. What distinguishes the big cats from the small, other than size?
6. Which shrub is called 'the Butterfly Bush'?

## 16

1. Emperor Hirohito of Japan.
2. Teddy Johnson.
3. In the fish bars owned by its creator, James Pimm.
4. The Banshee.
5. They gather into a dense formation.
6. An arbour or covered walk, formed by growing plants over trellis work.

## 92

1. Harry Houdini.
2. Alexander Plunkett Greene.
3. The black ones are picked later than the green.
4. Bow Street, because Queen Victoria complained that the blue lamp distracted her when she was attending the opera at Covent Garden.
5. Nine – four in each cheek and one between its teeth.
6. They are all wholly or partly poisonous.

## 168

1. Bedřich Smetana.
2. Gnasher.
3. It is Swedish for 'marinated salmon'.
4. An ornamental knot resembling a turban.
5. When crouched, the big cats stretch out their front legs; the small cats tuck theirs in.
6. Buddleia. When it is in flower, butterflies are attracted to it in great numbers.

## 17

1. Konrad Kujau was jailed for which crime in 1984?
2. What were we meant to pronounce on when the advertisement asked us, 'Which twin has the Toni?'
3. Which is the odd one out: *chorizo, Weisswurst, boudin blanc, pepperoni and kleftides*?
4. What links Groucho Marx and Robert Runcie, Archbishop of Canterbury?
5. What do the addax (from the Sahara) and the North American kangaroo rat never do?
6. Which festival became associated with CND in 1980?

## 93

1. A French priest and philosopher, Teilhard de Chardin, was involved in a famous scandal. Which?
2. What were Jeff Tracy, Lady Penelope and Parker the Butler?
3. What gastronomic predilection links the people of Nagasaki with those of the Rhondda?
4. In 1935, which versatile lamp came on the market?
5. What is published in *The Red Data Book*?
6. Which popular house plant is in danger of extinction in its natural habitat in Tanzania?

## 169

1. On 25 June 1876 'Long Hair' died. Who was he?
2. Which character did Honor Blackman play in *Goldfinger*?
3. With which wine would you serve the goat's cheese Crottin de Chavignol?
4. Which university did Indira Gandhi attend?
5. What is a collection of penguins known as?
6. To whom did the 1968 Countryside Act give the right to use bridleway rights of way?

# 17

1. Forging the so-called 'Hitler Diaries'.
2. Their hair. One twin had a professional style; the other had used a Toni home perm.
3. *Kleftides* are meatballs. The rest are sausages.
4. They were born on the same day, 2 October.
5. Drink water. They get all the moisture they need from their food.
6. The Glastonbury Festival.

# 93

1. The Piltdown Man scandal.
2. The original puppet stars of the television series *Thunderbirds*.
3. The love of seaweed.
4. The Anglepoise.
5. Lists of animals in need of protection.
6. The African violet. It has been named as one of the twelve most endangered species.

# 169

1. General Custer.
2. Pussy Galore.
3. Sancerre. The goats are reared cheek by jowl with the vineyards.
4. Oxford – she was at Somerville College.
5. A rookery.
6. Pedal cyclists.

## 18

1. What is unique about the Russian woman Yelena Nikolayev?
2. Which first-class-only service ceased in 1968?
3. What is beestings?
4. What is the shape of the DNA molecule?
5. Which is the largest species of monkey?
6. How could the Marquis of Bath bear to have thousands of arctophilists at Longleat on 27 May 1979?

## 94

1. Which composer spotted an unknown young woman at a British Embassy reception in South America and said, 'I'm going to marry that woman over there'?
2. Which was the BBC's first children's TV programme?
3. What was invented by John Woodger in the 1840s in Seahouses, Northumberland?
4. What is the US equivalent of the British motorway?
5. For what purpose were Spanish poodles kept in England until the 1920s?
6. Who might bore you with tales of gudgeon pins, poppet valves and tappets?

## 170

1. Who was born in Rochdale and died on Capri?
2. What was the name of the Bishop of Woolwich's book that caused so much controversy in 1963?
3. Which Italian dish literally means 'jump in the mouth'?
4. Who was the first Briton to use both the asterisk and the question mark?
5. Which New York precinct provides the setting for Ed McBain's novels?
6. Who or what in your household might suffer from velvet disease?

## 18

1. Both her parents have travelled in space. (Her mother is Valentina Tereshkova, her father Andrian Nikolayev.)
2. The postal service – it split into a two-tier system.
3. The milk from a cow that has recently calved; it is extra rich.
4. It is a double helix.
5. The mandrill.
6. He hosted 'The Great Teddy Bear Rally'. (The word 'arctophily' is derived from the Greek *arktos* meaning 'bear', and *philos* meaning 'love'.)

## 94

1. William Walton. (And he did.)
2. *Andy Pandy*.
3. The kipper. He adopted the process for kippering salmon.
4. The freeway or turnpike. (A highway is like a British A road.)
5. For sniffing out truffles.
6. A motorcycle or car enthusiast – they are all parts of an engine.

## 170

1. Gracie Fields.
2. *Honest to God.*
3. *Saltimbocca.*
4. Sir Philip Sidney, in *Arcadia*, in 1587.
5. The 87th precinct.
6. Aquarium fish.

# 19

1. For which periodical does Rabbi Lionel Blue write a cookery column?
2. Who had the glossiest lips in Britain in the 1960s?
3. Which cake is eaten around Guy Fawkes Night?
4. What, in 1963, were the Dog, the Monkey and the Fox?
5. When alarmed, the springbok will 'stot' or 'pronk', that is jump stiff-legged into the air. How high?
6. Where would you go to see Britain's wild cattle?

# 95

1. What have the following in common: Jack Dempsey, George VI, Casanova, Wellington, Mozart and Al Jolson?
2. What links a roll of lavatory paper with Ty Hardin?
3. Which member of the cabbage family would have been eaten by the characters in *Gone with the Wind*?
4. When does the bespoke tailor use his plonker?
5. The giant (five feet long) and the fairy (five inches long) are both species of which South American mammal?
6. Where would a Pennine poacher set his snares?

# 171

1. Which king visited his mistress at 9 o'clock, sometimes standing, watch in hand, awaiting the precise moment?
2. Which one-man band serenaded Rosy?
3. Brillat-Savarin relates that, having refused to pay forty francs for a vegetable, he saw two Englishmen snap it up, whistling 'God Save the King'. Which vegetable?
4. Who was Britain's best-known magician in the late 1950s?
5. Which is the world's largest amphibian?
6. Which craft is Honiton noted for?

# 19

1. A Roman Catholic newspaper, the *Universe*.
2. Kathy Kirby.
3. Parkin, made from oatmeal, treacle and ginger.
4. Dance crazes.
5. Ten to twelve feet in the air.
6. To Northumbria, where the famous, pale-coloured Chillingham cattle are to be found.

# 95

1. They were all Freemasons.
2. He played the role of Bronco Laine in the TV series of that name.
3. Collard greens – they are widely eaten in the southern United States.
4. During the final pressing of a suit. (A stroke of a heavy iron is followed up by dabs from a wooden block or plonker.)
5. The armadillo.
6. By the smoots, or small holes, that are built into the base of drystone walls to allow wild animals through.

# 171

1. George III.
2. Don Partridge.
3. Asparagus.
4. David Nixon.
5. The giant salamander.
6. Lace-making.

## 20

1. Which illustrious foreign correspondent gave an eye-witness account of the Bikini atom bomb explosion?
2. Two men disappeared in 1974. Name one of them.
3. How did steak tartare get its name?
4. How many storeys high is New York's Empire State Building?
5. How many kills made by a pride of lions are the work of the lionesses?
6. What makes 1985 noteworthy for the astronomist?

## 96

1. Who was Jimmy Jewell's partner in their comedy double-act?
2. Who said, 'It takes an awful lot of money to look this cheap'?
3. What is the name of the Mexican savoury dish of which the chief ingredient is avocado?
4. Where was the first staff canteen opened?
5. Male and female pet mice are called bucks and does. What are male and female guinea pigs called?
6. Which hobby is evoked by the mash, grist and wort?

## 172

1. Which great landscape painter was once a pastry cook?
2. Careful now . . . who was the lead singer in the Dave Clark Five?
3. Which is the only cereal of American origin?
4. Which religion advocates the use of *ganja*?
5. What is unusual about the walking pattern of a salamander?
6. Where would you most likely be if you heard the band playing *The Entry of the Gladiators*?

## 20

1. James Cameron.
2. Either John Stonehouse or Lord Lucan.
3. It is said that the Cossacks would put raw meat under their horses' saddles, so that it would be tenderized and salted after a day's ride.
4. One hundred and two. (Accept a margin of error of three each way.)
5. Ninety per cent. (When the kill is made, the lion has first go at the carcass; the lioness and the cubs follow.)
6. The reappearance of Halley's Comet.

## 96

1. Ben Warris.
2. Dolly Parton.
3. *Guacamole.*
4. In Robert Owen's New Lanark cotton mills in 1812.
5. Boars and sows.
6. Home-brewing.

## 172

1. Claude Lorrain.
2. Mike Smith.
3. Maize, confusingly called 'corn' by Anglo-Americans.
4. Rastafarianism. Believers smoke marijuana.
5. It walks diagonally, so it appears to move from left to right rather than straight ahead.
6. At the circus.

## 21

1. Who was Shelley's second mother-in-law?
2. Who played Jane to Johnny Weissmuller's Tarzan in the 1930s and early 1940s?
3. By what name are courgettes known in the United States?
4. From which quarry did Michelangelo take his marble?
5. In which animals is altruistic, or epimeletic, behaviour best developed?
6. Who would sigh nostalgically about the *Mallard* and the *Evening Star*?

## 97

1. Who was Fanny's bemonocled helper?
2. What were those stiff, bouffant 1950s petticoats made from?
3. Who would eat witchetty grubs?
4. Which planet was discovered in 1930?
5. What is the name for the scents that animals secrete and that act like hormones?
6. What would your hobby be if you used slip, a wheel and grog?

## 173

1. Who thinks better lying down than on his feet?
2. Where would you expect to see a 'CC41' symbol in the 1940s?
3. Which legume helped to elect a US President?
4. Which newspaper of international repute prints no photographs?
5. Queen Isabella of Spain was the first European to wear a coat made of the fur of which Andean rodent?
6. Turf, stone and hedge are all types of which puzzle?

## 21

1. Mary Wollstonecraft, writer of the early feminist tract *Vindication of the Rights of Woman*.
2. Maureen O'Sullivan.
3. Zucchini.
4. The quarry at Carrara, Italy.
5. In dolphins. If one is injured or unconscious, its companions will raise it to the surface so it can breathe.
6. A steam-train enthusiast. (The *Mallard* holds the world speed record for a steam locomotive (126 mph), and the *Evening Star* was the last steam locomotive built for British service.)

## 97

1. Johnny Cradock.
2. 'Paper nylon' – heavily starched, often stiffened at home with sugar and water.
3. Aborigines in the Australian bush – the grubs are a good source of protein.
4. Pluto.
5. Pheromones.
6. Pottery. (Slip is liquid clay and grog is fired ground clay.)

## 173

1. Edward de Bono, the inventor of lateral thinking.
2. Sewn into clothing – it indicated that a 'Utility' garment conformed to government regulations.
3. The peanut. It provided the wealth that allowed Jimmy Carter to run for President.
4. *Le Monde*.
5. The chinchilla, named after the Chincha Indians who trapped the animals at high altitudes.
6. The maze.

## 22

1. Of which colleague did Harold Wilson say, 'He immatures with age'?
2. Which schoolboy character did Anthony Buckeridge create in 1948?
3. Which food is given to the Chinese kitchen god just before his annual report to heaven?
4. Where does the popular term 'plonk' come from?
5. Which creature was the toast of the Jacobites?
6. What *must* a modern first edition have to be valuable?

## 98

1. Which book did Lloyd George say was the best ever written, 'not excepting Holy Writ'?
2. What was Ally's Army?
3. What is the American word for 'icing'?
4. Who was several times nominated for the Nobel Prize for literature and always rejected, dying a disappointed man?
5. Which high-voltage animal made its first appearance at Belle Vue, Manchester, in 1926?
6. Which island, off the coast of Mull, is considered by many to be Britain's most mystical site?

## 174

1. Which member of Captain Scott's team wrote, 'I dislike Scott intensely – he is not straight'?
2. What was the title of the Sex Pistols' 1977 album?
3. What was Sydney Smith's culinary idea of heaven?
4. What do Ethel Merman and Bob Dylan have in common?
5. Which animal, in Buddhism, symbolizes strength and restraint?
6. Who, in early July, sets out escorted by pikemen and musketeers because of King John's decree that he must be seen by Londoners?

# 22

1. Tony Benn.
2. Jennings – later to become a radio favourite in the 1950s.
3. A sticky ricecake to glue his jaws together or sweetmeats to ensure a favourable report.
4. It was brought back from France, after the First World War, by soldiers who had got used to asking for a bottle of *vin blanc*.
5. The mole. William of Orange was thrown and killed when his horse stumbled over a molehill.
6. The original dust wrapper. (Note: collectors never refer to dust jackets!)

# 98

1. *Les Misérables* by Victor Hugo.
2. The Scottish football team, ignominiously beaten in the World Cup in Argentina in 1978.
3. Frosting.
4. Leo Tolstoy.
5. An electric hare, at the greyhound race track.
6. Iona. (It is associated with St Columba.)

# 174

1. Captain Oates, in a letter to his mother.
2. *Never Mind the Bollocks . . . Here's the Sex Pistols*.
3. 'Eating *foie gras* to the sound of trumpets'.
4. They were born respectively Ethel and Robert Zimmerman.
5. The elephant. It is a title given to the Buddha.
6. The newly elected Lord Mayor at his Show.

## 23

1. Who revealed he wore no vest and so rocked the underwear manufacturers of America?
2. Who stepped into Roger Moore's shoes as Simon Templar in *The Saint*?
3. Where was *vichyssoise* first concocted?
4. What was the name of Lindbergh's famous aeroplane, in which he made the first solo transatlantic flight?
5. Margaret, John and Robert all gave their names to birds. Which ones?
6. What did Edwin Land invent that gives snappy results?

## 99

1. Of which continental European country was Elizabeth I invited to be queen?
2. Which football team did Alf Garnett support in *Till Death Us Do Part*?
3. What is the relation between *crème brûlée* and quantum physics?
4. What was known as a Tin Lizzie?
5. Which artist was known as 'the Horse Painter'?
6. Which architect invented the sash window in 1630?

## 175

1. Who, according to Wordsworth, was 'perhaps the most extraordinary man this country has ever produced'?
2. Which Python was appointed Rector of St Andrews University in 1971?
3. Where was the *Sachertorte* first created?
4. Which plants exchange carbon dioxide for oxygen at night?
5. In 1946, in an interview, Mao Tse-tung introduced a metaphorical animal into the language. Which?
6. Where do speleologists claim to do it?

## 23

1. Clark Gable, in *It Happened One Night*.
2. Ian Ogilvy.
3. At the Ritz-Carlton Hotel in New York, by the chef Louis Diat, in 1917.
4. *The Spirit of St Louis*.
5. Magpie, jackdaw and robin redbreast.
6. The Polaroid photographic system.

## 99

1. The Netherlands (in 1575); she declined.
2. West Ham.
3. Both were invented at Trinity College, Cambridge.
4. The Ford Model T car.
5. George Stubbs (1724–1806).
6. Inigo Jones.

## 175

1. James Wyatt, the Scottish engineer.
2. John Cleese.
3. In Vienna, at the eponymous hotel, Sacher's.
4. Cacti. Other plants do the opposite.
5. The 'paper tiger'.
6. Underground – they are pot-holers.

## 24

1. How old was Shirley Temple when she retired as an actress?
2. What was the name of the London nightclub opened by Peter Cook in 1961?
3. Of which country is *bigos* the national dish?
4. What is the literal translation of the word 'poltergeist'?
5. Over a distance of 700 yards, what speed can a cheetah reach?
6. Why would you be distressed to find a 'woolly bear' in your home?

## 100

1. Which great scientist was a friend of Coleridge and wrote poetry for two hours before breakfast?
2. Who produced the Mott the Hoople single 'All the Young Dudes'?
3. In which European wine-making area would you find the unlikely names of Lynch, Burke, Brown, Smith and Palmer?
4. What was striking about the *Daily Telegraph* crosswords in the first six months of 1944?
5. What colour does a chameleon become when it is angry?
6. Name two of England's four highest peaks.

## 176

1. Which son of a Suffolk railway employee was knighted for his services to British theatre?
2. Who played Mother in *The Avengers*?
3. From the milk of which animal is *mozzarella* made?
4. What is the name of the giant dam across the Nile?
5. For how long can a bedbug live without food?
6. Name the most southerly or the most northerly point of mainland Great Britain.

## 24

1. Ten years old.
2. The Establishment.
3. Poland.
4. 'Noisy spirit'.
5. Seventy miles per hour.
6. Because it is a carpet beetle in its early stages.

## 100

1. Sir Humphry Davy (1778–1829).
2. David Bowie.
3. Bordeaux – they are all names of *châteaux*.
4. The answers included many of the top-secret code names for the Normandy landings, including 'Overlord', the code for D-Day itself.
5. Black.
6. Scafell Pike, Sca Fell, Helvellyn and Skiddaw.

## 176

1. Sir Peter Hall.
2. Patrick Newall.
3. The European buffalo.
4. The Aswan Dam.
5. Up to two years.
6. Lizard Point is the most southerly and Easter Head the most northerly.

## 25

1. The 'Lily of Jersey' was born on that island and was famously beautiful. How was she otherwise known?
2. What was the name of the San Francisco district that was at the centre of the Flower Power movement?
3. What did the brothers Nicholas and François Appert invent in 1809?
4. In Esperanto *umdek* means a large but unspecified number. What is its English translation?
5. The stuffed body of which animal is on display at the Roy Rogers–Dale Evans Museum in California?
6. During the First World War tons of which pungent herb were used very effectively as a disinfectant?

## 101

1. Which biographer was advised by George III, 'There will be many foolish lives first, do you make the best'?
2. What was Billy Cotton's catchphrase?
3. Which word did Boulanger give to the world in 1765?
4. Once called Shangri-la, what is the American presidential retreat now called?
5. Where do the donkey and the elephant come into conflict?
6. What is a newel post?

## 177

1. Which Impressionist painter strapped his brushes to his rheumatoid wrists to continue painting?
2. What were Radios 1, 2, 3 and 4 formerly called?
3. In which Joan Crawford film did the eponymous heroine run a successful restaurant?
4. The Punic Wars between Carthage and Rome began in 264 BC. When did they formally end?
5. Which creature was associated with François I of France?
6. Which bean is planted earliest?

# 25

1. Lillie Langtry.
2. Haight-Ashbury.
3. The canning process. Cans were used immediately by Napoleon's armies in their attack on Russia.
4. 'Umpteen'.
5. Trigger, Roy Rogers's horse.
6. Garlic.

# 101

1. James Boswell (of his *Life of Johnson*.)
2. 'Wakey-wakey!' (it opened his Sunday lunchtime *Band Show* on the radio).
3. 'Restaurant'. Above his soup kitchen he hung a sign: *Boulanger débite des restaurants divins* ('Boulanger sells divine restoratives').
4. Camp David.
5. In the USA. (They are, respectively, the symbols of the Democratic and Republican parties.)
6. The principal post that supports the handrail at the top or bottom of a flight of stairs.

# 177

1. Auguste Renoir.
2. The Home Service, the Light Programme and the Third Programme.
3. *Mildred Pierce* (1945). She won her only Academy Award for her role in this film.
4. On 5 February 1985.
5. A salamander.
6. The broad bean.

## 26

1. Elizabeth Garrett Anderson could claim two 'firsts'. Name one.
2. Which 1960s fashion drove chiropodists to despair?
3. From which bakery does laver bread come?
4. In cards, 'trump' is said to be a corruption of which word?
5. Which animal's companions shouted out to him in glee, 'You'll go down in history!'?
6. Name a kitchen herb that does not conform to the botanical definition: 'a plant whose stem is not woody and persistent'.

## 102

1. What is the married name of Bernadette Devlin, once the youngest MP since Pitt?
2. What were loons?
3. What is galingale?
4. 'Ack emma' and 'pip emma' are old Army slang words for what?
5. Why was the bear Mischa so famous in 1980?
6. How old is the Cowthorpe Oak in North Yorkshire, said to be the oldest tree in Britain?

## 178

1. Which part of Mr John Roy's anatomy measures a record sixty-eight inches?
2. Who turned to the south for her comfort?
3. The mauve crocus of Asia Minor provides what?
4. Who coined the term 'global village'?
5. What was the name of Hopalong Cassidy's horse?
6. For what is Constance Spry best remembered?

## 26

1. She was the first English woman doctor and the first woman mayor (of Aldeburgh, Suffolk.)
2. Winklepickers (extravagantly pointed shoes, if you're too young to remember).
3. None. Laver is a seaweed, plucked from the rocks off the west coast of Great Britain and Ireland, which has a strong iodine taste. It is cooked to a mush and eaten with meat, preferably mutton.
4. Triumph.
5. Rudolph the Red-Nosed Reindeer's sleighmates.
6. Bay, rosemary, sage and thyme.

## 102

1. McAliskey.
2. Very wide bellbottomed hipster trousers, very fashionable in the early 1970s.
3. An aromatic root with the scent of damask roses. (Galingale syrup was poured over Chaucer's roast apples.)
4. A.m. and p.m.
5. He was the official mascot of the Moscow Olympics.
6. It seems to be over 1,500 years old.

## 178

1. His moustache.
2. Janis Joplin.
3. The dried stamens of the crocus provide saffron.
4. Marshall McLuhan.
5. Topper.
6. Flower-arranging.

## 27

1. Which monarch described smoking as 'a custom loathsome to the eye, hateful to the nose, harmful to the brain, dangerous to the lungs and . . . nearest resembling the horrible Stygian smoke of the pit that is bottomless'?
2. Who designed the costumes for the 1964 film version of *My Fair Lady*?
3. How would you make a Whisky Mack?
4. Where are you if you lie 'down among the dead men'?
5. Which cat loved his dog?
6. What is the maximum break at snooker?

## 103

1. Which British theatre and TV director is the great-nephew of Sigmund Freud?
2. When was *Time Out* first published?
3. Which eighteenth-century pastry cook from Bath gave her name to a teacake?
4. What is the Irish equivalent of the Scottish reel?
5. Which breed of dog is Snowy (or Milou), Tintin's companion?
6. Who designed the much admired garden at Hidcote Manor?

## 179

1. Who wrote the opera *Amelia di Liverpool*?
2. What do Stuart Sutcliffe and Pete Best have in common?
3. Which recipe did Marie Antoinette bring from Austria on her marriage to Louis XVI?
4. Where is the Parliament called the Tynwald?
5. What is the most valuable food fish in the world?
6. On poker dice, which colour is the Queen?

# 27

1. James I.
2. Cecil Beaton.
3. Add one-third of ginger wine to two-thirds of Scotch whisky.
4. Under the table, with the empty bottles.
5. Cat Stevens, in his song beginning 'I love my dog as much as I love you.'
6. One hundred and forty-seven.

# 103

1. Dr Jonathan Miller.
2. In 1968.
3. Sally Lunn.
4. The jig.
5. A white terrier.
6. Major Lawrence Johnston.

# 179

1. Gaetano Donizetti.
2. They were both early members of the Beatles.
3. A recipe for the *croissant.*
4. On the Isle of Man.
5. The herring.
6. Green.

## 28

1. Who got an honorary doctorate at Bob Jones University?
2. Whose poem did Mary Whitehouse find libellous?
3. Indian and Malay dishes are cooked in *ghee*. What is it?
4. Two public buildings were opened in 1852, one in Fleet Street, the other just off the Strand, but closed shortly after for lack of interest. What were they?
5. What is the easiest way to identify a natterjack toad?
6. What gave Tom Stephenson, a founder member of the Ramblers' Association, the idea of the Pennine Way?

## 104

1. Which playwright was ordered to be released from debtors' prison after James II had seen one of his plays?
2. When did the Campaign for Nuclear Disarmament begin?
3. Every schoolchild knows that the Duke of Clarence drowned in a butt of malmsey, but what is it exactly?
4. What does a sagger-maker's bottom-knocker make?
5. Why is a guillemot's egg pear-shaped?
6. The PET 2001 computer was launched around 1977. Which language did the beginner use?

## 180

1. Apart from Anton Karas, who is famous for playing the zither?
2. Why did millions of Americans suddenly grow up in 1971?
3. Which flavour of soup far outsells all others in Britain?
4. Francis Bacon said that three inventions had changed the world since classical times. Name two.
5. Fat-tailed, fat sand and naked-soled are all types of which rodent?
6. In which Cornish town must you beware the 'Obby 'Oss on May Day?

## 28

1. The Rev. Ian Paisley.
2. James Kirkup's. He wrote 'The Love that Dares to Speak its Name', published in *Gay News* in 1976.
3. Clarified butter made from buffalo's milk.
4. Gentlemen's and ladies' public lavatories.
5. It has a yellow line running down the middle of its back.
6. The example of the American Appalachian Way.

## 104

1. William Wycherley. (*The Plain Dealer* was the play.)
2. In 1958, a year after Britain exploded its first H-bomb.
3. It is a type of madeira, and the longest-lived wine in the world.
4. Pottery.
5. Because it is laid on a bare rock ledge and, if disturbed, will roll in a circle and not fall off.
6. BASIC.

## 180

1. Shirley Abicaire.
2. The age for enfranchisement was reduced to eighteen by the Twenty-Sixth Amendment.
3. Tomato soup.
4. Printing, gunpowder and the compass.
5. The gerbil or sand rat.
6. Padstow. (A large hat-shaped figure with the head of a horse is the focus of very lively May Day celebrations.)

## 29

1. Which writer said, 'I should like to be so famous that it would permit me to break wind in society'?
2. What do Kate Bush and Emily Brontë have in common?
3. What is the world's most important bean?
4. William Blake's poem 'Jerusalem' was inspired by a legend that Christ, as a youth, visited a Somerset town. Which town?
5. In North American Indian religions, which creature watched over the eastern gateway of the world and is often seen at the top of the totem pole?
6. Where would you go to see the British Grand Prix in 1989 but not in 1990?

## 105

1. Who became an MP at twenty-four and married Aneurin Bevan at twenty-seven?
2. What happened at Kent State University in 1970?
3. Where did madeira cake get its name?
4. What do the Cornish call 'Fair Maids'?
5. What is the 'twitch' that is used on a horse?
6. In which Scottish University town does the Kate Kennedy Procession take place in mid-April?

## 181

1. Who was the first Republican candidate for the US presidency to take the 'solid South' from the Democrats?
2. Who played the enigmatic lead in the TV series *Kung Fu*?
3. What is hard sauce better known as?
4. Which US state appears as a quadrilateral on the map?
5. What, in the Book of Revelation, is the number of the Beast?
6. What is the significance of a solid pink triangle on an Ordnance Survey map?

## 29

1. Honoré de Balzac.
2. *Wuthering Heights*. Emily Brontë wrote it; Kate Bush 'interpreted' it in a record of the same name in 1978.
3. Economically speaking, it is the soy bean, for it has both industrial and nutritional value.
4. Glastonbury.
5. The thunderbird, depicted as an eagle.
6. Silverstone. (It takes place at Silverstone in odd-numbered years and at Brands Hatch in even-numbered years.)

## 105

1. Jennie Lee.
2. US National Guards opened fire on students, killing several of them.
3. It was traditionally served with madeira wine.
4. Pilchards.
5. It is a rope that is twisted tightly around the upper lip to calm a nervous horse. (It may work on the acupuncture principle.)
6. St Andrews. (Male undergraduates dress up, one playing Kate Kennedy, a bishop's daughter who became the toast of the town.)

## 181

1. Richard Nixon, in 1972.
2. David Carradine.
3. Brandy butter.
4. Wyoming or Colorado.
5. Six hundred and sixty-six.
6. A Youth Hostel.

## 30

1. Who was the first woman to be awarded the American Film Institute's Life Achievement Award?
2. Who was the arch enemy of Dan Dare?
3. Name the seventeenth-century English dish of chopped meat, anchovies, eggs, onions, oil and condiments.
4. The Inquisition was carried out by a group sometimes called 'the hounds of the Lord'. Which group?
5. What was the name of the first living creature in space?
6. On what did Madame Tussaud base her original show?

## 106

1. Which English sculptor died tragically in a studio fire in St Ives in 1975?
2. How did Grace Metalious curl our hair in the 1950s?
3. Which society oversees the commercial preparation of kosher food?
4. Which former British colony has five times the land area of the UK?
5. Which pop group evokes one of T. S. Eliot's cats?
6. Which type of plants are calcifuge?

## 182

1. Who is the patron saint of postal, radio, telecommunication and television workers?
2. What were poppets?
3. What was the name of the nationally eaten, medieval English dish of hulled wheat boiled in milk?
4. What name did early Arab chemists give to residues that remained after the evaporation of their mixtures?
5. Which creature was sought after by sweltering Sidney Greenstreet and Peter Lorre, *inter alia*?
6. On a visit to which English cathedral would you see Graham Sutherland's tapestry of 'Christ in Glory'?

## 30

1. Bette Davis, in 1977.
2. The Mekon.
3. Salmagundi.
4. The Dominicans (*domini canes*).
5. Laika, a Samoyed husky bitch that went up in *Sputnik I* in 1957.
6. The death masks of guillotined heads that she had been forced to make during the French Revolution.

## 106

1. Dame Barbara Hepworth.
2. By the shocking goings-on of *Peyton Place*.
3. The Beth Din Society.
4. South Africa.
5. Mungo Jerry.
6. Those that cannot tolerate limy soils.

## 182

1. St Gabriel.
2. Chains of plastic beads that snapped on to each other. (Now they pass for money in the Club Mediterranée.)
3. Frumenty.
4. Alkali.
5. The Maltese Falcon.
6. Coventry.

# 31

1. The ladies of whose European court were ordered by decree to reduce their waists to 13 inches?
2. Who did Valerie Solanas shoot in 1968?
3. When Napoleon defeated the Austrians in 1800, what dish did his chef devise as a victory offering?
4. Which country has the greatest number of rugby clubs?
5. Why was Master Magrath famed in song?
6. What do St Helena, Pope Joan and Slippery Anne have in common?

# 107

1. Who recorded their first Number One hit in just one take of approximately three minutes?
2. Who had a bestseller about a seagull in 1970?
3. A Buck's Fizz is champagne and orange juice. What is a Bellini?
4. Where can we commonly see a picture of Nottingham Castle?
5. Jean de Brunhoff created which character from children's fiction?
6. When should autumn-fruiting raspberries be pruned?

# 183

1. Who was niece to one US President and cousin and wife to another?
2. What was *IT*?
3. In Alan Bennett's *A Private Function*, what was intended to be the main dish for the celebration dinner?
4. Which common eight-letter word has only one vowel?
5. According to Kafka, one morning Gregor Samsa woke up and found he had become . . . what?
6. Where, reputedly, is the highest pub in England?

# 31

1. Catherine de Medici's.
2. Andy Warhol.
3. *Poulet Marengo* – chicken with mushrooms, tomatoes, onions and brandy.
4. Japan.
5. He was a greyhound courser from 1867–73.
6. They are all card games.

# 107

1. The Beatles ('Please Please Me').
2. Richard Bach, author of *Jonathan Livingstone Seagull.*
3. Champagne and peach juice.
4. On the back of a packet of Players cigarettes.
5. Babar the Elephant.
6. February.

# 183

1. Eleanor Roosevelt.
2. *International Times*, a pillar of the underground press in the 1960s.
3. A secretly nurtured pig.
4. Strength.
5. A giant cockroach.
6. The Cat and Fiddle, Buxton, Derbyshire.

## 32

1. Whose exhibition of paintings was suppressed in 1928 because it depicted pubic hair?
2. Which quick cuppa came out of Switzerland in 1938?
3. Which American chef owned a restaurant in Suffolk called Hintlesham Hall?
4. Which was the first country to impose driving tests and issue driving licences?
5. Who invented the two-name system of nomenclature for the natural world?
6. Who would use an étrier, a piton and a chockstone?

## 108

1. Who is Martin Amis's mother?
2. Which workers' home inspired a 1960s hairstyle?
3. What is the special relationship between macaroni and spaghetti?
4. What were the first words ever recorded?
5. The blister beetle produces a poisonous substance that was used by Lucrezia Borgia and the Marquis de Sade, among others, for its supposed aphrodisiac qualities. What is it commonly known as?
6. What are a Basque knot, a bullion knot and a French knot?

## 184

1. Who instigated a mass suicide in Guyana in 1978?
2. What was special about Louise Brown?
3. Who is hostess of the biggest dinner party in the world?
4. What is a current account known as in the USA?
5. Which birds did Noah release to find out if there was any dry land?
6. Enthusiasts travel miles for a pint of Real Ale. Define Real Ale.

# 32

1. D. H. Lawrence's.
2. Instant coffee. Nescafé was produced by the Nestlé company.
3. Robert Carrier.
4. France. They were introduced in Paris in 1893 but not in Great Britain until 1935!
5. Linnaeus.
6. A rock climber.

# 108

1. Elizabeth Jane Howard.
2. The beehive.
3. When the centres are taken out of solid pasta, the hollow tubes are macaroni, and the centres are spaghetti.
4. 'Mary had a Little Lamb', spoken by Thomas Edison.
5. Spanish fly.
6. They are all embroidery stitches.

# 184

1. Jim Jones of Jonesville.
2. She was Britain's first test-tube baby.
3. Judy Chicago. Her *Dinner Party* is a work of art celebrating notable women throughout history.
4. A checking account.
5. First a raven, then a dove. (You must have both to get a point.)
6. It is beer brewed from traditional ingredients and allowed to mature naturally in the cask in a pub's cellar.

# Q

## 33

1. Who advertised himself as 'foot doctor to the world'?
2. Which island suffered a volcanic eruption in 1961?
3. What is verjuice?
4. What name is given to the strings of beads used as currency by North American Indians?
5. What is the Peruvian name for a llama (a word used for the fabric made from its wool)?
6. Who sponsors the Ideal Home Exhibition?

## 109

1. Who started out as an examiner at the Swiss Patents Office in Berne?
2. When did the ten-shilling note go out of circulation?
3. If you were eating rocket, what would it look like?
4. In what sublunar activity did 1,582 people take part in Seoul, South Korea, in 1970?
5. Why are the tails of many breeds of dog docked at birth?
6. Who would be interested in ammonites and 'Devil's toenails'?

## 185

1. Who was the second Briton to sail single-handed around the world?
2. Which animal began crossing the road in 1951?
3. What is metheglin?
4. For how many days must wood be smouldered to make charcoal?
5. What is the adult male gorilla sometimes known as?
6. Which leading British motorcycle manufacturer produced the two-stroke Baby, the Trophy and the Tiger?

## 33

1. William Scholl.
2. Tristan da Cunha.
3. The juice of unripe grapes, used like vinegar.
4. Wampum.
5. Alpaca.
6. The *Daily Mail*.

## 109

1. Albert Einstein.
2. In 1970.
3. Spinach leaves.
4. They got married in a ceremony conducted by the Rev. Sun Myung Moon.
5. This habit originated in the days when a curtailed dog was exempt from tax.
6. A fossil hunter. (Ammonites are sea-snail shells, and 'Devil's toenails' are the ends of large, tough oyster shells, curled like the nails on an animal's foot.)

## 185

1. Sir Alec Rose.
2. The zebra.
3. A type of spiced mead.
4. Fourteen days.
5. A silverback, from his silvery-white saddle.
6. Triumph.

## 34

1. Which twentieth-century American President was born Leslie King?
2. Who would have had a quiff and a DA?
3. *Farfalle, trenetti, pappardelle* and *fettucine* are all types of what?
4. Where would you be if you landed at Ringway Airport?
5. Which animal is the national animal of Canada?
6. To whom was the name 'Vulcanites' given in France in 1859?

## 110

1. Who was known as the Great American Malaprop?
2. In 1956 children were all wearing hats modelled on that of which character?
3. Mont Blanc is a dessert made from what?
4. In which country was the speaking clock first introduced?
5. Which animal was the star of a 1950s BBC children's programme?
6. Why do cinema usherettes have reason to be grateful to the British Mutoscope and Biograph Company?

## 186

1. Who is Charlotte Cornwell's brother?
2. Which American comedian had a radio show in which he created a myth about his own meanness?
3. French *marc* and Italian *grappa* are both types of what?
4. What name do the Chinese give to white Europeans and Americans?
5. Which animal did Noah omit to place in the Ark?
6. Where would Mrs Thatcher be most likely to play with her golliwog?

## 34

1. Gerald Ford. (He was renamed by his mother's second husband.)
2. A Teddy Boy – they were essential elements in his hairstyle.
3. Pasta.
4. Manchester.
5. The beaver.
6. Matchbox-label collectors.

## 110

1. Samuel Goldwyn, of 'Include me out' fame.
2. Davy Crockett.
3. Chestnut purée topped with whipped cream.
4. France. (M. Escalangon of the Paris Observatory invented it.)
5. Muffin the Mule.
6. They introduced the Ever Ready No. 1 torch to Britain in 1900.

## 186

1. John Le Carré.
2. Jack Benny.
3. Rough brandy made from the skins of grapes that have been pressed for wine.
4. Ghosts.
5. The unicorn.
6. At Chequers, where the original golliwog has remained since it was auctioned at Christie's in 1917 and presented to the Prime Minister of the day.

# 35

1. Who, in reply to Queen Victoria's query about the purpose of his studies, said, 'Madam, of what use is a baby?'?
2. Who designed the dream sequence in *Spellbound*?
3. Which biscuit has Proustian memories?
4. What was the first motorway in Britain?
5. The African white, the Javan and the Sumatran are among the five existing species of which animal?
6. What is scripophily?

# 111

1. What is missing from the ashes of Thomas Hardy, which lie in Westminster Abbey?
2. Name a man's suit, popular in the 1940s, consisting of a long, loose jacket and high-waisted, tapering trousers.
3. Which is the odd one out: *bordelaise*, *béarnaise*, *hollandaise*, *polonaise*?
4. What began life in 1894 as The Penny Bazaar at Cheetham Hill in Manchester?
5. Which bird derives its name from the river Phasis, which flows from Colchis into the Black Sea?
6. Which toy did the National Association of Toy Retailers elect 'Toy of the Year' in 1974, 1975 and 1979?

# 187

1. William Dampier (1652–1715) marooned this man but rescued him on a second voyage. Who was he?
2. Who was the mystery man from the *Daily News* who was much sought after in the 1920s and 1930s?
3. What was Hogarth's street girl selling?
4. What was the first Golden Disc?
5. Which animal is the symbol of the World Wildlife Fund?
6. Why would you use a dandy brush, and a curry comb?

## 35

1. Michael Faraday.
2. Salvador Dali.
3. The *madeleine*.
4. The 8½-mile Preston by-pass section of the M6.
5. The rhinoceros.
6. The love of, and collection of, bonds and share certificates.

## 111

1. His heart. It is buried with his first wife.
2. A zoot suit.
3. *Polonaise*; the first three are sauces, the last a slow, stately dance.
4. Marks and Spencer's chain of shops.
5. The pheasant (from the Greek *phasianos*).
6. Lego.

## 187

1. Alexander Selkirk (the inspiration for *Robinson Crusoe*).
2. Lobby Ludd. If you recognized and challenged him, you could win a prize.
3. Shrimps.
4. 'Chattanooga Choo Choo' by Glen Miller, recorded for RCA Victor in 1942.
5. The giant panda.
6. To groom a horse or pony.

## 36

1. What were Anne Bonny and Mary Read doing in the Caribbean in the early eighteenth century?
2. Where did British teenagers first go for a coffee and a hamburger in 1955?
3. A sprig of this herb, traditionally associated with remembrance, is worn in Australia to commemorate Anzac Day. What is it?
4. Wink Martindale is best known in Britain for which song?
5. What is the collective name for a group of owls?
6. Many motorcycle buffs would love to own a BSA machine. What do the letters stand for?

## 112

1. Which instrument did George Formby play?
2. Which singer walked the streets of London in 1974?
3. When is simnel cake traditionally eaten in England?
4. How many children did J. S. Bach father?
5. Why do walruses have tusks?
6. What did the British tobacco company W. D. and H. O. Wills introduce to Britain in 1885?

## 188

1. L. Ron Hubbard founded Scientology. What does the L. stand for?
2. Why did the Queen telephone the Lord Provost of Edinburgh from Bristol in 1958?
3. What does a carminative do?
4. Who is Blondie Bumstead's husband?
5. Which fish, when caught in Britain, must be presented or offered to the Crown?
6. What are known as 'glannies' in East London and 'taws' and 'glassies' elsewhere?

## 36

1. They were female pirates.
2. The Wimpy bar.
3. Rosemary.
4. 'Deck of Cards'.
5. A parliament.
6. Birmingham Small Arms (1906–71).

## 112

1. The ukulele banjo. (No penalty for saying just, 'The ukulele.')
2. Ralph McTell – it was his only Top Ten hit.
3. Formerly baked for Mothering Sunday, it is now eaten at Easter.
4. Twenty.
5. Although they are useful tools, they are used primarily to establish status.
6. Their packets were the first to contain picture cards, now much sought after by collectors.

## 188

1. Lafayette.
2. She was opening the subscriber trunk dialling (STD) service.
3. It is a drug that cures flatulence.
4. Dagwood, in the American comic strip by Chic Young.
5. The sturgeon.
6. Children's marbles.

# 37

1. As what are George Loveless, James Loveless, John Standfield, James Brine and James Hammett better remembered?
2. In 1959, just fifty years after Blériot made his cross-Channel flight, the Hovercraft made its maiden flight across the Channel. Who invented it?
3. What is stargazey pie?
4. Bell, book and candle are used in a ceremony carried out in the Roman Catholic Church. Which ceremony?
5. Which animal was always fretting about being late?
6. What is the result of a union between the cowslip and the primrose?

# 113

1. During the reign of which Roman Emperor was Christ crucified?
2. Which MP played Jet Morgan in *Journey into Space*?
3. What did the agronomist Antoine-Auguste Parmentier popularize?
4. Which card is known as the Curse of Scotland?
5. Caligula, in his insanity, appointed his horse consul. What was its name?
6. Who created the famous garden of Sissinghurst Castle?

# 189

1. Who wrote a famous modern English comedy in Shanghai?
2. Which kind of heels took over from stiletto heels?
3. What was the relationship between Anthelme Brillat-Savarin and Madame Récamier?
4. Who is known to the French as Marianne?
5. What was the true identity of Lassie in the first seven *Lassie* films?
6. What was 'Capability' Brown's baptismal name?

## 37

1. The Tolpuddle Martyrs.
2. Sir Christopher Cockerell.
3. A pie baked with pilchards. The heads protrude from the pastry, for, since the heads are not eaten, it would be a waste of pastry to cover them.
4. Excommunication.
5. The White Rabbit in Lewis Carroll's *Alice in Wonderland*.
6. The polyanthus (*Primula* × *variabilis*).

## 113

1. Tiberius (AD 14–37).
2. Andrew Faulds.
3. Potatoes (*à la Parmentier* indicates a dish served with potatoes).
4. The nine of diamonds.
5. Incitatus.
6. Vita Sackville-West and her husband, Sir Harold Nicolson.

## 189

1. Sir Noël Coward. (The play was *Private Lives*, written in 1930.)
2. Cuban heels.
3. They were cousins.
4. The female figure who represents France, as Britannia represents Britain.
5. A male collie called Pal.
6. Lancelot.

# 38

1. Which American shot a cigarette from Kaiser Wilhelm II's mouth in 1889?
2. For which US film studio did Graham Greene write *The Tenth Man* – published for the first time in 1985, forty years after he completed and then 'forgot' it?
3. By what name is fora filbert better known?
4. What is a ship's log?
5. Who or what is Grimalkin?
6. In 1952 a Long Island firm produced a game that rivalled Monopoly in popularity. Which game?

# 114

1. Who was the youngest Beatle?
2. Howard Hughes designed and built the largest aircraft ever flown, the Hercules. What was its more familiar nickname?
3. How are dishes prepared *à la hongroise*?
4. The new spectroscope of the 1850s made possible the discovery of helium, nebulium, coronium and geocoronium. Which is the odd man out?
5. In the shape of which animal does Hanuman, the Hindu god, appear?
6. When was the lawnmower invented?

# 190

1. According to whom did socialism plus electrification equal communism?
2. Whose career was launched in the film *Tiger Bay*?
3. Which American painter painted loners in diners?
4. Khartoum lies at a famous junction. Which?
5. What was the name of the intelligent horses whom Gulliver met on his travels?
6. What is an Irish Peach?

# 38

1. Annie Oakley, while touring Europe in the Buffalo Bill Wild West Show.
2. MGM.
3. The hazelnut. St Philbert's Day is 22 August, by which time hazelnuts are ripe.
4. The record of distance run through water.
5. It is another name for a cat, though in *Macbeth* it is a witch's familiar.
6. Scrabble.

# 114

1. George Harrison (born 1943).
2. The 'Spruce Goose'.
3. They are always cooked in cream and paprika.
4. Helium. The others do not exist.
5. The shape of a monkey.
6. In 1830.

# 190

1. Lenin.
2. Hayley Mills's.
3. Edward Hopper.
4. The confluence of the Blue and White Niles.
5. The Houyhnhnms.
6. An apple.

## 39

1. Which member of a famous partnership died at 75, after jumping into his private lake to help a woman in trouble?
2. Which 1970s group had an album called *The 5,000 Spirits, or the Layers of the Onion*?
3. Where is the white truffle to be found?
4. Where did the first Butlin's campers hear the cry, 'Wakey-wakey! Rise and shine!'?
5. Where does the cleaner fish live?
6. Which is the largest lake in the Lake District?

## 115

1. Which king is caricatured in the nursery rhyme 'Humpty Dumpty'?
2. Adam West and Burt Ward acted together in which 1960s television series?
3. Which part of the trout appealed most to the Romans?
4. What do the letters AM and FM, used in connection with broadcasting, represent?
5. Fossils of trilobites have been found in rocks 500 million years old. To which modern creature are they related?
6. To which area do British gourmets go in the asparagus season?

## 191

1. Who stood between Spurius Lartius and Herminius to face the Etruscans?
2. On which John Wyndham novel is the 1960 film *Village of the Damned* based?
3. What is *Eiswein*?
4. What is Calder Hall in Cumbria?
5. Which Poet Laureate is associated with the Loch Ness Monster?
6. Why would a pigeon-fancier describe a bird as 'tic-eyed'?

# 39

1. W. S. Gilbert, of the Gilbert and Sullivan operetta partnership.
2. The Incredible String Band.
3. In Piedmont, in the north of Italy. The centre of production is the town of Alba, equally well known for its wines.
4. In Skegness. (The camp could hold 1,000 people.)
5. Inside the jaws of a larger fish, picking off any parasites in the mouth.
6. Lake Windermere.

# 115

1. Richard III.
2. *Batman*. West played Batman, and Ward was Robin.
3. The cheek; they threw away the rest.
4. Amplitude modulation and frequency modulation.
5. The woodlouse.
6. The Vale of Evesham, where it is a popular local speciality.

# 191

1. Horatius (on the bridge).
2. *The Midwich Cuckoos*.
3. Wine made in Germany from grapes harvested after the autumn frosts. The must is reduced by freezing.
4. A nuclear power station. It was Britain's first.
5. Ted Hughes. He wrote about Nessie in one of his many animal poems.
6. Any bird with a little fleck of white feathering near the eye is called 'tic-eyed'.

## 40

1. Who was the last pope to be canonized?
2. The first stretch of motorway was opened in 1959. By whom?
3. What do we call the North American Indian food made of preserved meat mixed with melted fat?
4. What were started in 1939 to cope with the problems caused by the war?
5. Who or what is Greyfriars Bobby?
6. Where is the Royal Horticultural Society's 150-acre garden?

## 116

1. Why are Belisha beacons so called?
2. Which British opera was commissioned by the Arts Council for the Festival of Britain in 1951?
3. What is the North African speciality made with millet, chick peas, vegetable stock and meat?
4. Which unit of matter was named by Avogadro?
5. During the 1950s Donald O'Connor shared top billing with an animal in a series of very popular films. Which animal?
6. What is a gouge?

## 192

1. In 1781 William Herschel discovered the planet eventually named Uranus. What did he propose calling it?
2. What, according to Radio Luxembourg, was Friday night?
3. Name the young salmon that has been to sea only once.
4. Ringworm is a disease of the skin. What causes it?
5. What was the name of Napoleon's horse?
6. Where can you go on board Nelson's flagship HMS *Victory*?

# 40

1. Pius X (1903–14).
2. Ernest Marples.
3. Pemmican.
4. The Citizens' Advice Bureaux.
5. It is a statue found in Greyfriars churchyard in Edinburgh, erected in memory of a faithful dog who sat for years by his master's grave.
6. Wisley, Surrey.

# 116

1. After Sir Leslie Hore-Belisha, Minister of Transport at the time of their introduction in 1934.
2. *Billy Budd*, by Benjamin Britten.
3. *Couscous*.
4. The molecule.
5. Francis the Talking Mule.
6. A concave-bladed chisel used in carpentry.

# 192

1. George, or more precisely 'George Sidus', after George III.
2. 'Amami night'. Amami lotion would guarantee lovely locks for the weekend.
3. The grilse.
4. Fungi.
5. Marengo.
6. Portsmouth dockyard.

## 41

1. Widor, who composed works for the organ, joined forces with which other organist to write about J. S. Bach?
2. What drove Melina Mercouri into exile in 1967?
3. What became a sought-after delicacy when they were introduced to the court of Louis XIV from Italy?
4. What was Greta Garbo's job in Stockholm before she became a screen idol?
5. Which creature is known as 'the unicorn of the sea'?
6. What is the difference between breakdancing and bodypopping?

## 117

1. In 1972 Vigdis Finnbogadottir was director of the Reykjavik Theatre. What 'first' did she achieve in 1980?
2. Who was the other doctor that Drs Cameron and Finlay had to deal with?
3. Which fruit grows as far north as the Arctic Circle?
4. Which European country has the highest number of female pipe-smokers?
5. Which animal father carries his child round on his feet for two months?
6. Where do many seekers after King Arthur's Camelot go?

## 193

1. In which novel was a real-life Jacobite spy, William Drummond of Balhaldy, immortalized?
2. Where would you have found ashes of roses in the 1950s?
3. What is a mandolin used for in cookery?
4. On which London street are there only three houses, numbered 10, 11 and 12?
5. Which is Europe's most endangered bird?
6. Britain has miles of canals and navigable rivers open to the pleasure cruiser. Approximately how many?

# 41

1. Albert Schweitzer.
2. The Colonels seized power in Greece. She vowed to return only after democracy had been restored.
3. Peas – *petit pois*, to be precise.
4. She worked in a barber's shop, lathering customers' faces.
5. The narwhal, which has a long tusk.
6. Bodypoppers move with jerky, robot-like movements, while breakdancers spin and leap like acrobats.

# 117

1. She was the first woman to become a democratically elected head of state (of Iceland).
2. Dr Snoddie.
3. The gooseberry.
4. Denmark.
5. The emperor penguin.
6. To Cadbury Castle, north of Yeovil, Somerset.

# 193

1. R. L. Stevenson's *Kidnapped*.
2. In a scent bottle. Ashes of Roses was one of Woolworth's best-selling lines.
3. For finely slicing vegetables.
4. Downing Street.
5. The Spanish imperial eagle – fewer than 100 individuals of the species are alive at present.
6. 3,000 miles.

## 42

1. What did Jenny Geddes throw where?
2. Who played the repellent Master Blifil in the 1963 film *Tom Jones*?
3. Which beverage was created by a blind monk?
4. Which of your fingernails grows most quickly?
5. In Poland there is a famous Leonardo da Vinci portrait of a lady bearing an animal in her arms. Which animal?
6. What is the name given to plants that follow the sun (e.g. the sunflower)?

## 118

1. Who was known to his followers as James VIII of Scotland?
2. In 1963 who said, 'I am notorious. I will go down in history as another Lady Hamilton'?
3. A Martini is decorated with a twist of lemon. What is added to make it a Gibson?
4. Which religious order of women did St Francis help to found?
5. At any given time, how many more spiders than humans live in Britain?
6. How many elongated triangles, or points, are there on a backgammon board?

## 194

1. Which writer had a railway station named after one of his novels?
2. Which notorious murder trial took place in 1966?
3. *Rijstaffel* is the high point of which cuisine?
4. What is a ginnel?
5. Which animal is to be found on a tin of golden syrup?
6. Where would you find a copy of the Bible and the complete works of Shakespeare waiting for you?

# 42

1. A stool, in St Giles's Cathedral, Edinburgh, in protest at the use of the Anglican prayer book.
2. David Warner.
3. Champagne. At the time of Louis XIV he first used cork bark as a stopper instead of hemp rag.
4. The nail on the middle finger.
5. A ferret.
6. Girasol.

# 118

1. The Old Pretender (James), son of James II.
2. Mandy Rice-Davies, of the Profumo scandal.
3. A pearl onion. (In *The Long Goodbye* Philip Marlowe says he belongs in Idle Valley 'like a pearl onion belongs on a banana split'.)
4. The Poor Clares.
5. Between 40,000 and 50,000 times as many.
6. Twenty-four.

# 194

1. Sir Walter Scott. (The station is Waverley, in Edinburgh.)
2. The Moors murder trial, in which Myra Hindley and Ian Brady were found guilty of murdering three children.
3. Indonesian. It consists of a number of savoury dishes served all at the same time with rice.
4. In North-of-England dialect it means 'a narrow passage'.
5. A lion.
6. On the late Roy Plomley's desert island.

# 43

1. Which famous comedian ignored Christmas and sent his cynical cards in July?
2. In 1965 who told Mrs Brown she had a lovely daughter?
3. Pecorino, Reblochon, *speck*, *fetta* and Fribourg; which is the odd one out?
4. What colour is produced by healthy vegetation on the infra-red images sent back by Landsat satellites?
5. Peebles has a coat of arms with the motto 'Against the stream they multiply'. What is depicted on it?
6. What is the connection between a headpiece, a throat last and a brow band?

# 119

1. Just how old was Methuselah?
2. Who directed the 1963 underground film classic *Scorpio Rising*?
3. Who electrified Paris in the 1920s by singing the 'Ave Maria' clad in nothing but a girdle of bananas?
4. How many gates are there in the Thames Barrier?
5. Which famous engraver and illustrator gave his name to a type of swan?
6. British Moth, Firefly and Hornet are all types of what?

# 195

1. Percy Montrose wrote which famous mining song?
2. What caused a sharp intake of breath in October 1967?
3. In which novel did Mr Woodhouse suggest, 'An egg boiled very soft is not unwholesome'?
4. What was the first detective story?
5. Which cat is meant in the phrase 'not enough room to swing a cat'?
6. In which British festival city would you find Arthur's Seat?

## 43

1. W. C. Fields.
2. Herman's Hermits.
3. *Speck*. It is a spicy, paprika-flavoured, fatty pork, while the others are cheeses.
4. Red; blighted plants show up as dark grey.
5. Three salmon.
6. They are all parts of a bridle.

## 119

1. He was 969 years old. (Accept an error of ten years each way.)
2. Kenneth Anger.
3. Josephine Baker.
4. Ten. They are installed between abutments on each bank and nine concrete piers.
5. Thomas Bewick.
6. Sailing dinghies.

## 195

1. 'Oh My Darling Clementine'.
2. Barbara Castle introduced the breathalyser to a dismayed British public.
3. *Emma* by Jane Austen.
4. Edgar Allan Poe's *The Murders in the Rue Morgue*.
5. The 'cat o' nine tails', once much used in the Royal Navy.
6. Edinburgh. Arthur's Seat is a volcanic plug on the outskirts of the city.

# 44

1. Of whom did Margot Asquith say, 'If he was not a great man, at least he was a great poster'?
2. Which fashion designer put 'Gorgeous Gussy' Moran into frilly knickers for the 1949 Wimbledon matches?
3. What do Italians mean if they call a man *finocchio*, the Italian word for fennel?
4. Whose daughter is Jeanette Scott, actress and one-time 'close friend' of David Frost?
5. Which animals fall into Old and New World groups?
6. Name three of the four major London auction houses.

# 120

1. Which Oxford college bears the name of a regent and a king?
2. Who played Caligula in the 1970s TV series *I, Claudius*?
3. Which vegetable, dressed with vinegar, did Cato recommend should be eaten 'as much as possible' both before and after a feast?
4. Which psychologist formulated the theory of the collective unconscious?
5. Where, in France, are flocks of greater flamingoes found?
6. When, approximately, do the Chinese New Year celebrations begin?

# 196

1. Who is the earliest English composer known by name?
2. Name the tiny Italian popular car of the 1950s and 1960s.
3. What was in the mess of pottage that Esau sold his birthright for?
4. What, in the eighteenth century, was known as 'the necessary'?
5. Which part of the whale is the fluke?
6. What do stamp collectors understand by the letters OG?

## 44

1. Lord Kitchener.
2. Teddy Tinling.
3. They mean he is a homosexual.
4. Thora Hird's.
5. The monkeys.
6. Bonham's, Christie's, Phillips' and Sotheby's.

## 120

1. Balliol, named after John de Baliol, who was the regent and whose son became king of Scotland.
2. John Hurt.
3. Cabbage.
4. Carl Gustav Jung.
5. In the Camargue. The birds are attracted by its expanses of fresh- and salt-water marshes.
6. Between 21 January and 19 February.

## 196

1. John Dunstable (*c.*1380–1453).
2. The bubble car.
3. Lentils (Genesis 25:34).
4. The lavatory.
5. One of the lobes of its tail.
6. Original gum (a Good Thing, apparently).

## 45

1. What have the kings Edward the Confessor, Eric VIII of Sweden, Louis IX of France and Ferdinand III of Castile in common?
2. Who played Detective Inspector Barlow in *Z Cars*?
3. Blanket and honeycomb are the two main types of . . . what?
4. What was first opened in Fort Worth, Texas, on 18 April 1934 and fast became indispensable?
5. The southernmost mammal is the Weddel seal of the Antarctic. How does it get oxygen when the sea is frozen over?
6. What is the British Mecca for dog breeders?

## 121

1. Whose masterpiece was published at a shilling, reduced to a penny and bought up by Rossetti and Swinburne before it was sold for a guinea?
2. Who took unsuspecting customers to the cleaners when his company crashed in 1963?
3. How does American cheesecake differ from others?
4. What, in Middle English, was a *leman*?
5. Who was the pioneer of bird-song recording?
6. Why would a home mechanic use a feeler gauge?

## 197

1. Whom did Frank Muir describe as 'the thinking man's crumpet'?
2. Whose father's epitaph provided the inspiration for the Teddy Bears' hit 'To Know Him is to Love Him'?
3. What distinguishes bacon from gammon?
4. Which direction is widdershins?
5. Which bird swoops on to its prey at speeds of up to 80 mph?
6. Which organization supervises the authenticity of pedigree dogs?

# 45

1. They have all been venerated as saints.
2. Stratford Johns.
3. Tripe.
4. A laundrette.
5. It chews breathing holes in the ice.
6. Cruft's Dog Show, held in London annually.

# 121

1. Edward FitzGerald's *Rubáiyát of Omar Khayyám*.
2. John Bloom.
3. The American cheesecake is not baked but is set with gelatine.
4. A lover.
5. Ludwig Koch.
6. To set critical gaps, such as those for spark plugs, contact breaker and valves.

# 197

1. Joan Bakewell.
2. Phil Spector's.
3. Bacon comes from the body of the pig, gammon from the hind legs.
4. Counter-clockwise.
5. The peregrine falcon.
6. The Kennel Club.

# 46

1. Who said, 'In the sermon I have just preached, whenever I said Aristotle, I meant St Paul'?
2. Which Harvard professor argued that LSD and other psychedelic drugs were beneficial if properly controlled?
3. What exactly are sweetbreads?
4. What was remarkable about the night mail train that ran from Glasgow to London on 8 August 1963?
5. Six scientists, among them Fred Hoyle, now believe an evolutionary link may have been faked by the Victorians. Which creature is in question?
6. Which game was devised to pass the time during a cruise?

# 122

1. Whose epitaph reads, 'Where fierce indignation can no longer tear his heart'?
2. Which nightclub owner complicated matters for the Warren Commission?
3. What is *kir* made from?
4. For which *parfumier* did Lalique make crystal bottles?
5. How many locusts are there in an average swarm?
6. Where is the car park at a Youth Hostel usually situated?

# 198

1. Whose music, says Mark Twain, is 'better than it sounds'?
2. What were Black Cat, Target and Turf?
3. In the seventeenth century it was made from milk and spiced cider or ale. We eat a more sophisticated version of it nowadays. What is it?
4. What is special about the zoo at Schönbrunn, outside Vienna?
5. Which big cat lives on the slopes of the Himalayas?
6. Who is everyone's favourite fell companion?

## 46

1. The Rev. William Spooner.
2. Timothy Leary.
3. The thymus gland and the pancreas of a calf or lamb (known as the throat and heart respectively).
4. It was the train involved in the Great Train Robbery.
5. *Archaeopteryx*, the link between reptiles and birds.
6. Deck quoits.

## 122

1. That of Jonathan Swift.
2. Jack Ruby. He shot Lee Harvey Oswald, suspected of John Kennedy's assassination.
3. White wine and blackcurrant liqueur (*crême de cassis*). It was invented by Canon Félix Kir, a French Resistance hero.
4. Coty.
5. One thousand million.
6. Nowhere. Although the 'youth' aspect is often waived, travelling by car or motorcycle is frowned upon.

## 198

1. Wagner's.
2. All were brands of cigarettes, now stubbed out.
3. Syllabub.
4. It is the oldest in the world, founded by Emperor Franz in 1752.
5. The snow leopard.
6. Wainwright. (*Fell-walking with Wainwright* is a best-selling book.)

## 47

1. What links Peter Maxwell Davies and Violet Carson?
2. Which family committed multiple murders in 1969?
3. *Ackee*, one of Jamaica's staple foods, is the fruit of a tree taken there by which British sea captain?
4. How much money is a 'monkey'?
5. How does the sea otter open mussels, clams and other shellfish?
6. What is whitework?

## 123

1. Who is the earliest British poet known by name?
2. Why did Ms Lindi St Claire hit the headlines in 1980?
3. Why was a Roman pontifex not allowed even to mention broad beans?
4. When would you use an alcohol, rather than a mercury, thermometer?
5. Which species of the genus *Canis* (the dog family) is best known to us through Western films?
6. Where, in Britain, can you visit a recently excavated Viking town?

## 199

1. The painter Jacopo Robusti is better known as Il Tintoretto. What does that name mean?
2. What did Rudi Gernreich, the Californian designer who was popular in the 1960s, dispense with?
3. How many cauliflowers were destroyed by the EEC every minute of every day in 1984?
4. What was 'Kim' Philby's real first name?
5. How often may a pair of lions copulate in a period of twenty-four hours?
6. What would you be holding if you had a Märklin 4-4-0?

# 47

1. Violet Carson, a pianist as well as an actress, was the first person to give a public performance of one of his works.
2. Charles Manson's 'family', which killed Sharon Tate and several other people.
3. Captain William Bligh of the Bounty. Its botanical name is *Blighia sapida*.
4. £500.
5. By striking them against a stone balanced on its chest.
6. Any white fabric embroidered with white thread. The term is now generally reserved for fine embroidery on white muslin.

# 123

1. Caedmon (who lived in the seventh century, according to Bede).
2. She was the London prostitute who tried to register her enterprise as a company. The ensuing publicity attracted the attentions of the Inland Revenue, which presented her with a bill for £10,768.75.
3. Because they were a funereal plant – funerals traditionally ended in bean feasts.
4. When measuring very low temperatures.
5. The coyote.
6. At Coppergate, York.

# 199

1. 'The Little Dyer', from his father's trade.
2. The top half of the bikini. He created the monokini.
3. It averaged out at forty-one.
4. Harold.
5. Fifty times. (No comment.)
6. A toy train.

## 48

1. Who did Graham Greene think was 'the nearest we are likely to get to a human Mickey Mouse'?
2. What, in the 1960s, was the alternative to taking the money?
3. The Italians called it the golden apple; in Britain it was considered poisonous until the last century. What is it?
4. On the shores of which sea was the land where Jason found the Golden Fleece?
5. What is the animal equivalent to the Victoria Cross?
6. On which town is Mrs Gaskell's *Cranford* based?

## 124

1. Who was variously known as Ursa Major, the Great Bear and the Great Cham?
2. Why did Giuseppe Roncalli feature on the front cover of *Time* magazine at the end of the 1950s?
3. How did the word 'fool', as in gooseberry fool, originate?
4. Who gave rise to the expression 'like billio'?
5. How does the cheetah kill its prey?
6. Where in the world can you mine for Blue John?

## 200

1. What physical qualification did Frederick the Great demand of his Guards of Honour?
2. What name did the British Gold Coast take when it became independent in 1957?
3. Which bean pod is known as the 'date of India'?
4. How long does it take to ring a full peal of bells?
5. Which dog was bred into existence by North of England miners in the nineteenth century?
6. Where would you carry sulphur sticks, patches and french chalk?

# 48

1. Fred Astaire.
2. Opening the box, on the TV programme *Take Your Pick*.
3. The tomato.
4. The Black Sea.
5. The Dickin Medal.
6. The Cheshire town of Knutsford, where she was married, lived and died.

# 124

1. Samuel Johnson.
2. He was Man of the Year because of his outstanding qualities as Pope John XXIII.
3. It comes from the French word *fouler*, to crush.
4. One Joseph Billio, a Puritan divine from Maldon, Essex, who was particularly noted for his zeal and energy.
5. It suffocates the victim by biting the underside of its throat.
6. At Castleton, Derbyshire, the only place where this mineral is found.

# 200

1. They had to be at least 6 feet 6¾ inches tall.
2. Ghana.
3. The tamarind pod.
4. Approximately three hours.
5. The whippet.
6. In your saddlebag. They are contained in the standard rider's repair-kit tin.

# 49

1. Which playwright wrote over 2,200 plays, 100 of them reputedly taking only a day each?
2. Which Italian tractor manufacturer turned his attentions to producing cars in 1963?
3. Which liqueur is made at the Abbey of Fécamp?
4. When did Britain convert completely to decimal currency?
5. What do ostriches do that has given rise to the belief that they bury their heads in the sand?
6. How many people in Britain ride horses as a hobby?

# 125

1. Of which genius did El Greco say, 'He was a good sort of man but didn't know how to paint'?
2. Which popular singer of the 1950s and early 1960s never wore the same dress twice?
3. What was invented by the Chinese, imported from Italy by Charles I and known to the Arabs as sherbet?
4. Who led Rhodesia in its unilateral declaration of independence (UDI)?
5. Which creature, according to Pliny, had a glance that meant certain death?
6. Where would you go to visit Britain's most northerly cathedral?

# 201

1. By what name is Peggy Hookham, DBE, better known?
2. Which country built itself a new capital city in the 1960s?
3. What would a guard of honour be doing in your kitchen?
4. The first was published on 1 February 1930. What is it?
5. Which islands were given their name because of the large number of dogs to be found there?
6. Which game encourages a passion for world domination?

## 49

1. Lope de Vega (1562–1635), Spain's Shakespeare.
2. Ferrucio Lamborghini.
3. Benedictine.
4. In 1971.
5. Seeking camouflage against the pale sand, female ostriches flatten themselves over their scooped-out nests when threatened.
6. Two million.

## 125

1. Michelangelo.
2. Alma Cogan.
3. Ice-cream.
4. Ian Smith.
5. The basilisk.
6. Kirkwall, capital of the Orkneys. St Magnus's Cathedral was founded in 1137.

## 201

1. Margot Fonteyn.
2. Brazil. Rio de Janeiro gave way to Brasilia.
3. It is the name given to two best ends of neck of lamb joined together so that the bones criss-cross.
4. *The Times* crossword puzzle.
5. The Canary Islands (from the Latin *canes*, 'dogs'.)
6. Risk. The winner controls the globe.

# 50

1. Which statesman was born David Green?
2. Which American stuntman shot to fame in the 1970s?
3. Where would you find edible coral?
4. What is the name of the great ceremony of the Australian Aboriginals?
5. When a snake is ready to shed it, where does the old skin usually split?
6. What kind of doll is a Frozen Charlotte?

# 126

1. Who was the first person to receive a human heart transplant?
2. Through what would children suck the sherbet in a sherbet fountain?
3. What is a chafing dish?
4. The year 1797 saw the introduction of which unit of currency?
5. Which bird has been found capable of counting up to seven?
6. Which game was the Red Cross requested to provide for US prisoners of war during the Second World War?

# 202

1. Whose nickname was Schnozzle?
2. Where did the first 'love-in' take place?
3. Which is the most widely used herb in Swedish cooking?
4. From what metal are shoes for racehorses made?
5. By what name is the moose known in Europe and Asia?
6. In the exercise of which skill must you constantly rotate the gob on the end of your nose?

# 50

1. David Ben-Gurion. He chose the name for its biblical resonance.
2. Evel Knievel, who leapt over astonishing obstacles on his motorcycle.
3. In shellfish such as lobsters and scallops. It is the reddish ovary.
4. The Corroborree.
5. Around the lips. The snake then wriggles out.
6. A tiny china doll without movable limbs (supposedly named after a little girl who drowned), now a collectors' item.

# 126

1. Louis Washkansky, a South African dentist.
2. A hollow tube of liquorice – which always clogged.
3. A dish with a spirit burner for cooking food at the table.
4. The £1 note.
5. The raven.
6. Parcheesi. (Officials discovered, however, that only the dice were used.)

# 202

1. Jimmy Durante, because of his phenomenal nose.
2. At the Woodstock Festival, held in 1969.
3. Dill.
4. Aluminium. Mild steel is used for other types of horse.
5. The elk.
6. Glass-blowing. (The gob is molten glass, held by rotation to the nose, the thicker end of the blower's tube.)

# 51

1. Why was Miss Ethel Cain so correct from 1936 to 1956?
2. What was the name of the trail boss in the TV series *Rawhide*?
3. In which Western country was caviare farming successfully developed following the Russian Revolution?
4. What exactly is implanted in breast implants?
5. Which biblical prophet was fed by ravens?
6. What is the face value of the word 'quiz' in Scrabble?

# 127

1. Which famous poet's first wife was drowned in the Serpentine?
2. What did Whistling Jack Smith claim to be in 1967?
3. Which cheeses are used in Swiss *fondue*?
4. Seventy per cent of the world's hydrofoils are to be found in use in which country?
5. Which creature was the emblem of the Chinese emperor?
6. Many people die in the mountains from exposure. In climber's jargon, what is the other meaning of the word 'exposure'?

# 203

1. Cole Porter once served in this unique military organization. Which is it?
2. What was Nadsat?
3. On the menu of an Indian restaurant, what does *tandoori* imply?
4. What provides a motorway link between England and South Wales?
5. A flea can jump many times its own height. How many?
6. Which is the hardest grade of pencil?

# 51

1. She was the voice of Tim, the Speaking Clock.
2. Gil Favor.
3. France. Enterprising émigrés bred sturgeon in the Gironde estuary in south-west France.
4. Silicone rubber gel.
5. Elijah.
6. Twenty-two.

# 127

1. Percy Bysshe Shelley's.
2. Kaiser Bill's batman, in his Top Ten single of the same name.
3. Emmenthal and Gruyère.
4. The Soviet Union.
5. The dragon.
6. It indicates that there is a sheer drop below a certain piece of rock. A climb up a vertical wall would be described as 'exposed'.

# 203

1. The French Foreign Legion.
2. Anthony Burgess's invented dialect in his novel *A Clockwork Orange*.
3. The use of a clay oven in cooking meat or poultry.
4. The Severn Bridge.
5. One hundred and thirty times.
6. The hardest grade of pencil is 4H.

## 52

1. Who was known at school as 'Snobby Roberts'?
2. What were light, portable radios first popularly known as?
3. What is okra more popularly known as?
4. Which was the first country to guarantee freedom of worship?
5. Which animal is Byron reputed to have kept in his rooms at Cambridge?
6. Which British stamps are not listed in Stanley Gibbon's Catalogue?

## 128

1. Who was born Maurice Micklewhite?
2. Which 1950s writer coined the term 'the Beat generation'?
3. To whom was the first pineapple in England presented in 1657?
4. What is special about the Caucus race?
5. Which insect thrives on radiation?
6. Where were the original 35-millimetre cameras produced?

## 204

1. Who was the first Prime Minister to occupy 10 Downing Street?
2. In which TV programme did couples first take to the floor in 1951?
3. What is the principal ingredient in a treacle tart?
4. Who lives in the Élysée Palace?
5. Which football team is known as the Canaries?
6. What is a deltiologist's passion?

## 52

1. Mrs Thatcher.
2. 'Trannies' – from 'transistor' radios.
3. Ladies' fingers.
4. Transylvania (now part of Romania) in 1586.
5. A leopard.
6. The unofficial issues of British off-shore islands.

## 128

1. Michael Caine. (Not a lot of people know that.)
2. Jack Kerouac.
3. To Oliver Cromwell.
4. As the Dodo explained to Alice, you start when you like and you finish when you like.
5. The beetle (the confused flour beetle, to be precise).
6. The Tourist Multiple and the Simplex Multi-Exposure were produced in America in 1914.

## 204

1. Sir Robert Walpole, in 1735.
2. *Come Dancing*.
3. Golden syrup – no treacle is used.
4. The French President.
5. Norwich City.
6. The collecting of picture postcards.

## 53

1. To whom did the 'writing on the wall' appear?
2. What was the first James Bond book?
3. What is fermented pear juice called?
4. Tradescant's Ark, in South Lambeth, London, was the first of its kind. What was it?
5. How did Alexander the Great tame Bucephalus, his horse?
6. At which game did Paul Newman excel in *The Hustler*?

## 129

1. How is K'ung Fu-tzo, keeper of accounts for the province of Lu, better known?
2. What was Parliament's gift to Churchill on his eightieth birthday?
3. According to Dr Johnson, 'Claret is the liquor for boys; port for men; but . . . a hero must drink . . .' What?
4. Which means of communication was invented this century by Dr L. L. Zamenhoff?
5. In Hinduism, what is the significance of Nandi?
6. Round-head, cheese-head and square-head are all types of what?

## 205

1. What have Theodore Roosevelt, Henry Kissinger, Mother Theresa and Lech Wałesa in common?
2. Princess Margaret was discouraged from marrying whom?
3. What is *Danziger Goldwasser*?
4. Travelling westwards, Mean Solar Time varies about one minute for every how many miles?
5. What was the name of Tarzan's animal pal?
6. What do Daniel Deronda, W. E. Gladstone and Lady Betty Balfour have in common?

# 53

1. Belshazzar (Book of Daniel).
2. *Casino Royale.*
3. Perry.
4. The first public museum in England.
5. Having noticed that it shied at its own shadow, he mounted this ungovernable horse by facing it into the sun.
6. Pool.

# 129

1. Confucius (551–479 BC).
2. A Graham Sutherland portrait, which was subsequently burned by Lady Churchill.
3. Brandy.
4. Esperanto.
5. It is the white bull of Siva; they are usually depicted together.
6. Bolts.

# 205

1. They were all awarded the Nobel Prize for Peace (in 1906, 1973, 1979 and 1984 respectively).
2. Group Captain Peter Townsend.
3. Danzig *eau-de-vie* with flakes of gold leaf in it.
4. Eleven.
5. Cheetah the chimpanzee.
6. Each has a clematis named after him or her.

# Q

## 54

1. Which American writer explained to a prospective employer, 'Salary is no object. I only want to keep body and soul apart'?
2. Which architect from Pontefract ended up in a starkly simple, clean-lined cell in the 1960s?
3. Which central Chinese province favours spicier food than the rest of the nation?
4. Which wood is used for both Rolls-Royce dashboards and the stocks of sporting guns?
5. Which bear has a purely carnivorous diet?
6. What inanimate object can be categorized by its bridle, tail and wind?

## 130

1. What was the surname of the grandfather and grandson who were both presidents of the USA?
2. What did Lord Grade sink a lot of money into in 1979?
3. How heavy can a bunch of bananas be?
4. What do Russian Orthodox priests do on 7 January?
5. Which creature does the honey-guide bird call when it finds a bee's nest?
6. Which was the biggest-selling board game at Christmas 1984?

## 206

1. How old was Tutankhamun when he died?
2. Who was the top British fashion model in the 1950s?
3. Which vegetable is sold more often cooked than raw?
4. How many sides has an icosahedron?
5. What is the true identity of the legendary 'black panther'?
6. What are the equine equivalents of a car's four forward gears?

## 54

1. Dorothy Parker.
2. John Poulson.
3. Szechuan.
4. French walnut. The wood grows quickly enough in the French climate to ensure the necessary straight grain.
5. The polar bear, which eats seals.
6. A kite. The bridle is the line running the length of the kite to which the tow line is attached.

## 130

1. Harrison – William Henry (1773–1841) and Benjamin (1833–1901).
2. The unsuccessful epic *Raise the Titanic*.
3. Up to 80 pounds.
4. Celebrate Christmas Day according to the Russian Orthodox Calendar.
5. The honey badger, which breaks open the nest so they can both feed on it.
6. Trivial Pursuits.

## 206

1. Eighteen.
2. Barbara Goalen.
3. Beetroot.
4. Twenty.
5. It is a black-coated form of leopard.
6. Walk, trot, canter and gallop (hence the expression to put a horse through its paces).

## 55

1. The Hon. Hester Grenville was married to, mother of, sister and aunt to four . . . what?
2. Which US cigarette brand did Ronald Reagan advertise in the 1950s?
3. Its name comes from the Sanskrit *singi vera*, and we eat it in powdered and root form. What is it?
4. Which two men uncovered the tomb of Tutankhamun?
5. Who rules Narnia in the C. S. Lewis children's books?
6. How many different species of trout are native to Britain?

## 131

1. Which British Prime Minister exclaimed at being presented with a Fortnum and Mason game pie, 'My dear, you're more like a mistress than a wife'?
2. Which fourteen-storey building collapsed in South London in 1968?
3. Which condiment did the poet Schiller take only in moderation?
4. New York city is composed of five districts: Richmond, Manhattan . . . ?
5. Which kidnapping in Ireland in 1983 was never resolved?
6. What was George V's favourite hobby?

## 207

1. The patronage of the Prime Minister Robert Cecil, Lord Salisbury, is said to have given rise to which phrase?
2. Who were known as 'the Brylcreem boys'?
3. Which Scottish fish dish is made of Finnan haddock, milk and mashed potato?
4. How many publishers turned down the manuscript of Thor Heyerdahl's bestseller *The Kon-Tiki Expedition*?
5. Of which country is the white eagle the emblem?
6. Where is Legoland?

## 55

1. Prime Ministers (William Pitt the Elder, William Pitt the Younger, George Grenville and William Grenville).
2. Chesterfield.
3. Ginger.
4. Lord Carnarvon and Howard Carter.
5. Aslan, the Christian lion.
6. One – the sea trout and the brown trout differ only in colour from one habitat to another, but each may migrate and 'become' the other.

## 131

1. Benjamin Disraeli.
2. Ronan Point.
3. Pepper. Believing in its aphrodisiac qualities and being no longer tempted by his wife, he thought an excess might lead to an embarrassing slip-up.
4. Queens, Bronx and Brooklyn.
5. That of Shergar.
6. Stamp-collecting. The Queen also has a fine collection.

## 207

1. 'Bob's your uncle'.
2. The RAF.
3. Cullen skink.
4. Twenty.
5. Poland.
6. Denmark.

# 56

1. Whose first book is called Genesis?
2. In what circumstances did France and Britain reach an agreement about the letter E?
3. What is an ugli fruit, sometimes called a tangelo?
4. Who invented the telegraph?
5. Which bird carries all the droppings from its nest and puts them in a stream?
6. Which fish would be invited to a feast of Hare's Ear and Grouse and Orange?

# 132

1. What were the middle names of Oscar Wilde?
2. Why would you have needed to wear glasses at the cinema in 1952?
3. Over 1,000 years ago in Ethiopia local monks prized a bush known as *gavch* for its berries. What did the monks make from these?
4. Among Devon tanners, if a letter V represented 5, what number was represented by the letter Z?
5. When the Aborigines introduced the domestic dog into Australia about 30,000 years ago, it returned to the wild. By what name do we now know it?
6. Which game is known to Americans as Tic-tac-toe?

# 208

1. Who was the husband of Pamela Hansford Johnson?
2. 'Hip', 'hep', 'cool', 'square' and 'daddy-oh' come from the language of which group?
3. What are singing hinnies?
4. In 1863 the first stretch of the London Underground opened. Between which stations did it run?
5. Which animals were used as a croquet set by Alice?
6. When do grouse have to take cover?

# 56

1. Moses'.
2. They had to decide whether to name the supersonic airliner Concord (British) or Concorde (French).
3. A cross between a tangerine and a grapefruit.
4. Samuel Finley Breese Morse (1791–1872).
5. The lyrebird (the female, of course).
6. The trout. Both are the names of artificial flies.

# 132

1. Fingal O'Flahertie Wills.
2. To watch a film in 3-D.
3. They roasted the kernels and made coffee.
4. Seven – V for 'vive', Z for 'zeven' in the local dialect.
5. The dingo (*Canis dingo*).
6. Noughts and crosses.

# 208

1. Osbert Lancaster.
2. The Beatniks.
3. A Northumbrian speciality – griddle cakes that hiss or 'sing' when cooking.
4. Farringdon Street and Paddington.
5. Flamingoes and hedgehogs.
6. On the 'Glorious Twelfth' of August, when the grouse-shooting season opens.

## 57

1. Who started life as Bernard Schwartz?
2. Who played Mr Pastry in the 1950s children's television series?
3. What, according to legend, did the prophet Muhammad live on when meditating in the wilderness for forty days?
4. Which illustrious American writer contributed the story line to the 1930s comic strip 'Secret Agent X-9'?
5. In which position do spiny anteaters mate?
6. Which castle do Arthurians visit, believing it to be King Arthur's birthplace?

## 133

1. Whose voice did Walt Disney provide in his cartoons?
2. Who played bass with the original Shadows?
3. What is *tuoni e lampo*?
4. Which French President gave his name to the arts complex in Paris's Beaubourg area?
5. Which particular doggie in the window was a singer interested in?
6. Where are bearskins on show whenever the Queen is in residence?

## 209

1. Who has been the tallest Prime Minister since the First World War?
2. Which drug, issued in Britain by the Distillers Company, resulted in the birth of malformed babies?
3. Which well-known gastropod mollusc used to be eaten in Britain as a cure for catarrh and bronchitis?
4. Where was the original King's Bench?
5. The hair from the tail of which animal is used to make the best paint brushes?
6. Which national museum has introduced an entrance fee?

## 57

1. Tony Curtis. Bob Goldstein, a Hollywood producer, said to him, 'Schwartz ain't a name to get into the big time – not even George Bernard Schwartz.'
2. Richard Hearne.
3. Dates and goat's milk.
4. Dashiell Hammett.
5. Belly to belly or tail to tail. (The normal animal belly-to-back position is just too painful!)
6. Tintagel Castle.

## 133

1. That of Mickey Mouse.
2. Jet Harris.
3. A traditional Italian dish ('thunder and lightning'), in which chick peas are served with *vermicelli*.
4. Georges Pompidou.
5. The one with the waggly tail.
6. At Buckingham Palace for the Changing of the Guard.

## 209

1. James Callaghan, who stood 6 feet 1½ inches in his stockinged feet.
2. Thalidomide.
3. The snail.
4. In Westminster Hall.
5. The sable.
6. The National Maritime Museum at Greenwich.

# 58

1. Both the long and the short of the Chicago school of monetarism won a Nobel Prize for Economics. Name one.
2. In 1979 Norman Mailer published a 'non-fiction novel' concerning which murderer?
3. What are comfits?
4. Apart from felons and lunatics, which members of the House of Lords are not allowed to vote in general elections?
5. Which is the outstanding cannibal among British birds?
6. Walkers are inseparable from their Ordnance Survey maps. What is the scale used in the Landranger series?

# 134

1. Of whom did Coleridge say, 'To see [him] act, is like reading Shakespeare by flashes of lightning'?
2. When did *Oh! Calcutta!* first appear on the London stage?
3. Eccles cakes and Banbury cakes both contain what?
4. How is bright leaf, grown in the USA, better known?
5. How much of its life does the European hazel dormouse spend sleeping?
6. Which much loved British model railway was made at Binn's Road, Liverpool?

# 210

1. Which leading theologian and philosopher of medieval France is now best known for his affair with Héloïse?
2. Who headed the bill at the 1969 Isle of Wight pop festival?
3. Malabar Black is a prized variety of what?
4. What is the Cockney rhyming slang for a hat?
5. How does a rabbit prevent itself from getting rickets?
6. Which yoga posture is considered to be the best for meditation?

# 58

1. The long – George Stigler (1982 Nobel Prize); the short – Milton Friedman (1976 Nobel Prize).
2. Gary Gilmore.
3. Sugar-coated seeds, such as caraway or coriander, eaten as sweets.
4. The peers.
5. The herring gull.
6. One and a quarter inches to one mile.

# 134

1. Edmund Kean.
2. In July 1970, at the Roundhouse, Camden.
3. Spices and currants.
4. Virginia tobacco.
5. Up to 88 per cent.
6. The Hornby Dublo.

# 210

1. Peter Abelard.
2. Bob Dylan.
3. Pepper.
4. A tit for tat, hence a 'titfer'.
5. By frequently washing its ears, for it thus ingests an oil that reacts with sunlight to form vitamin D.
6. The lotus pose.

## 59

1. Whose adage was 'It's not the principle that counts, it's the money'?
2. What is the name of Steve Winwood's brother?
3. In which way are the Irish indisputably more mature than the Scotch?
4. How many cities are there, officially, in the UK?
5. How far can a skunk squirt its fluid?
6. What would you be doing if you opened with a Nimzo Indian or a Catalan?

## 135

1. The institution of the Eleven-plus exam was based on the findings of which educational psychologist?
2. What happened to Ernest Borgnine in *Willard*?
3. Where should large prawns come from if they are rightly to be called scampi?
4. Of what is the word 'spats' an abbreviation?
5. Name two of Britain's three native snakes.
6. Which 'Scottish magpie' left to the nation a collection that is housed some miles outside Glasgow?

## 211

1. Who was the real Henry Higgins?
2. Which 1960s pop star made a habit of splitting his trousers on stage?
3. What is the name for the crisp, yeast-raised pancakes that Russians serve with caviare?
4. The men of which European state voted to give women the franchise in 1984?
5. Which animal gives birth accompanied by one or two other females, who act as midwives?
6. What did the Ramblers' Association celebrate in 1985, under the presidency of Mike Harding?

# 59

1. Phil Silvers's.
2. Muff. He also played in the Spencer Davis Group in the 1960s.
3. Triple-distilled Irish whiskey must be, by law, at least five years old, while Scotch whisky need mature for only three years.
4. Fifty-eight.
5. As far as twelve feet – so stand well back!
6. Playing chess.

# 135

1. Sir Cyril Burt, later exposed as having falsified the results of some of his research.
2. He was eaten by rats.
3. The Bay of Naples.
4. Spatterdashers.
5. The adder (or northern viper), the grass snake and the smooth snake.
6. James Burrell.

# 211

1. A British bullfighter.
2. P. J. Proby.
3. Blini. (If you didn't know that, *how* have you been eating your caviare until now?)
4. Liechtenstein.
5. The elephant.
6. Its Golden Jubilee.

## 60

1. How was the partnership of Wiseman and Bartholomew better known?
2. When did Rudolf Nureyev leap across the Iron Curtain?
3. What is eaten at Thanksgiving in the USA?
4. Digital watches have an LCD: what is it?
5. Which reptile continually grows new teeth to replace its old ones?
6. Where would you be going armed with thin paper and heelball?

## 136

1. Who started in showbiz as the singing duo Tom and Gerry?
2. Of which material was a Sloppy Joe made?
3. What vegetable used to be popularly known as sparrowgrass?
4. What do Jack the Ripper, John McEnroe and George II have in common?
5. Which animal has a name which comes from the Afrikaans 'earth pig'?
6. What plaything, the first of its kind, was presented by the Duke of Saxony to his daughter in 1558?

## 212

1. Who was the second man on the moon?
2. In which year did Ena Sharples first call round at the Rover's Return?
3. Boletus, ceps and girolle are all edible types of what?
4. How many times a day do Muslims face Mecca and pray?
5. Why is the American jack rabbit poorly named?
6. Why would it be easy for a fromologist to sniff out a new item for his collection?

## 60

1. Morecambe and Wise.
2. In 1961.
3. Turkey with cranberry sauce, followed by pumpkin pie.
4. A liquid crystal display, on which the time is shown.
5. The crocodile.
6. Brass rubbing. (Heelball is hard black wax.)

## 136

1. Simon and Garfunkel.
2. Mohair. It was an oversized sweater, worn by girls in the 1960s.
3. Asparagus.
4. Left-handedness.
5. The aardvark.
6. A doll's house.

## 212

1. Buzz Aldrin. (The first was Neil Armstrong, by the way.)
2. In 1960 – *Coronation Street* has been running ever since.
3. Wild mushroom.
4. Five.
5. Because it is really a hare.
6. Because a fromologist collects cheese labels. (One collector is reputed to have more than 22,000 labels.)

# 61

1. Who was said to have alighted from an empty taxi outside No. 10?
2. What did 'your quiz inquisitor', Michael Miles, try to make you do?
3. What is the only take-away meal you can't buy on a Sunday?
4. What is the origin of the word snob?
5. Horses are measured in hands. What is the measurement of a hand?
6. What is known in France as 'baby-foot'?

# 137

1. Who auditioned for the part in *National Velvet* that went to Elizabeth Taylor, and subsequently became a British politician?
2. Why did Guy and Donald hit the headlines when they went abroad in 1951?
3. What is fenugreek?
4. What is an ampersand?
5. Which animal is depicted on the badge of Rome?
6. Where might you attend the Hallé Summer Proms?

# 213

1. John Betjeman called the Earl of Redesdale's daughters 'the Mitford Girls'. Name four of them.
2. What, during the 1960s, would a girl eat on Shrove Tuesday and put on her face the rest of the year?
3. What is 'Moors and Christians'?
4. Los Angeles has been host to the Olympic Games twice. In which years?
5. Which animal did Chas and Dave natter on about?
6. Which British town would you visit to see a complete two-mile circuit of medieval walls?

# 61

1. Clement Attlee. (This joke was current during his premiership and has been variously attributed.)
2. Say the forbidden words in the Yes/No interlude, in *Take Your Pick*.
3. Fish and chips – under legislation passed in the days before refrigeration was widespread.
4. It comes from the entry s. nob (*sine nobilitate*, without nobility) written against students' names on college lists.
5. Formerly it was three inches, now it is four. (Accept either.)
6. The café game, table-football.

# 137

1. Shirley Williams.
2. Because they were Burgess and Maclean, found to have been spying for the Russians.
3. A herb native to the Mediterranean. It has tiny reddish seeds and tastes like burnt sugar.
4. It is the printer's sign for 'and': &.
5. The she-wolf that supposedly suckled Romulus and Remus.
6. In Manchester, home of the Hallé Orchestra.

# 213

1. Unity, Jessica, Diana, Nancy, Deborah, Pam. They had one brother, called Tom.
2. Pancake. It was the name of a thick foundation make-up.
3. A black bean dish from Cuba, in which the black beans are cooked with rice and spices, black against white.
4. In 1932 and 1984.
5. Rabbit.
6. Chester.

## 62

1. Whose six-year-old seventh marriage, to John Warner, ended in divorce in November 1982?
2. Millicent Martin, David Kernan and Roy Kinnear all appeared in which 1960s TV programme?
3. What gives Earl Grey tea its distinctive flavour?
4. At which London theatre has a Twelfth Night cake been distributed to the cast since 1794?
5. Why do lions yawn so much during the day?
6. Which ancient art has been described as 'a discipline to achieve Union with the Divine, or the Infinite'?

## 138

1. Which famous artist produced over 13,000 paintings and 100,000 prints and engravings in seventy-eight years?
2. Which popular singer and songwriter of the 1970s wore an oversized cap, and braces?
3. What is the supposed origin of the expression 'to take the gilt off the gingerbread'?
4. Where would you apply if you wanted to become a lighthouse keeper?
5. Which two breeds provide guide dogs for the blind?
6. Which boxer might you find in your aquarium?

## 214

1. What do Sophia Loren and Ramsay MacDonald have in common?
2. Name the spaceship in *2001: A Space Odyssey.*
3. When do Germans traditionally eat carp cooked in beer?
4. When were the 'thirteen years of Tory misrule'?
5. Why does a kingfisher always swallow a fish head first?
6. Coquette, Calculation, Betrothal and Weddings are all variations of which card game?

# 62

1. Elizabeth Taylor.
2. *TW3* (*That Was The Week That Was*).
3. Oil of bergamot.
4. The Theatre Royal, Drury Lane.
5. To cool themselves by increased evaporation.
6. Yoga.

# 138

1. Pablo Picasso (1881–1973).
2. Gilbert O'Sullivan.
3. Gingerbread was traditionally decorated with cloves with gilded heads.
4. Trinity House, London.
5. The Labrador and the Alsatian.
6. Jack Dempsey. It is a small freshwater fish from the Amazon, named after the boxer because of its pugnacity.

# 214

1. They were both illegitimate.
2. The *Discovery*.
3. Christmas Eve.
4. 1951–64.
5. So the fins do not stick in its throat.
6. Solitaire.

# 63

1. Which post-war Prime Minister had a first-class degree in oriental languages?
2. Where did Bing Crosby get his first name?
3. What is the main ingredient of Palestine soup?
4. Who popularised the expression 'small is beautiful'?
5. Which animal is associated with Tin Pan Alley?
6. In Italy it's known as 'blind fly', in Germany as 'blind cow'. What is it?

# 139

1. What was unusual about Dr James Barry, Inspector-General of Hospitals in the British Army?
2. Who stepped into Jean Shrimpton's shoes as David Bailey's favourite model?
3. What are *tapas*?
4. In which way is Nicholas Brakespear unique?
5. Which is the largest flying bird in the world?
6. In England and Wales, 15 March–15 June is the statutory close season for which fish?

# 215

1. Which Bradford Grammar School boy had to forge his own certificate from the Royal College of Art and now lives in California?
2. Who had a hit with *Side Saddle* in 1959?
3. What is tofu?
4. Where is the Phoenix Park?
5. The musk used in making perfume comes from which animal?
6. Which is the most popular card game in Las Vegas?

# 63

1. Anthony Eden.
2. From a comic strip called the *Bingville Bugle* that he read as a schoolboy.
3. Jerusalem artichokes.
4. Schumacher (with his book of that title).
5. The dog pictured on the trademark of His Master's Voice.
6. Blind man's buff.

# 139

1. He was a woman, as revealed by an autopsy; 'his' real name was probably Miranda Stuart.
2. Penelope Tree.
3. Hors d'oeuvre, or appetizers, served with drinks in Spain.
4. He was the only English Pope, Adrian IV.
5. The condor. (It has a wingspan of ten feet.)
6. Coarse fish.

# 215

1. David Hockney.
2. Russ Conway.
3. It is soybean curd, sometimes known as 'vegetarian meat'.
4. In Dublin.
5. The civet.
6. Blackjack.

## 64

1. Who, on reading Dickens, said, 'One must have a heart of stone to read the death of Little Nell without laughing'?
2. Which cartoonist scripted Mike Nichols's *Carnal Knowledge* in 1971?
3. What is the Islamic equivalent of kosher food?
4. How was William Joyce raised to the nobility during the Second World War?
5. Which animal is said to have been 'built by a committee'?
6. Terry Wogan sang about it; it happens in Helston in Cornwall on 8 May. What is it?

## 140

1. Who, with reference to the art 'movement' of the early part of this century, was described as 'the mama of dada'?
2. Which Tolkien tale was published posthumously?
3. Shaggy parasol and lawyer's wig are types of . . . what?
4. What was unusual about Mr and Master Robinson, passengers on the liner *Montrose*?
5. What is the most common reason for a wolf howling?
6. In which dance do you 'raise the right hand level with the head and give the Cockney salute, shouting "Oi"'?

## 216

1. Who said, 'Be sure to show my head to the people. It's worth seeing'?
2. In 1976, the Tate Gallery dropped several . . . what?
3. Which town is said to produce the best olive oil in Italy?
4. If the average IQ for the UK is 100, what is it, to the nearest whole point, for Japan?
5. What, in theatrical slang, is an 'oyster' part?
6. Which annual event featured in the 1950s comedy film *Genevieve*?

# 64

1. Oscar Wilde.
2. Jules Feiffer.
3. Halal.
4. He was Lord Haw-Haw, who broadcast out of Germany for the Nazis.
5. The giraffe.
6. The Furry Dance, often misnamed the Floral Dance.

# 140

1. Gertrude Stein.
2. *The Silmarillion* – dubbed the Sellamillion by *Private Eye*.
3. Mushroom.
4. They were, in fact, Dr Crippen and his mistress, Ethel Le Neve.
5. If it is a pack animal, it howls to advertise the pack's location; if a lone wolf, it is ready to defend its territory.
6. The Lambeth Walk.

# 216

1. Georges-Jacques Danton.
2. Bricks – 128 of them, in Carl André's expensive arrangement on the floor of the gallery.
3. Lucca.
4. 106.6.
5. One in which the actor says one line, then keeps his mouth shut.
6. The London-to-Brighton veteran car rally.

# 65

1. Who was the first Englishwoman to support herself wholly by writing?
2. In 1952 Jacques Cousteau set sail on a four-year voyage to film the ocean depths. What was the name of his ship?
3. What is saké fermented from?
4. Which religious precept was agreed upon by a vote of 547 to 2 on 18 July 1870?
5. Which mammal has the largest number of teeth?
6. Playing which game might you be faced with the prospect of a simple or double squeeze?

# 141

1. Which world-famous figure was offered the presidency of Israel in 1948 but refused?
2. In 1950 an invaluable archaeological find was the cemetery of chamber tombs which revealed much about the Minoan civilization. Where were they found?
3. Who is the patron saint of pastry-cooks?
4. What is unusual about the British plants sundews and butterworts?
5. How many hours a day do elephants spend feeding?
6. In Britain there are three codes of Bowls: name two.

# 217

1. Who was the last Stuart monarch of Britain?
2. When would you have received your Coronation mug?
3. Who painted *The Roast Beef of Old England*?
4. Originally the badge of an intellectual clique of women in fifteenth-century Venice, readopted by a group of women in Paris in the 1590s . . . what?
5. How many times do horses chew each mouthful of food?
6. What are a Bermuda Three-Stick, an Indian Fighter and an Eddy?

# 65

1. Aphra Behn (1640–89), as novelist, playwright and poet.
2. *Calypso.*
3. Rice.
4. The doctrine of Papal Infallibility.
5. The killer whale; it has 260.
6. Bridge.

# 141

1. Albert Einstein.
2. Knossos.
3. St Honoré.
4. They are carnivorous.
5. Twenty-three.
6. Crown Green, Federation and Association.

# 217

1. Queen Anne.
2. In 1953.
3. William Hogarth, in 1748.
4. Blue stockings.
5. Forty-four times on average.
6. Types of kites.

# 66

1. Whose autobiography begins, 'Three passions, simple but overwhelmingly strong, have governed my life: the longing for love, the search for knowledge, and unbearable pity for the suffering of mankind'?
2. Which celestial figure showed his backside in 1959?
3. Which is the strongest of liqueurs?
4. The Spanish used to equate nobility with the whiteness of one's skin. Which expression has this given rise to?
5. How do frogs protect their eyes under water?
6. Why would a Mamba not be suitable for an amateur herpetologist to keep?

# 142

1. Which radio and TV personality lived with his mother, the 'Duchess', until she died?
2. Which TV show measured success with a 'clappometer'?
3. How should true Yorkshire Pudding be cooked?
4. Name the propulsants used in aerosol sprays.
5. Which bird makes the longest migratory journey?
6. Every computer hobbyist has heard of hardware and software, but what is firmware?

# 218

1. Who was accused of condoning police brutality at the Democratic Convention in Chicago in 1968?
2. Why were Lt William Calley and Staff Sgt David Mitchell put on trial in the US in 1969?
3. The name of which drink is 'little water'?
4. What put a white collar among the blue collars in 1943?
5. For how long may the male and female Orange tip butterflies copulate?
6. Why would a home handyman have Mole grips in his toolbox?

# A

## 66

1. Bertrand Russell's.
2. The man in the moon, photographed by the Russian satellite Lunik III.
3. Green Chartreuse.
4. Blue-blooded. (Veins appear blue under white skin.)
5. By drawing transparent lids across them.
6. It is a venomous snake, which requires special handling and rearing as its bite can be fatal. (A herpetologist is a reptile expert).

## 142

1. Jimmy Savile.
2. Hughie Green's *Opportunity Knocks*.
3. It should lie underneath a joint secured on a jack, so that the meat juices drop down into the pudding.
4. Freons.
5. The Arctic Tern. (It travels, on average, 11,250 miles from its Arctic breeding grounds to its summer quarters in Antarctica.)
6. Programs permanently resident in the machine, having been blown on to ROM (read only memory) chips.

## 218

1. Mayor Daley.
2. They were accused of having taken part in the My Lai massacre in Vietnam.
3. Vodka.
4. The founding of the worker–priest movement.
5. For up to one week!
6. They are self-gripping pliers (named after the original makers) and useful when a 'third hand' is needed for a job.

## 67

1. Which old boy of Dulwich College took the name of his most popular creation from an Elizabethan dramatist?
2. Which form of transport did Barry Goldwater choose in his campaign against Johnson to win the Presidency?
3. What did medieval pilgrims to the shrine of St James, at Compostela in Spain, wear in their hats?
4. How did the bike-riding Hell's Angels get their name?
5. Which type of snake fought Rikki-Tikki-Tavi?
6. Mancala, which involves moving pebbles, is the oldest game in the world. Where is it still practised?

## 143

1. Who wrote, 'As no man is born an artist, so no man is born an angler'?
2. Who was the pilot of the U-2 spy-plane, shot down over Russia in 1960?
3. Which region of the Soviet Union is famous for its walnut sauces?
4. Who invented the saxophone?
5. Which sex symbol became the animals' best friend?
6. At which monument do English Druids gather on Midsummer Eve for their most important ceremony?

## 219

1. Who said, 'I remain . . . a clown. It places me on a much higher plane than any politician'?
2. In which district of Los Angeles did the worst race riots take place in 1966?
3. What is the sweetmeat *rahat lokum* better known as?
4. Who was the last woman to be hanged in Britain?
5. Which animal can reputedly see the wind?
6. What can you see at Cerne Abbas, Dorset, and Wilmington, Sussex, that you can't see elsewhere in England?

## 67

1. Raymond Chandler. (Philip Marlowe was born of Christopher ('Kit') Marlowe.)
2. He rode around on a white horse.
3. A scallop-shell badge.
4. From Howard Hughes's film, *Hell's Angels*, about First World War fighter pilots.
5. The cobra.
6. Throughout Africa, though it has spread, as part of the Muslim culture, as far east as the Philippines.

## 143

1. Isaac Walton.
2. Gary Powers.
3. Georgia.
4. Adolph Sax, of course!
5. Brigitte Bardot.
6. Stonehenge.

## 219

1. Charlie Chaplin.
2. Watts.
3. Turkish delight.
4. Ruth Ellis.
5. The pig.
6. They boast the only chalk giants on English hillsides.

# 68

1. Who lodged in John Evelyn's house and, according to Wren's estimate, caused £150 worth of damage?
2. From whom did Castro seize power in 1959?
3. What is believed to be at the root of the leek's special connection with Wales?
4. Which couturier was a partner of Christian Dior's before going on to found his own fashion house?
5. What is the technical term for coming into heat?
6. What would you be doing if you engaged in an Open Telemark and Cross Hesitation, a Whisk and Chassé, and a Drag Hesitation and Backward Lock?

# 144

1. Which headmaster's object was to make Christian men, 'for Christian boys I can hardly hope to make'?
2. Who first said 'fuck' on television?
3. Of which vegetable did Dr Johnson write, '. . . [it] should be well sliced, and dressed with pepper and vinegar, and then thrown out, as good for nothing'?
4. Which organization 'brainwashed' Patty Hearst?
5. What name do we give a mainly fruit-eating animal?
6. What do Hindus celebrate each year around October?

# 220

1. Which writer described himself as looking 'like a wedding cake that has been left out in the rain'?
2. Which illustrator created a striking series of jacket covers for Shakespeare plays in the 1960s?
3. Which vegetable is attacked by the Colorado beetle?
4. What was the original meaning of 'blackmail'?
5. Which creature is the voice of conscience for Pinocchio?
6. The smallest church in England is just 12 feet wide and not accessible by car. Where would you go to see it?

# 68

1. Peter the Great of Russia.
2. Batista.
3. It is thought that Phoenicians trading in Welsh tin brought them to Wales.
4. Yves Saint Laurent.
5. Coming into oestrus.
6. Waltzing.

# 144

1. Thomas Arnold.
2. Ken Tynan, thereby causing a furore.
3. The cucumber.
4. The Symbionese Liberation Army.
5. A frugivore.
6. Diwali – the New Year festival, when lamps are lit and presents are exchanged.

# 220

1. W. H. Auden.
2. Milton Glaser.
3. The potato.
4. It was protection money paid to outlaws operating along the English–Scottish borders.
5. Jiminy Cricket.
6. Culbone, by Exmoor Forest.

## 69

1. How, according to legend, was Pope Joan revealed to be a woman?
2. Living beyond your means became easier in 1950. Why?
3. What is the French upside-down apple cake called?
4. Holyhead lies on the tip of an island off an island off an island. What are the three islands?
5. A legend encircles the head of the lion which announces MGM films. What does it say?
6. When sailing down the Thames, you can see where Queen Elizabeth I was born, reigned and died. Name two of the three places.

## 145

1. Which famous contemporary English playwright was born in Czechoslovakia?
2. The BBC lost its monopoly in 1955. What was the first advertisement seen on British TV screens?
3. What is the French word for a coffee-house with smoking facilities?
4. In 1955 in Montgomery, Alabama, Rosa Parks hit the headlines by refusing to do . . . what?
5. Who is the love object of Miss Piggy?
6. Where is the oldest galleried inn in London?

## 221

1. Who changed her name from Frances Gumm, having started as one of the 'Gumm Sisters Kiddie Act'?
2. Who moved from *High Society* to high society in 1956?
3. Name Rex Stout's gourmet private detective.
4. Which is the highest type of cloud formation?
5. Who is known as Topolino in Italy, Musse Pig in Sweden and Miki Kuchi in Japan?
6. Where is the smallest house in Britain said to be?

# 69

1. She gave birth during a papal procession through Rome.
2. The first credit card – Diners Club – was introduced.
3. Tarte Tatin.
4. Holy Island, Anglesey and Britain.
5. *Ars Gratia Artis*.
6. Greenwich, Whitehall and Richmond.

# 145

1. Tom Stoppard.
2. An advertisement for Gibbs SR.
3. An *estaminet*.
4. Sit at the back of a bus with the other black passengers, away from the part reserved for whites.
5. Kermit the Frog, in the *Muppets*.
6. The George Inn, Borough High Street.

# 221

1. Judy Garland.
2. Grace Kelly, star of the film *High Society*. She married Prince Rainier.
3. Nero Wolfe.
4. Cirrus.
5. Mickey Mouse.
6. In Conwy.

# 70

1. To whom did Dorothy Parker leave the bulk of her estate when she died in 1967?
2. Who were among the victims of a 1958 plane crash at Munich airport?
3. What sort of wine is Château d'Yquem?
4. What was Operation Dynamo, in the Second World War?
5. When Rinka the Great Dane was shot in 1975, the long-term repercussions led to the Old Bailey and the House of Commons. Why?
6. What is a plashed hedge?

# 146

1. Whose name, according to Milton, 'in arms through Europe rings and fills all mouths with envy and amaze'?
2. What were the findings of the Wolfenden Report?
3. What are an animal's lights?
4. Which early Austrian car had the number-plate A 111 118?
5. In Greek myth, what was the name of the winged horse Bellerophon tamed?
6. Name one of the architect Robert Adam's lesser-known brothers.

# 222

1. Who is the patron saint of accountants, bankers and book-keepers?
2. Alec Issigonis designed it, and it was unveiled in 1959. What was it?
3. What is the Hungarian national dish?
4. Which NATO member has a standing army of 630 men?
5. What was the name of That Pig in the P. G. Wodehouse stories?
6. Where can you see a red pagoda in West London?

# 70

1. Martin Luther King.
2. Members of the Manchester United football team.
3. Sauternes.
4. The Dunkirk evacuation.
5. Rinka was Norman Scott's dog, and it was claimed Jeremy Thorpe had hired a killer to rid him of the potentially embarrassing Mr Scott.
6. One in which the growths have been intertwined and plaited to strengthen it and render it impenetrable to animals.

# 146

1. Thomas Fairfax, the parliamentary general in the Civil War who distinguished himself particularly at the Battle of Marston Moor.
2. Prostitution should be kept off the streets and male homosexuality should be permissible between consenting adults.
3. Its lungs.
4. The car in which the Archduke Ferdinand was assassinated.
5. Pegasus.
6. James or John.

# 222

1. St Matthew.
2. The Mini.
3. Goulash.
4. Luxembourg.
5. The Empress of Blandings.
6. In Kew Gardens.

# 71

1. Who was the last bearded British Prime Minister?
2. Who warned us that TV advertisers might be planting subliminal messages?
3. The Hippophagic Society was formed in London in the seventeenth century to popularize what?
4. Every Japanese learns there are four things to fear: earthquakes, thunder, fire and . . . ?
5. What was the name of the performing dog which belonged to Sissy Jupe's father in *Hard Times*?
6. What do Sue Lawley, Derek Nimmo and Anna Ford have in common?

# 147

1. Which New Zealand cartoonist was knighted?
2. Which restaurant did Woody Guthrie's son eat at?
3. When was the traditional season for killing pigs?
4. How did *Uncle Tom's Cabin* create a literary 'first'?
5. Name the animals found in the traditional Punch and Judy story.
6. What is a gazebo?

# 223

1. Which of Byron's lovers was married to a future Prime Minister?
2. How did Uncle Mac sign off, at the end of *Children's Favourites*?
3. What do you understand by Bath chaps?
4. Albert Einstein and Leo Szilard jointly filed a patent on a domestic machine. Which?
5. What is the ancient animal found at Uffington in Berkshire?
6. Which type of soil do rhododendrons need?

## 71

1. The Marquis of Salisbury, 1830–1903.
2. Vance Packard, in his book *The Hidden Persuaders*.
3. The eating of horseflesh.
4. One's father.
5. Merrylegs.
6. They all have roses named after them.

## 147

1. Sir David Low. He worked for the *Evening Standard* and the *Manchester Guardian*.
2. *Alice's Restaurant*, Arlo Guthrie's 1970s film.
3. Autumn, when every part except the squeak was used.
4. It was the first novel to sell a million copies.
5. Toby, the dog, and the Crocodile.
6. A small look-out tower, or summerhouse with a view.

## 223

1. Caroline Lamb. She was the wife of William Lamb, later Lord Melbourne.
2. 'Goodbye, children (slight pause) everywhere.'
3. It is a cold brawn-like mould, made from the jowls of pigs.
4. The refrigerator.
5. A pre-Roman white horse, cut into the hillside.
6. A lime-free soil.

# 72

1. Which British King was tattooed in his youth, much to the annoyance of his mother?
2. In which West End play did Richard Attenborough and Sheila Sim star together in 1952?
3. What is the Russian name for white sturgeon of the Black and Caspian seas?
4. How many members of the Order of Merit can there be?
5. If a vampire bat decides to suck your blood, which part of the body is it most likely to go for?
6. When were jigsaw puzzles invented?

# 148

1. Which famous London statue was erected in honour of Lord Shaftesbury, campaigner against child labour?
2. Which American TV series was prefaced by '. . . only the names have been changed to protect the innocent'?
3. Which cheese did Marie Harel perfect in 1790?
4. Shah Jehan's wife is immortalized by this. What is it?
5. What, on a snake, is Jacobson's organ?
6. How do you make granny or Afghan squares?

# 224

1. Who lived to be 101 and started painting at 67?
2. Who first performed Vaughan Williams's *Harmonica Concerto*?
3. What are angels on horseback?
4. Which oil tanker caused the first major oil spillage in the English Channel?
5. How does a flying fish fly?
6. People engaging in what activity might 'Shoot the Owl', 'Chase the Squirrel' and 'Box the Gnat'?

# 72

1. George V.
2. *The Mousetrap*.
3. Beluga.
4. Twenty-four living members.
5. The nose or the ear.
6. In 1760, by John Spilsbury, a London print-shop owner.

# 148

1. Eros, erected in Piccadilly Circus in 1885.
2. *Dragnet*.
3. Camembert.
4. The Taj Mahal.
5. It is a double scent cavity on the roof of the mouth by which snakes smell.
6. By crocheting.

# 224

1. Grandma (Anna) Moses.
2. Larry Adler.
3. Oysters wrapped in bacon.
4. The Torrey Canyon, in 1967.
5. It has two enlarged pectoral fins and uses its tail to propel itself out of the water.
6. Country dancing.

## 73

1. Which brother of a world-famous Shakespearean actor turned world-famous assassin?
2. Who or what was Veruschka?
3. What do you understand by VSOP?
4. What did George C. Scott and Marlon Brando both refuse?
5. Where can one see a full-sized suit of armour for an elephant?
6. Which plant, brought from France as an ornamental plant, is now a common vegetable?

## 149

1. Which chemistry teacher and founder of a women's medical school is now best remembered for two symphonies, two string quartets and an opera?
2. Which actress made her reputation as the Brummie Monica in the radio programme *Educating Archie*?
3. Mekong is a much favoured drink in Thailand. What is it?
4. What is ZAPU?
5. What species of deer, now extinct in the wild, was discovered by a French missionary in 1865?
6. At roulette, what does a gambler betting on 'manque' hope?

## 225

1. Who saw his sister murder their mother with a carving knife, and went on to write with her?
2. What posed a global threat in the 1954 horror film classic, *Them!*?
3. What is the distinguishing feature of Buck Rarebit?
4. What is a rebus?
5. Which prominent London citizen keeps newts?
6. The British island of Lundy derives its name from the old Norse word for which bird?

## 73

1. John Wilkes Booth, brother of Edwin Booth and assassin of Lincoln.
2. A top model in the 1960s.
3. Very superior old pale; it is a term used in the liquor trade.
4. Their respective Oscar awards.
5. In the Tower of London. The armour was used at the battle of Plassey, India, in 1757.
6. The runner-bean.

## 149

1. Alexander Porfyrievich Borodin.
2. Beryl Reid.
3. It is a kind of rice whisky.
4. Nkomo's Zimbabwe African People's Union.
5. Père David's deer. (They can be seen at Woburn.)
6. That a number between one and eighteen will come up.

## 225

1. Charles Lamb. His sister was Mary.
2. Giant, man-eating ants.
3. It is Welsh Rarebit with a poached egg on top.
4. A riddle in picture form, or a puzzle where the syllables of a word are given in puns.
5. Ken Livingstone.
6. The puffin.

## 74

1. Which two national leaders have been refused honorary degrees by Oxford University?
2. What is the name of Dame Edna's husband?
3. What does the epithet 'Crécy' mean on a menu?
4. At what time of the day does the evening primrose open?
5. Which is the tallest breed of dog in the world?
6. For whom did Lord Snowdon design a house in Regent's Park?

## 150

1. Whose verses, according to James I, were 'like the peace of God; they pass all understanding'?
2. Which writing partnership created the Glumm family?
3. What is Bombay duck?
4. The motto of which organization is *Service before Self*?
5. Which animal is referred to by the adjective 'anserine'?
6. In which English town can you go shopping in 'The Shambles'?

## 226

1. How is Sally Olwen, singer and actress and one-time top female vocalist in France, better known?
2. Which rock and roll TV show was broadcast for the first time from the stage of the Hackney Empire in June 1958?
3. What is a *merguez*?
4. What happens to the profits of the Irish Sweepstakes scheme?
5. Fireflies are not really flies at all. What are they?
6. Which village is sometimes dubbed the 'Blackpool of the Cotswolds'?

# 74

1. Mrs Thatcher (in 1985) and President Bhutto of Pakistan (in 1975).
2. Norm.
3. Carrots. The centre of carrot production is Crécy-en-Brie, to the east of Paris.
4. At six o'clock.
5. The Irish wolfhound. (J. P. Donleavy owns one.)
6. The birds. He designed the Northern Aviary in association with Cedric Price and Frank Newby.

# 150

1. John Donne's.
2. Frank Muir and Denis Norden.
3. Dried fish.
4. Rotary International.
5. The goose.
6. In York. They are part of a web of narrow, medieval streets.

# 226

1. Petula Clark.
2. *Oh Boy*.
3. A spicy North African sausage made from lamb or beef, never from pork.
4. They go into a fund for hospitals.
5. Female beetles, lighting up to attract the males.
6. Bourton-on-the-Water.

## 75

1. Which French king died at Esher in Surrey?
2. The most-decorated American hero of the Second World War took up film acting after the war. Who was he?
3. Who created the Lobster Telephone in 1936?
4. Which place was once called 'The Island of Cloves'?
5. What was the name of the creature that led us through Kit Williams's book *Masquerade*?
6. How many different species of cacti are there?

## 151

1. Of which English queen is Jane Fonda a descendant?
2. Who sang the theme tune to *High Noon*?
3. Which New York restaurant commissioned Mark Rothko to paint seven paintings, which they rejected, and which now hang in the Tate?
4. Which planets are known to have rings?
5. Christopher Smart wrote a long poem eulogizing his cat. What was its name?
6. What was the landscape gardener's last laugh over cattle?

## 227

1. Which two poets have the most entries in the *Oxford Dictionary of Quotations*?
2. In *The Wild Ones*, Marlon Brando played the leader of one motorcycle gang. Who was the leader of the other?
3. How many bottles of champagne does a nebuchadnezzar hold?
4. Which name appears on Swiss stamps?
5. In *David Copperfield*, with whom did David have to compete for Dora's affections?
6. In which town in Kent can you visit the Pantiles?

## 75

1. Louis Philippe, the 'Citizen King', in 1850.
2. Audie Murphy.
3. Salvador Dali.
4. Zanzibar.
5. Jack Hare.
6. Approximately 2,000.

## 151

1. Jane Seymour, Henry VIII's third wife.
2. Tex Ritter.
3. The Four Seasons.
4. Jupiter, Saturn and Uranus.
5. Geoffrey.
6. The ha-ha.

## 227

1. Shakespeare and Tennyson.
2. Lee Marvin.
3. Twenty.
4. Helvetia.
5. Jip, her dog.
6. In Royal Tunbridge Wells.

## 76

1. The motto hanging in her Streatham kitchen read: 'My home is CLEAN enough to be healthy . . . and DIRTY enough to be happy.' Jailed in 1978 for keeping a disorderly house, who is she?
2. Who played the part of Caruso in the 1951 film biography?
3. What do you understand by Spätlese?
4. According to Norse mythology, what was the name of the hall reserved for dead heroes?
5. Which animals lurk on the London Underground map?
6. What is a bag of rubby dubby?

## 152

1. Which inventor of an indispensable household instrument devoted himself to the education of deaf-mutes?
2. Who was the Rolling Stones' first manager?
3. What are known in Italy as 'the bread of the mountains'?
4. What do Bernstein, Prokofiev, Berlioz and Tchaikovsky have in common?
5. Which animal is the focus of the annual Puck Fair in Co. Kerry?
6. In which game are the balls referred to as 'pioneer', 'pivot' or 'pilot', according to where they lie on the court?

## 228

1. What did Sir Arthur Conan-Doyle train as?
2. Who played Jim Hardy in the 1950s TV series *Wells Fargo*?
3. What would you unpack from a carpet-bag steak?
4. The old French word *bougette* means 'little bag'. Which English word derives from it?
5. Which famous breed of dog originally came from Bingley, in Yorkshire?
6. Which fruit bush is attacked by Big Bud?

# 76

1. Cynthia Payne.
2. Mario Lanza.
3. It is a German term for wine made from grapes picked late in the harvest, thus resulting in a smooth, fuller-bodied wine.
4. Valhalla.
5. The Elephant (and Castle) and Blackhorse (Road).
6. Fish, finely chopped, bagged and used as bait.

# 152

1. Alexander Graham Bell, inventor, of course, of the telephone.
2. Andrew Loog Oldham.
3. Edible chestnuts.
4. They have all written music inspired by *Romeo and Juliet*.
5. The goat.
6. Croquet.

# 228

1. A doctor.
2. Dale Robertson.
3. An oyster – the steak is slit open and an oyster slipped inside.
4. Budget.
5. The Airedale terrier.
6. The blackcurrant.

# Part 3
# The Sports Quiz

## Edited by David Robins

with

| | |
|---|---|
| Alkis Alkiviades | Jim Cuddon |
| Jon Nash | Jonathon Green |
| Ted Gruetzner | |

# Introduction to The Sports Quiz

Which cricketer was offered the vacant throne of Albania? In ring-a-ring-of-roses, what happens after the second a-tishoo? Who manages Neasden FC? And which US Pro footballer, asked if he preferred Astroturf to grass, replied, 'I don't know. I never smoked Astroturf'?

And we have not forgotten the old adage: ONE PERSON'S TRIVIA IS ANOTHER'S PROFUNDITY. If you jog ten miles daily, play a couple of team games a week, watch darts and snooker continuously on the box, and then spend what's left of your time memorizing the results on the sports pages, then there is much here to challenge you in the way of Serious Sports Facts and Significant Statistics.

This section is a compendium of trivia, both pure and ultimate, drawn from the endlessly expanding world of sports and games, and is divided into six categories:

1. **Football.** These questions will test your true Trivia Retention Level when it comes to football – mostly Association, but with the occasional dip into Rugby, Australian, Gaelic and American.
2. **Cricket.** Contains ephemera from the world of willow on leather and the questions range from the essential (to cricket buffs) to the esoteric, as in the case of the woman who invented round-arm bowling.
3. **Allsports.** Many questions here are in the category of Solid Knowledge. Feats of champions, game rules and rituals, sports terms and phrases, from jammers and bunts to Rudies and Randies.
4. **Mixed Bag.** Here is where you'll find the Sports Trivia that refuses to be labelled.
5. **Personalities.** Who first said, 'Nice guys finish last'? Who was the Brit sporting hero who on retirement announced that he didn't just want to be the name above three greengrocer's shops?

6 **Sportscreen.** Isn't this the true realm of sport in our time? In films and television, not only as 'live coverage', but packaged and programmed, and as quiz games, and as part of

popular entertainment generally. And here you'll also find questions on sport in songs, books and plays. So, when did Sylvester Stallone co-star with Pelé? And in which film are baseballs treated with a material that makes them repellent to baseball bats?

The aim, then, is SPORTS TRIVIA FOR ALL – from aspiring Masterminds to weekend buffs. You would have to have lived on Mars not to have heard of Muhammad Ali, John McEnroe, 'Hurricane' Higgins, George Best and the rest. But in all categories, and particularly 4, 5 and 6 there are questions that even people who hate sports, and recoil every time they hear the theme music for 'Match of the Day', can join in and score well at.

David Robins

## 1

1. Who is Scottish rugby's record scorer with 273 points?
2. What was Christina Willes's contribution to cricket?
3. How many red balls are used in a game of snooker?
4. In what game is 'it' animal, vegetable or mineral?
5. What was the nickname of the ice hockey star Maurice Richard?
6. What was Werner Herzog's film about a world ski jumping champion?

## 77

1. Which US President tried to offer tactics to an American football team?
2. Which England batsman shot himself, believing he was afflicted with an incurable disease?
3. In what sport is it well worth learning the herringbone step?
4. In charades, what does pushing away mean?
5. In what sport was Richard Bergman outstanding?
6. Who co-starred as American football players in *Semi Tough*?

## 153

1. Who won the Milk Cup in 1985?
2. Who got a hat-trick in a test match in 1957?
3. If you were at the Brickyard, what sport would you be watching?
4. Which chess piece moves on diagonal lines only?
5. What was baseball star Babe Ruth's real first name?
6. Which comedy team had a sketch about a philosophers' football team?

# 1

1. Andy Irvine.
2. She invented round-arm bowling.
3. Fifteen.
4. 'Twenty Questions'.
5. 'Rocket'.
6. *The Great Ecstasy of Woodcarver Steiner*.

# 77

1. Richard Nixon (to the Washington Redskins).
2. Arthur Shrewsbury.
3. Skiing.
4. You're 'cold'!
5. Table tennis.
6. Kris Kristofferson and Burt Reynolds.

# 153

1. Norwich City.
2. Peter Loader (for England against West Indies at Headingley).
3. Motor racing (it's the nickname for the Indianapolis circuit).
4. The bishop.
5. Herman.
6. 'Monty Python's Flying Circus'.

## 2

1. When was the last time Great Britain won an Olympic gold medal at soccer?
2. In cricket, who was 'The Champion'?
3. In what country is Buzkashi widely played?
4. In what game can you bunt?
5. Which jump jockey became a best-selling author?
6. Who does Shorty race against in the song 'Cut Across Shorty'?

## 78

1. Which Olympic 100m. gold medallist became even more famous as a Pro footballer?
2. How many times had Sussex won the County Cricket Championship by 1984?
3. What sporting event takes place at Uttoxeter?
4. In what game is a 'ten second lawn' described as 'slow'?
5. Which eighteenth-century prizefighter was known as 'The Light of Israel'?
6. What was film star Jim Brown's game?

## 154

1. In American football, where do the Bears come from?
2. Which Australian batsman was dismissed for a pair within two hours by Jim Laker at Old Trafford in 1956?
3. In what sport do you have to be on the lookout for the Venturi Effect?
4. Who did the cricket writer Neville Cardus say was 'as much an Australian as God'?
5. Who described Soviet athlete Vladimir Kuts as 'nature's attempt at an engine in boots'?
6. In which film are baseballs made of a special material repellent to baseball bats?

## 2

1. 1912 (they beat Denmark 19–1).
2. W. G. Grace.
3. Afghanistan.
4. Baseball.
5. Dick Francis.
6. Dan.

## 78

1. Bob Hayes.
2. None.
3. Horse racing.
4. Bowls.
5. Daniel Mendoza.
6. Pro football.

## 154

1. Chicago.
2. Neil Harvey.
3. Hang-gliding.
4. Keith Miller.
5. A. P. Herbert.
6. *It Happens Every Spring*.

## 3

1. Who scored 19 points for Ireland against Australia at rugby in 1979?
2. Who was Australia's outstanding woman cricketer of the 1950s?
3. In curling, how many shots are allowed for each player?
4. If you slam dunked, what game would you be playing?
5. What is Mick Jagger's favourite game?
6. In which film does Clark Gable play a boxer in love with an actress?

## 79

1. Where was the first rugby club?
2. Which cricketer is nicknamed 'Smokey'?
3. Who was 1984 world 500cc motor cycle champion?
4. What is black, frozen, and measures 3in. by 1in.?
5. Baseball player Randy Moffitt has a famous sister – name her.
6. Who plays chess with Boris Karloff in *The Black Cat*?

## 155

1. Who played seventeen times for the British Lions between 1962 and 1975?
2. In Australian cricket, what is the term meaning 'the end of the day's play'?
3. Who was the first boxer to win three Olympic gold medals?
4. In charades, what does counting on fingers mean?
5. According to Sir William Fraser in 1889 where was the Battle of Waterloo won?
6. In which song do 'the players try for a forward pass'?

## 3

1. Ollie Campbell.
2. Betty Wilson.
3. Two.
4. Basketball.
5. Cricket.
6. *Cain and Mabel.*

## 79

1. Guy's Hospital (1843).
2. Viv Richards.
3. Eddie Lawson.
4. Ice hockey puck.
5. Billy Jean King.
6. Bela Lugosi.

## 155

1. Willie John McBride.
2. Stumps.
3. Lazlo Papp (Hungary).
4. Plural.
5. On the playing fields of Eton.
6. 'American Pie' (by Don Maclean).

## 4

1. Name the soccer team which included the former captains of Brazil, Holland and West Germany?
2. Who scored 1,834 runs in Australian cricket in 1983?
3. Who contests baseball's 'World Series'?
4. From what material are snooker balls made?
5. Which athlete models clothes for C & A?
6. In the film *Trouble Along the Way*, who says: 'Winning is not everything. It's the only thing'?

## 80

1. Name the two soccer managers who joined the 'Anti-Nazi League'.
2. Which cricketer is nicknamed 'Diamond'?
3. What bat and ball team game is 'the origin of baseball'?
4. In what country was the game of Trivial Pursuit invented?
5. Whose autobiography is entitled *Faster! A Racer's Diary*?
6. Who wrote the screenplay of *Chariots of Fire*?

## 156

1. From what country is the soccer club Penarol?
2. What do cricketers ask the umpires if they think a batsman is out?
3. Ronald Rawson was the last Englishman to do what?
4. On what day are pancake races run?
5. Name the playwright who was once a professional at rugby league.
6. In what sport was W. Barrington Dalby well known as a commentator?

# 4

1. New York Cosmos.
2. Graham Yallop.
3. The winners of the National League and the winners of the American League.
4. Crystallite.
5. Seb Coe.
6. John Wayne.

# 80

1. Brian Clough and Jack Charlton.
2. Wayne Daniel.
3. Rounders.
4. Canada.
5. Jackie Stewart.
6. Colin Welland.

# 156

1. Uruguay.
2. 'How's that?' (or 'Owzat').
3. Win an Olympic heavyweight gold medal.
4. Shrove Tuesday.
5. David Storey.
6. Boxing.

## 5

1. What was J. P. R. Williams's profession outside rugby?
2. Which newspaper does Clive Lloyd read?
3. Who was 500cc world motor cycle champion in 1977?
4. Which sporting scene did Degas paint?
5. What was Archie Moore's nickname?
6. When does Elizabeth Taylor get to ride in the Grand National?

## 81

1. Who was the captain of Argentina sent off in the 1966 World Cup game against England?
2. How many overs are allotted to each side in a Benson & Hedges cup match?
3. Who won the *Tour de France* in 1978?
4. Who was snooker's first ever 'billiards only' professional?
5. Who said: 'angling is the name given to fishing by people who can't fish'?
6. What team do the girls in *Those Glory Glory Days* support?

## 157

1. Who remarked about American football: 'It has become so complicated that the student will find it a recreation to go to classes'?
2. What is the Australian name for a googly?
3. In basketball, what is the word for a pass to an unguarded team-mate which results in an immediate score?
4. Who commentated: 'For those of you with black-and-white sets, Liverpool are in the all-red strip'?
5. Which legendary glider flew too near the sun?
6. What was *The Mean Machine*?

## 5

1. Doctor.
2. The *Guardian*.
3. Barry Sheene.
4. Horse racing.
5. 'The Mongoose'.
6. In *National Velvet*.

## 81

1. Rattin.
2. Fifty-five.
3. Bernard Hinault.
4. Norman Dagley.
5. Stephen Leacock.
6. Spurs.

## 157

1. T. S. Eliot.
2. A bosie.
3. Assist.
4. David Coleman.
5. Icarus.
6. A prison American football team.

## 6

1. What game is Subbuteo modelled on?
2. How many runs does a batsman get for hitting a ball clear over the boundary without it bouncing?
3. At darts, which score is called 'bed and breakfast'?
4. On which river does the Henley regatta take place?
5. With what game is Dan Maskell associated?
6. Name the BBC's chess series.

## 82

1. In American football, what city do the Seahawks come from?
2. Who wrote *The Story of Spedegues Dropper*?
3. Who was undefeated in singles at Wimbledon from 1919 to 1926?
4. From which kind of wood are championship darts boards made?
5. Which snooker player is known as 'the grinder'?
6. Who was the tennis bum in the television series *I Spy*?

## 158

1. Who saved a penalty in 1980 with his first touch of the ball in first-class football?
2. How old was W. G. Grace when he first captained England?
3. In what sport does Rudi Hartono excel?
4. Where are the TT races held?
5. Who once shouted out in the middle of a world title fight: 'Ma, he's killing me!'?
6. Which *Blue Peter* presenter went on to introduce televised darts?

## 6

1. Soccer.
2. Six.
3. Twenty-six.
4. Thames.
5. Tennis.
6. *The Mastergame*.

## 82

1. Seattle.
2. Arthur Conan Doyle.
3. Susanne Lenglen.
4. Elm.
5. Cliff Thorburn.
6. Robert Culp.

## 158

1. Tony Coton (for Birmingham City against Sunderland).
2. Forty.
3. Badminton.
4. Isle of Man.
5. Max Baer.
6. Peter Purves.

## 7

1. Who was voted European Footballer of the Year in 1968?
2. Which son of a former England test captain made his own test cricket debut in 1984?
3. What is the traditional form of wrestling in Japan?
4. What state is known as 'the gambling state of America'?
5. Which former chairman of the Conservative Party was ranked eleventh over 400 yards in 1954?
6. What sport does Clint Eastwood practise in *The Eiger Sanction*?

## 83

1. What trophy is at stake in an England–Scotland rugby union match?
2. Which Australian businessman was responsible for 'World Series Cricket'?
3. In 1984 the skier Hanni Wenzel won the first ever Olympic gold medal for which country?
4. If scissors cuts paper, and paper wraps stone, what does stone do?
5. Which British Olympic gold medallist holds a degree in Economics from Loughborough University?
6. Who were 'tennis chumps'?

## 159

1. Of which American football team was Vince Lombardi coach?
2. Who scored 365 not out for the West Indies in 1957?
3. What is basketball's equivalent to a kick-off?
4. Which baseball player married Marilyn Monroe?
5. Which champion darts player is known as 'the crafty cockney'?
6. What game is the subject of the film *This Sporting Life*?

# 7

1. George Best.
2. Christopher Cowdrey.
3. Sumo.
4. Nevada.
5. Cecil Parkinson.
6. Mountaineering.

# 83

1. The Calcutta Cup.
2. Kerry Packer.
3. Lichtenstein.
4. Blunts scissors.
5. Seb Coe.
6. Tom and Jerry.

# 159

1. The Green Bay Packers.
2. Garfield Sobers.
3. A tip-off.
4. Joe DiMaggio.
5. Eric Bristow.
6. Rugby league.

## 8

1. Which two English soccer grounds are 400 yards apart and separated by a river?
2. Which Pommy-hating Aussie cricketer was known as 'Slasher'?
3. What is the score for potting a red ball at billiards?
4. What is a Nimbus 2, a Skylark 3B and an ASW 17?
5. Who founded the modern Olympics?
6. In what film does Kirk Douglas point out that: 'Einstein couldn't kick a football across this dance floor, but he changed the shape of the universe'?

## 84

1. Which has been Northern Ireland's most successful soccer club?
2. Which English cricket captain was born in Milan?
3. Where are the US Open tennis championships currently held?
4. Which nineteenth-century British artist is famous as a painter of thoroughbred racehorses?
5. Who is Steve Davis's manager?
6. What is the setting for the film *Walk Don't Run*?

## 160

1. What is soccer star Liam Brady's nickname?
2. What is the name for a delivery which flies over the batsman's head without bouncing?
3. Cinzano SCP, Team Fiat and Maccabi Tel Aviv compete in which sport?
4. What is 'Annie's Room' at darts?
5. What was the tennis star Ann Jones's name before marriage?
6. In what film does Stirling Hayden steal $2 million from a racetrack?

# 8

1. Nottingham Forest and Notts County.
2. Ken Mackay.
3. Three points.
4. They are gliders.
5. Baron de Coubertin.
6. *A Letter to Three Wives*.

# 84

1. Linfield.
2. Ted Dexter.
3. Flushing Meadow.
4. George Stubbs.
5. Barry Hearne.
6. Tokyo Olympics.

# 160

1. 'Chippy'.
2. Beamer.
3. Basketball.
4. Double one.
5. Haydon.
6. *The Killing*.

# 9

1. Which leading soccer manager was a Queen's Guardsman?
2. Which England cricket captain's initials are M.C.C.?
3. In showjumping, what is the name for a competition in which the emphasis is on the height of a decreasing number of obstacles?
4. What is the second most played sport in France?
5. Which former world champion wrote a book on Muhammad Ali entitled *Sting Like a Bee*?
6. Name the Hollywood Tarzan who won swimming gold medals in the Olympics of 1924.

# 85

1. What is the nickname for the New Zealand rugby team?
2. Who 'died' during an England–New Zealand cricket test in 1975?
3. Who beat Björn Borg in a Wimbledon final?
4. Blind Hughie, Matador and Sebastopol are all versions of which game?
5. Who said: 'If I had my life over again, I'd have ended up as a sports writer'?
6. Which group had a hit with a song entitled 'We Are the Champions'?

# 161

1. Who plays in goal for Neasden FC?
2. How many runs did Don Bradman make in his last test innings?
3. How high is a netball post?
4. What was the ancient Greek name for a racecourse?
5. Which basketball team's signature tune is 'Sweet Georgia Brown'?
6. Which film is about a marathon dance contest?

# 9

1. Laurie McMenemy.
2. Cowdrey.
3. Puissance (or test).
4. *Boules* (or *petanque*).
5. José Torres.
6. Johnny Weissmuller.

# 85

1. The All Blacks.
2. A. E. Chatfield (his heart stopped beating for several seconds after he was hit by a bouncer).
3. John McEnroe.
4. Dominoes.
5. Richard Nixon.
6. Queen.

# 161

1. Wally Foot (one-legged).
2. None.
3. 3·05m. (10 ft).
4. Hippodrome.
5. Harlem Globetrotters.
6. *They Shoot Horses, Don't They?*

# 10

1. Which soccer club started as the St Domingo Church Sunday School club?
2. Which England cricketer was offered the vacant throne of Albania?
3. Who won seven swimming golds at the Munich Olympics in 1972?
4. Who invented the term 'gamesmanship'?
5. Which tennis master was brought up in New York but born in Germany?
6. What sport is portrayed in Walt Disney's *The Happiest Millionaire*?

# 86

1. Which soccer club's ground is literally a stone's throw from the Thames?
2. Who were the three Ws?
3. How many times did Lester Piggott win the Derby?
4. How many points have been scored in tennis if the umpire calls 'love'?
5. What was President Eisenhower's favourite game?
6. Name the two British athletes on whom the film *Chariots of Fire* was based?

# 162

1. Who is the chief soccer reporter of the *Sunday Times*?
2. What is cricket's answer to the Bible?
3. Which sport has been described as 'a form of aquatic gymnastics'?
4. What is the oldest international sporting trophy?
5. What was known as 'Enery's 'Ammer?
6. Which Hitchcock film features a tennis match?

# 10

1. Everton.
2. C. B. Fry.
3. Mark Spitz.
4. Stephen Potter.
5. John McEnroe.
6. Boxing.

# 86

1. Fulham.
2. Worrell, Walcott and Weekes.
3. Nine.
4. None.
5. Golf.
6. Harold Abrahams and Eric Liddell.

# 162

1. Brian Glanville.
2. *Wisden's Almanack.*
3. Synchronized swimming.
4. The Americas Cup (yacht racing).
5. Henry Cooper's left hook.
6. *Strangers on a Train.*

## 11

1. Who was the first black footballer in an FA Cup final?
2. In cricket, what is the name for a very short loose delivery which the batsman has plenty of time to hit?
3. Who did Stan Smith defeat to win Wimbledon in 1972?
4. Which British fighter took Ali five rounds in 1976?
5. Who are the hooligan fans that follow Neasden FC?
6. In which sport was Sonja Henie a champion before she went into films?

## 87

1. Who was transferred to Arsenal from Ipswich in 1979, and later became president of the PFA?
2. Which famous cricketer became High Commissioner for Trinidad and Tobago?
3. Name the world-famous horse auctioneers in Newmarket.
4. What is the lowest score not possible with one dart?
5. Which French monarch installed a billiards table at Versailles?
6. In which film does Warren Beatty fix a deck of cards in order to win in the casino?

## 163

1. Who won the 1981 rugby Grand Slam?
2. Who was the first person to hit six sixes in an over of first-class cricket?
3. In sailing, what is the term for reducing the area of sail in a high wind?
4. Complete the couplet: 'Float like a butterfly, sting like a bee –'
5. Where is Steve Ovett's home town?
6. In which film does a prisoner train for a place in the Olympic team?

## 11

1. Albert Johannson (Leeds United).
2. Long hop.
3. Ilie Nastase.
4. Richard Dunne.
5. Sid and Doris Bonkers.
6. Ice skating.

## 87

1. Brian Talbot.
2. Sir Learie Constantine.
3. Tattersalls.
4. Twenty-three.
5. Louis XIV.
6. *Kaleidoscope.*

## 163

1. Scotland.
2. Garfield Sobers.
3. Reefing down.
4. – His hands can't hit what his eye can't see.
5. Brighton.
6. *The Jericho Mile.*

## 12

1. Which Scottish soccer club's ground has a Gaelic name meaning 'hill of dung'?
2. Which cricketer's autobiography was entitled *I Don't Bruise Easily*?
3. Who won the race between the tortoise and the hare?
4. In golf, what is the word for play without errors and flukes?
5. Which US President was a keen jogger?
6. Which game does Jack Nicholson play in *Five Easy Pieces*?

## 88

1. In American football, what city do the Dolphins come from?
2. Which batswoman has scored more test runs than any other?
3. In what game do players use sticks fitted with nets?
4. In skating, what is the word for a jump in which one and a half turns are made in mid-air?
5. Who would 'rather be at Twickenham than Number 10'?
6. Who directed the film *The Goalkeeper's Fear of the Penalty*?

## 164

1. Who played each other for the first time at Lansdowne Road, Dublin on 20 September 1978?
2. Test cricketer Sarah Potter is the daughter of which well-known playwright?
3. In boxing, what is 'a punch delivered with a straight arm'?
4. Where is the Circus Maximus?
5. William Hill and Joe Coral are familiar names in the high street. Why?
6. Who starred in the boxing film *Champion*?

## 12

1. Aberdeen (Pittodrie).
2. Brian Close.
3. Tortoise.
4. Par.
5. Jimmy Carter.
6. Bowling.

## 88

1. Miami.
2. Rachel Heyhoe-Flint.
3. Lacrosse.
4. Axel.
5. Dennis Thatcher.
6. Wim Wenders.

## 164

1. Republic of Ireland and Northern Ireland.
2. Dennis Potter.
3. Jab.
4. Rome.
5. They are betting-shop chains.
6. Kirk Douglas.

## 13

1. In what town is the soccer club Juventus?
2. What is the name for the pieces of wood laid across cricket stumps?
3. Which British oarsman won medals in five consecutive Olympics?
4. What fantasy game is often called D & D?
5. What was the middle name of Cassius Clay?
6. Who played the tennis bum's coach in the television series *I Spy*?

## 89

1. Which 'Greek philosopher' captained Brazil?
2. Who wrote: 'If the French noblesse had been capable of playing cricket with their peasants, their châteaux would never have been burned'?
3. What is Australia's most prestigious horse race?
4. In honour of which God did the ancient Greeks hold the Olympic Games?
5. Who tossed the coin to start the 1985 Superbowl?
6. What sport features in the film *Accident*?

## 165

1. What soccer club is nicknamed 'The Irons'?
2. What game did Bob Willis take up after his retirement from cricket?
3. What piece of sports equipment is made up of fletching, cresting, shaft and pile?
4. What is 'conkers' usually played with?
5. What was the profession of the shot putter Geoff Capes?
6. In which film does Warren Oates race James Taylor?

## 13

1. Turin.
2. Bails.
3. Jack Beresford.
4. Dungeons & Dragons.
5. Marcellus.
6. Bill Cosby.

## 89

1. Socrates.
2. G. M. Trevelyan.
3. The Melbourne Cup.
4. Zeus.
5. President Reagan.
6. Cricket.

## 165

1. West Ham United.
2. Tennis.
3. Arrow.
4. Horse chestnuts.
5. Policeman.
6. *Two Lane Blacktop*.

# 14

1. What American football team did Joe Namath play for?
2. Who said: 'The sound of the ball hitting the batsman's skull was music to my ears'?
3. In which two sports do you find the 'piste'?
4. In tennis, what is the name for a stroke that puts clockwise spin on the ball?
5. Who in basketball was known as 'Wilt the Stilt'?
6. Who chaired the original *What's My Line*?

# 90

1. In American football, where are the Vikings from?
2. Which cricketer has three gods in his surname?
3. What is the top master's grade in judo?
4. Name the BBC radio quiz programme where teams from different schools compete.
5. Which fighter is known as 'The Hit Man' or 'The Motor City Cobra'?
6. Why was 'Spearchucker Jones' really brought in to join medics in *MASH*?

# 166

1. What is the total length of an American football field?
2. What is the name for an off-break delivered with a leg-break action?
3. Ring Taw and Spangy are forms of what game?
4. Who declaimed: 'There is no greater glory for a man than that which he wins by his own hands and feet'?
5. Who is the BBC's longest-serving racing commentator?
6. Who was filming the American football game in *The Fortune Cookie*?

## 14

1. New York Jets.
2. Jeff Thomson.
3. Fencing and skiing.
4. Slice.
5. Wilt Chamberlain.
6. Eamonn Andrews.

## 90

1. Minnesota.
2. Sivaramakrishnan.
3. Tenth Dan.
4. *Top of the Form.*
5. Thomas Hearns.
6. To play American football.

## 166

1. 120 yards (109·8m.).
2. Googly.
3. Marbles.
4. Homer.
5. Peter O'Sullivan.
6. Jack Lemmon.

# Q

## 15

1. In American football, each team has four 'downs' to travel how far?
2. Which cricketer is nicknamed 'Big C' and 'Hubert'?
3. In tennis, what is the score 40-all called?
4. In what sport was Eamonn Andrews once proficient?
5. Which snooker player is renowned for his impersonations of other players?
6. About what sport is the film *Below the Belt*?

## 91

1. Which two sets of brothers once played in the same team for Wales?
2. Which county did W. G. Grace play for?
3. What sport was banned in Derby in 1846 by using troops and special constables, and reading the Riot Act?
4. What is the only team sport which allows players to fight without risk of banishment from the game?
5. What does Fred Trueman smoke?
6. What was Terry McCann of *Minder* before he went to prison?

## 167

1. Who was Arsenal's manager in the 1930s?
2. Who was 'The Nonpareil'?
3. What are the dimensions of a baseball field?
4. In chess, what is the name for checkmate in two moves?
5. Who said: 'When the public is hungry I sell 'em fish. When they're bloodthirsty I fix up fights'?
6. In which film does Janette Scott win the Miss Globe title?

## 15

1. Ten yards.
2. Clive Lloyd.
3. Deuce.
4. Boxing.
5. John Virgo.
6. Women's wrestling.

## 91

1. Len and Ivor Allchurch and John and Mel Charles (at soccer).
2. Gloucestershire.
3. Football.
4. Ice hockey.
5. A pipe.
6. A boxer.

## 167

1. Herbert Chapman.
2. F. W. Lillywhite.
3. There are no standard dimensions.
4. Fools' mate.
5. Jack Solomons (boxing promoter and fishmonger).
6. *The Beauty Jungle.*

## 16

1. Which soccer team is nicknamed 'The Dons'?
2. Where is the urn that holds the Ashes kept?
3. What is the word for a stroke in tennis that sends the ball over the opponent to drop into the back of the court?
4. What is the name for a big marble?
5. Which golfer recovered from a bad car crash to win the US Open?
6. In which film do two girl athletes fall in love?

## 92

1. Where is 'The Shed'?
2. Who sponsors test cricket in England?
3. How many does an in-off red score at billiards?
4. For what sport did The Marquess of Queensberry make the rules?
5. Who could 'never understand tennis players who wore nice dresses but showed dreary garments underneath'?
6. Name the Mr Universe who played Hercules?

## 168

1. Which rugby player was known as 'Pine Tree'?
2. Who was 'Tittlemouse'?
3. In what sport do MV, Matchless and Yamaha battle it out?
4. Who wrote *Homo Ludens*?
5. Who threw the first televised ten-dart 501?
6. In what city was the film *The Games* set?

## 16

1. Aberdeen.
2. Lords.
3. Lob.
4. Dobber.
5. Ben Hogan.
6. *Personal Best.*

## 92

1. Chelsea F.C.
2. Cornhill Insurance.
3. Three points.
4. Boxing.
5. Teddy Tinling (tennis costume designer).
6. Steve Reeves.

## 168

1. Colin Meades.
2. Fred Titmus.
3. Motor cycle racing.
4. Huisinga.
5. Alan Evans.
6. Rome.

## 17

1. In American football, which city are the Cardinals from?
2. In what competition do Australian state cricket teams take part?
3. In which sport do you have 'hanging fives' and 'hot dogs'?
4. Who was world pool champion nineteen times?
5. At which game did Paul Robeson excel, before taking to the stage?
6. What was the film *The Championship Season* about?

## 93

1. Who was the first French soccer international to play in the English first division?
2. Who was the first woman cricketer to hit a six in a test match?
3. What is the word for a running attack in fencing?
4. On a snakes and ladders board, which are higher, the snakes or the ladders?
5. Which boxer's namesakes have been 'Top of the Pops'?
6. Who presents *Mastermind*?

## 169

1. How many officials are in charge of an American football game?
2. How many umpires are required for a game of cricket?
3. What is the name for a saloon car specially prepared for racing with a 'safety roll cage' inside?
4. What sport is followed by 'gentlemen of the turf'?
5. In what game is Val Robinson famous?
6. Who played Jim Corbett in *Gentleman Jim*?

## 17

1. St Louis.
2. Sheffield Shield.
3. Surfing.
4. Ralph Greenleaf (USA).
5. American football.
6. High school basketball.

## 93

1. Didier Six.
2. Rachel Heyhoe-Flint (at Lords, 1952).
3. Flêche.
4. Snakes.
5. Roberto Duran (the group is Duran Duran).
6. Magnus Magnusson.

## 169

1. Six.
2. Two.
3. Stock car.
4. Horse racing.
5. Hockey.
6. Errol Flynn.

## 18

1. Who called an election presuming that England would still be in contention for the World Cup on polling day?
2. How many test centuries did Len Hutton score?
3. What is the first race in US horse racing's 'triple crown'?
4. Who commentated: 'and referee Thomas blows his watch'?
5. Who were Wyomia Tyus, Edith Maguire, Iris Davis and Martina Watson known as?
6. What sport is Marion taught in the film *Pauline à la Plage*?

## 94

1. Which Australian Rules football ruckman had the nickname 'Captain Blood'?
2. Which cricketer was nicknamed 'The Big Ship'?
3. Who was a Wimbledon finalist at the age of nineteen and again at thirty-nine?
4. In tennis, what is the word for a good return of an awkward ball?
5. Which two competitors in the 1984 world professional snooker championships were born in Tredegar?
6. What was the television quiz game based on noughts and crosses?

## 170

1. How many of Argentina's World Cup-winning squad signed for English clubs the following season?
2. Which county cricket club did Alan Knott play for?
3. What sport is contested at the ASA championships?
4. How many one-eyed jacks are in a pack of playing cards?
5. What was the favourite sport of the Pasha of Marrakesh, T'hami el Glaoui?
6. Which television series was co-written by Terry Venables?

# 18

1. Harold Wilson (in 1970 – England lost to West Germany a few days before).
2. Nineteen.
3. The Kentucky Derby.
4. Hugh Johns.
5. The Tennessee Tigerbelles (US Olympic sprint relay gold medallists, 1968).
6. Windsurfing.

# 94

1. Jack Dyer.
2. W. W. Armstrong.
3. Ken Rosewall.
4. A get.
5. Cliff Wilson and Ray Reardon.
6. *Criss Cross Quiz*.

# 170

1. Three.
2. Kent.
3. Swimming.
4. Two.
5. Golf.
6. *Hazell*.

## 19

1. In what year was the Football League founded?
2. Who are the two cricket-mad passengers in *The Lady Vanishes*?
3. For what sport do you need a dropping-zone controller and a jumpmaster?
4. For what game do you need a shuttlecock?
5. Which seventy-one-year-old scored a hole in one at the 1973 British Open?
6. Which former heavyweight boxer starred in *Mandingo*?

## 95

1. What shape is the field in Australian Rules football?
2. Who wrote 'Play up! play up! and play the game!'?
3. In what game is Jocky Wilson famous?
4. In which Waddington's game do you play at detectives?
5. Who retired in 1973 after winning his third world drivers' championship?
6. Who won the race at the end of *The Loneliness of the Long Distance Runner*?

## 171

1. Of which soccer club was Eric Morecambe a director?
2. Which cricket reporter was also a renowned music critic?
3. Where is the Observer Gold Cup run?
4. What is the name for a tennis stroke played before the ball hits the ground?
5. Who was the BBC commentator who covered England's World Cup win in 1966?
6. Which famous baseball star did William Bendix play?

## 19

1. 1888.
2. Charters and Caldicott.
3. Parachuting.
4. Badminton.
5. Gene Sarazen.
6. Ken Norton.

## 95

1. Oval.
2. Sir Henry Newbolt (from *Vitae Lampador*, 1877).
3. Darts.
4. Cluedo.
5. Jackie Stewart.
6. James Fox.

## 171

1. Luton Town.
2. Neville Cardus.
3. Doncaster.
4. Volley.
5. Ken Wolstenholme.
6. Babe Ruth.

## 20

1. What is the name for the players in rugby whose job is to win possession for the backs?
2. Who scored a hundred in each of his first three tests in 1984–5?
3. Who is the only athlete in modern times to win gold medals in four successive Olympics?
4. Who once made a 100 break at billiards in 27.5 seconds?
5. Who said on retirement: 'I don't want to just be the name above three greengrocer's shops"?
6. Who hosted *Double Your Money*?

## 96

1. With which club was Santiago Bernabeau player, director and eventually president?
2. Who was known as 'Plum"?
3. Where were the 1984 Winter Olympics held?
4. In tennis, what is the name for a full-blooded shot played above shoulder height?
5. With what sport is Max Boyce associated?
6. In what sport is Sylvester Stallone involved in *Paradise Alley*?

## 172

1. Which American footballer was known as 'O. J.'?
2. How many test hundreds did Jim Parks score?
3. Who rode 149 National Hunt winners in his first championship season?
4. What is the name for the total amount of money paid by spectators at a sporting event?
5. In what sport is Chester Barnes famous?
6. Who directed *The Chess Players*?

# 20

1. Forwards.
2. Azharuddin.
3. Al Oerter (discus).
4. Walter Lindrum.
5. Henry Cooper.
6. Hughie Green.

# 96

1. Real Madrid.
2. Pelham Warner.
3. Sarajevo, Yugoslavia.
4. Smash.
5. Rugby.
6. Pro wrestling.

# 172

1. O. J. Simpson.
2. Two.
3. Jonjo O'Neill.
4. The gate money (or gate receipts).
5. Table tennis.
6. Satyajit Ray.

## 21

1. Which soccer team is nicknamed 'The Saints'?
2. Who took thirty-three wickets for England in the 'bodyline' series against Australia in 1932–3?
3. In what sport do you use asymmetric bars?
4. What game features in Bernard Malamud's novel *The Natural*?
5. What is Martina Navratilova's country of origin?
6. What race does Paul Newman compete in at the end of the film *Winning*?

## 97

1. Where is the headquarters of the Welsh Rugby Union?
2. Which England captain shot himself?
3. What board game is known as checkers in America?
4. Who carried off the Bolero routine to perfection in 1984?
5. Which former Wimbledon champion was arrested in a protest against apartheid?
6. Which BBC television series helped popularize snooker in the 1970s?

## 173

1. How many players are there in a Gaelic football team?
2. Which nineteenth-century poet received a black eye from a white cricket ball?
3. In which sport do you find the snatch, the jerk, and the clean and press?
4. What is the only chess piece which can cross a square occupied by another chess piece?
5. What was Jack Dempsey's nickname?
6. In which film does a rabbit called Thumper try ice skating?

## 21

1. Southampton.
2. Harold Larwood.
3. Gymnastics.
4. Baseball.
5. Czechoslovakia.
6. The Indianapolis 500.

## 97

1. Cardiff Arms Park.
2. A. E. Stoddart.
3. Draughts.
4. Jayne Torvill and Christopher Dean.
5. Arthur Ashe.
6. Pot Black.

## 173

1. Fifteen.
2. John Keats in 1819.
3. Weightlifting.
4. The knight.
5. 'The Manassa Mauler'.
6. *Bambi.*

## 22

1. How many times have West Germany won the World Cup?
2. Which cricketer was nicknamed 'Dolly'?
3. In volleyball, can points be scored against service?
4. In boxing, what is the name for sparring against an imaginary opponent?
5. Which top British rider's name denotes 'two fingers'?
6. Which comedy duo did a baseball sketch called 'Who's on first'?

## 98

1. Who won the soccer competition in the 1984 Olympics?
2. Which England bowler was also a published poet?
3. How many cards are used in pinochle?
4. Who are Neasden's greatest rivals in the North Circular Relegation League?
5. Who wrote *A Sportsman's Notebook*?
6. What sport is Simon MacCorkingdale good at in the film *The Riddle of the Sands*?

## 174

1. Who was Britain's first '£100 a week' footballer?
2. Who faced the first ball bowled in test cricket?
3. In what game can you have a line drive?
4. What game was invented by Alfred Butts in 1931?
5. Who was 'The Orchid Man'?
6. What was the occupation of Bill Cosby in *The Bill Cosby Show*?

# 22

1. Twice (1954, 1974).
2. Basil D'Oliveira.
3. No.
4. Shadow boxing.
5. Harvey Smith.
6. Abbott and Costello.

# 98

1. France.
2. John Snow.
3. Forty-eight.
4. Dollis Hill Academicals.
5. Ivan Turgenev.
6. Yachting.

# 174

1. Johnny Haynes.
2. Charles Bannerman.
3. Baseball.
4. Scrabble.
5. Georges Carpentier.
6. Athletics coach.

## 23

1. Which club kept the FA Cup for seven years?
2. Which former England cricket captain was busted for drugs?
3. In what sport do you find a Hereford round?
4. Who coined the phrase 'bread and circuses'?
5. In snooker, who is 'The Hurricane'?
6. Who played the *Raging Bull*?

## 99

1. Where do France play most of their rugby union internationals?
2. From what kind of wood are cricket bats made?
3. What was the most noticeable new safety feature of the 1984 Olympic boxing competition?
4. Which Prussian baron was a three-time Wimbledon finalist?
5. For services to which game did M. Bottvinik receive the Order of Lenin in 1957?
6. In what Swedish film does the hero play chess with death?

## 175

1. Which soccer teams are known as 'the auld firm'?
2. Who said: 'Pray God, no professional shall ever captain England'?
3. In what game do the chief shots include the trail, the draw, the tap and the guard?
4. Who wrote a novel about boxing entitled *Cashel Byron's Profession*?
5. Who skippered *Morning Cloud*?
6. What sport is featured in the film *Damn Yankees*?

# A

## 23

1. Portsmouth (they won it in 1939, and kept it for seven years because of the War).
2. Ian Botham.
3. Archery.
4. Juvenal.
5. Alex Higgins.
6. Robert DeNiro.

## 99

1. Parc des Princes, Paris.
2. Willow.
3. The boxers wore headguards.
4. Gottfried von Cramm.
5. Chess.
6. *The Seventh Seal*.

## 175

1. Celtic and Rangers of Glasgow.
2. Lord Hawke.
3. Bowls.
4. George Bernard Shaw.
5. Edward Heath.
6. Baseball.

## 24

1. Which soccer club's supporters stand in 'The Loft'?
2. Which cricket club had its headquarters at the Bat and Ball Inn, Broadhalfpenny Down, Hampshire?
3. What is the name for training a horse in obedience and deportment?
4. What is the most famous US amateur boxing tournament?
5. Who was Britain's greatest woman cyclist from the 1950s to the 1980s?
6. In which film does Gregory Peck play table tennis with Chairman Mao?

## 100

1. Which Russian prince played rugby for England?
2. What is the distance between cricket stumps and popping crease?
3. What do Nicolaus Silver, Gay Trip and Rag Trade have in common?
4. What board game was improved with the innovations of 'doubling' and 'chouette'?
5. Who said: 'No Viet Cong ever called me nigger'?
6. Who uses wheels with knives in the big chariot race in *Ben Hur* (the remake)?

## 176

1. How many times have Italy won the World Cup?
2. Who in 1963 became the youngest bowler ever to take 100 wickets in an English season?
3. Streatham Redskins and Nottingham Panthers compete in which sport?
4. Which British hospital has a fully equipped sports stadium in its grounds?
5. Who was the first television snooker commentator?
6. In which thriller does a London soccer club feature?

## 24

1. Queens Park Rangers.
2. Hambledon.
3. Dressage.
4. The Golden Gloves.
5. Beryl Burton.
6. *The Most Dangerous Man in the World.*

## 100

1. Alexander Obolensky.
2. Four feet.
3. They all won the Grand National.
4. Backgammon.
5. Muhammad Ali.
6. Stephen Boyd.

## 176

1. Three (1934, 1938, 1982).
2. Derek Underwood (aged 18).
3. Ice hockey.
4. Stoke Mandeville.
5. (Whispering) Ted Lowe.
6. *The Great Arsenal Stadium Mystery.*

## 25

1. What was the original name of Arsenal FC?
2. Who captained the 1984–5 England women's cricket team to Australia?
3. Where is the Italian 500cc motor cycle Grand Prix held?
4. What is 'the noble art'?
5. Who was the first man to win an Olympic athletics gold medal for Cuba?
6. In which television series does Lloyd Bridges go scuba diving?

## 101

1. Of what soccer club was Tommy Trinder a director?
2. Which county won the 1984 Benson & Hedges Cup?
3. When was the Epsom Derby first run?
4. Who would win a sprint race between a racehorse and an antelope?
5. Who won the world professional snooker title at his first attempt in 1979?
6. In what film does a game of chess end in seduction?

## 177

1. In soccer, how many steps may a goalkeeper take before releasing the ball?
2. Which county has three scimitars on its cricket badge?
3. In what game do you come across the Nimzowich, the Sicilian and the Queen's Gambit Declined?
4. Which newspaper for many years sponsored the major darts championship?
5. Who won the 5,000 and 10,000 metres and marathon in the same Olympics?
6. In which film does Bill Murray blow up a golf course?

## 25

1. Woolwich Arsenal.
2. Jan Southgate.
3. Monza.
4. Boxing.
5. Alberto Juantorena.
6. *Sea Hunt*.

## 101

1. Fulham.
2. Lancashire.
3. 1780.
4. Antelope.
5. Terry Griffiths.
6. *The Thomas Crown Affair*.

## 177

1. Four.
2. Essex.
3. Chess.
4. *News of the World*.
5. Emil Zatopek.
6. *Caddyshack*.

## 26

1. Who headed the winning goal in the 1984 Wembley five-a-side soccer finals?
2. Who is the only Nobel literature prize-winner to appear as a player in *Wisden*?
3. For what cross-country event will you need a map and a compass?
4. What is the value of the blue ball at snooker?
5. What was supposed to be the golfer Tony Lema's favourite drink?
6. Who filmed the 1936 Berlin Olympics?

## 102

1. Who won the Olympic rugby title in 1970?
2. How many runs have you scored if you are out for a duck?
3. Who was the first Australian to win the US Open golf championship?
4. Who won the Derby twice and the St Leger in his last race?
5. Name the Olympic medallist who is a member of the royal family?
6. At what game does Sergeant Bilko excel?

## 178

1. What position does Eddie Niedzwiecki play?
2. How many runs have you scored if you have made a ton?
3. Who won the first 'open' Wimbledon?
4. What is the Indianapolis 500 motor race known as?
5. What did John Erikson achieve at the age of fourteen?
6. When does Spencer Tracy manage multi-sport champion Katherine Hepburn?

## 26

1. Nobody. Heading is illegal in five-a-side.
2. Samuel Beckett.
3. Orienteering.
4. Five.
5. Champagne.
6. Leni Riefenstahl.

## 102

1. USA.
2. None.
3. David Graham.
4. Mick the Miller (the greyhound).
5. Captain Mark Phillips.
6. Poker.

## 178

1. Goalkeeper.
2. A hundred.
3. Rod Laver.
4. The Indy.
5. He swam the channel.
6. In the film *Pat and Mike*.

## 27

1. What song was known in the 1960s as 'the battle hymn of the Liverpool Kop'?
2. What side was once 0 for 4 wickets in a test in 1952?
3. What international sporting event is held at Stoke Mandeville Hospital?
4. Which sports league competition has been won by Cradley Heath, Belle Vue, and Reading?
5. In what sport is Anna Maria Carrasco of Venezuela famous?
6. Name a television series about a soccer club?

## 103

1. What is the Jules Rimet Trophy?
2. Who is Bob Willis's favourite singer?
3. What is played at Carnoustie?
4. What sports event takes twenty-three days and costs more than £1,000 million?
5. Who in the snooker world is 'Steady Eddie'?
6. Who starred in the film *Pumping Iron*?

## 179

1. Which former Liverpool and Scotland striker is now a television presenter?
2. Which England batsman played in thirty-one tests before scoring his first test century?
3. In what sport do you find a safety, a guard and a post player?
4. What is the word meaning 'to box in training'?
5. Who won the 1971 European equestrian championships on Doublet?
6. What film starring Dustin Hoffman and Laurence Olivier is named after an Olympic event?

# 27

1. 'Walk On' ('You'll Never Walk Alone').
2. India.
3. Paraplegic Games.
4. Speedway.
5. Water skiing.
6. *United* or *Murphy's Mob*.

# 103

1. The soccer World Cup.
2. Bob Dylan.
3. Golf.
4. Tour de France.
5. Eddie Charlton.
6. Arnold Schwarzenegger.

# 179

1. Ian St John.
2. Mike Gatting.
3. Basketball.
4. Spar.
5. Princess Anne.
6. *Marathon Man*.

# Q

## 28

1. Name the outstanding Polish World Cup goalkeeper who Brian Clough branded 'a clown'?
2. What is the maximum score off a six-ball over?
3. In boxing, what is 'a short punch delivered with a circular motion and a bent elbow'?
4. Which popular board game was known as 'Tables' in England, and 'Scripta Dodecim' by the Romans?
5. What was the horse on which Colonel Harry Lewellyn won a gold medal for Britain in the Helsinki Olympics?
6. In which film does Gert Frobe cheat at cards with the aid of a woman in a bikini and a large pair of binoculars?

## 104

1. From whom did Gordon Banks make his 'miracle save' in the 1970 World Cup in Mexico?
2. Who won the John Player League in 1984?
3. When was the first modern Olympic Games held?
4. What game does FIDE govern?
5. Which government minister was an FA referee?
6. In what film does Jane Fonda support Anthony Perkins playing basketball?

## 180

1. What is the nickname of the Australian rugby team?
2. Who said: 'Try explaining cricket to an intelligent foreigner – it is far harder than explaining Chomsky's generational grammar'?
3. How many times did Jonah Barrington win the British Open squash championships?
4. What equipment do you need to play Pelmanism?
5. Who was Charlie Smirke?
6. In which film does Esther Williams swim the channel?

# 28

1. Tomaszewski.
2. An infinite number.
3. Hook.
4. Backgammon.
5. Foxhunter.
6. *Goldfinger*.

# 104

1. Pelé.
2. Essex.
3. 1896.
4. Chess.
5. Dennis Howells.
6. *Tall Story*.

# 180

1. 'Wallabies'.
2. C. P. Snow.
3. Six.
4. A pack of cards.
5. A jockey.
6. *Dangerous When Wet*.

## 29

1. Which country has 1·5 million registered senior footballers?
2. Whose autobiography was entitled *Pace Like Fire*?
3. Karen Biggs has won two world and three European titles in which sport?
4. What game is also known as ping-pong?
5. Who completed a hat-trick of world speedway championships in 1970?
6. In which film does John Lennon help make a cricket pitch in the desert during World War II?

## 105

1. Who won the European Cup in 1977?
2. The grandson of which Poet Laureate captained England?
3. What is the name for a ski competition where competitors have to turn round flags or sticks?
4. Which top snooker player is known as 'Joe 90'?
5. Who was Henry Cooper's manager?
6. When does Dirk Bogarde get trapped in a greyhound racing stadium?

## 181

1. Which former Arsenal and Scotland goalkeeper is now a television presenter?
2. Who was dropped after making 246 not out for England in a test?
3. In racing, what is 'the tote' short for?
4. What game is Napoleon recorded as having played on St Helena?
5. Who called a Wimbledon Umpire 'the pits of the world'?
6. In what film was Steve McQueen a rodeo star?

# 29

1. China.
2. Wes Hall.
3. Judo.
4. Table tennis.
5. Ivan Mauger.
6. *How I Won the War*.

# 105

1. Liverpool.
2. Tennyson.
3. Slalom.
4. Dennis Taylor.
5. Jim Wicks ('The Bishop').
6. In *The Blue Lamp*.

# 181

1. Bob Wilson.
2. Geoffrey Boycott.
3. Totalisator.
4. Solitaire.
5. John McEnroe.
6. *Junior Bonner*.

# 30

1. Who wrote *The Glory Game*?
2. In which century is the first recorded reference to cricket found?
3. Who did John McEnroe beat to win Wimbledon in 1984?
4. What chess piece is represented by a horse's head?
5. Who raised his fist in a black power salute when presented with an Olympic gold medal?
6. What soccer ground does Albert Finney take his son to in *Charlie Bubbles*?

# 106

1. Who called Argentinians 'animals' in 1966?
2. What is the term for being out *first ball* in both innings?
3. In high-jumping, what is the method of jumping head first and landing on your back?
4. In what game are there ruffs, pianolas, and informatory doubles?
5. With which sport was Raymond Baxter associated?
6. Which two former prizefighters play mobsters in *On the Waterfront*?

# 182

1. Who were football league champions in 1962?
2. Who pursued Ian Chappell through a Sydney traffic jam after a bar-room argument?
3. As what was the World Cup of golf formerly known?
4. What was once known as inanimate bird shooting?
5. What hair lotion did Denis Compton endorse in the 1950s?
6. Who does Jackie Gleason play in the film *The Hustler*?

## 30

1. Hunter Davies.
2. The thirteenth century (Prince Edward is recorded playing 'creag' in 1272).
3. Jimmy Connors.
4. The knight.
5. Tommy Smith.
6. Old Trafford.

## 106

1. Alf Ramsey.
2. King pair.
3. The (Fosbury) flop.
4. Bridge.
5. Motor racing.
6. Tony Galento and Tami Mauriello.

## 182

1. Ipswich Town.
2. Ian Botham.
3. Canada Cup.
4. Clay pigeon shooting.
5. Brylcream.
6. Minnesota Fats.

# 31

1. Which goalkeeper was killed in the Munich air disaster?
2. Who was the first bowler to take 200 wickets in tests?
3. How many national darts titles did Jim Pike win?
4. What do 'the bells of Old Bailey' say?
5. Who was first dubbed 'the golden girl of British athletics'?
6. In what musical does a floating crap game take place in a sewer?

# 107

1. Which former Welsh international became 'Mr Soccer' in the USA?
2. In cricket, can you be out for hitting the ball twice?
3. In what sport do competitors negotiate a hogsback and a double oxer?
4. In what ancient Roman sport were fans divided into Blues, Greens, Whites and Reds?
5. For his brilliance at what is Ty Page nicknamed 'Mr Incredible'?
6. About which sports hero did Count Basie write a song, with lyrics by Richard Wright, which was sung by Paul Robeson?

# 183

1. In soccer, whose nickname meant 'the little bird'?
2. Who captained England to victory in the test series in Australia in 1971?
3. In ten-pin bowling, how many strikes must you score for a perfect game?
4. What is a hand in poker of three of a kind and a pair?
5. Which baseball star was nicknamed 'Jolting Joe'?
6. Which writer compared life to 'a football game with everyone offside and the referee gotten rid of'?

# 31

1. Frank Swift.
2. Clarrie Grimmett.
3. None.
4. 'When will you pay me'.
5. Mary Bignall Rand.
6. *Guys and Dolls*.

# 107

1. Phil Woosnam.
2. Yes.
3. Showjumping.
4. Chariot racing.
5. Skateboarding.
6. Joe Louis.

# 183

1. 'Garrincha' (Brazil; real name M. F. dos Santos).
2. Ray Illingworth.
3. Twelve.
4. Full house.
5. Joe DiMaggio.
6. F. Scott Fitzgerald (in *This Side of Paradise*).

# 32

1. Which soccer team does the Stretford End follow?
2. How many no-balls is a bowler allowed to bowl in an over?
3. In what sport do you have Rudies and Randies?
4. What is the motto of the Olympic Games?
5. Who did 'Meadowlark' play for?
6. Who directed *Chariots of Fire*?

# 108

1. Who 'first took the ball in his arms and ran with it' in 1823?
2. Who was Percy Holmes's opening partner for Yorkshire in the 1930s?
3. How many points away if the white ball goes in when you are playing a red in snooker?
4. What do Americans call the darts game known in Britain as Mickey Mouse?
5. Who set eighteen world records as a distance runner, but never won an Olympic title?
6. In which Danny Kaye film does a milkman become a prizefighter?

# 184

1. For which British soccer club did Israel's Avi Cohen play?
2. What was the result of the Australia–West Indies test at Brisbane, 1960?
3. Who won the British Open golf championship in 1967?
4. What do 'the bells of Shoreditch' say?
5. What nationality is speedway's Ivan Mauger?
6. What was Burt Lancaster in *The Killers*?

# 32

1. Manchester United.
2. An infinite number.
3. Trampolining.
4. *Citius – altius – fortius* (Faster – higher – stronger).
5. The Harlem Globetrotters.
6. Hugh Hudson.

# 108

1. William Webb Ellis.
2. Herbert Sutcliffe.
3. Four.
4. Cricket.
5. Ron Clarke (Australia).
6. *The Kid From Brooklyn.*

# 184

1. Liverpool.
2. A tie.
3. Roberto de Vicenzo (Argentina).
4. 'When I grow rich'.
5. New Zealander.
6. A boxer.

## 33

1. Which former centre forward for fourth division Swansea went on to play for Italy and the New York Cosmos?
2. What is the name for a fielder positioned as a back-up to the wicketkeeper?
3. In motor racing, what is 'a pair of tight turns in opposite directions in a straight stretch of course'?
4. Which country holds the Americas Cup?
5. What nationality was tennis star Maria Bueno?
6. In which film does Tippi Hedren go to the races with Sean Connery?

## 109

1. Who is 'Kaiser Franz'?
2. If an umpire raises his arm and touches his shoulder with his fingertips, what is he signalling?
3. What is hockey's version of a kick-off?
4. Who described angling as 'a stick and a string with a worm at one end and a fool at the other'?
5. Who was 'The Brown Bomber'?
6. Did Elvis Presley ever play a boxer?

## 185

1. In what city is the soccer club Ferencvaros based?
2. Can a batsman be out off a no-ball?
3. How many fences are there in the Grand National?
4. How many points is the following snooker break worth: red, blue, red, pink, red, yellow?
5. For what extraordinary feat is Karl Wallenda famous?
6. Who wrote *The Dice Man*?

# 33

1. Giorgio Chinaglia.
2. Long stop.
3. Chicane.
4. Australia.
5. Brazilian.
6. *Marnie*.

# 109

1. Franz Beckenbauer.
2. One run short.
3. Bully-off.
4. Dr Samuel Johnson.
5. Joe Louis.
6. Yes (in *Kid Galahad*).

# 185

1. Budapest.
2. Yes.
3. Thirty.
4. Sixteen.
5. Tightrope walking.
6. Luke Rhinehart.

## 34

1. Which first division goalkeeper fought in the civil war in Zimbabwe?
2. Who said: 'Cricket is the greatest thing that God ever created'?
3. Who won all three Wimbledons for which she entered?
4. Who described life as 'the great game'?
5. At what game does Omar Sharif excel?
6. Who starred in *The Greatest*?

## 110

1. Which Spurs footballer was killed by lightning?
2. Who wrote *Tales from a Long Room*?
3. What game is also known as twenty-one, vingt-et-un, pontoon, and vanjohn?
4. Name snooker champion Steve Davis's home town?
5. Whose fans are known as 'Arnie's Army'?
6. Who is the subject of the boxing documentary *Pound for Pound*?

## 186

1. Which soccer star was falsely accused of stealing a bracelet from a shop in Bogotá?
2. What have you collected if you are out for nought in both innings?
3. Which skier won the women's alpine overall World Cup six times between 1971 and 1979?
4. What is the term for two people passing a ball between them, while a third attempts to intercept?
5. Who did Anne Packer run to after she won an Olympic gold?
6. Who directed the film *Grand Prix*?

## 34

1. Bruce Grobbelaar.
2. Harold Pinter.
3. Maureen Connolly ('Little Mo').
4. Rudyard Kipling.
5. Bridge.
6. Muhammad Ali.

## 110

1. John White.
2. Peter Tinniswood.
3. Blackjack.
4. Romford.
5. Arnold Palmer.
6. Sugar Ray Robinson.

## 186

1. Bobby Moore.
2. A pair.
3. Annemarie Moser Pröll (Austria).
4. Pig-in-the-middle.
5. Robbie Brightwell.
6. John Frankenheimer.

## 35

1. What shape is a rugby ball?
2. Which cricketer was 'The Master'?
3. Which skier won the downhill World Cup five times from 1975 to 1983?
4. What is the basic unit of measurement of a game of bridge?
5. In what sport is Mike Hazelwood famous?
6. Which film about boxing stars Jeff Bridges?

## 111

1. Who are 'The Baa-baas'?
2. Which cricket great was born in Cootamundra, New South Wales?
3. Who won the 1981 New York Marathon?
4. What is another name for the 'castle' in chess?
5. In what sport did Milon of Croton win six Olympic titles in 600 BC?
6. Which World Cup takes place in the film *Goal!*?

## 187

1. What do Bobby Charlton and Yul Brynner have in common?
2. What is the name for a low-order batsman sent out before close of play to prevent the loss of further wickets?
3. Where is the Irish Sweeps Derby held?
4. Where was the world's first motor racing circuit?
5. Who was British professional 1,000m. cycling champion at the age of fifty-four?
6. Who wrote *The Loneliness of the Long Distance Runner*?

## 35

1. Oval.
2. Jack Hobbs.
3. Franz Klammer.
4. Rubber.
5. Water skiing.
6. *Fat City*.

## 111

1. The Barbarians.
2. Don Bradman.
3. Alberto Salazar.
4. The rook.
5. Wrestling.
6. The 1966 World Cup in England.

## 187

1. Baldness.
2. Night watchman.
3. The Curragh.
4. Brooklands.
5. Reg Harris.
6. Alan Sillitoe.

## 36

1. Who took seventy-three years to beat Liverpool away?
2. Who was the only bowler to dismiss Bradman twice in tests for nought?
3. Who wrote *The Compleat Angler*.
4. What is 'clickety-click' in Bingo?
5. Which Olympic champion was also called Wa-Tho-Huck, meaning 'Bright Path'?
6. Which sports presenter went on to front breakfast television?

## 112

1. Where is the Football Association's National Soccer School?
2. Who made 221 for India against England in 1979?
3. The name of which Japanese martial art means 'way of the sword'?
4. What is SANROC?
5. Who was 'the leading English sports writer of the nineteenth century'?
6. Which soccer manager gets a mention by the Beatles?

## 188

1. Which England international held a degree from Manchester University?
2. Who scored 247 and 133 in a single test against New Zealand in 1974?
3. Who was 1985 world professional billiards champion?
4. Which Roman emperor abolished the Olympics?
5. Who said: 'People go to Laver to talk about tennis – they come to me to talk about abortions'?
6. In what film does Robert Ryan play a washed-up fighter?

# 36

1. Tottenham.
2. Alec Bedser.
3. Isaac Walton.
4. Sixty-six.
5. Jim Thorpe.
6. Frank Bough.

# 112

1. Lilleshall.
2. Sunil Gavaskar.
3. Kendo.
4. South African Non-Racial Olympic Committee.
5. Pierce Egan.
6. Matt Busby.

# 188

1. Steve Coppell.
2. Greg Chappell.
3. Ray Edmonds.
4. Theodosius.
5. Billy Jean King.
6. *The Set Up*.

## 37

1. What is Canadian football's version of the FA Cup?
2. Which cricket umpire was Yorkshire Personality of the Year 1977?
3. What game do members of 'I Zingari' play?
4. Who won the 180m. sprint in the Olympics of 776 BC?
5. Who saved Unipart oil filters?
6. Who hosted *Take Your Pick*?

## 113

1. What is the name for an employee of a soccer club whose job is to seek out new talent?
2. Which ITN news reporter wrote a biography of Viv Richards?
3. How many players in an ice hockey team?
4. What is the IAAF?
5. Which Olympic champion was known as 'Queen of the Track'?
6. Name the ex-world-champion boxer who starred in *I Married a Monster from Outer Space*.

## 189

1. Which soccer manager won seven cups, two league championships, and two promotions to the first division in eleven years?
2. Which test cricket ground was vandalized by supporters of the 'Free George Davis' campaign?
3. In what sport do 'jammers' win the contest?
4. In darts, what is the score of 77 known as?
5. Whose autobiography is entitled *Chess is My Life*?
6. Which rock band had the Liverpool Kop Choir on its LP?

# 37

1. The Grey Cup.
2. Dickie Bird.
3. Cricket.
4. Coroebus.
5. Pat Jennings.
6. Michael Miles.

# 113

1. Scout.
2. Trevor McDonald.
3. Six.
4. International Amateur Athletics Federation.
5. Irena Szewinska (Poland).
6. 'Slapsie Maxie' Rosenbloom.

# 189

1. Brian Clough.
2. Headingley.
3. Roller derby.
4. Sunset Strip.
5. Viktor Korchnoi.
6. Pink Floyd.

# 38

1. Which French player was carried off on a stretcher after being knocked down by the German goalkeeper in the 1982 World Cup?
2. Who played cricket for England at the age of eighteen in 1949?
3. What athletic event is sometimes called the hop, step and jump?
4. In what sport is S. Smildzinya of the Soviet Union regarded as one of the great women players of the century?
5. What was Paavo Nurmi's nickname?
6. What game does Donald Duck play in the cartoon *Slide, Donald, Slide*?

# 114

1. Which nation's soccer team is known as 'The Leopards'?
2. In which city is Sabina Park cricket ground?
3. In athletics, how many times can a runner make a false start before being disqualified?
4. Which rowing club is named after Hero's lover?
5. What is the nickname of the golfer Graham Marsh?
6. Who announced the prizes on *Take Your Pick*?

# 190

1. Who scored fourteen goals in World Cup games in 1970 and 1974?
2. For which county cricket club does David Gower play?
3. How many players in a volleyball team?
4. In what game can you set a leg trap?
5. Who won both singles titles at Wimbledon in 1974 and then announced their engagement?
6. Name a film about the Monte Carlo Rally?

## 38

1. Battiston.
2. Brian Close.
3. Triple jump.
4. Basketball.
5. 'The Flying Finn'.
6. Baseball.

## 114

1. Zaïre.
2. Kingston, Jamaica.
3. Twice.
4. Leander.
5. 'Swampy'.
6. Bob Danvers Walker.

## 190

1. Gerd Muller (West Germany).
2. Leicestershire.
3. Six.
4. Cricket.
5. Jimmy Connors and Chris Evert.
6. *Monte Carlo or Bust*.

## 39

1. What soccer club plays in 'The Den'?
2. Which cricketer once tried to use an aluminium bat?
3. Who did George Foreman beat to become heavyweight champion in 1973?
4. Which novelist once played in goal for Algiers?
5. In snooker, who is often called 'The People's Champion'?
6. When did Jack Warner captain England?

## 115

1. Can a goal in soccer be scored direct from a goal kick?
2. In the calypso 'Cricket Lovely Cricket', who were 'those two little friends of mine'?
3. In darts, what is the name of the raised line from which players throw?
4. In bowls, what is the small white porcelain ball called?
5. Which television commentator won the Manchester Mile in 1949?
6. In which film does Montgomery Clift play a rodeo bum?

## 191

1. Who did Italy beat in the semi-finals of the 1982 World Cup?
2. Which Prime Minister was president of the MCC?
3. What game did Dr James Naismith invent in 1892?
4. What is known as 'the roaring game'?
5. What is Neil Kinnock's favourite game?
6. What is Cary Grant playing when he meets Katherine Hepburn in *Bringing Up Baby*?

## 39

1. Millwall.
2. Dennis Lillee.
3. Joe Frazier.
4. Albert Camus.
5. Alex Higgins.
6. In the film *The Final Test*.

## 115

1. No.
2. Ramadhin and Valentine.
3. The oche.
4. The jack.
5. David Coleman.
6. *The Misfits*.

## 191

1. Poland.
2. Sir Alec Douglas Home.
3. Basketball.
4. Curling.
5. Rugby.
6. Golf.

# 40

1. What is the Italian word for football?
2. In which city is Trent Bridge cricket ground?
3. Who won the 1983 world professional darts championship?
4. What is the value of the yellow ball in snooker?
5. Which soccer team did television's Jimmy Hill play for?
6. In which film is a racehorse hidden in a girls' dormitory?

# 116

1. Which soccer club's theme song is 'We're Forever Blowing Bubbles'?
2. Who topped the English batting averages in 1984?
3. Who won an Olympic gold for Britain in the javelin in 1984?
4. Name the BBC Saturday afternoon television sports programme.
5. What is Joe Frazier's pop group called?
6. When does Raquel Welch play a roller derby star?

# 192

1. Who won the European Nations' Cup in 1984?
2. Which former test cricketer became Bishop of Liverpool?
3. What is the only ball on the snooker table which may be struck with the cue?
4. What fighter changed his name to Marvelous?
5. What is Joel Garner's nickname?
6. What do they play in the movie *Big Deal at Dodge City*?

# 40

1. *Calcio.*
2. Nottingham.
3. Keith Deller.
4. Two points.
5. Fulham.
6. *The Belles of St Trinians.*

# 116

1. West Ham United.
2. Mike Gatting.
3. Tessa Sanderson.
4. *Grandstand.*
5. The Knockouts.
6. In *Kansas City Bomber*.

# 192

1. France.
2. David Shepherd.
3. The white ball.
4. Marvin Hagler.
5. 'Big Bird'.
6. Poker.

## 41

1. What is the word in soccer for kicking a ball through an opponent's legs?
2. How many stumps were used in early forms of cricket?
3. Which country proclaimed 'Sport For All'?
4. What game did Konrad Koch introduce in Germany at the end of the last century?
5. What was the showjumper Lucinda Green's name before marriage?
6. In what film does the hero suggest: 'How about a little game of Get the Guests'?

## 117

1. What is France's leading soccer magazine?
2. Who was 'The Croucher'?
3. Where did Bobby Fischer and Boris Spassky contest the world chess championship?
4. What is another name for board sailing?
5. Who once commented: 'And Juantorena opens his legs and shows his class'?
6. Who does John Hurt play in *Champions*?

## 193

1. Who was Fleet Street's first woman soccer reporter?
2. Who captained England in the 'bodyline' series?
3. Who was the first man to win two Olympic marathon medals?
4. Who won the Greyhound Derby in 1973?
5. Who wrote a book on the Ali–Foreman clash entitled *The Fight*?
6. Which group had a hit with 'Surfin' USA'?

# 41

1. Nutmeg.
2. Two.
3. East Germany (GDR).
4. Handball.
5. Prior-Palmer.
6. *Who's Afraid of Virginia Woolf?*

# 117

1. *France Football.*
2. Gilbert Jessop.
3. Reykjavik, Iceland.
4. Windsurfing.
5. David Coleman.
6. Bob Champion.

# 193

1. Julie Welch.
2. Douglas Jardine.
3. Abebe Bikila.
4. Dolores Rocket.
5. Norman Mailer
6. The Beach Boys

## 42

1. How many times did Bobby Moore play for England?
2. Who said: 'What is human life but a game of cricket?'
3. As what is the Tour of Britain cycle race also known?
4. In tiddly-winks, what is the name for the large flat disk used to make the winks jump?
5. Who became world champion racing driver posthumously in 1970?
6. Who wins the big chariot race in *Ben Hur* (the remake)?

## 118

1. How many players are there in a rugby league team?
2. What was Trevor Bailey's nickname?
3. What is the first big race of the English flat racing season?
4. What are Littlewoods and Vernons?
5. What is the nickname of the West Indies cricket team?
6. Who plays Gossage the games mistress in *The Happiest Days of our Lives*?

## 194

1. Which team plays at Turf Moor?
2. How did Dr Heath, headmaster of Eton, react to the school's defeat at cricket by Westminster?
3. Who got beaten for the world flyweight title by Sot Chitalada in February 1985?
4. Which sporting event does Diomedes win in Book XXIII of the *Iliad*?
5. Which jockey, winner of the US 'triple crown', is also a winner of the English 2,000 Guineas?
6. Who won the race in *Those Magnificent Men in their Flying Machines*?

# A



## 42

1. One hundred and eight.
2. The Duke of Dorset in 1777.
3. The Milk Race.
4. The Squidger.
5. Jochen Rindt.
6. Charlton Heston as Ben Hur.

## 118

1. Thirteen.
2. 'Barnacle Bill'.
3. The Lincoln.
4. Football pools promoters.
5. 'Windies'.
6. Joyce Grenfell.

## 194

1. Burnley.
2. He flogged the whole side (including the scorer).
3. Charlie Magri.
4. The chariot race.
5. Steve Cauthen.
6. James Fox.

## 43

1. Which rugby club is for Welsh exiles?
2. What was the Oval before it was a cricket ground?
3. In baseball, what is the name for the player who stands behind the home plate and catches unhit pitches?
4. Which people have a God of Sports called Louo-i-ka-Makahiki?
5. Who once commentated: 'And your carpenter is Harry Commentator'?
6. What was the audience novelty game featured in *Sunday Night at the London Palladium*?

## 119

1. Which soccer club is nicknamed 'The Hatters'?
2. What is the name for a delivery in cricket which pitches at or very near the batsman's blockhole?
3. What game is played at Yad Eliyahu, Tel Aviv?
4. In which game may teams employ the *catenaccio*?
5. By what name was the tennis player Ricardo Gonzalez better known?
6. Which ex-basketball star played the co-pilot in *Airplane*?

## 195

1. What was the former West Ham striker Brian Robson's nickname?
2. At which sport, apart from cricket, did W. G. Grace captain England?
3. In tennis, what is the name for a pre-match period when players are allowed to practise on court?
4. In baseball, where are the Orioles from?
5. Who is 'Britain's answer to Evel Knievel'?
6. In which film does James Coburn play Omar Sharif at pool?

## 43

1. London Welsh.
2. Market garden.
3. Catcher.
4. Hawaiians.
5. David Coleman.
6. 'Beat the Clock'.

## 119

1. Luton Town.
2. Yorker.
3. Basketball.
4. Soccer.
5. 'Pancho'.
6. Kareem Abdul-Jabaar.

## 195

1. 'Pop'.
2. Bowls.
3. Knock-up.
4. Baltimore.
5. Eddie Kydd.
6. *The Baltimore Bullet*.

## 44

1. In American football, what is the game played between the two leading college teams?
2. Which cricket county was once captained by Robin Marler?
3. Where is the Cesarewitch held?
4. What was the professional wrestler Billy Two Rivers's favourite weapon?
5. Who fell with Zola Budd?
6. What was the game of *The Cincinnati Kid?*

## 120

1. Who were the last amateurs to win the FA Cup?
2. Who hit six sixes in a six-ball over in 1985?
3. In what year was the first 'open' Wimbledon?
4. In what game is the winner the last person to evade bankruptcy?
5. In what game are events named after Bing Crosby and Glen Campbell?
6. Who wrote *The Golden Boy*?

## 196

1. How old was Stanley Matthews when he retired?
2. Which poet 'together join'd in cricket's manly toil' by playing for Harrow in 1805?
3. What is the USA's premier sports magazine?
4. What game is played with a *cochonnet*?
5. How many people with the name Davis have been world snooker champion?
6. Who were the first captains on *A Question of Sport*?

# 44

1. Rose Bowl.
2. Sussex.
3. Newmarket.
4. The tomahawk chop.
5. Mary Dekker.
6. Poker (five-card stud).

# 120

1. Old Etonians (in 1882).
2. Ravi Shastri.
3. 1968.
4. Monopoly.
5. Golf.
6. Clifford Odets.

# 196

1. Fifty.
2. Lord Byron.
3. *Sports Illustrated*.
4. *Pétanque* (or *boules*).
5. Three (Joe, Fred and Steve).
6. Cliff Morgan and Henry Cooper.

## 45

1. In what city is the soccer club Rapid SK?
2. What did Mike Gatting and Graeme Fowler achieve for England for the first time against India at Madras in 1985?
3. In what game can you use a penholder grip?
4. What do 'the bells of St Clements' say?
5. Which showjumping rider is also a professional wrestler?
6. In *The Girl Can't Help It*, what is Edmond O'Brien's favourite pastime?

## 121

1. Which soccer club's original name was Newton Heath?
2. Who was the 'Governor-General'?
3. Where is the Royal and Ancient golf club based?
4. What is the name for a racehorse which has never won a race?
5. Who was the first round-the-world yachtswoman?
6. Who caught Alan Bates on the boundary in *The Go-Between*?

## 197

1. How many players are there in a Canadian football team?
2. Which England cricket captain scored more than 1,000 runs on tour then dropped himself from tests because of poor form?
3. In what game do you 'peg out'?
4. In tennis, what is the name for winning a game against the opponents' serve?
5. Who was killed on Coniston Water in Bluebird in 1967?
6. At what game do Ben Gazzara and John Cassavetes work out in *Husbands*?

# 45

1. Vienna.
2. They each scored double centuries in the same innings.
3. Table tennis.
4. 'Oranges and lemons'.
5. Harvey Smith.
6. Shooting.

# 121

1. Manchester United.
2. G. G. Macartney.
3. St Andrews.
4. Maiden.
5. Clare Francis.
6. Dominic Guard.

# 197

1. Twelve.
2. Mike Denness.
3. Cribbage.
4. Service break.
5. Donald Campbell.
6. Basketball.

## 46

1. Who made sixty-nine appearances for Ireland at rugby?
2. Who once took ninety-five minutes to get off the mark?
3. At what game was Maureen Flowers British champion in 1982?
4. What was introduced into billiards in 1835?
5. Who was Muhammad Ali's corner man?
6. What sport was popularized in *Love Story*?

## 122

1. Who won the European Cupwinners' Cup in 1983?
2. Who was the first man to take 100 catches in test matches?
3. In what type of athletics meetings do they toss the caber?
4. What Simon and Garfunkel song mentions Joe DiMaggio?
5. Who was Britain's first black boxing champion?
6. In which film does Tyrone Power play a bullfighter?

## 198

1. What was ITV's answer to *Match of the Day*?
2. Which cricketer's nicknames include 'Goose', 'Harold', and 'Swordfish'?
3. If you were an Oiler, Leafer or King, what sport would you be playing?
4. In charades, what does a beckoning signal mean?
5. Who said: 'If you are fit you don't need it; if you're not you shouldn't risk it'?
6. Which soccer club did Alf Garnett's son-in-law support?

## 46

1. Mike Gibson.
2. Godfrey Evans (v. Australia at Adelaide, 1947).
3. Darts.
4. Rubber cushions.
5. Bundini Brown.
6. Ice Hockey.

## 122

1. Aberdeen.
2. Wally Hammond.
3. Highland Games.
4. 'Mrs Robinson'.
5. Dick Turpin.
6. *Blood and Sand.*

## 198

1. *The Big Match.*
2. Bob Willis.
3. Ice-hockey.
4. You're 'warm'.
5. Henry Ford.
6. Liverpool.

## 47

1. Who was Sweden's manager in the 1958 World Cup?
2. The grandfather of Ian and Greg Chappell also captained Australia. Who was he?
3. What sport does the Royal Toxophilite Society pursue?
4. What game is called in France *jeu de paume*?
5. Which sport was E. W. Swanton most associated with?
6. Name the bad guy in *Whacky Races*.

## 123

1. Which club pawned everything and bought Diego Maradona in 1984?
2. How much should a regulation cricket ball weigh when new?
3. How many players in a baseball team?
4. In what game would you find a cross pilot?
5. Which Wimbledon tennis commentator was also chairman of *Going for a Song*?
6. In which film does John Derek play American football?

## 199

1. Who was 'The Doog'?
2. In cricket, what happens if the ball is struck on to a fielder's helmet which is lying on the ground?
3. What is the highest-value ball in snooker?
4. As what is The Skol Sprint better known?
5. In what sport is Shirley Babashoff famous?
6. Who was a bullfighter in the film *The Bullfighter and the Lady*?

## 47

1. George Raynor.
2. Victor Richardson.
3. Archery.
4. Real tennis.
5. Cricket.
6. Dick Dastardly.

## 123

1. Napoli.
2. Five and a half ounces.
3. Nine.
4. Shuffleboard.
5. Max Robertson.
6. *Saturday's Hero*.

## 199

1. Derek Dougan.
2. Five runs are awarded to the batsman.
3. The black.
4. The Powderhall.
5. Swimming.
6. Robert Stack.

## 48

1. Who did Bobby Robson succeed as England soccer manager?
2. In cricket, what is the name for a bowler who can make the ball deviate in the air?
3. At which racetrack is the Rowley mile course?
4. Who threw herself in front of the King's horse at the Epsom Derby in 1913?
5. In which sport has Prince Charles represented his country?
6. In what film is James Caan the undisputed world champion?

## 124

1. Which soccer club plays at the Baseball Ground?
2. What do the letters MCC stand for?
3. How many times did Björn Borg win the US Open tennis championships?
4. In ring-a-ring-of-roses, what happens after the second a-tishoo?
5. Which retired greengrocer sailed round the world in 1967?
6. Who played the challenger Clubber Lang in *Rocky*?

## 200

1. Which Brazilian footballer was born Artur Antunes Coimbra?
2. Which country sent a women's cricket touring team to England in 1984?
3. What sport does FITA govern?
4. What team does Ron Knee manage?
5. By what name is Walker Smith better known?
6. What sport is featured in the film *Breaking Away*?

## 48

1. Ron Greenwood.
2. Swing bowler.
3. Newmarket.
4. Emily Davison, suffragette.
5. Polo.
6. *Rollerball.*

## 124

1. Derby County.
2. Marylebone Cricket Club.
3. None.
4. We all fall down.
5. Sir Alec Rose.
6. Mr T.

## 200

1. Zico.
2. New Zealand.
3. Archery.
4. Neasden FC (in *Private Eye*).
5. Sugar Ray Robinson.
6. Cycling.

# 49

1. Who scored a goal in every round of the 1970 World Cup?
2. Who scored five centuries in a test series in 1954–5?
3. Who won the world amateur snooker title in 1980 at the age of eighteen?
4. Who is Sweden's number one darts player?
5. What was 'Sonny' Liston's first name?
6. Who wins the steeplechase in *The Quiet Man*?

# 125

1. Which nation's soccer team is called 'The Green Eagles'?
2. Which cricketer played 114 times for England?
3. Who won the women's 800m. and 1,500m. in the 1976 Olympics?
4. What is the word for a quoit which circles the pin?
5. In what sport is Willy Mays a legend?
6. In which film does Harold Lloyd take up boxing?

# 201

1. In American football, which city are the 49ers from?
2. In cricket, what is the name for a ball which, when hit by the bat, strikes the ground immediately and bounces up?
3. In what sport did Lu Liang Huan once win the hearts of the British public?
4. What word does an athlete hear before the gun?
5. What did Muhammad Ali call his tactic of lying on the ropes and letting an opponent wear himself out?
6. What was *Man's Favourite Sport* in the Rock Hudson film?

## 49

1. Jairzinho.
2. Clyde Walcott (against Australia).
3. Jimmy White.
4. Stefan Lord.
5. Charles.
6. John Wayne.

## 125

1. Nigeria.
2. Colin Cowdrey.
3. Tatiana Kazankina (Soviet Union).
4. Ringer.
5. Baseball.
6. *The Milky Way*.

## 201

1. San Francisco.
2. Bump ball.
3. Golf.
4. 'Set'.
5. Rope-a-dope.
6. Angling.

## 50

1. What is the name for the field in American football?
2. Who wrote about a cricket-mad brigadier?
3. In billiards, what is the name for a ball that touches both the red ball and the opponent's ball?
4. In which game does a blindfolded person try to catch people?
5. Which journalist, Oxford Blue, and son of a famous artist is coach of the women's national rowing squad?
6. What rally does *Genevieve* take part in?

## 126

1. Which soccer player was officially scheduled 'a national asset'?
2. What is the distance between the wickets in cricket?
3. In baseball, what is the name for an area where relief pitchers limber up during a game?
4. What game was once known as 'slide-thrift' and 'push penny'?
5. Which golfer is nicknamed 'The Golden Bear'?
6. Who directed *Tokyo Olympiad*?

## 202

1. How many people watched the game between Leicester City and Stockport County on 7 May 1921?
2. Who founded the Hollywood Cricket Club?
3. With which game are the 'bleachers' associated?
4. What sport takes place at Oulton Park?
5. Who said: 'I'd give up golf like a shot. It's just that I've got so many sweaters'?
6. What sport is featured in *Rocco and his Brothers*?

## 50

1. Gridiron.
2. Peter Tinniswood.
3. Cannon.
4. Blind man's buff.
5. Dan Topolski.
6. London to Brighton.

## 126

1. Pelé.
2. Twenty-two yards.
3. Bullpen.
4. Shove ha'penny.
5. Jack Nicklaus.
6. Kon Ichikawa.

## 202

1. Thirteen.
2. C. Aubrey Smith.
3. Baseball.
4. Motor racing.
5. Bing Crosby.
6. Boxing.

# 51

1. Which soccer club is nicknamed 'The Blades'?
2. Who performed the double of 1,000 runs and 100 wickets in 1984?
3. In what sport do you use a dumb-bell?
4. What were the ITV Seven?
5. Which Belgian rider won the Tour de France five times?
6. What is the surname of *Rocky*?

# 127

1. Who led three different clubs to victory in the rugby league Challenge Cup?
2. Who 'felt like a boy who had killed a dove' after bowling Trumper?
3. At what game is Gillian Gilks a leading player?
4. Who beat Bustino at Ascot in 1975 and smashed the course record?
5. Which Prime Minister won the Sydney to Hobart yacht race?
6. What is the play *Outside Edge* about?

# 203

1. Which was the first FA Cup final at Wembley to end in a draw?
2. Who won the county cricket championship seven times in a row between 1952 and 1958?
3. Who retired from baseball in 1976 with a career record of 755 home runs?
4. What did A. T. Myers do at Wimbledon in 1888 that revolutionized tennis?
5. Who is 'Big Bren'?
6. Which soccer club has a hit with 'Blue is the Colour'?

## 51

1. Sheffield United.
2. Richard Hadlee (Nottinghamshire).
3. Weightlifting.
4. Horse races (televised on *World of Sport*).
5. Eddie Merckx.
6. Balboa.

## 127

1. Alex Murphy.
2. Arthur Mailey.
3. Badminton.
4. Grundy.
5. Edward Heath.
6. Cricket.

## 203

1. Chelsea v. Leeds, 1970.
2. Surrey.
3. Hank Aaron (of the Atlanta Braves).
4. Served overarm.
5. Brendan Foster.
6. Chelsea.

## 52

1. Who scored the winning goal for Spurs in the hundredth FA Cup final?
2. Which was the first county to win the Gillette Cup?
3. Which horse won racing's 'triple Crown' in 1970?
4. What game – Chinese name wei-ch'i – is more than 3,000 years old?
5. In what sport is Angelo Parisi famous?
6. What film has the following exchange: '"Was it the Rose Bowl he made his famous run?" "It was the Punch Bowl, honey"'?

## 128

1. Which soccer luminary co-wrote a novel called *They Used to Play On Grass*?
2. Which teams played in de Selincourt's cricket match?
3. How many players in a basketball team?
4. The Oxford–Cambridge Boat Race runs from where to where?
5. Who was John Newcombe's doubles partner?
6. What sport does Ben Kingsley play with Jeremy Irons in *Betrayal*?

## 204

1. In what game did Billy Boston and Alex Murphy become famous?
2. Who once commentated: 'And Brian Toss wins the Close'?
3. In what sport do riders often carry their bicycles?
4. In which country was orienteering invented?
5. How many classic winners did Arkle sire?
6. What exercise did the POWs take up in Stalag Luft III?

# 52

1. Ricardo Villa.
2. Sussex (1963).
3. Nijinsky.
4. Go.
5. Judo.
6. *Cat On a Hot Tin Roof*.

# 128

1. Terry Venables.
2. Tillingfold and Ravely.
3. Five.
4. Putney to Mortlake on the Thames.
5. Tony Roche.
6. Squash.

# 204

1. Rugby League.
2. Henry Blofeld (Radio 2).
3. Cyclo cross.
4. Sweden.
5. None – Arkle was a gelding.
6. Vaulting (over *The Wooden Horse*).

# 53

1. In what country is the soccer club Fluminese?
2. Which cricketer was nicknamed 'Toey'?
3. Which sport needs a velodrome?
4. How many squares are there on a chess board?
5. Which tennis star's wife wrote a book entitled *Love Match*?
6. What game does Warren Beatty play in *Heaven Can Wait*?

# 129

1. What have Watford and 'Rocket Man' in common?
2. Who was the first man in cricket history to take 300 test wickets?
3. What game is played with a chistera against a fronton?
4. Who trained Sir Ivor, Nijinsky, Roberto and The Minstrel?
5. Which speedway ace was nicknamed 'The Ball of Fire'?
6. Which black champion is the hero of *The Great White Hope*?

# 205

1. Which team plays at Molyneux?
2. Which England test captain stood as Conservative parliamentary candidate in the 1960s?
3. Where were the 1980 Winter Olympics held?
4. What is different about Thai boxing?
5. Name the expert on bringing up babies who won an Olympic gold in rowing in 1924?
6. In what film do 'the pros from Dover' appear?

## 53

1. Brazil.
2. Hugh Tayfield.
3. Cycling.
4. Sixty-four.
5. Mariana Borg.
6. American football.

## 129

1. Elton John.
2. Fred Trueman.
3. Pelota (or Jai-alai).
4. Vincent O'Brien.
5. Ove Fundin.
6. Jack Johnson.

## 205

1. Wolverhampton Wanderers.
2. Ted Dexter.
3. Lake Placid, USA.
4. Competitors may kick.
5. Dr Benjamin Spock.
6. *MASH*.

## 54

1. Who was the first soccer player to be transferred for one million pounds?
2. Who was 'Fiery Fred'?
3. In what sport does the referee signal 'soremade' when he sees an 'ippon'?
4. What game has been called 'the national card game of the United States'?
5. What is Jimmy Connors's nickname?
6. Who played middleweight champ Rocky Graziano in the film *Somebody Up There Likes Me*?

## 130

1. In which season did Arsenal do the double?
2. In which novel does a cricket match take place between Dingley Dell and All-Muggleton?
3. How many pieces are there at the start of a chess game?
4. Which game involves one player counting slowly to a hundred while the others hide?
5. What sport did Henry Longhurst cover for the BBC?
6. In what film do they play tennis without a ball?

## 206

1. What is American football's answer to the FA Cup?
2. What do Booker T and the MGs have to do with cricket?
3. In boxing, what is the term for an illegal blow to the back of the head?
4. What is another name for tick-tack-toe?
5. What is the title of the golfer and television commentator Peter Alliss's biography?
6. Who starred in *Downhill Racer*?

## 54

1. Trevor Francis (from Birmingham City to Nottingham Forest, 1979).
2. F. S. Trueman.
3. Karate.
4. Poker.
5. 'Jimbo'.
6. Paul Newman.

## 130

1. In 1970–71.
2. *The Pickwick Papers* by Charles Dickens.
3. Thirty-two.
4. Hide and seek.
5. Golf.
6. *Blow Up*.

## 206

1. The Superbowl.
2. Their record 'Soul Limbo' is the television cricket signature tune.
3. Rabbit punch.
4. Noughts and crosses.
5. *Alliss through the Looking Glass*.
6. Robert Redford.

## 55

1. Who managed Manchester City in 1971?
2. Which fictional hero was ‘perhaps the very finest slow bowler of his generation’?
3. What do Jesse Owens and Carl Lewis have in common?
4. Which ball game is referred to in Shakespeare’s *Henry V*?
5. What is Henry Kissinger’s favourite sport?
6. In what movie does George Segal play baseball in a London park?

## 131

1. Where is the headquarters of the Football League?
2. What is the name for an over in cricket where no runs are scored?
3. Which heavyweight champion lost his title sitting in his corner?
4. Who covers all the games at Neasden Bridge Stadium?
5. What was Evonne Cawley’s name before her marriage?
6. Who were *The Bad News Bears*?

## 207

1. In which year did Tottenham do the double?
2. What was W. G. Grace’s favourite headgear?
3. In what year did Lester Piggott ride his first winner?
4. Who is John McEnroe’s doubles partner?
5. What is snooker player Ray Reardon’s nickname?
6. In which film is a girl tennis player spurred on by her ambitious mother?

## 55

1. Malcolm Allison.
2. Raffles.
3. Four gold medals in 100m., 200m., long jump, and relay in one Olympics.
4. Tennis.
5. Soccer.
6. *A Touch of Class*.

## 131

1. Lytham St Annes.
2. Maiden.
3. Sonny Liston.
4. E. I. Addio (in *Private Eye*).
5. Goolagong.
6. Junior baseball team.

## 207

1. In 1961.
2. An MCC cap.
3. In 1948.
4. Peter Fleming.
5. 'Dracula'.
6. *Hard, Fast and Beautiful*.

## 56

1. What is the largest soccer club ground in England?
2. Which test captain had only one eye?
3. Where is the Prix de l'Arc de Triomphe horse race run?
4. Who sponsors the world professional snooker championships?
5. Which prizefighter, when questioned about Shakespeare, said: 'I'll moider da bum!'?
6. Who played 'The Man' in *The Cincinnati Kid*?

## 132

1. What was the UEFA Cup known as before 1972?
2. How many stumps are there on a cricket pitch?
3. What is the PGA?
4. From which bird's feathers are darts flights usually made?
5. What was Ken Rosewall's nickname?
6. Who wrote *The Harder They Fall*?

## 208

1. Which Spanish club did Johann Cruyff play for?
2. Of which county is Geoff Boycott a native?
3. For what trophy do British women golfers compete against Americans?
4. Where are the 1988 summer Olympics to be held?
5. Which is John Conteh's home town?
6. What game is featured in the film *The Hustler*?

## 56

1. The Valley (Charlton Athletic).
2. The Nawab of Pataudi (India).
3. Longchamps, Paris.
4. Embassy.
5. 'Two Ton' Tony Galento.
6. Edward G. Robinson.

## 132

1. European Fairs Cup.
2. Six.
3. Professional Golfers Association.
4. Turkey.
5. 'Muscles' (he was also called 'The Little Master').
6. Budd Schulberg.

## 208

1. Barcelona.
2. Yorkshire.
3. Curtis Cup.
4. Seoul, South Korea.
5. Liverpool.
6. Pool.

## 57

1. Who kept goal for the Soviet Union in three World Cups?
2. What was the name for the annual game between professionals and amateurs in cricket?
3. In which sport did Heather Mckay win the British Open sixteen times in a row?
4. In ten-pin bowling, what is the word for knocking down all ten pins with your first ball?
5. Which 1956 Olympic gold medallist was originally disqualified, but eventually reinstated?
6. On what sport is the film *Players* based?

## 133

1. Who was the most outstanding African-born soccer player of the 1960s?
2. What does lbw stand for?
3. In what game do teams compete for the Stanley Cup?
4. In what game might you build Nelson's column after completing lobster pots?
5. Name Henry Cooper's twin?
6. Which Olympic gold medallist played Flash Gordon?

## 209

1. Who was the Celtic goalkeeper who died following a collision with a Rangers player in 1937?
2. Which cricket ground is in St John's Wood?
3. Members of the North of England Homing Union are engaged in which sport?
4. What kind of club is Isis?
5. Which Wimbledon favourite hailed from Lookout Mountain, Tennessee?
6. In what film do Peter Sellers and Orson Welles face each other across the baccarat table?

# 57

1. Lev Yashin.
2. Gentlemen v. Players.
3. Squash.
4. Strike.
5. Christopher Brasher.
6. Tennis.

# 133

1. Eusebio.
2. Leg before wicket.
3. Ice hockey.
4. Five stones.
5. Jim.
6. Clarence 'Buster' Crabbe.

# 209

1. John Thomson.
2. Lord's.
3. Pigeon racing.
4. Rowing club (of Oxford University).
5. Roscoe Tanner.
6. *Casino Royale*.

## 58

1. In rugby, what is the name for the player nearest the referee in the front row of the scrum?
2. What is significant about Kent v. Worcestershire at Tunbridge Wells, 15 June, 1960?
3. In what game can you have an 'Indian check'?
4. In Scrabble, how many bonus points are awarded to a player who uses seven tiles in a single turn?
5. In which sport is Eric Tabarly famous?
6. Half of *Movie Movie* is a boxing film. What is it called?

## 134

1. Who captained Czechoslovakia in the 1962 World Cup?
2. How many hundreds did Jack Hobbs score in first-class cricket?
3. What is the maximum break in snooker?
4. In badminton, can you score points against service?
5. Which Greek hero's chariot horses were called Xanthus and Balius?
6. What sport is the film *Our Winning Season* about?

## 210

1. As what is the Argentinian rugby touring team known?
2. Can a batsman be out for handling the ball?
3. What world event took place in 1922 in the Pershing Stadium, Paris?
4. In which country is the Gezira sporting club?
5. In what sporting event is Ilona Slupanick of East Germany a former world record holder and Olympic champion?
6. In which film does an American girl win three gold medals at the Moscow Olympics?

## 58

1. Loose head prop.
2. It ended in a day.
3. Lacrosse.
4. Fifty.
5. Sailing.
6. *Dynamite Hands*.

## 134

1. Josef Masopust.
2. One hundred and ninety-seven.
3. Without a 'free ball', 147.
4. No.
5. Achilles.
6. High school athletics.

## 210

1. 'The Pumas'.
2. Yes.
3. The Women's World Games.
4. Egypt.
5. Shot put.
6. *Goldengirl*.

## 59

1. Which rugby club are 'The Wizards of the West'?
2. Which England cricketer also played for Southampton in the FA Cup final?
3. Which sport is contested at Bisley?
4. Who won the Olympic boxing light heavyweight gold medal in Rome, 1960?
5. Who married Chris Evert?
6. Who plays *Rocky*?

## 135

1. Who made ninety-six appearances for Liverpool in European competitions between 1964 and 1977?
2. Who took 16 wickets for 137 runs in his test debut?
3. How many times did Rod Laver win Wimbledon?
4. Which game is best played on the pavement and involves not treading on the lines?
5. What is the nationality of the champion marathon runner Greta Waitz?
6. What sport features in the film *Silver Dream Racer*?

## 211

1. What soccer club is nicknamed 'The Canaries'?
2. Which England cricket captain trained as a psychotherapist?
3. How many metres long is a basketball court?
4. For what field sport would you need a hood and jesses?
5. Who was the first black player to win a Wimbledon title?
6. Who rides the winner in *A Day at the Races*?

# 59

1. Aberavon.
2. C. B. Fry.
3. Shooting.
4. Muhammad Ali.
5. John Lloyd.
6. Sylvester Stallone.

# 135

1. Ian Callaghan.
2. Bob Massie (for Australia against England at Lord's, 1972).
3. Four.
4. Hopscotch.
5. Norwegian.
6. Grand Prix motor cycle racing.

# 211

1. Norwich City.
2. Mike Brearley.
3. Twenty-six.
4. Falconry.
5. Althea Gibson.
6. Harpo Marx.

## 60

1. Which Italian soccer club did Denis Law once play for?
2. Which cricketer is nicknamed 'Arkle'?
3. What is the highest score possible with three darts?
4. Who wrote *The Compleat Gamester* in 1674?
5. Who was known as 'The Human Windmill'?
6. In which film does Spencer Tracy referee Mickey Rooney in a boxing match?

## 136

1. Who took over from Alf Ramsey as England soccer manager?
2. For which county cricket club did Garfield Sobers play?
3. How many black squares are there on a chess board?
4. Who once beat his brother to win a world championship?
5. Which cyclist was described as 'the most popular loser the sport has known'?
6. Who compèred *The Sky's the Limit*?

## 212

1. In which country is there a soccer club called Videoton?
2. How much must a cricket bat weigh?
3. What do the New York Knickerbockers play?
4. What game is known as 'poor man's golf'?
5. Who presents *Sport on Four*?
6. Name a song by Paul Simon about baseball?

## 60

1. Torino.
2. Derek Randall.
3. One hundred and eighty.
4. Charles Cotton.
5. Harry Greb (prizefighter).
6. *Boys Town.*

## 136

1. Joe Mercer.
2. Nottinghamshire.
3. Thirty-two.
4. Joe Davis beat his brother Fred to win the world snooker title.
5. Raymond Poulidor (France).
6. Hughie Greene.

## 212

1. Hungary.
2. There is no legal restriction.
3. Basketball.
4. Knur and spell.
5. Tony Lewis.
6. 'Night Game'.

## 61

1. Who was Brian Clough's other half at Nottingham Forest and Derby County?
2. In cricket, who was 'The Prince'?
3. Who was the first woman to win a major car rally?
4. What game was originally played with sheep knucklebones?
5. Which tennis player has 'the body of an Adonis, a name like a skin disease'?
6. Who performs the theme music of *Chariots of Fire*?

## 137

1. Which quarterback was nicknamed 'Broadway Joe'?
2. Who won the World Cup of cricket in 1985?
3. What is the name for a hand of cards all of the same suit?
4. Who wrote: 'It takes more "cojones" to be a sportsman when death is a close party to the game'?
5. What was racing tipster Clive Graham's pen name?
6. What was John Houston's sport before he became a film director?

## 213

1. What is the equivalent in American football to a try in rugby?
2. Which cricket law was altered in 1970?
3. At what athletics event does Kjell Isaakson excel?
4. What is the most powerful piece on a chessboard?
5. Which top horsewoman wrote books about horses for children?
6. Who played *The Iron Man*?

## 61

1. Peter Taylor.
2. J. S. Ranjitsinhji.
3. Pat Moss (Liège–Rome Rally, 1960).
4. Five stones.
5. Vitas Gerulaitis.
6. Vangelis.

## 137

1. Joe Namath.
2. India.
3. Flush.
4. Ernest Hemingway.
5. The Scout.
6. Boxing.

## 213

1. Touchdown.
2. Lbw.
3. Pole vaulting.
4. The queen.
5. Pat Smythe.
6. Lew Ayres.

## 62

1. Which rugby club has no ground, no club house, no entry fee and virtually no money?
2. Who was the leading Indian wicket-taker in the 1984–5 test series against England?
3. What piece of sports equipment is a sandwich of wood, sponge and rubber?
4. What does 'screw' mean in snooker?
5. Who is generally regarded as the greatest 400m. hurdler of all time?
6. In which film does Marlon Brando reckon: 'I coulda been a contender'?

## 138

1. What part of your anatomy was Norman Hunter supposed to bite?
2. Which cricketer was a long jump champion but missed the Olympics because he didn't know they were on?
3. Who were regarded as golf's 'big three' in the 1960s?
4. What is the modern name for Lotto, Housey-Housey and Tombola?
5. What is Ilie Nastase's country of origin?
6. Who played *The Swimmer*?

## 214

1. Who said: 'In England soccer is a grey game played on grey days by grey people'?
2. How many times does Shakespeare mention cricket?
3. In motor cycling's TT races, what does the TT stand for?
4. What happens if you burn more fuel in ballooning?
5. Who did Muhammad Ali defeat in 'the rumble in the jungle'?
6. What sport do the inmates play in *One Flew Over the Cuckoo's Nest*?

## 62

1. The Barbarians.
2. Sivaramakrishnan.
3. Table tennis bat.
4. Putting backspin on the cue ball.
5. Edwin Moses.
6. *On the Waterfront*.

## 138

1. Your legs.
2. C. B. Fry.
3. Arnold Palmer, Jack Nicklaus, Gary Player.
4. Bingo.
5. Romania.
6. Burt Lancaster.

## 214

1. Rodney Marsh.
2. None.
3. Tourist Trophy.
4. You go up.
5. George Foreman.
6. Basketball.

## 63

1. Which soccer club is nicknamed 'The Owls'?
2. Which cricketer's party trick was 'to leap backwards from carpet to mantelpiece from a standing start'?
3. Where is the Champion Hurdle run?
4. Who won the world professional snooker championship between 1957 and 1964?
5. Who was known as 'the memory man' of sport?
6. In what television series did James Garner play a professional gambler?

## 139

1. Which Manchester United player scored 5 goals in European Cup games and was killed in the Munich air crash?
2. In cricket, what is the name for lifting one leg and glancing the ball under it towards fine leg?
3. In tennis, what is the name for an undecided rally which is played again?
4. What is the minimum number of darts required to finish 501 (straight in, double out)?
5. Who is Frank Bruno's manager?
6. In what film does Kenneth Moore play golf on artificial legs?

## 215

1. What was the name of the official 1982 World Cup film?
2. What is the maximum permitted width of a cricket bat?
3. In what game are there birdies, albatrosses and eagles?
4. Who spins a roulette wheel?
5. Who in tennis was known as 'Nasty'?
6. Name the original *What's My Line* panel.

## 63

1. Sheffield Wednesday.
2. C. B. Fry.
3. Cheltenham.
4. No one – it was not held.
5. Leslie Welsh.
6. *Maverick*.

## 139

1. Tommy Taylor.
2. Dog-leg cut.
3. Let.
4. Nine.
5. Terry Lawless.
6. *Reach For The Sky*.

## 215

1. *G'Olé*.
2. Four and a quarter inches.
3. Golf.
4. The croupier.
5. Ilie Nastase.
6. David Nixon, Barbara Kelly, Isobel Barnett, Gilbert Harding.

# 64

1. Which soccer star said: 'The most important thing is not the players, not the clubs, but the fans'?
2. Can a batsman be stumped off a wide ball?
3. Who did Larry Holmes defeat to win the WBC heavyweight title in 1978?
4. Who did A. Karpov beat in Manila in 1978 to stay world chess champion?
5. Who had a bad fall in the Grand National in 1839 and became a household name?
6. What American football team does Robert DeNiro support in *The Deerhunter*?

# 140

1. In what game can a team employ the shotgun?
2. Who scored 337 in 999 minutes in 1958?
3. What game has the Swaythling Cup?
4. Round the Clock and Shanghai are popular forms of which game?
5. Who covered both rugby league and *It's a Knockout*?
6. What sport did Henry Winkler follow in *The One and Only*?

# 216

1. How wide is the goal in soccer?
2. What is a cricket umpire signalling if he extends one arm horizontally?
3. In what sport did Denise Parry captain her country in 1968?
4. How much is the following break worth in snooker: red, black, red, brown, red, green?
5. Which Welsh world champion flyweight was known as 'The Mighty Atom'?
6. Which famous comedy team starred in *The Caddy*?

## 64

1. Kevin Keegan.
2. Yes.
3. Ken Norton.
4. Viktor Korchnoi.
5. Captain Becher (whence Becher's Brook).
6. Pittsburgh Steelers.

## 140

1. American football.
2. Hanif Mohammad.
3. Table tennis.
4. Darts.
5. Eddie Waring.
6. Wrestling.

## 216

1. Eight yards (7·32m.).
2. No-ball.
3. Hockey.
4. Seventeen.
5. Jimmy Wilde.
6. Dean Martin and Jerry Lewis.

# 65

1. Which club resigned from the football league on 6 March 1962?
2. Why did Graham Gooch not play test cricket between 1982 and 1985?
3. How many players are there in a netball team?
4. Who painted card players from 1890 to 1894?
5. At what sport was Sammy Davis Jnr once proficient?
6. What sport is featured in the film *North Dallas Forty*?

# 141

1. Which former 'bad boy of football' was voted Footballer of the Year in 1978?
2. Who wrote a study of West Indian cricket and society entitled *Beyond a Boundary*?
3. Who won two Olympic gold medals and later became a top woman golfer?
4. What is the term for balancing a motor bike on its rear wheels?
5. What is Daley Thompson's home town?
6. Which soccer club did Alf Garnett support?

# 217

1. In American football, where do the Redskins hail from?
2. When was the first women's test match played at Lord's?
3. What does a grand master excel at?
4. What do Julio Iglesias and Bob Wilson have in common?
5. Which tennis player was known as 'The Bounding Basque'?
6. What film starred Sylvester Stallone, Pelé and Bobby Moore?

## 65

1. Accrington Stanley.
2. He was banned for playing in South Africa.
3. Seven.
4. Cézanne.
5. Boxing.
6. American football.

## 141

1. Kenny Burns.
2. C. L. R. James.
3. Babe Didrikson.
4. Wheelie (or wheelstand).
5. London.
6. West Ham United.

## 217

1. Washington DC.
2. In 1976.
3. Chess.
4. They are both former soccer goalkeepers.
5. Jean Borotra.
6. *Escape to Victory*.

# 66

1. Whose autobiography was called *This One's on Me*?
2. What trophy is at stake in a test series between England and the West Indies?
3. In darts, what is the maximum check-out number at 501 or 301?
4. Who won the first Observer single-handed yacht race in 1960?
5. Who rode Sunsalve and Mr Softee?
6. Who wrote *Professional Foul*?

# 142

1. Which soccer club is nicknamed 'The Toffees'?
2. Name the openers who put on 359 for England against South Africa in 1948?
3. Who won five gold medals in the 1980 Winter Olympics?
4. Who would win a sprint race between a racehorse and a greyhound?
5. Who, when asked if he preferred Astroturf to grass, replied: 'I don't know. I never smoked Astroturf'?
6. About what sport is the play *Zigger Zagger*?

# 218

1. What happened to England at Belo Horizonte in 1950?
2. Who took 8 wickets for 43 runs against Australia at Headingley in 1981?
3. Who won his eighth national table tennis singles title in 1985?
4. What happened to Cambridge in the 1978 Boat Race?
5. Who in snooker is 'The Whirlwind'?
6. Who starred in the film version of *The Natural*?

# 66

1. Jimmy Greaves.
2. The Wisden Trophy.
3. One hundred and seventy.
4. Sir Francis Chichester (in *Gipsy Moth III*).
5. David Broome.
6. Tom Stoppard.

# 142

1. Everton.
2. Hutton and Washbrook.
3. Eric Heiden.
4. Racehorse.
5. Joe Namath.
6. Soccer.

# 218

1. They lost 1–0 to the USA and went out of the World Cup.
2. Bob Willis.
3. Desmond Douglas.
4. They sank.
5. Jimmy White.
6. Robert Redford.

# 67

1. Which two soccer grounds are the closest together in Britain?
2. What is G. O. B. Allen's nickname?
3. How long is the Epsom Derby?
4. What US magazine calls itself 'The Bible of Boxing'?
5. Which Roman Emperor killed his wife after she scolded him for going to the races?
6. What sport is featured in the movie *One on One*?

# 143

1. Which soccer club was once called Small Heath?
2. Who came bottom in the county cricket championship for the first time in 1983?
3. As what is the San Francisco Marathon also known?
4. Which great indoor sports arena is built over a railway station?
5. Who owns Goodwood racecourse?
6. What sport do Woody Allen and Diane Keaton play in *Annie Hall*?

# 219

1. Who was the first footballer to be knighted?
2. Who resigned as captain of Australia during the 1984–5 series against the West Indies?
3. At darts, what number are you on if you are 'in the basement'?
4. In what country did snooker originate?
5. Who said: 'When I make that jump I'll be competing against the toughest opponent of all – death'?
6. Who reckoned: 'Jesus would have made the best little All-American quarterback in the history of football'?

## 67

1. Dundee and Dundee United (Dens Park and Tannadice are a goal kick apart).
2. 'Gubby'.
3. A mile and a half.
4. *The Ring*.
5. Nero.
6. Basketball.

## 143

1. Birmingham City.
2. Yorkshire.
3. The Bay to Breakers.
4. Madison Square Garden.
5. The Duke of Richmond.
6. Tennis.

## 219

1. Stanley Matthews (in 1965).
2. Kim Hughes.
3. Double three.
4. India.
5. Evel Knievel.
6. Burt Lancaster as *Elmer Gantry*.

## 68

1. Who succeeded Bill Shankly as manager of Liverpool?
2. What is the Australian term for extras in cricket?
3. Who was the first non-Japanese competitor to win an Olympic gold medal in judo?
4. Which Olympic gold medallist died from a traffic accident in Addis Ababa?
5. Who was known as 'The Ambling Alp'?
6. In which film is a girl picked to play soccer for her school?

## 144

1. In what year was the FA Cup first played at Wembley Stadium?
2. How many overs are allotted to each side in John Player League matches?
3. Which British woman won an Olympic fencing gold medal in 1956?
4. In 1896 the Indian board game Pachisi was modified and introduced into England under what name?
5. As what were Lacoste, Cochet, Borotra and Brugnon known?
6. Which world sporting event takes place in the film *King Boxer*?

## 220

1. Who is the only soccer player to have played for England at five levels?
2. Name Manchester's test match ground?
3. Who won the Derby in 1981?
4. In what game do you find the Leonard Trophy?
5. Which snooker professional receives tax relief on his lager consumption?
6. Which Olympic star is in the film *Ski Raiders*?

## 68

1. Bob Paisley.
2. Sundries.
3. Anton Geesink.
4. Abebe Bikila.
5. Primo Carnera.
6. *Gregory's Girl.*

## 144

1. In 1923.
2. Forty.
3. Gillian Sheen.
4. Ludo.
5. 'The Four Musketeers' of tennis.
6. All-China Boxing Trophy.

## 220

1. Terry Venables.
2. Old Trafford.
3. Shergar.
4. Bowls.
5. 'Big' Bill Werbeniuk.
6. Jean-Claude Killy.

## 69

1. Which player ended Arsenal's 1979–80 season with a penalty miss?
2. From which island in the West Indies is Viv Richards?
3. What is the most popular participant sport in France?
4. What is the main piece of equipment in Tug-of-war?
5. Who was the first woman to train a Grand National winner?
6. In what film is Paul Newman involved in an egg-eating contest?

## 145

1. Which soccer club chairman called his fans 'scum' over the PA and offered to forfeit a match'?
2. Which US writer described baseball as 'a state of mind and you can't learn it'?
3. In what game did Victor Barna excel?
4. In chess, what is the name for a pawn which has a clear run with no hostile pawns on flanking files?
5. Who sang 'The Star Spangled Banner' at the start of the 1983 Superbowl?
6. Who played a 'pinball wizard'?

## 221

1. Which ex-public schoolboy played for Arsenal in 1984–5?
2. What is the name for a delivery in cricket which travels mostly along the ground?
3. Why was the 1877 Oxford–Cambridge Boat Race 'the most remarkable in history'?
4. Who beat Bobby Riggs at the Houston Astrodome in 1973 and struck a blow for women?
5. Who said: 'Until I was ten I was a rather sickly child'?
6. Who starred in the remake of *The Champ*?

## 69

1. Graham Rix (the penalty miss against Valencia cost Arsenal the Cupwinners' Cup).
2. Antigua.
3. Cycling.
4. A rope.
5. Jenny Pitman.
6. *Cool Hand Luke*.

## 145

1. Ken Bates of Chelsea.
2. John Steinbeck.
3. Table tennis.
4. Passed pawn.
5. Barry Manilow.
6. Roger Daltry in *Tommy*.

## 221

1 Stewart Robson.
2. Daisycutter.
3 It ended in a dead heat.
4 Billy Jean King.
5 Arnold Schwarzenegger.
6. John Voight.

# 70

1. How much *actual playing time* is there in an American football game?
2. Who is the only batsman to have made two scores of more than 400?
3. Where is England's leading indoor athletics track?
4. Which drugs do athletes take – illegally – to put on weight?
5. What is the nationality of the chess player Gary Casparov?
6. In what film does Gig Young know more about baseball than Clark Gable?

# 146

1. What club did Tom Finney play for?
2. In which year were eight-ball overs tried in English cricket?
3. Who won Britain's only individual gold medal in the 1976 Montreal Olympics?
4. Who described bullfighting as having 'the formality of classicism, the expressiveness of romanticism'?
5. Who said: 'Nice guys finish last'?
6. Which BBC television quiz game is contested by teams of families?

# 222

1. Who captained Italy in the 1982 World Cup?
2. Who took seven wickets in eleven balls in 1972?
3. In darts, what is the official throwing distance?
4. Where was the first public billiards room in England?
5. Who clocked 301 m.p.h. at the Bonneville salt flats, Utah in 1935?
6. In what film do René Fromage and Kit Mambo compete in the Olympics?

# 70

1. 60 minutes.
2. W. Ponsford.
3. Cosford.
4. Anabolic steroids.
5. Russian.
6. *Teacher's Pet.*

# 146

1. Preston North End.
2. In 1939.
3. David Wilkie.
4. Kenneth Tynan.
5. Leo Durocher (baseball manager, 1946).
6. *Ask the Family.*

# 222

1. Dino Zoff.
2. Pat Pocock.
3. Seven feet, nine and one-quarter inches (2.37m.).
4. The Piazza, Covent Garden.
5. Malcolm Campbell.
6. *Animalympics.*

# 71

1. What was the crowd attendance for the World Cup final of 1950 between Brazil and Uruguay?
2. Who scored two double tons in the same match in 1938?
3. Who rode Sir Ivor to victory in the Washington International in 1968?
4. What is the penalty at snooker if a player plays a ball which runs along the rail and into a pocket?
5. Which ex-world boxing champion established a restaurant on Broadway, New York?
6. Which songwriter never dreamt of making the team because his heart belonged to Daddy?

# 147

1. Who scored three goals in the final of the European Cup and ended up on the losing side?
2. Which county has a leaping fox on its cricket badge?
3. In what sport do Manchester United regularly meet Hemel Hempstead?
4. Who wrote a book about bullfighting called *Death in the Afternoon*?
5. Who won the Derby in 1964 on Santa Claus?
6. Which soccer manager has a television series on angling?

# 223

1. Who was the first Dutchman to play for Manchester United?
2. Who won the 1984 Whitbread Village Championship?
3. What game is played in a pit 32 ft long and 21 ft high, surrounded by walls?
4. Who would win a sprint race between a greyhound and a hare?
5. Who was the first person to reach 600 m.p.h. on land?
6. About what sport is the film *Gipsy Moths*?

## 71

1. Estimated at 200,000.
2. Arthur Fagg.
3. Lester Piggott.
4. None – the break continues.
5. Jack Dempsey.
6. Cole Porter.

## 147

1. Ferenc Puskas (for Real Madrid against Benfica).
2. Leicestershire.
3. Basketball.
4. Ernest Hemingway.
5. Scobie Breasley.
6. Jack Charlton.

## 223

1. Arnold Mühren.
2. Marchwiel.
3. Squash.
4. Hare.
5. John Cobb.
6. (Free fall) parachuting.

# 72

1. What is the more familiar name for Heart of Midlothian?
2. Who captained Australia more times, Ian or Greg Chappell?
3. Who took the heavyweight title from Muhammad Ali in 1978?
4. How much treacle do you need to pop the weasel?
5. Who was the first ever Olympic champion from Wales?
6. Which Evelyn Waugh novel describes a hilarious school sports day?

# 148

1. Who scored a hat-trick in the 1953 'Matthews' Cup final?
2. Which batsman's career average was 99·94 over 52 tests?
3. In basketball, what is the name for taking up position between attacker and basket?
4. What is the fastest animal in the world?
5. Who carried news of battle from Marathon to Athens, a distance of 25 miles?
6. In which film do the Marx Brothers play college football?

# 224

1. Who beat Bon Accord 36–0 in the Scottish Cup of 1885?
2. Who said: 'Truly, I think I could get more runs if England had some faster bowlers'?
3. What is the term used to describe an outright service winner in tennis?
4. Why is Wimbledon unique among major present-day tennis tournaments?
5. Who was 'The Flying Dutchwoman'?
6. About what sport is the play *Up'n'Under*?

# A

## 72

1. Hearts.
2. Greg.
3. Leon Spinks.
4. Half a pound.
5. Lynn Davies.
6. *Decline and Fall.*

## 148

1. Stan Mortensen.
2. Don Bradman.
3. Blocking out.
4. Cheetah.
5. Pheidippides.
6. *Horse Feathers.*

## 224

1. Arbroath.
2. Viv Richards.
3. Ace.
4. It is the only one on grass.
5. Fanny Blankers-Koen.
6. Rugby league.

## 73

1. How many 'set pieces' are there in a game of soccer?
2. In which year did New Zealand first beat England in a test?
3. How many times did Sir Gordon Richards win the Derby?
4. How many times did Jacques Anquetil win the Tour de France?
5. Which soccer club did the novelist Italo Svevo support?
6. Who starred in the film *Le Mans*?

## 149

1. Which soccer player, a university graduate, was known as 'Little Bamber'?
2. What birds are depicted on the badge of Sussex cricket club?
3. Who won four women's swimming golds at the 1976 Olympics?
4. Which London hall was for sixty years the venue of all major snooker tournaments?
5. Which nineteenth-century jockey was known as 'the backer's best friend'?
6. What sport features in the television series *Ripcord*?

## 225

1. Which soccer club is nicknamed 'The Magpies'?
2. Which Australian cricketer played in every test match in which a Chappell was captain?
3. How long is the Boat Race?
4. Name the no-holds-barred combat event of the Ancient Olympics?
5. Who was the first man to swim the channel?
6. For what are the competitors awarded points in the film *Death Race 2000*?

# 73

1. Seven (corner, goal kick, free kick, throw-in, kick-off, penalty, indirect free kick).
2. In 1978.
3. Once (on Pinza in 1953).
4. Five.
5. Charlton Athletic.
6. Steve McQueen.

# 149

1. Brian Hall.
2. Martlets.
3. Kornelia Ender (GDR).
4. Leicester Square Hall.
5. Fred Archer.
6. Sky diving.

# 225

1. Newcastle United.
2. Rodney Marsh.
3. Four and one-quarter miles.
4. Pankration.
5. Captain Matthew Webb.
6. Human casualties.

# 74

1. For which rugby club did Barry John and Phil Bennett play?
2. Which two batsmen put on 555 for the first wicket for Yorkshire in 1932?
3. What sport's name is derived from a Greek word meaning 'naked'?
4. Who was given the OBE in 1966 for services to chess?
5. Who wrote songs about fighters called 'Hurricane', 'The Boxer' and 'Who Killed Davey Moore'?
6. Name the hit record of the 1970 England World Cup squad?

# 150

1. For which club did Gerd Muller play?
2. Who has scored 8,114 runs in tests?
3. How many times did Red Rum win the Grand National?
4. Which Olympic athlete was called 'The Shifter'?
5. Who is the richest sportswoman in the world?
6. In what ITV television drama series did Liverpool footballers appear?

# 226

1. Which Liverpool winger, a university graduate, was known to his team-mates as 'Big Bamber'?
2. For which trophy is the West Indies inter-island tournament played?
3. Who won the Wimbledon women's singles in 1977?
4. Who was Muhammad Ali's trainer?
5. Which Irish Prime Minister was all-Ireland hurling champion?
6. What game took place at the end of the alley in *Top Cat*?

## 74

1. Llanelli.
2. Sutcliffe and Holmes.
3. Gymnastics.
4. Harry Golombek.
5. Bob Dylan.
6. 'Back Home'.

## 150

1. Bayern Munich.
2. Geoffrey Boycott.
3. Three.
4. Miruts Yifter.
5. Martina Navratilova.
6. *Scully*.

## 226

1. Steve Heighway.
2. Shell Shield.
3. Virginia Wade.
4. Angelo Dundee.
5. Jack Lynch.
6. Ten-pin bowling.

## 75

1. Who wrote: 'And life itself is but a game of football'?
2. Who was known as 'Typhoon'?
3. Who beat the United States to win the 1984 Davis Cup?
4. What is the name for underwater hockey?
5. Which golfer was known as 'King of the Jungle'?
6. What was actor Brian Glover's former profession?

## 151

1. Which rugby star was known as 'Mighty Mouse'?
2. Which England cricketer's biography is called *With Time to Spare*?
3. Who is 'The Undisputed King of Bowls'?
4. At what weight did Alan Minter become a world boxing champion?
5. Which world champion racing driver also won the Le Mans 24 Hours and the Indianapolis 500?
6. What film is about a women's tag wrestling team?

## 227

1. Which London soccer hero was known as 'Chopper'?
2. Which fruit features on the badge of Worcestershire cricket club?
3. Who finished fourth in a Grand Prix race in 1976, six weeks after he was given the last rites?
4. How many times did Red Rum come second in the Grand National?
5. Which world religious leader is a leading racehorse owner?
6. Which pop singer starred in *I Gotta Horse*?

# 75

1. Sir Walter Scott.
2. Frank Tyson.
3. Sweden.
4. Octopush.
5. Severiano Ballesteros.
6. Wrestler.

# 151

1. Ian MacLauchlan.
2. David Gower.
3. David Bryant.
4. Middleweight.
5. Graham Hill.
6. *California Dolls*.

# 227

1. Ron Harris.
2. Pear.
3. Nicki Lauda.
4. Twice.
5. The Aga Khan.
6. Billy Fury.

## 76

1. Who in rugby was 'The King'?
2. Which team was admitted into the county cricket championship in 1921?
3. If you were sitting in the hack, worrying about being shot rock, what sport would you be playing?
4. In charades, what does a finger on the nose mean?
5. Who said: 'To play billiards well is the sign of a mis-spent youth'?
6. What was Albert Tatlock's game in *Coronation Street*?

## 152

1. Which club did soccer managers John Bond, Malcolm Allison and Ken Brown once play for?
2. Who played cricket for England, Leicestershire, Surrey and Western Australia?
3. Where is the Cresta Run?
4. What is the 'referee' called in Dungeons & Dragons?
5. In what sport is 'Maltese Joe' pre-eminent?
6. In what movie does the Pro footballer Boom Boom Jackson appear?

## 228

1. Which team has won the 'Rugby Sevens' tournament most times?
2. Who is nicknamed 'Guy The Gorilla'?
3. What sport started with the use of a stuffed rabbit towed by a motorcycle?
4. In poker, what is the name for the compulsory bet before the deal?
5. Why is the 1919 Chicago White Sox baseball team famous?
6. What game is played in *The Four Musketeers*?

## 76

1. Barry John.
2. Glamorgan.
3. Curling.
4. You're right.
5. Herbert Spencer (1870).
6. Dominoes.

## 152

1. West Ham United.
2. Tony Lock.
3. St Moritz, Switzerland.
4. The Dungeon Master.
5. Pool.
6. *The Fortune Cookie*.

## 228

1. Richmond.
2. Ian Botham.
3. Greyhound racing.
4. Ante.
5. They fixed the World Series.
6. Real tennis.

# Part 4
# The Music Quiz

## Edited by John Denny

with

Roxy Beaujolais
Richard Beswick
Ian Bradley
Hugh Bredin
Geraldine Cooke
Simon Frazer
Steve Gibson
Andrew Keener
Nicholas Reader
Robin Robertson
Monica Schertzer
Antonia Till
Andrew Walpole

# Introduction to The Music Quiz

How many symphonies did Beethoven compose? 'Nine', you say. Ah, but what about the *Battle* Symphony which he wrote for a mechanical instrument to celebrate Wellington's victory over Napoleon in 1813? Then there's the *Jena* Symphony, which we would not know had *not* been written by Beethoven at all had not a gentleman named H.C. Robbins Landon told us otherwise.

Which Harry Lauder song did Winston Churchill play incessantly during the dark days of the Second World War to keep up his spirits? And which is the only song that Prince Charles says he knows by heart?

What is a 'B-52', a 'Jefferson airplane', a 'Steely Dan' or a 'bo diddley'? How did Cilla Black, The Bee Gees and The Sex Pistols get their names? And who was Eric Clapton's 'Layla', Jim Morrison's 'Queen of the Highway' or The Pretenders' 'Kid'?

If these are the sort of things you love knowing and have an insatiable appetite for knowing more of, then you can safely count yourself one of the select band of Truly Trivial Persons. Here is a compendium of facts which no sensible person ought to know, compositions which no sensible composer ought to have written, and deeds which can only be accounted for as expressions of the flip side of genius. How else can you explain the castrato who was employed by Philip V of Spain on an annual salary of 50,000 francs to sing to him the same four songs every night for twenty-five years; the tap-dancers who danced the carioca on top of seven white grand pianos; the rock star who set his hair on fire on *Top of the Pops*; the singer who shot himself back-stage playing Russian roulette; the erotic madrigalist who assassinated his wife and her lover after discovering them *in flagrante delicto*?

The horizons are limitless, for there are no heights unscaled nor depths unplumbed in the extremes to which musicians go in eccentricity, banality, venality or sheer depravity – as John Gay's Polly says, 'Music might tame and civilize wild beasts, but 'tis evident it never yet could tame and civilize musicians'!

So prepare your mental lumber-room for an onslaught of undreamed-of absurdity by the facts in this section. The questions and their answers are divided very broadly into six subject categories:

1. **Top Twenty.** Chart-topping rock and pop from Duran Duran to Doo-wop, Shalamar to the Shirelles, Band Aid to The Band.

2. **Stage and Screen.** Broadway to Drury Lane, Hollywood to Pinewood, *film noir* to spaghetti westerns.

3. **Radio Three.** Boccherini for breakfast, Bax for snacks, Lully for lunch, Ligeti for tea and D'Indy for dinner.

4. **A Night at the Opera.** 'Bach interwoven with Spohr and Beethoven'. Puccini to Peri, Menotti to Patti, and Britten and Wagner and Offenbach too.

5. **Oldies.** Golden Oldies, your father's Golden Oldies, plus jazz and blues: everyone who listens to Radio Two will know most of these.

6. **Rag-bag.** Anything that won't fit into the above: birds that sing, nymphs that turn into reed-pipes, national anthems, strange instruments and even noise. In fact, be prepared for anything!

John Denny

# Q

## 1

1. What is the most obvious similarity between Edgar and Johnny Winter?
2. Neil Diamond's*The Jazz Singer* makes how many versions?
3. Which German poet inspired Paul Dukas's *Sorcerer's Apprentice*?
4. What is the full title of Wagner's *Tannhäuser?*
5. Whose farewell to music hall in 1922 was 'A Bit of a Ruin that Cromwell Knocked About a Bit'?
6. Why is 'With a Song in My Heart' redolent of loved ones far away?

## 77

1. Who was christened Genevieve and is nicknamed Alf?
2. In the 1944 movie *Atlantic City*, which opera was the heroine listening to and learning?
3. Who wrote *Apparitions*, *Ramifications*, an *Artikulation* and a *Poème Symphonique* for 100 metronomes?
4. Which Met soprano was nicknamed 'la donna immobile'?
5. With whom did Harry Belafonte sing 'There's a Hole in My Bucket' in 1961?
6. What phenomenon causes a train whistle to change pitch as it passes by?

## 153

1. Which DJ, born John Ravenscroft, once managed a band called The Misunderstood?
2. When did Lucille Ball 'bring Dixie back to Dixieland'?
3. Who composed *In a Monastery Garden*?
4. In which opera do a tobogganer and a skier collide?
5. When 'Bean' met 'Prez', who met whom?
6. Which heroine in a 1911 novel said, 'I don't know anything about music really, but I know what I like'?

# 1

1. They are albino.
2. Three.
3. Johann Wolfgang Goethe.
4. *Tannhäuser and the Singing Contest at the Wartburg*.
5. Marie Lloyd's.
6. It was the *Forces Favourites* theme tune.

# 77

1. Alison Moyet.
2. *Norma* (Bellini).
3. György Ligeti.
4. Zinka Milanov.
5. Odetta.
6. The Doppler effect.

# 153

1. John Peel.
2. In the 1974 movie *Mame*.
3. Albert Ketèlby.
4. *Intermezzo* (Richard Strauss).
5. Coleman Hawkins met Lester Young.
6. Zuleika Dobson (Beerbohm).

# 2

1. Whose Kings Road shop was named Sex?
2. In which 1945 movie did Lauren Bacall and Hoagy Carmichael sing together?
3. Which composer, as a printer's devil, nearly died after mistaking a glass of acid for water?
4. Which Gilbert and Sullivan character was 'never, never sick at sea . . . well, hardly ever!'?
5. Whose trombone playing did Sinatra imitate vocally?
6. What shape is a kazoo?

# 78

1. Which record company turned down The Beatles but signed up The Rolling Stones?
2. Who lived at 5135 Kensington Avenue?
3. Which Beethoven symphony has five movements?
4. Into which order did Rossini's 'Italian Girl' enrol Mustapha, Bey of Algiers?
5. According to the Andrews Sisters, what does 'Bei Mir Bist Du Schön' mean?
6. Which popular music magazine started in 1926?

# 154

1. After which city are Tamla-Motown Records named?
2. Which British team of hit-makers contemplated a show based on the Cuban missile crisis?
3. Who married Anna Magdalena and wrote music in her notebooks?
4. What was Gershwin's other opera called?
5. Which Benny Goodman 'killer-diller' swing number inspired a Carnegie Hall audience to jive in the aisles?
6. What are boobams – percussion instruments – made of?

## 2

1. Malcolm McLaren's.
2. *To Have and Have Not.*
3. Carl Maria von Weber.
4. Captain Corcoran (*HMS Pinafore*).
5. Tommy Dorsey's.
6. Cigar shaped.

## 78

1. Decca.
2. Esther (Judy Garland; *Meet Me In St Louis*).
3. The *Pastoral* (No. 6).
4. The 'Pappatacci'.
5. 'You're Grand'.
6. *Melody Maker.*

## 154

1. Detroit ('Motortown').
2. Rice–Lloyd Webber.
3. J. S. Bach.
4. *Blue Monday.*
5. 'Sing, Sing, Sing'.
6. Bamboo.

## 3

1. Who said of the French, 'They managed to stop our lamb, but they couldn't stop me'?
2. Which Ellington vocalist sang 'All God's Chillun Got Rhythm' in the Marx Brothers' *A Day at the Races*?
3. Which child said to a friend, 'Your violin is tuned sharper than my butter fiddle by half a quarter of a tone'?
4. Which was the first opera written specifically for TV?
5. Of whom did Benny Goodman in 1939 say, 'Who the hell wants to hear an electric guitar player' – then hired him?
6. Which fish beats a drum rhythm on its air bladder to warn other fish of impending danger?

## 79

1. Who was the Sheffield Gas Board fitter who with a little help got back up where he belonged?
2. What was *South Pacific*'s 'magical island' called?
3. Which piece of music did Mark Gottlieb perform submerged in a swimming pool in Washington in 1975?
4. Which soprano's farmer father made her milk the cows before her audition at the Swedish Royal Opera?
5. Who is the Viennese Weather Reporter?
6. If you suffered from diplacusis, what would you be?

## 155

1. What is Madonna's surname?
2. Who is the 'Silver Fox' in *Every Which Way But Loose*?
3. What was the name of Mozart's composer son?
4. In which Donizetti opera would you see Christians, lions and three leading tenors?
5. Which American vaudeville star 'could never take my corset off/To the music of Rimsky-Korsakoff' or find 'sailors who would pay/To see me strip to Massenet'?
6. What is a hydrodaktulopsychicharmonica?

# 3

1. Boy George.
2. Ivie Anderson.
3. Wolfgang Amadeus Mozart.
4. *Amahl and the Night Visitors* (Menotti).
5. Charlie Christian.
6. The sea catfish.

# 79

1. Joe Cocker.
2. Bali Ha'i.
3. Handel's *Water Music*.
4. Birgit Nilsson's.
5. Joe Zawinul.
6. Tone deaf.

# 155

1. Ciccone.
2. Charlie Rich.
3. Franz Xaver.
4. *Poliuto*.
5. Gypsy Rose Lee.
6. A variety of musical glasses.

# 4

1. In which country was Cliff Richard born?
2. Which (then) husband-and-wife team wrote the song 'Valley of the Dolls' for the 1967 movie of the same title?
3. One of whose symphonies was *Inextinguishable*?
4. What is the name of Bellini's 'La Sonnambula'?
5. 'I'd Climb the Highest Mountain' was a posthumous hit for which composer?
6. Where might you find a fire-extinguisher in G# or hear 'O Come All Ye Faithful' played on a cash till?

# 80

1. Who named his daughter Tulip after his 1968 hit?
2. Which Broadway hit is credited to both Oscar Hammerstein and Bizet?
3. To whose music is sung 'Deutschland über Alles'?
4. Who was the first woman to compose an opera?
5. Which bandleader's wife's legs were insured for one million dollars?
6. What might a Scot refer to as a 'kist o' whistles'?

# 156

1. The brothers Jermaine, Marlon, Michael, Sigmund and Toriano formed which vocal quintet?
2. To which real-life *non*-pianist did Ingrid Bergman say, in *Casablanca*, 'Play it, Sam, play "As Time Goes By"'?
3. For which instrument did Berlioz compose for Paganini his *Harold In Italy*?
4. Which drawing-room anthem from Henry Bishop's opera *Clari* did Donizetti plagiarize in *Anna Bolena*?
5. Of whom did Ethel Waters say, 'She sings like her shoes are too tight'?
6. Which war inspired the song, 'We Don't Want To Fight But By Jingo If We Do'?

# 4

1. India.
2. André and Dory Previn.
3. Carl Nielsen's (No. 4).
4. Amina.
5. Anton Dvořák (*Humoresque*).
6. The BBC Radiophonic Workshop.

# 80

1. Tiny Tim ('Tiptoe Through the Tulips').
2. *Carmen Jones*.
3. Joseph Haydn's.
4. Francesca Caccini (*La Liberazione di Ruggiero*, 1625).
5. Harry James's (he was married to Betty Grable).
6. A pipe organ.

# 156

1. The Jackson 5.
2. Dooley Wilson.
3. The viola.
4. 'Home, Sweet Home'.
5. Billie Holiday.
6. The Russo–Turkish War (1877–9).

# 5

1. What was Yosef Islam's former name?
2. *Cocksucker Blues* was a 1976 film about which rock band?
3. Why in 1976 was Rodrigo's *Guitar Concierto de Aranjuez* No. 1 in the UK charts for only three hours?
4. In which Savoy opera do they 'Dance the Cachucha, Fandango, Bolero' – all at once?
5. What was the maximum number of 'Pennies' at any one time in Red Nichols's Five Pennies?
6. Which of Liverpool's Great George, London's Big Ben or St Paul's Great Paul is the heaviest chiming bell?

# 81

1. Who was Martha in Paul McCartney's 'Martha, My Dear'?
2. In which 1929 musical did Chevalier first sing 'Louise'?
3. Which conductor signed a six-year recording contract at the age of 94, but died at 96?
4. Who sowed the seeds of the English National Opera in the Royal Victorian Coffee Music Hall in 1880?
5. Which famous blues derived from an 18th-century Bristol folk song?
6. Which philosopher believed that the 'music of the spheres' was a physical phenomenon caused by the planets?

# 157

1. Which American band had a 'Psychotic Reaction' in 1966 and never recovered?
2. Which song did the Marx Brothers sing in herring barrels in *Monkey Business*?
3. Which Khachaturian ballet features the *Sabre Dance*?
4. What is a *souffleur* or *maestro suggeritore*?
5. Whose magic piano 'could talk and play itself'?
6. What effect does Beethoven's *Kreutzer Sonata* have on the main protagonists in Tolstoy's novel?

## 5

1. Cat Stevens.
2. The Rolling Stones.
3. Because of a computer error.
4. *The Gondoliers*.
5. Fourteen.
6. Great Paul (334 cwt.).

## 81

1. His dog.
2. *Innocents of Paris*.
3. Leopold Stokowski.
4. Lilian Baylis.
5. 'St James Infirmary Blues'.
6. Pythagoras.

## 157

1. Count Five.
2. 'Sweet Adeline'.
3. *Gayane*.
4. The prompter.
5. Sparky's (Danny Kaye).
6. They commit adultery.

# 6

1. If Frankie Goes To Hollywood were the second band to chart No. 1 with their first three singles, who were the first?
2. Which 1963 film gave birth to the song 'More'?
3. Which composer wrote *Mozartiana*?
4. In which Massenet opera does the heroine bid adieu to a table?
5. 'Spring Is Here, Why Doesn't My Heart Go Dancing'?
6. How many grand pianos played together at the opening of the 1984 Los Angeles Olympic Games?

# 82

1. Which much-banned American gospel-rock singer in 1974 recorded 'Let's Go Streaking' in the nude?
2. In which 1981 film did Diana Rigg sing 'You're the Top'?
3. Which English university gave Haydn a doctorate?
4. Which tenor was made a Vatican Count?
5. Which comedy duo had a posthumous hit in 1975 with their 1937 recording of 'Trail of the Lonesome Pine'?
6. Which American sewing-machine heiress was also a patron of French music?

# 158

1. Who is the famous stepfather of Brian Jones's son Julian?
2. Who was the café guitarist in Losey's *The Servant*?
3. Which composer was known as 'the British Orpheus'?
4. Which vegetarian composer once published a diatribe against 'the abominable practice of flesh-eating'?
5. What was Harry Woods's remedy for 'women who get weary wearing the same shabby dress'?
6. Which English novelist was a first-class pianist, a friend of Liszt, and entertained the Wagners in 1877?

# 6

1. Gerry and the Pacemakers ('How Do You Do It', 'I Like It', 'You'll Never Walk Alone'; 1963).
2. *Mondo Cane.*
3. Pyotr Tchaikowsky (his Suite No. 4).
4. *Manon.*
5. 'Maybe it's because nobody loves me' (Rodgers–Hart).
6. Eighty.

# 82

1. Hank Ballard.
2. *Evil Under the Sun.*
3. Oxford University.
4. John McCormack.
5. Laurel and Hardy.
6. Princesse Edmond de Polignac (Winaretta Singer).

# 158

1. Donovan.
2. Davey Graham.
3. Henry Purcell.
4. Richard Wagner.
5. 'Try a Little Tenderness'.
6. George Eliot.

## 7

1. Which band made a single inspired by a girl random killer whose excuse was 'I don't like Mondays'?
2. For whom was it springtime when the chorus sang 'Don't be stoopid, be a smarty/Come and join the Nazi Party'?
3. Which composer's daughter deterred both Bach and Handel from succeeding him as organist in Lübeck because the post was conditional on marriage with her?
4. Which Russian composer's brother wrote the libretto for Rachmaninov's operatic failure, *Francesca da Rimini*?
5. Which torch singer was tried for murdering her millionaire husband in 1932?
6. What kind of instrumentalist uses 'combinations'?

## 83

1. Which singer turned The Beatles on to marijuana?
2. Who was the hillbilly banjoist in *Deliverance*?
3. Which British conductor thought that 'no woman was worth the loss of a night's sleep'?
4. Placido Domingo's American debut in *Lucia* was also the last performance of which legendary coloratura?
5. What was Cole Porter suggesting in 'Let's Do It'?
6. What is colophony?

## 159

1. Engel and Maus are real names of two of which Brothers?
2. Who had 'Tea for Two' in *No, No, Nanette*?
3. Which composer's music – so he thought – was 'best understood by children and animals'?
4. Which American president gaffed when he introduced to his White House guests, 'Beverly Stills, who can sing everything from Verdi ballads to Strauss operations'?
5. 'Limehouse Blues' evoked an area of which city?
6. Who composed 'Onward Christian Soldiers'?

# 7

1. The Boomtown Rats.
2. Hitler (*The Producers*).
3. Dietrich Buxtehude's.
4. Pyotr Tchaikovsky's (Modest).
5. Libby Holman.
6. An organist (of stops).

# 83

1. Bob Dylan.
2. Eric Weissberg.
3. Sir Thomas Beecham.
4. Lily Pons.
5. 'Let's Fall In Love'.
6. Bow resin.

# 159

1. The Walker Brothers.
2. Bernice Claire and Alexander Gray (Nanette and Tom).
3. Igor Stravinsky's.
4. Gerald Ford.
5. London (the East End).
6. Arthur Sullivan.

## 8

1. What year was the Monterey rock festival?
2. *West Side Story* is based on which Shakespeare play?
3. Which waltz did Brahms inscribe on Johann Strauss II's widow's fan with the words, 'Unfortunately not by Brahms'?
4. What kind of singers does the opera *Koanga* call for?
5. Jean Cocteau wrote, 'Paris has two monuments, the Eiffel Tower and' – which singer?
6. Which Second World War air raid inspired the song, 'Praise the Lord and pass the ammunition'?

## 84

1. Which record producer defined 'Zip-a-Dee-Doo-Dah' and 'Da Doo Ron Ron' as his 'little symphonies for the kids'?
2. Who was the original 'Entertainer' in *The Sting*?
3. Which American popular song was adapted by Anton Dvořák in the finale of his *New World* Symphony?
4. In which opera is the heroine killed by Jack the Ripper?
5. Of which Fats Waller song was the inspiration the ample posterior and small bosom of singer Kitty Murray?
6. Which French decadent poet preferred to Wagner the music 'of a cat hung up by its tail outside a window and trying to stick to the panes of glass with its claws'?

## 160

1. Which 'King' first sang 'Awopbopaloomopalopbamboom'?
2. What was Shakespeare's version of *Kiss Me Kate* called?
3. Which legendary Austrian conductor at a rehearsal once exploded, 'Your damned nonsense can I stand twice or once, but sometimes always, by God, never!'?
4. Whose play provided the plot for *Madam Butterfly*?
5. Whose old man said 'Follow the van'?
6. What date is patron saint of music St Cecilia's day?

# 8

1. 1967.
2. *Romeo and Juliet*.
3. *The Blue Danube*.
4. Black singers (Delius).
5. Maurice Chevalier.
6. Pearl Harbor (Frank Loesser).

# 84

1. Phil Spector.
2. Scott Joplin.
3. 'Yankee Doodle'.
4. *Lulu* (Berg).
5. 'All That Meat and No Potatoes'.
6. Charles Baudelaire.

# 160

1. Little Richard ('Tutti Frutti').
2. *The Taming of the Shrew*.
3. Hans Richter.
4. David Belasco's.
5. Marie Lloyd's.
6. 22 November.

# 9

1. Whose 'Boots Were Made For Walkin'' in 1966?
2. Which singer spoke the first words ever heard in a full-length movie: 'Wait a minute, you ain't heard nothin' yet'?
3. Which composer tried to drown himself in the river after which his Third Symphony is named?
4. Which opera begins with the singing of the numbers 'Five – ten – twenty – thirty – thirty-six – forty-three'?
5. Who was blues singer Gertrude Melissa Nix Pridgett?
6. What did the Apollo IX astronauts sing on 8 March 1969?

# 85

1. The composer of 'For Your Love', 'Bus Stop' and 'No Milk Today' went on to play bass for which band?
2. Which singing actress once said, 'I used to be Snow White, then I drifted'?
3. Which German composer wrote a 'gay Viennese ballet' on the subject of *Whipped Cream*?
4. How many nights, according to the title of his memoirs, did Rudolf Bing spend at the opera?
5. Which Handy composition was first named 'Mr Crump'?
6. Which British bird holds the record with a repertory of fifty different songs and a range of 300 notes?

# 161

1. 'Puppy Love' and 'Too Young' were which teen idol's hits?
2. From which Noël Coward comedy came the line, 'Strange how potent cheap music is'?
3. Which composer once declined an invitation to go boating saying 'No thank you, I'm contrapuntal'?
4. Which Romantic opera features a hermit, the Black Hunter and seven magic bullets?
5. What make of guitar is B. B. King's 'Lucille'?
6. Who played the theme from *Harry's Game*?

## 9

1. Nancy Sinatra's.
2. Al Jolson (*The Jazz Singer*).
3. Robert Schumann (the *Rhenish* Symphony).
4. *The Marriage of Figaro* (Mozart).
5. Ma Rainey.
6. 'Happy Birthday to You'.

## 85

1. 10cc (Graham Gouldman).
2. Mae West.
3. Richard Strauss.
4. 5000.
5. 'Memphis Blues'.
6. The meadowlark.

## 161

1. Donny Osmond's.
2. *Private Lives*.
3. Edward Elgar.
4. *Der Freischütz* (Weber).
5. A Gibson.
6. Clannad.

# 10

1. Which would-be MP appeared on stage in a coffin?
2. Who sang 'They Call Me Wicked Lola' in *Blue Angel*?
3. Which Italian composer wrote a fugue after seeing his cat walking on the keyboard of his harpsichord?
4. Which Richard Strauss heroine seals her fate with a glass of water?
5. Which singing actress's son is 'J. R.' in *Dallas*?
6. Which Prussian king used to compose military marches to celebrate his own victories?

# 86

1. Which band in their efforts to entice Sandie Shaw to record with them sent her nude pictures of themselves?
2. 'O-he-o-hi-o-ho', sang Robert Mitchum in which 1948 film?
3. Which composer of thirty-two symphonies was seventy-eight before any of them were performed?
4. Whose operatic daughter ended up, stabbed, in a sack?
5. What does MJQ stand for?
6. A motif from which piece of music was the call-sign of the BBC Overseas Service during the Second World War?

# 162

1. Which John Lennon song was inspired by a police two-tone siren?
2. With whom was Dolly Parton 'Sneakin' Around' in *The Best Little Whorehouse in Texas*?
3. Which dodecaphonic composer died from a bee sting?
4. Which Japanese Imperial Army war-song did Gilbert and Sullivan appropriate for *The Mikado*?
5. Which pianist died in a Chicago dance-hall shoot-out?
6. Whose music gave Madame Verdurin a headache in Proust's *À la Recherche du Temps Perdu*?

## 10

1. Screaming Lord Sutch.
2. Marlene Dietrich (von Sternberg).
3. Domenico Scarlatti (the *Cat Fugue*).
4. Arabella.
5. Mary Martin's (Larry Hagman).
6. Frederick the Great.

## 86

1. The Smiths.
2. *Rachel and the Stranger*.
3. Havergal Brian.
4. Rigoletto's (Verdi).
5. The Modern Jazz Quartet.
6. Beethoven's Fifth Symphony.

## 162

1. 'I am the Walrus'.
2. Burt Reynolds.
3. Alban Berg.
4. 'Miya Sama, Miya Sama'.
5. Pinetop Smith.
6. Richard Wagner's.

## 11

1. George Harrison in 1971 organized a concert in Madison Square Garden in aid of famine relief for which country?
2. Who played Glenn Miller in *The Glenn Miller Story*?
3. On which universal theme did Borodin write a variation in his *Coteletten Polka*?
4. Who said, 'Give me a laundry list and I'll set it to music'?
5. Who was the composer of 'On a Clear Day' who once said, 'I don't like my music, but what is my opinion against that of millions of others?'?
6. In which Aldous Huxley novel is a man shot after a poignant rendition of Beethoven's *Heiliger Dankgesang*?

## 87

1. What is Ms Adu widely known as?
2. To which traditional melody does Henry Fonda dance with Jane Darwell in *The Grapes of Wrath*?
3. Which Vincent Youmans number did Shostakovich orchestrate as *Tahiti Trot* in 1928?
4. A number from which Offenbach opera later became the US Marines' hymn?
5. Which Oscar Hammerstein II song was inspired by the Nazi occupation of France?
6. *Der Tannenbaum* became the anthem of which US state?

## 163

1. Who went from Squeeze to *The Tube*?
2. In which 1948 movie did Bob Hope and Jane Russell have a hit with 'Buttons and Bows'?
3. Which virtuoso greeted his audiences by making his violin mimic the words 'good evening'?
4. From where in Spain did Don José and Micaela come?
5. Who left law to partner Al Rinker in vaudeville in 1924?
6. Which piece of music introduced *Desert Island Discs*?

# 11

1. Bangladesh's.
2. James Stewart.
3. 'Chopsticks'.
4. Gioacchino Rossini.
5. Frederick Loewe.
6. *Point Counter Point*.

# 87

1. Sade.
2. 'Red River Valley'.
3. 'Tea for Two'.
4. *Geneviève de Brabant*.
5. 'The Last Time I Saw Paris'.
6. Maryland.

# 163

1. Jools Holland.
2. *The Paleface*.
3. Niccolò Paganini.
4. Navarre (*Carmen*).
5. Bing Crosby.
6. 'By the Sleepy Lagoon' (Eric Coates).

## 12

1. What have Shane Fenton, Bernard Jewry and Alvin Stardust in common?
2. Whose original recording of 'Drum Boogie' is heard on the soundtrack of *Raging Bull*?
3. Which battle did Haydn's *Nelson* Mass celebrate?
4. In which opera is the heroine shot by a gamekeeper?
5. Who had a 1948 hit with 'Red Roses for a Blue Lady'?
6. Which British comedian arranged to have 'In the Mood' played to mourners at his funeral in 1980?

## 88

1. *Q Are We Not Men*?
2. Which musical starred the Red Shadow?
3. Which composer's music did Debussy say was 'like a pink bon-bon filled with snow'?
4. Which operatic heroine worked in a cigar factory?
5. Which was 'The Biggest Little Band in the Land'?
6. With which number did the Royal Scots Dragoon Guards Band reach No. 1 in the UK charts in 1972?

## 164

1. Whose peel-off banana featured on the sleeve of Velvet Underground's first album?
2. Who was the 'Cinderella with the husky voice' who sang 'Either It's Love Or It Isn't' to Bogart in *Dead Reckoning*?
3. Which Spanish composer sank with HMS *Sussex* in 1916?
4. In which opera does the fourth act begin with a search for a missing pin?
5. Which blues singer in 1924 claimed that her 'Black Bottom' was better than anyone else's?
6. To which composer did comedian Jimmy Durante pay tribute in 'The Guy Who Found "The Lost Chord"'?

## 12

1. They are the same person.
2. Gene Krupa's.
3. Aboukir Bay (1798).
4. *The Cunning Little Vixen* (Janáček).
5. Vaughn Monroe.
6. Peter Sellers.

## 88

1. *A. We Are Devo!*
2. *Desert Song*.
3. Edvard Grieg's.
4. Carmen (Bizet).
5. The John Kirby Sextet.
6. 'Amazing Grace'.

## 164

1. Andy Warhol's.
2. Lizabeth Scott.
3. Enrique Granados.
4. *The Marriage of Figaro* (Mozart).
5. Ma Rainey.
6. Arthur Sullivan.

## 13

1. Who was the lead singer of Aphrodite's Child which had one hit with 'Rain and Tears' in 1968, who later produced a double concept album about the Apocalypse called *666*?
2. Nat King Cole and Stubby Kaye appear as wandering western minstrels in which 1965 movie?
3. Which German composer in 1927 wrote a cantata on the subject of Lindbergh's flight across the Atlantic?
4. Which bel canto heroine disposes of her husband before the wedding breakfast is over?
5. Whose swing band was the first to feature a string quartet?
6. Where would you find a nazard, a larigot and a quint?

## 89

1. Which singer has been backed by The Rockets, The Shocking Pinks, The Stray Gators and Crazy Horse?
2. In which movie was Harvey Keitel a concert pianist?
3. Whose mistress was Mathilde Wesendonck?
4. In which opera are wedding bells a cue for a massacre?
5. Who wrote an 'Opera in Vout (Groove Juice Symphony)'?
6. Who painted the HMV bull-terrier trade mark?

## 165

1. Which Stones album had a zip on its sleeve?
2. In which biographical film did Vanessa Redgrave sing Jerome Kern's 'They Didn't Believe Me'?
3. Which composer wrote, 'A symphony must be like the world, it must embrace everything'?
4. Whose child was Trouble?
5. From where did Allan Sherman sing his letter home to the tune of Ponchielli's *Dance of the Hours*?
6. Which instrument did Ambrose Bierce describe as 'a parlour utensil for subduing impenitent visitors'?

## 13

1. Demis Roussos.
2. *Cat Ballou.*
3. Kurt Weill (*Der Lindberghflug*).
4. Lucia di Lammermoor (Donizetti).
5. Artie Shaw's.
6. In a pipe organ.

## 89

1. Neil Young.
2. *Fingers.*
3. Richard Wagner's.
4. *I Vespri Siciliani* (Verdi).
5. Slim Gaillard.
6. Francis Barraud.

## 165

1. *Sticky Fingers.*
2. *Agatha* (Christie).
3. Gustav Mahler.
4. Madam Butterfly's (Puccini).
5. Camp Grenada ('Hello Muddah, Hello Faddah').
6. The piano.

## 14

1. Stevie Wonder sang 'Happy Birthday' in 1980 for whom?
2. On which instrument did Spencer Tracy accompany himself to 'Don't Cry Little Fish' in *Captains Courageous*?
3. Which French composer's only quartet arose out of his being in a concentration camp where the only other musicians were a cellist, a clarinettist and a violinist?
4. Which opera score calls for eighteen anvils?
5. Which Glenn Miller number earned him the first true golden disc?
6. King Phumiphon Adumet, monarch of which country, wrote a pop song called 'His Majesty's Blues'?

## 90

1. Which football team did the Dave Clark Five play for?
2. In which film did Audrey Hepburn sing 'La Vie en Rose' to Humphrey Bogart?
3. Which of his fugues did J. S. Bach base on the hymn tune to which is sung 'O God Our Help In Ages Past'?
4. Which diva inspired the main character in a novel by Beverley Nichols?
5. Who was the 'Nabob of Sob' whose 1952 hit was 'Cry'?
6. Which US general was 'Marching Through Georgia' in 1864?

## 166

1. With which Beatles song did Del Shannon have a hit in the States before they ever did?
2. In which movie did Rex Harrison 'Talk to the Animals'?
3. Which of his waltzes did Johann Strauss II dedicate to the Vienna Journalists' Association?
4. Who made an opera of Greene's *Our Man in Havana*?
5. Where did Fats Domino 'find his thrill'?
6. Which tune was on the first-ever musical recording?

## 14

1. Martin Luther King.
2. The hurdy-gurdy.
3. Olivier Messaien (*Quartet for the End of Time*).
4. *Das Rheingold* (Wagner).
5. 'Chattanooga Choo-Choo'.
6. Thailand.

## 90

1. Tottenham Hotspurs.
2. *Sabrina Fair*.
3. The *St Anne* Fugue.
4. Dame Nellie Melba.
5. Johnnie Ray.
6. General Sherman.

## 166

1. 'From Me to You'.
2. *Doctor Dolittle*.
3. *Morgenblätter* ('Morning Papers').
4. Malcolm Williamson.
5. On 'Blueberry Hill'.
6. 'Yankee Doodle' (played by cornettist Jules Levy in 1878).

## 15

1. Which reincarnated seventeenth-century witch appeared on stage with a live boa constrictor?
2. Who were the 'Two Sleepy People' in the 1938 movie *Thanks for the Memory*?
3. Which composer, at the end of his 1914 published recording of *Shepherd's Hey*, is heard saying 'I think we'd better do that again' – but obviously didn't?
4. Which Russian author inspired Shostakovich's opera about an official's nose which comes to life?
5. Who was the original 'Henery the Eighth I Am'?
6. Which eleventh-century musical theorist is remembered chiefly for his hand, with which he notated music?

## 91

1. Who sang 'God Must Be a Boogie Man'?
2. Which London theatre usually hosts Broadway musicals?
3. What was Joseph Haydn's composer brother's name?
4. Which number in *Carmen* did Bizet describe as 'merde'?
5. Who died playing Russian roulette in 1954?
6. What is the Belgian national anthem?

## 167

1. To whom did Public Image Ltd pay tribute with *The Flowers of Romance*, the name of his first band?
2. Who was 'Baby' when Cary Grant sang 'I Can't Give You Anything But Love, Baby' in 1938?
3. Into which of his symphonies did Beethoven incorporate the tune of 'God Save the King'?
4. Which diva sang Tosca's 'Vissi d'Arte' lying on the floor?
5. Which Eric Coates number was the signature tune for the Thirties BBC variety series *In Town Tonight*?
6. Which folksong commemorates a Tudor priest who changed religion with each succeeding monarch?

## 15

1. Alice Cooper.
2. Bob Hope and Shirley Ross.
3. Percy Grainger.
4. Nikolai Gogol (*The Nose*).
5. Harry Champion.
6. Guido d'Arezzo.

## 91

1. Joni Mitchell.
2. The Theatre Royal, Drury Lane.
3. Michael.
4. The Toreador's Song.
5. Johnny Ace.
6. *La Brabançonne*.

## 167

1. Sid Vicious.
2. A leopard (*Bringing Up Baby*).
3. The *Battle* Symphony.
4. Maria Jeritza.
5. The *Knightsbridge March*.
6. 'The Vicar of Bray'.

## 16

1. The Detergents' 'Leader of the Laundromat' was an answer to which band's 1965 hit?
2. What did Audrey Hepburn sing sitting on a fire-escape in *Breakfast at Tiffany's*?
3. Which French composer wrote *Memoirs of an Amnesiac*?
4. Which is the largest opera house in the world?
5. Who sang 'Gonna put myself aboard the Santa Fé and go, go, go', and then he died on the *Santa Fé Chief* in 1943?
6. Which instrument did Leonardo da Vinci play?

## 92

1. Who was Porter Wagoner's 'Dumb Blonde'?
2. In which of his films did Groucho Marx sing 'Lydia, the Tattooed Lady'?
3. Which composer did Stravinsky describe as 'six feet of Russian gloom'?
4. Whose *Europa Riconosciuta* opened La Scala in 1778?
5. Who would 'Never Do a Tango With an Eskimo' – perhaps because she couldn't 'Tell a Waltz From a Tango'?
6. Who was 'Mary, Mary, Quite Contrary'?

## 168

1. Who legally changed his name to '?', leader of ? and the Mysterians?
2. Which wandering minstrel was played by Paul Nicholas?
3. Which Haydn symphony was named when a chandelier crashed to the ground but missed the audience?
4. What are the names of Wagner's three Rhinemaidens?
5. Which Nazi-sympathist song did Churchill ask Noël Coward to sing seven times in one evening?
6. Which sound in Hindu and Vedanta tradition symbolizes the Creative Word?

## 16

1. The Shangri-Las' ('Leader of the Pack').
2. 'Moon River'.
3. Erik Satie.
4. The Metropolitan Opera House, New York.
5. Fats Waller.
6. The lira da braccio (viola).

## 92

1. Dolly Parton.
2. *The Marx Brothers at the Circus.*
3. Sergei Rachmaninov.
4. Antonio Salieri's.
5. Alma Cogan.
6. Mary, Queen of Scots.

## 168

1. No one knows his real name.
2. *Blondel.*
3. The *Miracle* Symphony (No. 96).
4. Wellgunde, Woglinde and Flosshilde (The *Ring*).
5. 'Don't Let's Be Beastly to the Germans'.
6. 'Om' (or 'Aum').

# 17

1. Which two Beatles sons are now professional musicians?
2. The Count Basie Band appears in the desert in which 1974 western parody?
3. Which was the first symphony to include trombones?
4. In which opera do characters think they are on the moon?
5. 'She didn't say yes, she didn't say no' – 'what *did* she do'?
6. Which Mediterranean country's national orchestra is bigger than its army?

# 93

1. Which eponymous rock band leader, born Don Van Vliet, named one of his albums, *Lick My Decals Off, Baby*?
2. In which 1958 movie did Sophia Loren sing 'Bing! Bang! Bong!' with a chorus of children?
3. Who wrote 'Purcell's' *Trumpet Voluntary*?
4. Which famous Italian tenor's singing teacher advised him that his voice was 'like gold at the bottom of the Tiber – hardly worth digging for'?
5. Whose guitar read 'This Machine Kills Fascists'?
6. How many finger holes does a penny whistle have?

# 169

1. Who had the 1972 hit 'Give Ireland Back to the Irish'?
2. How many Fred and Ginger movies were there?
3. Which Spanish composer could play the piano with his back to the keyboard'?
4. Upon hearing a gramophone record for the first time in 1905, of which singer did Adelina Patti exclaim, 'Quelle voix! Quelle artiste!'?
5. Which music-hall star was 'Almost a Gentleman'?
6. Which English monarch, a proficient player of the lute and virginals, thought it ill-bred to make music in public?

# A

## 17

1. Julian Lennon and Zak Starkey.
2. *Blazing Saddles*.
3. Beethoven's Fifth.
4. *Il Mondo della Luna* (Haydn).
5. 'She did just what you'd do too'.
6. Monaco's.

## 93

1. Captain Beefheart.
2. *Houseboat*.
3. Jeremiah Clarke.
4. Enrico Caruso's.
5. Woody Guthrie's.
6. Six.

## 169

1. Paul McCartney and Wings.
2. Ten.
3. Isaac Albéniz.
4. Herself (singing 'Voi che Sapete').
5. Billy Bennett.
6. Elizabeth I.

# 18

1. Who had a hit 'In the Year 2525' in 1969?
2. In which movie did Dorothy Lamour sing 'Silent Night'?
3. Which 1870 ballet is subtitled 'The girl with enamel eyes'?
4. How many overtures did Beethoven compose for *Fidelio*?
5. What was the name of Chas McDevitt's female vocalist?
6. Which Irish folk tune, sung to the words 'Danny Boy', did Hubert Parry call 'the most beautiful tune in the world'?

# 94

1. Which rock band was named after an American tractor?
2. Which David Bowie album was originally conceived as a soundtrack for a projected film of Orwell's *1984*?
3. Which of Benjamin Britten's works, commissioned for the 2600th anniversary of the Japanese Mikado dynasty, was rejected because of its references to the Catholic liturgy?
4. Which Savoy opera, styled by its composer a 'dramatic cantata', is the only one without spoken dialogue?
5. Which bandleader always ended his radio show with 'Here's to the Next Time'?
6. Which symbol did Stradivari sign his violins with?

# 170

1. Which band had a hit with 'Rock Lobster' and were named after a Fifties hairdo?
2. Who played piano, and the character Cricket, in Howard Hawks's *To Have and Have Not*?
3. Which teenager's symphony began with a *Boisterous Bourrée* and ended with a *Frolicsome Finale*?
4. Which French heroine is first described as 'neither boy, nor girl, nor woman'?
5. Who sang 'Something Stupid' with his daughter in 1967?
6. What was the theme music of the original *Lone Ranger*?

## 18

1. Zager and Evans.
2. *Donovan's Reef.*
3. *Coppélia* (Delibes).
4. Four.
5. Nancy Whisky.
6. The Londonderry Air.

## 94

1. Buffalo Springfield.
2. *Diamond Dogs.*
3. *Sinfonia da Requiem.*
4. *Trial By Jury.*
5. Henry Hall.
6. A Maltese Cross and his initials inside a double circle.

## 170

1. The B-52s.
2. Hoagy Carmichael.
3. Benjamin Britten's (*Simple* Symphony).
4. *Mignon* (Ambroise Thomas).
5. Frank Sinatra (with Nancy).
6. The *William Tell* Overture (Rossini).

## 19

1. Who is 'the Divine Miss M.'?
2. Whose musical autobiopic featured open-heart surgery?
3. Which composer in 1695 used a march intended for Shadwell's *The Libertine* in Queen Mary's funeral music?
4. In which French opera does the heroine's hair have an important scene?
5. Who invented scat singing when he forgot the words of 'Heebic Jeebies' during a 1926 recording session?
6. Which show was the first Radio One broadcast?

## 95

1. Which Everly Brothers classic had been rejected by more than thirty acts before they made it a hit in 1957?
2. Who was the unwitting composer of the soundtrack of *Death in Venice*?
3. In which of his works did Debussy use the 'Keel Row'?
4. If the name Cinderella is *La Cenerentola* in Italian (Rossini), what is it in French (Massenet)?
5. Who was 'the Singing Brakeman'?
6. E. F. Benson's Lucia was noted for her playing of which piece of music?

## 171

1. What was the first complete song broadcast on Radio One?
2. Which Rodgers and Hart musical featured an elephant?
3. Which composer founded a 'League of David' (*Davidsbündler*) in order to fight the philistines of art?
4. In which Meyerbeer opera is a ballet danced by the spectres of apostate nuns?
5. What was Eamonn Andrews's only hit, in 1956?
6. Which impresario put Bessie Smith, Billie Holiday, Pete Seeger and Bob Dylan *On Record*?

# A

## 19

1. Bette Midler.
2. Bob Fosse's (*All That Jazz*).
3. Henry Purcell.
4. *Pelléas et Mélisande* (Debussy).
5. Louis Armstrong.
6. The *Tony Blackburn Show*.

## 95

1. 'Bye Bye Love'.
2. Gustav Mahler.
3. *Images* (*Gigues*).
4. *Cendrillon*.
5. Jimmie Rodgers.
6. The *Moonlight* Sonata.

## 171

1. 'Flowers in the Ring'.
2. *Jumbo*.
3. Robert Schumann.
4. *Robert le Diable*.
5. 'Shifting Whispering Sands'.
6. John Hammond.

# 20

1. Which band wears baggy trousers?
2. Which cartoon character was given songs by Alan Price?
3. Which composer of German parentage was born in Bradford, lived in Florida and died in Grez-sur-Loing?
4. Which Rossini opera is subtitled 'The Useless Precaution'?
5. Which clarinet player, 'confused by an excess of success', in 1939 deserted his band and fled to Mexico?
6. What is the title of George Martin's Radio One jingle?

# 96

1. Why were The Bee Gees so called?
2. Which band's final performance was filmed in Martin Scorsese's 1978 film *The Last Waltz*?
3. To which composer's works do Hoboken numbers apply?
4. After which prima donna is a raspberry sauce named?
5. Which jazz classic did Spencer Williams name after his aunt's bordello in New Orleans?
6. What did Ambrose Bierce describe as 'an instrument to tickle human ears by friction of a horse's tail on the entrails of a cat'?

# 172

1. Which artist's 'Subterranean Homesick Blues' gave the Weathermen their name?
2. Which 1962 musical combined Plautus with burlesque?
3. Which Mannheim composer died, along with his family, after mistaking toadstools for mushrooms?
4. Which 1831 opera describes the life and times of Henry VIII's second wife?
5. Which is the only other instrument, besides the trumpet, that Louis Armstrong has played on a recording?
6. Who compèred BBC TV's *Juke Box Jury*?

# 20

1. Madness.
2. Andy Capp.
3. Frederick Delius.
4. *The Barber of Seville*.
5. Artie Shaw.
6. *Theme One*.

# 96

1. They were the *b*rothers *G*ibb.
2. The Band's.
3. Joseph Haydn's.
4. Dame Nellie Melba.
5. 'Mahogany Hall Stomp'.
6. The violin.

# 172

1. Bob Dylan's.
2. *A Funny Thing Happened on the Way to the Forum*.
3. Johann Schobert.
4. *Anna Bolena* (Donizetti).
5. The penny whistle (on King Oliver's 'Sobbin' Blues').
6. David Jacobs.

## 21

1. Who is 'Little Miss Dynamite'?
2. Which Rodgers and Hammerstein musical begins in heaven?
3. Name the first English composer to be made a life peer?
4. Which French novelist was Ravel's librettist for *L'Enfant et les Sortilèges*?
5. Which singing group, featuring Billy, Deek, Hoppy and Charlie, began as railway porters and in 1980 celebrated their fiftieth year in show business?
6. What name is given to wild music made in honour of Dionysius?

## 97

1. Which 'Tres Hombres' appeared on stage with snakes, buffalo and cactus on their 1976 tour?
2. What was Oliver selling when he sang, 'Who Will Buy'?
3. Which composer was known as 'the black Mahler'?
4. Which 'King of the High Cs' shared a wet-nurse with Mirella Freni?
5. What were the colours of Perez Prado's first million-seller?
6. What does SPAM stand for?

## 173

1. To what did Brian Epstein change Priscilla White's name?
2. Who washed her hair eight times a week for three and a half years?
3. Who wrote 'Haydn's' *Toy* Symphony?
4. What is the name of Brünnhilde's horse?
5. Where is Dixieland?
6. Which musical instrument is made out of a log hollowed out by termites?

## 21

1. Brenda Lee.
2. *Carousel.*
3. Baron Britten of Aldeburgh.
4. Colette.
5. The Ink Spots.
6. Dithyramb.

## 97

1. ZZ Top.
2. 'This Wonderful Morning'.
3. Samuel Coleridge-Taylor.
4. Luciano Pavarotti.
5. 'Cherry Pink and Apple-Blossom White'.
6. Society for the Publication of American Music.

## 173

1. Cilla Black.
2. Mary Martin as Ensign Nellie Forbush (*South Pacific*).
3. Mozart's father, Leopold.
4. Grane (The *Ring*).
5. The Southern States, USA.
6. The didgeridoo.

## 22

1. Which Who member's father was lead reed-player in the Forties dance band The Squadronnaires?
2. Who was 'Tony', of the Awards for the Best Musical?
3. Which German orchestra, the earliest extant, until 1906 always performed standing up?
4. How many operas did Donizetti compose (± ten)?
5. Which swing instrument is called a 'liquorice stick'?
6. With 1477 stops, 33,112 pipes and a 365-horse-power engine, which is the largest organ in the world?

## 98

1. Which band began with 'Roll Over Beethoven', made a *New World* album and toured in a giant hamburger?
2. Who sang the theme music of *For Your Eyes Only*?
3. Which composer set to music Blake's 'Jerusalem'?
4. When Verdi's *Ernani* became the first complete recording of any opera, how many record sides did it occupy?
5. Which music-hall star used to recite 'I like the girls who do, I like the girls who don't, I hate the girl who says she will and then she says she won't?
6. Which Shakespeare character sings, 'Where the bee sucks, there suck I'?

## 174

1. What was the true title of The Beatles' 'White Album'?
2. How many von Trapp children were there?
3. Who thought 'the best thing you can be is a dead composer, and the next best thing you can be is a German composer. The worst thing you can be is an American composer'?
4. Which opera gave rise to 'Here Comes the Bride'?
5. Who is the nine-fingered 'King of the Keyboard'?
6. For what product did Chas and Dave sing 'Gertcha'?

## 22

1. Pete Townsend's.
2. Antoinette Perry.
3. The Leipzig Gewandhaus Orchestra.
4. Sixty-six.
5. The clarinet.
6. The Auditorium Organ, Atlantic City.

## 98

1. Electric Light Orchestra.
2. Sheena Easton.
3. Hubert Parry.
4. Forty.
5. Max Miller's.
6. Ariel (*The Tempest*).

## 174

1. *The Beatles*.
2. Seven.
3. Milton Babbitt.
4. *Lohengrin* (Wagner).
5. Bill McGuffie.
6. Courage beer.

## 23

1. What nationality were Tangerine Dream?
2. How many roles does the leading man in *Little Me* have?
3. Which composer was married before an audience of 20,000 in the Hollywood Bowl in 1928?
4. Privalof's opera *Dreams of the Volga* was scored entirely for which instruments?
5. Which jazz pianist-composer's father was a butler in the White House?
6. Who normally plays the Aeolian harp?

## 99

1. Which band had a 1970 hit with 'The Green Manalishi (With the Two-Pronged Crown)'?
2. How did Gwen Verdon then Liza Minnelli get away with murder?
3. Which modern composer thinks 'We are all transistors'?
4. In which Italian opera are there three Masks and three Enigmas?
5. Where was 'Storyville'?
6. Who feared that 'Hell is full of musical amateurs'?

## 175

1. The father of three members of which Californian band used to punish them by removing his glass eye and making them stare into the empty socket?
2. Which 1941 film features the *Warsaw* Concerto?
3. Which nineteenth-century arbiter of taste in art wrote, 'Beethoven always sounds to me like the upsetting of bags of nails, with here and there also a dropped hammer'?
4. What was 'Fidelio's' real name?
5. What were the Andrews Sisters' first names?
6. How many semihemidemisemiquavers in a breve?

# A

## 23

1. West German.
2. Seven.
3. Percy Grainger.
4. Balalaikas.
5. Duke Ellington's.
6. Aeolus (the wind).

## 99

1. Fleetwood Mac.
2. As Roxie Hart in *Chicago*.
3. Karlheinz Stockhausen.
4. *Turandot* (Puccini).
5. New Orleans.
6. George Bernard Shaw.

## 175

1. The Beach Boys (Murray Wilson).
2. *Dangerous Moonlight* (Richard Addinsell).
3. John Ruskin.
4. Leonora.
5. Patty, Maxine and Laverne.
6. 256.

## 24

1. Which electric Australian group features a guitarist in short trousers?
2. In which film did Inspector Clouseau sing 'Come to Me'?
3. Which composer's own name for his Second Symphony in C was *Symphony of Heavenly Length*?
4. How many children did Cherubini's Medea have?
5. According to Sammy Fain and Irving Kahal, what goes with a 'Sunbonnet Blue'?
6. Which German music-hall song became the Nazi anthem?

## 100

1. Which blind vocalist sang the line, 'Lately I've been staring in the mirror'?
2. Who was the unwitting composer of *Kismet*?
3. Which English composer complained, 'If I write a tune you all say it's commonplace – if I don't, you all say it's rot'?
4. Which composer once referred to the diva Marietta Alboni as 'the elephant that swallowed a nightingale'?
5. Which jazz pianist-composer's first piano teacher's name was Mrs Clinkscales?
6. To which tune do the Grenadier Guards march on parade?

## 176

1. What was the French stage-name of the Singing Nun?
2. Which American president befriends Orphan Annie?
3. Which critic, when Mahler and Bruckner were new to English audiences, said 'we don't want them here'?
4. Which French poet became a *verismo* hero?
5. What was Michael Holliday's autobiographical hit of 1958?
6. Which Boer War song became the unofficial anthem of white South Africans?

## 24

1. AC/DC.
2. *The Pink Panther Strikes Again.*
3. Robert Schumann's.
4. Two.
5. 'A yellow straw hat'.
6. The Horst Wessel Song.

## 100

1. Stevie Wonder.
2. Alexander Borodin.
3. Edward Elgar.
4. Gioacchino Rossini.
5. Duke Ellington's.
6. The March from *Scipio* (Handel).

## 176

1. Sœur Sourire.
2. Theodore Roosevelt.
3. Eric Blom.
4. Andrea Cheniér (Giordano).
5. 'The Story of My Life'.
6. 'Sarie Marais'.

## 25

1. Whose skiffle recording of 'Rock Island Line' inspired Phil Spector to buy his first guitar?
2. Which one-eyed guitarist provided the soundtrack for Walter Hill's *The Long Riders*?
3. Which French composer set to music five *Banalities*?
4. Which famous castrato sang the same four songs every night for twenty-five years to Philip V of Spain?
5. Which of Rudolf Friml's little songs ended up as 'The Donkey Serenade'?
6. Where in New York was the original Tin Pan Alley?

## 101

1. Who wrote the single 'Spasticus Autisticus' for the United Nations Year of the Disabled only to have it rejected?
2. Duran Duran were named after a character in which Roger Vadim movie?
3. What is the name of Kyung-Wha and Myung-Wha's pianist brother?
4. Which Verdi heroine is buried alive?
5. Whose singing was censured in Parliament as 'sentimental, sloppy muck in the Forces Programme'?
6. Where would one normally sing a threnody?

## 177

1. Who sang about Van Gogh in 'Vincent'?
2. For which 1960 Billy Wilder comedy did piano-duo Ferrante and Teicher play the theme?
3. Balakirev, Borodin, Mussorgsky, Rimsky-Korsakov and which other composer formed 'the Mighty Handful'?
4. Which singer's name when translated into English means 'Betty Blackhead'?
5. Which Dinah Shore hit was based on a Jewish folk song?
6. Who most famously didn't compose *Greensleeves*?

# 25

1. Lonnie Donegan's.
2. Ry Cooder.
3. Francis Poulenc (Apollinaire).
4. Farinelli.
5. 'Chansonette'.
6. 28th Street.

# 101

1. Ian Dury.
2. *Barbarella*.
3. Myung-Whung (Chung).
4. Aïda.
5. Vera Lynn's.
6. At a funeral.

# 177

1. Don McLean.
2. *The Apartment*.
3. César Cui.
4. Elizabeth Schwarzkopf's.
5. 'Yes, My Darling Daughter'.
6. King Henry VIII of England.

# 26

1. Who said, during a 1967 court hearing, 'We are not old men . . . we are not worried about petty morals'?
2. Who was the popular black singer in Fred Zinnemann's 1953 *Member of the Wedding*?
3. Which composer died saying, 'I shall hear in heaven'?
4. Who entitled her memoirs, *Men, Women and Tenors*?
5. Which US disc-jockey called himself 'the fifth Beatle'?
6. Who was the *Guardian*'s most musical cricket writer?

# 102

1. Who was arrested in 1965 for entering America with a guitar-case full of pep-pills, appeared on stage with Billy Graham and had a hit song about a transvestite?
2. Which opera featured in *Sunday, Bloody Sunday*?
3. Which composer taught at *St Paul's* Girls' School, *Brook Green*, *Hammersmith*, London?
4. Which Norwegian soprano when asked, 'What do you need to sing Wagner?' replied, 'A pair of comfortable shoes'?
5. Who was the 'Sentimental Gentleman of Swing'?
6. Which tune does the BBC World Service share with the Orange party?

# 178

1. 'Heads Down No Nonsense Mindless Boogie' by Alberto Y Lost Trios Paranoias was a parody of which group?
2. Which Lloyd Webber flop had an Ayckbourn libretto?
3. Who was Elgar's 'Nimrod'?
4. Which Tippett opera features a far-sighted character from T. S. Eliot's *The Waste Land*?
5. What kind of bird did Marie Lloyd have as a pet?
6. In English folk song, whose 'father he makes cabbage-nets/And through the streets does cry them?

# 26

1. Keith Richard.
2. Ethel Waters.
3. Ludwig van Beethoven.
4. Frances Alda.
5. Murray 'the K' Kaufmann.
6. Neville Cardus, also music critic.

# 102

1. Johnny Cash ('A Boy Named Sue').
2. *Così fan tutte* (Mozart).
3. Gustav Holst.
4. Kirsten Flagstad.
5. Tommy Dorsey.
6. 'Lilliburlero'.

# 178

1. Status Quo.
2. *Jeeves*.
3. August Jaeger (his editor).
4. *The Midsummer Marriage* (Madame Sosostris).
5. A cock linnet.
6. 'Sally (in our Alley')'s.

# 27

1. The subject of whose 1962 song for children 'Puff the Magic Dragon' was thought to be psychedelic drugs?
2. Who were Renaldo and Clara in *Renaldo and Clara*?
3. Which composer wrote, 'I am disposed towards harmony, but organically I am incapable of a tune'?
4. In which opera are the heroes 'magnetically revived'?
5. Which jazz musician used to perform with 'flute, tenor, manzello, stritch and siren'?
6. Which English poet was attracted to music because 'it can be made anywhere, is invisible and does not smell'?

# 103

1. In which city did The Beatles have their first success?
2. To whom did Tommy Steele give *Half a Sixpence*?
3. Which Austrian pianist prided himself not on the notes he played but on the spaces in between?
4. In which opera does an emperor sing a love-song to a tree?
5. Which jazz pair recorded *Back to Back* and *Side by Side*?
6. Who would be familiar with purfling, f-holes and a frog?

# 179

1. Which two singer-songwriters addressed singles to each other, respectively titled 'Oh Neil' and 'Oh Carol'?
2. What was the title of the 1942 hit from *Bambi*?
3. Which rock star narrated in a 1977 recording of Prokofiev's *Peter and the Wolf*?
4. In Offenbach's *Tales of Hoffmann*, which opera is playing next door to the Inn where the hero tells his tales?
5. Which music-hall song was written to promote a well-known brand of sparkling wine?
6. What do singers do when given the injunction *bocca chiusa* or *bouche fermée*?

## 27

1. Peter, Paul and Mary's.
2. Bob Dylan and Joan Baez.
3. Arnold Schoenberg.
4. *Così fan tutte* (Mozart).
5. Roland Kirk.
6. W. H. Auden.

## 103

1. Hamburg.
2. Marti Webb.
3. Artur Schnabel.
4. *Xerxes* (Handel).
5. Duke Ellington and Johnny Hodges.
6. A string player.

## 179

1. Carole King and Neil Sedaka.
2. 'Love is a Song'.
3. David Bowie.
4. *Don Giovanni* (Mozart).
5. 'Champagne Charlie' (Moët).
6. They hum.

## 28

1. What happened on Max Yasgur's farm in August 1969?
2. In which 1935 musical were Fred and Ginger dancing 'Cheek to Cheek'?
3. Which work by Charles Ives is subtitled 'A Contemplation of Nothing Serious'?
4. For what sum is Smetana's Bride Bartered?
5. Which of his rivals did Jelly Roll Morton describe as 'the most dastardly impostor in the history of music'?
6. What is known in German as a *dudelsack*?

## 104

1. Which 'Rock 'n' Roll Animal' in 1975 released a double album consisting entirely of mechanical noise?
2. *With a Song in My Heart* was a 1952 biopic of whom?
3. For which one-armed pianist did Ravel, Prokofiev and Franz Schmidt write concertos?
4. For which diva – also his wife – did Rossini compose arias 'designed specifically to expose her virtues and disguise her very considerable deficiencies'?
5. Which American boxer inspired an album by Miles Davis?
6. What is a 'thunder stick'?

## 180

1. Which rock band debuted with a transcription of Mussorgski's *Pictures at an Exhibition*?
2. The screen version of *Guys and Dolls* featured which two stars not best known for their singing?
3. Referring to whom did Robert Schumann exclaim, 'Hats off, gentlemen, a genius'?
4. In which Meyerbeer opera does a character die from the effects of perfume from a tree?
5. Who was Louis Armstrong's 'Papa Joe'?
6. Which tune was played as the *Titanic* sank in 1912?

## 28

1. The Woodstock Music Festival.
2. *Top Hat.*
3. *Central Park in the Dark.*
4. 300 gulden.
5. W. C. Handy.
6. The bagpipe.

## 104

1. Lou Reed (*Metal Machine Music*).
2. Jane Froman.
3. Paul Wittgenstein.
4. Isabella Colbran.
5. Jack Johnson.
6. A bull-roarer.

## 180

1. Emerson, Lake and Palmer.
2. Marlon Brando and Jean Simmons.
3. Fryderyk Chopin.
4. *L'Africaine.*
5. 'King' Oliver.
6. 'Nearer My God to Thee' (or 'Autumn', according to some).

## 29

1. A member of which band in 1966 asserted, 'We're more popular than Jesus Christ right now'?
2. Which Johnny Mercer song did Louis Armstrong sing to a horse in the 1938 film *Going Places*?
3. Which American composer in his *Composition 1960* No. 2 builds a fire in front of the audience?
4. In which operetta does 'The Last Rose of Summer' feature?
5. Which jazzman played a white plastic saxophone?
6. What does ASCAP stand for?

## 105

1. To whom did Bob Dylan sing 'It Ain't Me Babe'?
2. Which Broadway heroine has a dog named Sandy?
3. Which composer died of gangrene after striking his foot with a pole?
4. Which opera has a proposal made from a phone booth?
5. Which big-band leader was stabbed to death by one of his drummers during a tour of America in 1919?
6. Which blustering American president said, 'I don't give a damn about "The Missouri Waltz" but I can't say it out loud because it's the song of Missouri'?

## 181

1. Who appeared in 'Cars' and now flies aeroplanes?
2. 'The Lambeth Walk' appears in which Noël Gay show?
3. Which royal couple when they married in 1960 started a vogue for using Widor's *Toccata* at weddings?
4. Whose prescription for music-hall singers was to make them listen to 'Bach interwoven/With Spohr and Beethoven/At Classical Monday Pops'?
5. What do the initials stand for in Reinhardt–Grappelli's 'H.C.Q. Strut'?
6. Area Code 615's 'Stone Fox Chase' was the signature tune for which TV show?

## 29

1. The Beatles (John Lennon).
2. 'Jeepers Creepers'.
3. La Monte Young.
4. *Martha* (Flotow).
5. Ornette Coleman.
6. American Society of Composers, Authors and Publishers.

## 105

1. Joan Baez.
2. Annie Mudge (*Annie*).
3. Jean-Baptiste Lully.
4. *The Telephone* (Menotti).
5. James Europe.
6. Harry S. Truman.

## 181

1. Gary Numan.
2. *Me and My Girl*.
3. The Duke and Duchess of Kent.
4. The Mikado's (Gilbert and Sullivan).
5. The Hot Club Quintet.
6. *Old Grey Whistle Test*.

# Q

## 30

1. Whose gesturing middle finger on Moby Grape's debut album was airbrushed out after causing a furore?
2. Who was Rudy Vallee serenading with 'Goodnight Sweetheart' in *The Palm Beach Story*?
3. Which English composer wrote *Three Little Funeral Marches* for a statesman, a canary and a rich aunt?
4. Whose tiny hand was frozen?
5. Which black jazz player was known as 'the fifth Goon'?
6. Which Shakespearean character says, 'If music be the food of love, play on'?

## 106

1. Which 'Two Virgins' held a 'Bed-In For Peace' in 1969?
2. What was the title of the musical adaptation of George Bernard Shaw's *Arms and the Man*?
3. Of a family of which no less than fifty-three were professional musicians, who was the greatest?
4. Which suicidal heroine is a freelance ballad singer?
5. Who played cornet for the Wolverines?
6. What are, or were, *bassanelli, ottavini* and *piccoli*?

## 182

1. Who sang back-up vocal on and was conjecturally the subject of Carly Simon's 'You're So Vain'?
2. Joan Crawford starred in MGM's 1928 screen version of which operetta?
3. Which national anthem is quoted in Schumann's *Faschingsschwank* and Elgar's *Music Makers*?
4. Which operatic courtesan signalled her readiness for love by the colour of the flowers she wore?
5. Whose 'bad-assed tenors' were Herschel Evans and Lester Young in the late Thirties?
6. What is the difference between a *tromba marina* and a nun's fiddle?

## 30

1. Don Stevenson's.
2. Claudette Colbert.
3. Lord Berners.
4. Mimi's (*La Bohème*).
5. Ray Ellington.
6. Orsino (*Twelfth Night*).

## 106

1. John Lennon and Yoko Ono.
2. *The Chocolate Soldier.*
3. Johann Sebastian Bach.
4. 'La Gioconda' (Ponchielli).
5. Bix Beiderbecke.
6. Wind instruments.

## 182

1. Mick Jagger.
2. *Rose-Marie.*
3. The *Marseillaise.*
4. Violetta (*La Traviata*; Verdi).
5. Count Basie's.
6. None.

# 31

1. Which artist went gold with a double-album bootleg called *Great White Wonder*?
2. Pat Boone had a hit in 1956 with the theme from which western movie?
3. Whose *Clavier* was *Well-Tempered*?
4. In which Romantic opera is the heroine mute?
5. Which between-the-wars singing star went on to become Mrs Dale in *Mrs Dale's Diary*?
6. Which dance according to legend is both the symptom and the cure for a bite from a poisonous spider?

# 107

1. Which comedy actress in 1963 had a hit with 'All I Want For Christmas Is a Beatle'?
2. In Truffaut's *Jules et Jim*, who sings 'Le Turbillon'?
3. Which now-forgotten composer was hailed by Robert Schumann as 'a thorough Englishman, a glorious artist, and a beautiful and poetic soul'?
4. Which opera did Joseph Kerman describe as 'a shabby little shocker'?
5. Who began his singing career with *Welsh Rarebit*?
6. After which Italian town is a drinking song named?

# 183

1. Which female singer started out filleting fish in Aberdeen?
2. In which movie was Robert de Niro a bandleader?
3. Which composer of symphonies for the piano is falsely reputed to have died after being crushed by a bookshelf?
4. In which city was the first opera house opened?
5. Which music-hall star once appeared in a stage play called *The A.B.C. Girl* ('or Flossie the Frivolous')?
6. What shape were John Broadwood's square pianos?

## 31

1. Bob Dylan.
2. *Friendly Persuasion* ('Thee I Love').
3. J. S. Bach's.
4. *The Dumb Girl of Portici* (Auber).
5. Jessie Matthews.
6. The *tarantella*.

## 107

1. Dora Bryan.
2. Jeanne Moreau.
3. William Sterndale Bennett.
4. *Tosca* (Puccini).
5. Harry Secombe.
6. Brindisi.

## 183

1. Annie Lennox.
2. *New York, New York*.
3. Alkan.
4. Venice (1637).
5. Marie Lloyd.
6. Rectangular.

# 32

1. Who is known as 'the Cool Ruler' and 'the Lonely Lover'?
2. For which film did Walton write a *Spitfire* Prelude?
3. Which Dutch composer's middle name was Pieterszoon?
4. Which symphonic intermezzo depicts a repentant courtesan journeying to a convent?
5. Who temporarily renounced his singing career after a concert in 1957 with the words, 'If you want to live for the Lord, you can't rock and roll too. God doesn't like it'?
6. Which comedian says, 'If music be the food of love, then play us a tune on your jam buttie'?

# 108

1. Which band was sued by Harold Wilson for portraying him on publicity material in bed with his secretary?
2. Which singer was prevented by a drink-driving charge from appearing in the 1930 movie *The King of Jazz*?
3. What does Tchaikovsky's *1812* Overture commemorate?
4. Whose brother-in-law was turned into a swan before the opera begins?
5. From whom did Tommy Dorsey borrow his 'Song of India'?
6. Which orchestra had a hit with the 'Superman' theme?

# 184

1. What was Keith Moon's real name?
2. In which 1942 movie did Veronica Lake, as a singing magician, sing, 'Now You See It, Now You Don't'?
3. Which composer's dogs were named Marco and Mina?
4. Of which great tenor was it said that 'he made the gramophone and the gramophone made him'?
5. Who in 1935 became the first black jazzman to appear in public in America with a white band?
6. Who has written *The Definitive History of P D.Q. Bach*, 'history's most justifiably neglected composer'?

# 32

1. Gregory Isaacs.
2. *The First of the Few.*
3. Jan Sweelinck's.
4. *Meditation* (*Thaïs*; Massenet).
5. Little Richard.
6. Ken Dodd.

# 108

1. The Move.
2. Bing Crosby.
3. Napoleon's retreat from Moscow.
4. Lohengrin's (Wagner).
5. Nicolai Rimsky-Korsakov.
6. The London Symphony Orchestra.

# 184

1. Keith Moon.
2. *This Gun For Hire.*
3. Edward Elgar's.
4. Enrico Caruso.
5. Teddy Wilson (with Benny Goodman).
6. The composer Peter Schickele.

## 33

1. Which Russian folksong in translation made a hit for Mary Hopkin in 1968?
2. Which popular singer supplied the voices for both Siamese cats in *The Lady and the Tramp*?
3. Which work was Stravinsky's 'little concerto in the style of the *Brandenburg* Concertos'?
4. Which Gilbert and Sullivan character 'sipped no sup and he craved no crumb as he sighed for the love of a lady'?
5. Why must you 'Be sure it's true when you say, "I love you"'?
6. What was David Hare's play about a rock band?

## 109

1. One of which car-obsessive's albums features 'Cadillac Ranch', 'Drive All Night' and 'Wreck on the Highway'?
2. In which horror film did Vincent Price play the trumpet?
3. What was the title of Henze's 'popular and military oratorio' which caused a riot in Hamburg in 1968?
4. Who lived in a house named 'Wahnfried' – 'Peace from Madness'?
5. 'Wiv a ladder and some glasses/You could see ter 'Ackney Marshes/If it wasn't for – ' what?
6. Who danced from London to Norwich in 1599?

## 185

1. What was the name of Elvis Presley's house in Memphis?
2. As what did *All About Eve* receive a Broadway ovation?
3. Who wrote a bagatelle for his girlfriend, Elise?
4. In which historical operatic war did the king and queen of France take opposing sides?
5. Who married Howlin' Wolf's sister?
6. Who wrote the novel *The Phantom of the Opera*?

## 33

1. 'Those Were the Days'.
2. Peggy Lee.
3. The *Dumbarton Oaks* Concerto.
4. Jack Point (*Yeoman of the Guard*).
5. Because 'It's a Sin To Tell a Lie'.
6. *Teeth 'n' Smiles*.

## 109

1. Bruce Springsteen's (*The River*).
2. *The Abominable Dr Phibes*.
3. *The Raft of the Medusa*.
4. Richard Wagner.
5. 'If it wasn't for the 'ouses in between'.
6. William Kemp.

## 185

1. Graceland.
2. *Applause!*
3. Ludwig van Beethoven (*Für Elise*).
4. The 'War of the Buffoons' (1752–4).
5. Sonny Boy Williamson.
6. Victor Hugo.

## 34

1. Elkie Brooks and Robert Palmer played together in which Seventies band?
2. Before *A Star is Born* begins, what is Vicki Lester's name?
3. Which sixteenth-century Prince of Venosa and composer of erotic madrigals had his wife and her lover assassinated after finding them *in flagrante delicto*?
4. Which thespian heroine dies from sniffing a bunch of poisoned violets?
5. Whose last hit, in 1959, was 'It Doesn't Matter Any More'?
6. Who wrote the *Coronation Street* theme music?

## 110

1. Who is 'Keith Partridge' of the Partridge Family?
2. Which dance does Anna teach the King of Siam?
3. Which composer had 'Musical Moments'?
4. How many versions of *The Bartered Bride* did Smetana compose?
5. Who had four stabs at the UK charts with 'Mack the Knife'?
6. How many strings does a balalaika have?

## 186

1. Which band were famous for spending 'Saturday Night at the Movies', 'Kissing in the Back Row'?
2. What was the working title of *West Side Story*?
3. Of which composer did Handel say, 'He knows no more of contrapunto as mein cook'?
4. What was 'La Traviata's name?
5. To which British king did Louis Armstrong dedicate a performance with the words, 'This one's for you, Rex'?
6. What name is given to violent music made with household utensils for the humiliation of social outcasts?

# 34

1. Vinegar Joe.
2. Esther Blodgett.
3. Carlo Gesualdo.
4. Adriana Lecouvreur (Cilea).
5. Buddy Holly's.
6. Eric Spear.

# 110

1. David Cassidy.
2. The polka.
3. Franz Schubert (*Moments Musicales*).
4. Five.
5. Bobby Darin.
6. Three.

# 186

1. The Drifters.
2. *East Side Story*.
3. Christoph Willibald von Gluck.
4. Violetta Valery (Verdi).
5. King George V.
6. Charivari.

## 35

1. The original members of Genesis all went to which English public school?
2. In which film did Sigmund Romberg score for Eddy–Macdonald an opera based on Tchaikovsky's Fifth Symphony?
3. Whose music, according to Ernest Newman in 1921, 'used to be original. Now it is aboriginal'?
4. In which two places would you find Gluck's *Iphigenia*?
5. Who sang 'I'm a G-nu'?
6. Which was the 'Deep River' of the Negro spiritual?

## 111

1. Under what name did the vocal duo Tom and Jerry become famous?
2. Whose life story was *The Lady Sings the Blues*?
3. Which composer wrote, 'Beethoven can write music, thank God – but he can do nothing else on earth'?
4. Which Italian composer had a passion for duck shooting?
5. Which popular performer, asked if the critics upset him, coined the phrase, 'I cry all the way to the bank'?
6. Of which country was the legendary 'Good King Wenceslas' monarch?

## 187

1. Which rock star used the pseudonyms Rev. Thumbs Ghurkin, Dr Winston O'Boogie and Dwarf McDougal?
2. Which famous tenor acted and sang the part of another famous tenor in a 1950 movie?
3. Who wrote a concerto for Woody Herman's 'ebony stick'?
4. Which opera made Gay rich and Rich gay?
5. Who was 'the Tragi-Comedian of Jazz with the Gas-Pipe Clarinet'?
6. Who wrote the *Listen With Mother* signature tune?

## 35

1. Charterhouse.
2. *Maytime* (*Czaritza*).
3. Igor Stravinsky's.
4. *In Aulis* and *In Tauris*.
5. Michael Flanders (with Donald Swann).
6. The river Jordan.

## 111

1. Simon and Garfunkel.
2. Billie Holiday's.
3. Ludwig van Beethoven.
4. Giacomo Puccini.
5. Wladziu Valentino Liberace.
6. Bohemia.

## 187

1. John Lennon.
2. Mario Lanza (*The Great Caruso*).
3. Igor Stravinsky (his *Ebony* Concerto).
4. *The Beggar's Opera*.
5. Ted Lewis.
6. Gabriel Fauré (*Dolly Suite*).

## 36

1. Which single did Miss Chuckle Cherry's 'My Pussycat' parody?
2. Which was Broadway's longest-running musical?
3. Which composer was known as 'the Red Priest'?
4. What is the name of the Merry Widow?
5. In which street in London is Ronnie Scott's jazz club?
6. Which American president said, 'I know only two tunes. One of them is "Yankee Doodle" and the other isn't'?

## 112

1. Which nineteenth-century English Prime Minister returned to fame with Cream in 1967?
2. Of whom did Christopher Plummer say, 'Working with her is like being hit over the head with a Valentine card'?
3. Who wrote 'Handel in the Strand'?
4. Which composer was associated with the 1848 revolutionary slogan 'Vittorio Emmanuele, Re d'Italia'?
5. Which jazz band used to bill itself as 'Fifty Joy-Whooping Sultans of High-Speed Syncopation'?
6. What were 'platters' made of?

## 188

1. Who thought The New Yardbirds would 'sink like a lead balloon' unless they changed their name?
2. Which bandleader premièred *Rhapsody in Blue* with Gershwin and starred in the movie *King of Jazz*?
3. Which pianist, also known as 'Michel Dvorsky', once said, 'Music is the most expensive of all noises'?
4. Which composer did Clive James describe as 'Mozart without the brains'?
5. How old was Al Jolson's 'Sonny Boy'?
6. In which Thomas Mann novel does a small boy play Mahlerian improvisations on the piano?

# 36

1. (Chuck Berry's) 'My Ding-a-Ling'.
2. *A Chorus Line.*
3. Antonio Vivaldi.
4. Anna Glawari.
5. Frith Street.
6. Ulysses S. Grant.

# 112

1. Benjamin Disraeli (*Disraeli Gears*).
2. Julie Andrews.
3. Percy Grainger.
4. Giuseppe Verdi (V.E.R.D.I.).
5. The Original Dixieland Jazz Band.
6. Shellac (78s).

# 188

1. Keith Moon (Led Zeppelin).
2. Paul Whiteman.
3. Josef Hofmann.
4. Gioacchino Rossini.
5. Three.
6. *Buddenbrooks*.

## 37

1. Who wrote 'Wild Thing' for The Troggs and 'Angel of the Morning' for Merrilee Rush?
2. How many dancers did Zach want in *Chorus Line*?
3. Which virtuoso pianist once arranged the *William Tell* Overture for thirty-two hands on eight pianos?
4. Which play did Verdi intend for his fourth Shakespearean opera after *Macbeth, Otello* and *Falstaff*?
5. Who was the original 'Ta-ra-ra-boom-de-ay' girl?
6. Musical instruments are classed as chordophones, membraphones, aerophones and which other category?

## 113

1. Which rock guitarist failed an audition to join The Monkees because of his teeth?
2. Which film-maker, adapted Beethoven's Sixth Symphony for one of his films, saying, 'Gee, this'll make Beethoven'?
3. Which composer heard the Devil trill?
4. Which opera since the Revolution has been known in Russia as *Ivan Susanin*?
5. Which famous Canadian clarinettist is also a cartoonist for two British newspapers?
6. How many fiddlers did Old King Cole call for?

## 189

1. Who was called 'the Thin White Duke'?
2. Which golfing song features in *Bridge on the River Kwai*?
3. Which famous jazzman commissioned works from Bartók, Copland and Hindemith?
4. Which composer was nicknamed 'Signor Crescendo'?
5. Which jazzman was 'happy on the shelf' with 'no one to talk to but myself'?
6. What was a 'Waltzing Matilda'?

## 37

1. Chip Taylor.
2. Eight.
3. Karl Czerny.
4. *King Lear*.
5. Lottie Collins.
6. Idiophones (percussion).

## 113

1. Stephen Stills.
2. Walt Disney (*Fantasia*).
3. Giuseppe Tartini (Violin Sonata in G minor).
4. *A Life for the Tsar* (Glinka).
5. Wally Fawkes ('Trog').
6. Three.

## 189

1. David Bowie.
2. 'Colonel Bogie'.
3. Benny Goodman.
4. Gioacchino Rossini.
5. Fats Waller ('Ain't Misbehavin'').
6. An Australian swagman's knapsack.

## 38

1. Who cuts himself with broken glass on stage and recorded an album called *The Idiot*?
2. Shakespeare's *The Comedy of Errors* provided the plot for which Rodgers and Hart musical?
3. Which of Beethoven's contemporary composers was a torchbearer at his funeral?
4. What was Tosca's first name?
5. Who played sax on the 1964 hit 'Girl From Ipanema'?
6. Which instrument did Sir Thomas Beecham describe as 'two skeletons copulating on a galvanized tin roof'?

## 114

1. Who was the first Briton to win the Eurovision Song Contest?
2. Rusty, Belle, Electra, Joule, Volta and Greaseball are all in which show?
3. How many of Schubert's symphonies were unfinished?
4. In which opera is the heroine almost executed for a crime committed by a bird?
5. What was a 'tickler'?
6. Who was the 'Daring Young Man on the Flying Trapeze'?

## 190

1. Whose bare feet on a zebra crossing fuelled a 1969 rumour that he was dead?
2. In which film did Julie Andrews play Gertrude Lawrence?
3. Which composer was an avid train-spotter and pigeon-fancier?
4. Which operatic courtesan was converted by a monk who died for love of her?
5. In which Harlem night-club was bebop music born?
6. What did Johann Nepomuk Maelzel do for music?

## 38

1. Iggy Pop.
2. *The Boys From Syracuse.*
3. Franz Schubert.
4. Floria.
5. Stan Getz.
6. The harpsichord.

## 114

1. Sandie Shaw (with 'Puppet On a String').
2. *Starlight Express.*
3. Three (Nos. 7, 8 and 10).
4. *The Thieving Magpie* (Rossini).
5. A jazz piano player.
6. Léotard.

## 190

1. Paul McCartney's (on the sleeve of *Abbey Road*).
2. *Star!*
3. Anton Dvořák.
4. Thaïs (Massenet).
5. Minton's Playhouse.
6. He invented the metronome (1814).

## 39

1. Which band had a hit with Khachaturian's *Sabre Dance*?
2. What is the name of the fictitious impresario in whose theatre Sondheim's *Follies* takes place?
3. Which of 'Beethoven's' symphonies was not by him?
4. Which Mozart opera parodies two prima donnas?
5. Which 1955 Frank Sinatra album resulted from his break-up with Ava Gardner?
6. 'God Bless the Prince of Wales' is the official tune of which of Her Majesty's forces?

## 115

1. Who is Peggy Seeger's singing daughter?
2. What is the Hollywood connection between Shirley MacLaine and Puccini?
3. Which author inspired Stravinsky's *Le Baiser de la Fée*?
4. What was the name of 'Il Trovatore'?
5. Who in 1954 asked 'How Do You Speak To An Angel'?
6. Which royal musical establishment under Richard III sent press-gangs out to kidnap choristers from other choirs?

## 191

1. Mott the Hoople's first hit single, 'All the Young Dudes', was written for them by which star performer?
2. Which show originally starred its author, with Zena Dare, and was later filmed with Anna Neagle and Errol Flynn?
3. Which eighteenth-century composer's wife used to line her pastry tins with his manuscripts?
4. Which opera, based on the 1647 revolution in Naples, sparked off another revolution in Brussels in 1830?
5. Who is 'Ol' Blue Eyes'?
6. In the law of which empire was it written, 'If any person has sung or composed . . . a song such as was causing slander or insult to another, he shall be clubbed to death'?

# 39

1. Love Sculpture.
2. Dimitri Weisman.
3. The *Jena* Symphony.
4. *The Impresario.*
5. *In the Wee Small Hours.*
6. The Royal Air Force.

# 115

1. Kirsty MacColl.
2. The movie *My Geisha.*
3. Hans Christian Andersen (*The Ice Maiden*).
4. Manrico.
5. Dean Martin.
6. The Chapel Royal.

# 191

1. David Bowie.
2. *King's Rhapsody* (Ivor Novello).
3. Joseph Haydn's.
4. *The Dumb Girl of Portici* (Auber).
5. Frank Sinatra.
6. The Roman (*The Twelve Tables*, 449 B.C.).

## 40

1. Who once appeared on stage in a fox's head and red gown, and later dressed as a flower?
2. Whose last starring role coincided with Yul Brynner's first in Broadway's *The King and I*?
3. Of whom did Mendelssohn quip, 'He has many fingers but few brains'?
4. Who was the eponymous hero of *Louise*'s sequel?
5. Who sang the 'Bluebottle Blues' in 1956?
6. Which mute bird reputedly sings only when about to die?

## 116

1. For whom was 'Annie's Song' written?
2. Who were 'The Waiter, the Porter and the Upstairs Maid' in the 1941 movie *The Birth of the Blues*?
3. For whom did Verdi compose his *Requiem*?
4. Which one-act, one-character 'tragedie lyrique' dramatizes a telephone conversation?
5. What did 'every little breeze seem to whisper' to a lip-jutting Parisian?
6. Which piece of music did E. M. Forster describe in *Howard's End* as 'the most sublime noise that has ever penetrated into the ear of man'?

## 192

1. Which was the first rock band to appear in the Proms?
2. Peter Sellers sang which film title song with The Hollies?
3. Which major Baroque composer's entire output runs to only six opus numbers?
4. Which opera did Sullivan have to re-compose in New York, having left all the music back in England?
5. Which fat blues shouter was called 'Mr Five By Five'?
6. Which Greek philosopher invented the monochord to show the mathematical relationship between different notes?

# 40

1. Peter Gabriel.
2. Gertrude Lawrence's.
3. Franz Liszt.
4. Julien (Charpentier).
5. The Goons.
6. The swan.

# 116

1. John Denver's wife.
2. Bing Crosby, Jack Teagarden and Mary Martin.
3. Alessandro Manzoni.
4. *La Voix Humaine* (Poulenc).
5. 'Louise' (Chevalier).
6. Beethoven's Fifth Symphony.

# 192

1. Soft Machine (1970).
2. 'After the Fox'.
3. Arcangelo Corelli's.
4. *The Pirates of Penzance*.
5. Jimmy Rushing.
6. Pythagoras.

# 41

1. Who was the 'Glossy-Lipped Golden Girl of Pop'?
2. Which conductor co-starred with Mickey Mouse?
3. Who was the 'hero' in Richard Strauss's *Ein Heldenleben*?
4. Where did the world première of *Aïda* take place?
5. Who fought Bing Crosby in 'the Battle of the Baritones'?
6. Which Hawaiian instrument's name translates as 'flea'?

# 117

1. Who got his name from his black-and-yellow-striped jersey and sang Binnie Hale's motto song for Denis Potter?
2. Which Ingmar Bergman film inspired *A Little Night Music*?
3. Which popular sixteenth-century song, used in a number of mass settings, contained the words, 'Christ, if my love were in my armes/And I in my bedde again'?
4. Which Puccini heroine plays poker to save her tenor's life?
5. Which composer's first published song was Sophie Tucker's 1916 hit, 'When You Want 'Em, You Can't Get 'Em, When You've Got 'Em, You Don't Want 'Em'?
6. Which brass instrument does the performer have to get inside to play?

# 193

1. Who was the composer of 'Good Vibrations' who after listening to a Beethoven symphony said, 'I've just realized I'm a musical midget'?
2. Whose first screen test assessment ran, 'Can't act, can't sing. Slightly bald. Can dance a little'?
3. Which 'decomposed' composer's music was 're-composed' by Stravinsky in *Pulcinella*?
4. By which dancing marauders was Prince Igor captured?
5. Who was the most famous of Whiteman's 'Rhythm Boys'?
6. What are song-posts?

## 41

1. Kathy Kirby.
2. Leopold Stokowski (*Fantasia*).
3. Strauss himself.
4. Cairo.
5. Russ Colombo.
6. The ukelele.

## 117

1. Sting ('Spread a Little Happiness').
2. *Smiles of a Summer Night*.
3. 'Western Wynde'.
4. Minnie (*La Fanciulla del West*).
5. George Gershwin's.
6. The sousaphone.

## 193

1. Brian Wilson (The Beach Boys).
2. Fred Astaire's.
3. Giovanni Pergolesi's.
4. The Polovtsians (Borodin).
5. Bing Crosby.
6. Birds' territorial singing positions.

## 50

1. Who sings 'Like a Bat Out of Hell'?
2. 'September Song' comes from which Kurt Weill show?
3. In honour of which conductor was the NBC Symphony Orchestra created in 1937?
4. Which Janáček heroine is 337 years old?
5. Which singer had a hit with 'Stormy Weather' before becoming Mrs Lennie Hayton?
6. Which American saxophonist has recorded duets between himself and animals in the wild?

## 126

1. Who was 'Pearl' on the 1971 album *Pearl*?
2. In which 1979 movie is a napalm attack accompanied by *The Ride of the Valkyries*?
3. What was Karl von Dittersdorf's middle name?
4. By which of his librettists was Debussy once challenged to a duel?
5. Whose 1944 hit was 'Is You Is Or Is You Ain't Ma Baby?'?
6. Which Goons number has Prince Charles admitted to being the only song he knows by heart?

## 202

1. Who was the subject of Eric Clapton's 'Layla'?
2. Which song was Doris Day singing in *The Man Who Knew Too Much*?
3. Who finished Mahler's unfinished Tenth Symphony?
4. With which famous ballet did Puccini's first opera, *Le Villi*, share its plot?
5. Who was the 'Down Yonder Girl', 'Queen of the Ragtime Pianists'?
6. Which nation's anthem has also been that of America, Austria, Ireland, Prussia, Sweden and Switzerland?

# 50

1. Meat Loaf.
2. *Knickerbocker Holiday*.
3. Arturo Toscanini.
4. Emilia Marty (*The Makropulos Affair*).
5. Lena Horne.
6. Paul Winter.

# 126

1. Janis Joplin.
2. *Apocalypse Now*.
3. Ditters.
4. Maurice Maeterlinck.
5. Louis Jordan's.
6. The 'Ying Tong Song'.

# 202

1. Patti Boyd (whom he married).
2. 'Que Será, Será'.
3. Deryck Cooke.
4. *Giselle*.
5. Del Wood.
6. Britain's.

## 51

1. Who was Marie Lawrie of The Luvvers?
2. Which 1965 musical is about a Brooklyn girl's struggle to give up smoking?
3. Which ballet was based on Charles Perrault's 'La Belle au Bois Dormant'?
4. In which opera would you see an auto-da-fé?
5. In whose band did 'O'Briens and Ryans and Sheehans and Meehans and Hennessy Tennessee play'?
6. At what time is the *Last Post* sounded in British Army barracks?

## 127

1. Who 'Did It My Way' but 'killed a cat' in the process?
2. *Lilac Time* featured whose life and music?
3. Whose *Seven Last Words* did Haydn set to music?
4. In which composer's 1740 masque *Alfred* did 'Rule Britannia' bring the house down?
5. Whose is 'the face in the misty light' ( – 'she gave your very first kiss to you')?
6. How would you respond if instructed to play *minaccevolmente*?

## 203

1. Under what names did Salvatore Bono and Cherilyn Sarkasian become famous?
2. One member of which folk group composed the music for the 1975 Stanley Kubrick film *Barry Lyndon*?
3. Which composer's First Symphony did Hans von Bülow dub 'Beethoven's Tenth'?
4. Who was 'the Swedish Nightingale'?
5. Which English jazz singer is famous for falling off the stage at the end of his rendition of 'Frankie and Johnnie'?
6. 'Of all noises' who thought 'music the least disagreeable'?

## 51

1. Lulu.
2. *On a Clear Day You Can See Forever.*
3. *Sleeping Beauty.*
4. *Don Carlos* (Verdi).
5. 'Macnamara's Band'.
6. 10 p.m.

## 127

1. Sid Vicious.
2. Franz Schubert's.
3. *Our Saviour*'s (*From the Cross*).
4. Thomas Arne's.
5. 'Laura's'.
6. Menacingly.

## 203

1. Sonny and Cher.
2. The Chieftains.
3. Johannes Brahms's.
4. Jenny Lind.
5. George Melly.
6. Samuel Johnson.

## 52

1. Which MP appeared with Tracy Ullman on video?
2. Who played the piano for Roger Daltrey in *Lisztomania*?
3. The 1887 concert-overture *The Land of the Mountain and the Flood* was an evocation of which country?
4. Who was Verdi's 'Bismarck of music criticism'?
5. What is the name 'Satchmo' short for?
6. What is an epithalamium?

## 128

1. Which singer had four consecutive hits with 'Hold Me', 'Together', 'Somewhere' and 'I Apologize'?
2. Which Irving Berlin musical satirized Washington hostess Pearl Mesta?
3. Which three towns host the Three Choirs Festival?
4. Which Franco-Italian heroine dies on the shores of Louisiana?
5. Against which 'Prowling Prude' did Winston Churchill defend the music hall's 'Ladies of the Promenade'?
6. What kind of song is the Italian *ninna-nanna, ninnarella*?

## 204

1. Rick Wakeman and pop duo Hudson-Ford played together in which folk-rock group?
2. Which British musical united Keith Waterhouse and Michael Crawford?
3. Which libertine English composer was noted by the Archbishop of Canterbury for being 'as famous for marrying of virginity as for fingering of organs and virginals'?
4. Which hoydenish heroine dies in an avalanche?
5. Who was the 'Man Who Broke the Bank at Monte Carlo'?
6. In which street was London's Tin Pan Alley?

## 52

1. Neil Kinnock.
2. David Wilde.
3. Scotland (Hamish McCunn).
4. Eduard Hanslick.
5. 'Satchel Mouth' (Louis Armstrong).
6. A wedding hymn.

## 128

1. P. J. Proby.
2. *Call Me Madam*.
3. Gloucester, Hereford and Worcester.
4. Manon Lescaut (Puccini).
5. Mrs Ormiston Chant.
6. A cradle song.

## 204

1. The Strawbs.
2. *Billy*.
3. John Bull.
4. 'La Wally' (Catalani).
5. Charles Coburn.
6. Denmark Street.

## 53

1. Which Brontë novel was given a boost by Kate Bush?
2. To whose voice did Rita Hayworth lip-synch 'Put the Blame on Mame' in the 1946 movie *Gilda*?
3. Who was the industry's first record producer who committed much of Edward Elgar's music to disc?
4. Which opera had such an effect on Emma Bovary that it 'sent a vibration . . . through her whole being, as if the bows of the violins were being drawn across her nerves'?
5. 'When Cootie Left the Duke', who left whom?
6. Which king of England was a renowned troubadour?

## 129

1. How many Beatles were there altogether?
2. In which 1938 musical did Judy Garland sing 'Zing, Went the Strings of My Heart'?
3. Who thought 'the goose is a most inconvenient bird, too much for one and not enough for two'?
4. Which Bizet operetta has an 'Omelette Quartet'?
5. Stan Kenton composed *Homage to the Princess* for whom?
6. What is a bumbass?

## 205

1. Which original Roxy's middle names are Peter George St John de Baptiste de la Salle?
2. Who was the former child star who played Mrs Chipping in the 1969 re-make of *Goodbye Mr Chips*?
3. What, in sixteenth-century music, was a salad?
4. Which Rossini opera on its first performance ran from 7 p.m. until one o'clock in the morning?
5. Which popular songwriter could 'only play on the black notes' – in F# major?
6. Which music degree is in the gift of the Primate of the Church of England?

# 53

1. *Wuthering Heights* (Emily Brontë).
2. Anita Ellis's.
3. Fred Gaisberg.
4. *Lucia di Lammermoor*.
5. Cootie Williams left Duke Ellington.
6. Richard I.

# 129

1. Six (Pete Best, George Harrison, John Lennon, Paul McCartney, Ringo Starr and Stu Sutcliffe).
2. *Listen, Darling*.
3. George Frideric Handel.
4. *Doctor Miracle*.
5. Princess Grace of Monaco.
6. A bladder and string instrument.

# 205

1. Brian Eno's.
2. Petula Clark.
3. A macaronic (multi-lingual) choral piece.
4. *William Tell*.
5. Irving Berlin.
6. The 'Lambeth' or Canterbury degree.

## 54

1. Who was the inspirational 'Great Beast' in whose house Jimmy Page of Led Zeppelin lives?
2. In which 1954 film did Kay Kendall play the trumpet?
3. Of which composer did Ambroise Thomas exclaim, 'This is not a woman composer, but a composer-woman!'?
4. What are the names of Turandot's three ministers?
5. Who in 1953 'Saw Mommy Kissing Santa Claus'?
6. To which opera does the hero of Iris Murdoch's *The Black Prince* go?

## 130

1. Who was treated for rabies in 1981 after biting off the head of a bat during a performance?
2. Who stripped while singing 'Take It Off the E-String, Play It On the G-String' in *Striptease Lady*?
3. Which pianist-composer's *Ocean* Symphony did Mussorgsky describe as 'a puddle'?
4. Which operetta has also been presented as *Champagne Sec, The Merry Countess* and *A Wonderful Night*?
5. What will happen 'When the Swallows Come Back to Capestrano'?
6. Who were the nine choristers of the Delphic Oracle?

## 206

1. Whose brother was Peter of Peter and Gordon?
2. In which Broadway hit did an American diplomat (male) fall in love with an English aristocrat (male) in Paris?
3. Which twelve-tone composer vainly hoped that his music would one day 'be whistled in the street by errand boys'?
4. How many Valkyries are there at the end of *Die Walküre*?
5. Of which dance did Eartha Kitt sing, 'You've just got to stand there and just sort of do it'?
6. Who wrote the words of 'Come Into the Garden, Maud'?

## 54

1. Aleister Crowley.
2. *Genevieve*.
3. Cécile Chaminade.
4. Ping, Pang and Pong.
5. Jimmy Boyd.
6. *Der Rosenkavalier*.

## 130

1. Ozzy Osbourne.
2. Barbara Stanwyck.
3. Anton Rubinstein's.
4. *Die Fledermaus*.
5. 'That's the day you promised to come back to me'.
6. The Muses.

## 206

1. Jane Asher's.
2. *Boy Meets Boy*.
3. Arnold Schoenberg.
4. Eight.
5. 'The New Fangled Tango'.
6. Alfred Lord Tennyson.

## 55

1. Who does hand-stands on his piano keyboard?
2. Who played Pink in *The Wall*?
3. Which orchestra has its home in the Severance Hall?
4. In which inn does Offenbach's Périchole dine too well?
5. Which much-married American bandleader wrote a book called *I Love You, I Hate You, Drop Dead*?
6. Which Thracian king sang and played the lyre with such art that savage beasts and even trees would follow him?

## 131

1. In which Irish rock band does 'The Edge' play?
2. In which 1971 film did Peter O'Toole sing 'Dry Bones'?
3. Whose *Miserere*, closely guarded by the Vatican, was 'stolen' by the boy Mozart who memorized and reproduced it after only one hearing?
4. Which golden-voiced Spanish soprano's first job was in a handkerchief factory?
5. Which heart-throb singer of 'In a Shady Nook By a Babbling Brook' was in 1949 feared 'to have an unhealthy effect on young girls'?
6. Which Communist state's national anthem is 'Arise! We Are Slaves No Longer'?

## 207

1. Which Seventies band took its name from a dildo in William Burroughs's novel *Naked Lunch*?
2. *Divorce Me, Darling* was the sequel to which pastiche?
3. Which ballet is subtitled 'the Wilis'?
4. A chicken and pasta dish is named after which diva who for charity once went up in a biplane and sang a high C?
5. At which cabaret star's funeral in 1926 did the mourners sing 'Bye, Bye Blackbird'?
6. What was the name of Galileo's composer father?

# 55

1. Elton John.
2. Bob Geldof.
3. The Cleveland Orchestra.
4. The Three Cousins.
5. Artie Shaw.
6. Orpheus.

# 131

1. U2.
2. *The Ruling Class.*
3. Gregorio Allegri's.
4. Monserrat Caballé's.
5. Donald Peers.
6. The People's Republic of China.

# 207

1. Steely Dan.
2. *The Boy Friend.*
3. *Giselle* (Adam).
4. Luisa Tetrazzini.
5. Florence Mills's.
6. Vincenzo Galilei.

## 56

1. Which Beatle's pseudonym was adopted by the Ramones?
2. Which 1909 musical brought nymphs and shepherds to the races?
3. *In the South* of which country did Elgar compose his concert overture?
4. Which Scots-American diva had her *Salome* banned by Chicago police as 'an affront to public morality'?
5. Which of the Hoboken Four first found fame with Tommy Dorsey?
6. Which Reformation leader did not see why 'the Devil should have all the best tunes'?

## 132

1. Which London country music band is fronted by a practising family-planning doctor?
2. In which adaptation of a novel by a nine-year-old did Alfred Marks star in 1969?
3. Who was brought up at Esterháza, taught by Salieri, kissed by Beethoven and ordained in St Peter's, Rome?
4. In which opera does the tenor bear 40,000 children?
5. Of whom did Duke Ellington say, 'he played piano like one of those high-school teachers in Washington'?
6. Neither English nor a horn, what is an English horn?

## 208

1. How many are the Thompson Twins?
2. What does M*A*S*H stand for?
3. Of which orchestral work did its composer state that its principal theme '"goes" but is not played'?
4. How many operas did Robert Schumann write?
5. How many notes are played on possibly the world's shortest single, Les Paul's 'Magic Melody Part Two'?
6. What kind of song did Venetian gondoliers sing?

# 56

1. Paul McCartney's ('Phil Ramone' of The Silver Beatles).
2. *The Arcadians*.
3. Italy (Alassio).
4. Mary Garden.
5. Frank Sinatra.
6. Martin Luther.

# 132

1. Hank Wangford.
2. *The Young Visiters*.
3. Franz Liszt.
4. *Les Mamelles de Tiresias*.
5. Jelly Roll Morton.
6. An oboe.

# 208

1. Three.
2. Mobile Army Surgical Hospital.
3. The *Enigma Variations* (Edward Elgar).
4. One (*Genoveva*).
5. Two.
6. The barcarolle.

## 57

1. Which band covered 'I Fought the Law' but was arrested for shooting prize pigeons?
2. As which character did Bing Crosby sing 'Too-ra-loo-ra-loo-ral' in *Going My Way*?
3. Which composer wrote 'Songs Without Words'?
4. Which composer, during a rehearsal with the intransigent diva Cuzzoni, threatened to throw her out of the window?
5. Whose wife's phone number was 'Pennsylvania 6-5000'?
6. Which Pope is a patron saint of music?

## 133

1. Who was the 'Black Elvis' who in 1967 set his guitar on fire during a concert?
2. Who was Pete Townsend's first choice to sing the Acid Queen in *Tommy* before Tina Turner?
3. Who is Nicola LeFanu's mother, also a composer?
4. What was the title of Wagner's first opera?
5. Who wrote the lyrics for 'I Wished On the Moon'?
6. Which of Jane Austen's heroines said, 'If I give up music, I shall take up carpet work'?

## 209

1. Which album was Marvin Gaye ordered to make in 1976 by an alimony-court judge?
2. In the making of which 1972 biopic did Diana Ross refuse to lip-synch to old recordings?
3. Which romantic piano piece was adapted by Diaghilev's Russian Ballet in *La Spectre de la Rose*?
4. Which prima donna wrote a short story about Richard Strauss playing skat in heaven?
5. Which Harry Lauder song did Churchill play incessantly during the Second World War to keep his spirits up?
6. Which James M. Cain thriller has an operatic setting?

## 57

1. The Clash.
2. Father Chuck O'Malley.
3. Felix Mendelssohn.
4. George Frideric Handel.
5. Glenn Miller's.
6. Pope Gregory the Great.

## 133

1. Jimi Hendrix.
2. Tiny Tim.
3. Elizabeth Maconchy.
4. *Die Feen* (The Fairies).
5. Dorothy Parker.
6. Emma Woodhouse.

## 209

1. *Here, My Dear*.
2. *Lady Sings the Blues*.
3. *Invitation to the Waltz* (Weber).
4. Lotte Lehmann.
5. 'Keep Right On to the End of the Road'.
6. *Serenade*.

# 42

1. Which actor played Biggles on TV then launched a pop career with 'Johnnie, Remember Me'?
2. Which show celebrated the American Bicentennial?
3. Which chamber music ensemble carries its own performance hall around with it on tour?
4. In Donizetti's comic opera, what is 'L'Elisir d'Amore'?
5. What was the 'Yellow Dog' in W. C. Handy's 'Yellow Dog Blues'?
6. On whose radio show *'Ave a Go* did Violet Carson play the piano before going on to *Coronation Street*?

# 118

1. Which Moody Blues album took its title from a mnemonic for the lines of the treble stave?
2. Which Broadway heroine had a cold for fourteen years?
3. Which composer wrote in his diary, 'I have played over the music of that scoundrel Brahms. What a giftless bastard!'?
4. Who was the playwright of *The Barber of Seville*, in which a character says, 'That which is not worth saying is sung'?
5. Which British jazz singer collects surrealist art?
6. What was the official full name of the wartime troupe who brought the troops 'Every Night Something Awful'?

# 194

1. Why does Roy Orbison wear dark glasses?
2. Which Broadway hit, advertised as 'The musical of the Eighties', was set in Motown?
3. Which composer thought that 'the best music results from ecstasies of logic'?
4. Which soprano, smelling liquor on Caruso's breath during a recording of *Madam Butterfly*, sang 'he had a highball' instead of 'si per la vita'?
5. What was the title of the Great War 'stuttering song'?
6. Who wrote the words of 'Drink to Me Only'?

# 42

1. John Leyton.
2. *1776*.
3. Domus (a geodesic dome).
4. Cheap wine.
5. The Yazoo Delta Railroad.
6. Wilfred Pickles's.

# 118

1. *Every Good Boy Deserves Favour*.
2. Miss Adelaide (*Guys and Dolls*).
3. Pyotr Tchaikovsky.
4. Pierre-Augustin de Beaumarchais.
5. George Melly.
6. Entertainments National Services Association (ENSA).

# 194

1. Because he is cross-eyed.
2. *Dreamgirls*.
3. Alban Berg.
4. Geraldine Farrar.
5. 'K-K-K-Katy' ('the only g-g-g-girl that I adore').
6. Ben Jonson.

## 43

1. Who began his singing career dressed as a clown?
2. Who were satirized as the Swiss Family Whittlebott in Noël Coward's 1922 revue, *London Calling*?
3. For which now obsolete instrument did Haydn compose?
4. What nationality were Bizet's Pearl Fishers?
5. Who, 'Up in Harlem at a table for two', complained, 'Your pedal extremities really are obnoxious?
6. With which tune does the British Army bid farewell?

## 119

1. Which Charles Dickens-inspired band's first album was called *Very 'eavy, Very 'umble*?
2. Which song, written for a singing-lesson scene, became one of Noël Coward's biggest hits?
3. Which song, alluding to empty bottles under the tables, gave its title to a book by Bernard van Dieren?
4. Of which Italian opera was there a Victorian parody entitled *The Roof Scrambler*?
5. Who sang like Sinatra on 'Songs for Swinging Sellers"?
6. What do 'hairpins' mean to musicians?

## 195

1. Who wrote 'Twisting the Night Away' and 'Bring it on Home to Me', and was Rod Stewart's favourite singer?
2. Which sultry beauty was the original 'Maid of the Mountains' and subsequently Nell Gwynne?
3. What was Salieri's Christian name?
4. Which German Romantic opera was set to a libretto by the English dramatist, J. R. Planché?
5. What is it that 'the Japanese don't care to' and 'the Chinese wouldn't dare to' do?
6. What kind of instrumentalist would use a 'high hat'?

## 43

1. Leo Sayer.
2. The Sitwells (Edith, Osbert and Sacheverell).
3. The baryton.
4. Ceylonese.
5. Fats Waller ('Your Feet's Too Big').
6. 'The Girl I Left Behind Me'.

## 119

1. Uriah Heep's.
2. 'I'll See You Again'.
3. 'Down Among the Dead Men.'
4. *La Sonnambula* (Bellini).
5. Matt Monro.
6. *Crescendo* and *decrescendo*.

## 195

1. Sam Cooke.
2. José Collins.
3. Antonio.
4. *Oberon* (Weber).
5. 'Go Out In the Midday Sun' ('Mad Dogs and Englishmen').
6. A drummer.

## 44

1. Who was travelling in a hearse when he first met Stephen Stills?
2. *Apocalypse Now* opens with which song?
3. How old was Sir Robert Mayer when he died in 1985?
4. Which Rossini heroine claims to be 'a viper' with a hundred tricks?
5. Who might have played 'Misterioso' 'Round Midnight'?
6. Which novelist preferred 'The Soldier's Lament' and 'The Yellow-Haired Laddie' to Haydn and Mozart?

## 120

1. Which Napoleon sang 'They're Coming to Take Me Away, Ha-Haaa!' in 1966?
2. With whose voice did Snow White sing 'Whistle While You Work' in Walt Disney's 1937 picture?
3. From which Bach cantata did Procul Harem derive their 1967 classical rock hit 'A Whiter Shade of Pale'?
4. Which London theatre was formerly the Royal English Opera House?
5. Which veteran 'Urban Folk' singer did the poet Carl Sandberg dub 'America's tuning fork'?
6. Which US comedian at the age of eighty-four had a hit in 1980 with 'I Wish I Was Eighteen Again'?

## 196

1. Which rock poet had a hit with a triangular single?
2. On which instrument did Bing Crosby accompany himself singing 'True Love' to Grace Kelly in *High Society*?
3. Which work did Elgar dedicate to Elizabeth II?
4. Which composer, according to Rossini, had 'beautiful moments but awful quarter hours'?
5. What was the subject of Fats Waller's 'Viper's Drag'?
6. Whose shofar band blew down the walls of Jericho?

## 44

1. Neil Young.
2. 'The End' (The Doors).
3. 105.
4. Rosina (*The Barber of Seville*).
5. Thelonious Monk.
6. Jane Austen.

## 120

1. Napoleon XIV.
2. Adriana Caselotti's.
3. *Wachet Auf.*
4. The Palace Theatre, Cambridge Circus.
5. Pete Seeger.
6. George Burns.

## 196

1. John Cooper Clarke ('¡Gimmix! Play Loud').
2. A concertina.
3. His *Nursery Suite* (in 1931, when she was five).
4. Richard Wagner.
5. Marijuana.
6. Joshua's.

# 45

1. Who played didgeridoo on Kate Bush's 'The Dreaming'?
2. For which film did Schoenberg compose his *Accompaniment to a Film Scene*?
3. For which instrument did Bach write his *Fiddle* Fugue?
4. Who thought that 'Wagner is evidently mad'?
5. Which pioneer trumpeter was tempted out of retirement in 1942 with a set of false teeth?
6. Which Roman nymph pined away for love of Narcissus?

# 121

1. Which band's 1984 best-selling first album made prominent use of the pink triangle?
2. What was the name of the Berlin night-club in which *Cabaret* opens?
3. What was the title of Arthur Honegger's 1924 evocation of a steam locomotive?
4. What did Iago believe in foremost in his 'Credo'?
5. Which ex-professional baseball player was turned on by 'Distant Drums'?
6. In which E. M. Forster novel is a game of tennis substituted for an erratic piano rendition of *Parsifal*?

# 197

1. Who in 1963 sang 'It's My Party' and went on to write lyrics for the movie *Fame*?
2. Who sang the *Butch Cassidy* hit theme song, 'Raindrops Keep Falling On My Head'?
3. Where do the accents go on Leos Janacek's name?
4. In which town in Japan is *Madam Butterfly* set?
5. Whose 'Hit and Miss' was the signature tune for BBC's *Juke Box Jury*?
6. In which kind of music does a performer continue to play, rather than stop, when he 'takes a break'?

## 45

1. Rolf Harris.
2. None (it is 'pure' film music).
3. The organ.
4. Hector Berlioz.
5. Bunk Johnson.
6. Echo.

## 121

1. Bronski Beat (*Age of Consent*).
2. The Kit-Kat Klub.
3. *Pacific 231*.
4. 'A cruel god'.
5. Jim Reeves.
6. *A Room With a View*.

## 197

1. Lesley Gore.
2. B. J. Thomas.
3. Leoš Janáĉek.
4. Nagasaki.
5. The John Barry Seven's.
6. Jazz.

## 46

1. Which ex-*Vogue* model put her 'Nipple to the Bottle'?
2. Which three movie queens are identified by their song from 1942's *Star Spangled Rhythm*, 'A Sweater, a Sarong and a Peek-a-Boo Bang'?
3. The choleric, melancholic, sanguine and which other did Carl Nielsen describe in his *Four Temperaments*?
4. What is the nickname of the diva Beverly Sills?
5. Whose theme tune was 'Flying Home'?
6. Which Jane Austen character thought 'music a very innocent diversion, and perfectly compatible with the profession of a clergyman'?

## 122

1. To what did Robert Zimmerman change his name in 1962?
2. Where was the film *Jazz on a Summer's Day* set?
3. Which composer wrote six 'Haydn' Quartets?
4. Of which opera is Chabrier's *Souvenirs de Munich* a skit?
5. Which song, brought back by British soldiers from the Crimean Wars, was a 1927 hit for Frank Crumit?
6. Which American newspaper editor wrote, 'There are only two kinds of music: German music and bad music'?

## 198

1. With which poem did Mick Jagger commemorate Brian Jones in Hyde Park in 1969?
2. Which German classic inspired *Cabin in the Sky*?
3. Which composer did Osbert Sitwell once describe as 'every inch the personification of Colonel Bogey'?
4. Three chairs, a cup, a tea-pot and an ottoman are characters in which French opera?
5. Whose old man was a dustman?
6. Which 1927 popular dance craze was inspired by Charles Lindbergh's pioneering transatlantic flight?

## 46

1. Grace Jones.
2. Paulette Goddard, Dorothy Lamour and Veronica Lake.
3. The phlegmatic.
4. 'Bubbles'.
5. Lionel Hampton's.
6. Mr Collins (*Pride and Prejudice*).

## 122

1. Bob Dylan.
2. Newport, Rhode Island.
3. Wolfgang Amadeus Mozart.
4. *Tristan und Isolde* (Wagner).
5. 'Abdul Abulbul Amir'.
6. H. L. Mencken.

## 198

1. Shelley's *Adonis*.
2. *Faust* (Goethe).
3. Edward Elgar.
4. *L'Enfant et les Sortilèges* (Ravel).
5. Lonnie Donegan's.
6. The 'Lindy Hop'.

## 47

1. What 'unprecedented' invitation was extended to The Platters in Italy in 1958?
2. In which 1968 musical did Barbra Streisand say, 'You think beautiful girls are going to stay in style forever?'?
3. How many symphonies did Wagner write?
4. A 1955 production of which Gilbert and Sullivan opera starred Lena Horne, Louis Armstrong and Eartha Kitt?
5. Whose was the first American band to play in Britain after a 22-year trade-union ban dating from 1934?
6. Which instrument did Chaucer's Miller play?

## 123

1. Who wrote 'We Are the World' for USA for Africa?
2. From which movie did the hit song 'Moon River' come?
3. Which Italian conductor did Sir Thomas Beecham refer to as 'the Military Bandmaster'?
4. Which seventeenth-century opera was written for Sir Josias Priest's Boarding School for Girls?
5. Who sang, 'If women like them like men like those then why don't women like me'?
6. For which TV theme tune did Ron Grainer ask the BBC sound workshop for sounds like 'windbubbles and clouds'?

## 199

1. Which band did Sid Vicious leave to join the Sex Pistols?
2. For which 1955 movie did Elmer Bernstein write the music, Shorty Rodgers play it and Frank Sinatra sing it?
3. What was the name of the renowned (now forgotten) nineteenth-century 'three-handed' pianist?
4. Which was Wagner's favourite opera?
5. Which singer in 1954 had a hit with 'Gilly Gilly Ossenfeffer Katzenellen Bogen By the Sea'?
6. What is a song of unrequited love called?

# 47

1. To an audience with the Pope (Pius XII).
2. *Funny Girl*.
3. One (in C).
4. *The Mikado*.
5. Stan Kenton's.
6. The bagpipes.

# 123

1. Michael Jackson and Lionel Richie.
2. *Breakfast at Tiffany's* (Henry Mancini).
3. Arturo Toscanini.
4. *Dido and Aeneas* (Purcell).
5. George Formby.
6. *Dr Who*.

# 199

1. Siouxsie and the Banshees.
2. *Man With the Golden Arm*.
3. Sigismond Thalberg.
4. *Norma* (Bellini).
5. Max Bygraves.
6. A torch song.

## 48

1. Which Radio One DJ featured in a 1979 Pretenders hit?
2. For which 1944 Ginger Rogers psychiatric comedy did Kurt Weill write the music?
3. Which composer gave J. S. Bach a Brazilian beat?
4. In which Shostakovich opera is the 'hero' nearly pickled in vodka and vinegar?
5. Which alto player got his nickname after the van in which he was touring ran over a chicken?
6. Which Greek musician, after rebuffing the Thracian women, had his head torn off by them?

## 124

1. Whose place in the Yardbirds was later taken by Eric Clapton, Jimmy Page and Jeff Beck respectively?
2. Who created the jazz soundtrack on *Last Tango in Paris*?
3. Which Elgar work was written for the 1912 Delhi Durbar?
4. Which mezzo-turned-soprano was once known as 'die schwarze Venus'?
5. Who wrote the 30s hit 'The Waltzing Game'?
6. What is the musical term for the instruction, 'go back to the beginning and start again'?

## 200

1. Which Dutch band regularly climaxed their performance with the drummer being catapulted over his drumkit?
2. From which classical source was drawn the story of *Seven Brides for Seven Brothers*?
3. What did Stravinsky write for Barnum and Bailey?
4. What were the destinations of Mr Brouček's Excursions?
5. Which American Civil War melody provided Vaughn Monroe with a hit in 1949?
6. What are lithophonic bells made out of?

## 48

1. David 'Kid' Jensen.
2. *Lady In the Dark.*
3. Heitor Villa-Lobos (*Bachianas Brasileiras*).
4. *The Nose.*
5. Charlie 'Bird' Parker.
6. Orpheus.

## 124

1. Anthony 'Top' Topham's.
2. Gato Barbieri.
3. *The Crown of India.*
4. Grace Bumbry.
5. Kurt Weill.
6. *Da capo.*

## 200

1. Golden Earring.
2. The Rape of the Sabine Women.
3. *Circus Polka* (*For a Young Elephant*).
4. To the moon and to the fifteenth century (Janáček).
5. 'When Johnny Comes Marching Home'.
6. Stone.

# 49

1. Who is Crystal Gayle's 'Coal Miner's Daughter' sister?
2. Which Walt Disney cartoon used Pearl Bailey and Louis Prima's voices?
3. To which symphony did the film score of *Scott of the Antarctic* give rise?
4. Which composer's music did Bill Nye assert was 'really better than it sounds'?
5. Which great trumpeter was turned on to jazz by a present from Gracie Fields of a gramophone and six records?
6. Which opera does Gogol's Government Inspector claim to have seen?

# 125

1. Who was the graffiti hero, subject of Pink Floyd's 'Shine On You Crazy Diamond' and 'Wish You Were Here'?
2. In which 1964 film did Anthony Quinn dance the sirtaki?
3. What kind of dance did Debussy's *Golliwog* do?
4. Which singer, overhearing Nellie Melba practising at the Savoy hotel, inquired of the manager, 'And how many cats have you in your lovely hotel?'?
5. Who wrote about life *Beneath the Underdog*?
6. In which country did the polka originate?

# 201

1. Who sang for The Buggles and Yes and now produces records for Frankie Goes to Hollywood?
2. Which South Sea islander is named after a cocktail?
3. Which Debussy work depicts a nymph who, fleeing from Pan, becomes a reed-bed from which he makes his pipe?
4. Which effervescent mezzo is known as 'Flicka'?
5. On 'the day that music died', who died along with Buddy Holly, ensuring the success of his only hit, 'Donna'?
6. Which historical event inspired 'Ring o' Ring o' Roses'?

## 49

1. Loretta Lynn.
2. *The Jungle Book*.
3. The *Sinfonia Antarctica* (Vaughan Williams).
4. Richard Wagner's.
5. Nat Gonella.
6. *The Marriage of Figaro*.

## 125

1. Syd Barrett.
2. *Zorba the Greek*.
3. The Cakewalk.
4. Luisa Tetrazzini.
5. Charlie Mingus.
6. Bohemia.

## 201

1. Trevor Horn.
2. Bloody Mary (*South Pacific*).
3. *Syrinx*.
4. Frederica von Stade.
5. Ritchie Valens.
6. The Great Plague.

## 58

1. Who, among Bryan Ferry, Keith Emerson, Hank B. Marvin and David Essex, is not a Geordie?
2. Which 1966 Joseph Losey film about a comic-strip heroine was scored by Johnny Dankworth and Benny Green?
3. Which German humorist made a cartoon version of Ravel's *L'Enfant et les Sortilèges*?
4. Which Victorian diva caused a scandal when she acquired from a freak show a midget named General Mite?
5. Whose daughter was 'a bit of an ugly duckling, you honestly must confess, And the width of her seat would surely defeat her chances of success'?
6. With which country is the *fado* associated?

## 134

1. Who is LKJ in the 1981 album *LKJ in Dub*?
2. In which Disney movie did 'Some Day My Prince Will Come' – 'the Kodak song' – appear?
3. Which composer's *Prometheus* called for a 'keyboard of light' to project colours onto a screen?
4. What are Tosca's last words?
5. Which Folies-Bergères star used to perform wearing a banana skirt and accompanied by two cheetahs?
6. In Greek myth, who had to win a musical contest with a satyr to affirm his supremacy as god of music?

## 210

1. What was the Liverpool football team's hit single called?
2. When did Yul Brynner sing 'Mad About the Boy' in drag?
3. Whose favourite musical instruction was '*nobilmente*'?
4. Which opera did Gilbert suggest be subtitled 'Not So Good as *The Mikado*'?
5. Which fascist dictator had a jazz pianist son?
6. What is the Welsh National Anthem?

## 58

1. David Essex.
2. *Modesty Blaise.*
3. Gerard Hoffnung.
4. Adelina Patti.
5. Mrs Worthington's.
6. Portugal.

## 134

1. Linton Kwesi Johnson.
2. *Snow White.*
3. Alexander Scriabin's.
4. 'O Scarpia, we meet before God'.
5. Josephine Baker.
6. Apollo.

## 210

1. 'We Can Do It'.
2. In the movie *The Magic Christian.*
3. Edward Elgar's.
4. *Ruddigore.*
5. Benito Mussolini.
6. 'Land of Our Fathers'.

## 59

1. Who received the Freedom of the City of London after giving a concert on the eve of Prince Charles's wedding?
2. 'White Christmas' was first sung in which 1942 movie?
3. Which composer wrote a Symphony No. 0?
4. What was Ponchielli's first name?
5. What aristocratic titles ennobled Joe Oliver, Edward Ellington, William Basie, and Billie Holiday?
6. Uncle Matthew in Nancy Mitford's *The Pursuit of Love* played which diva's recordings at the wrong speed?

## 135

1. What was the title of Terry Wogan's one and only hit?
2. Who dubbed Danny Kaye's trumpet in *The Five Pennies*?
3. Who spent *Evenings in the Orchestra*?
4. Which heroine's name does Tchaikovsky share with Gilbert and Sullivan?
5. On which classic blues number did Joe Stafford base her 1954 hit 'Make Love to Me'?
6. Which Greek philosopher designed a water-powered organ-clock which would play tunes every hour?

## 211

1. About which American band was there a Marvel Comic book reputedly printed in ink containing their blood?
2. Under what title is the soundtrack of the documentary film *The Instruments of the Orchestra* now known?
3. What distinction did Nicholas Staggins, John Eccles, Walter Parratt and Arnold Bax share?
4. Which Vaughan Williams heroine has deadly lips?
5. Where will you see the sun go down 'if you ever go across the sea to Ireland'?
6. Which American statesman's bear-hunting trip in 1904 inspired 'The Teddy Bear's Picnic'?

## 59

1. Mike Oldfield.
2. *Holiday Inn.*
3. Anton Bruckner.
4. Amilcare.
5. 'King', 'Duke', 'Count' and 'Lady' ('Lady Day').
6. Amelita Galli-Curci's.

## 135

1. 'Floral Dance'.
2. Red Nichols.
3. Hector Berlioz.
4. Iolanthe (Yolanta).
5. 'Tin Roof Blues'.
6. Plato.

## 211

1. Kiss.
2. *The Young Person's Guide to the Orchestra* (Britten).
3. Master of the King's Musick.
4. Tormentilla (*The Poisoned Kiss*).
5. Galway Bay.
6. Theodore Roosevelt's.

## 60

1. Which singer began his solo career in McDonald's hamburger commercials and later sang 'It's a Miracle'?
2. Which composer wrote the first-ever film score?
3. Which British conductor was known as 'Glorious John'?
4. Which of his operas did Wagner designate 'a stage-consecrating festival-play'?
5. Who was 'the Sentimental Gentleman of Swing'?
6. What kind of dance was the Black Bottom?

## 136

1. Who are 'the Glimmer Twins'?
2. Which Jerry Herman stage hit was set on a kibbutz?
3. Which J. S. Bach work was written to ease insomnia?
4. An aria from which opera is performed annually at the Remembrance Day Service at the Cenotaph in London?
5. Which songwriter, born within twenty-four hours of Gershwin in the same city (New York), also shared with him his lyricist, music publisher and Broadway producer?
6. How does a *gusla* differ from a *gusli*?

## 212

1. Which is Prince Charles's favourite singing group?
2. Which instruments did Jack Lemmon and Tony Curtis play in an all-girl orchestra in *Some Like It Hot*?
3. Which British conductor was nicknamed 'Flash Harry'?
4. Which composer, dubbed (inaccurately) by Stravinsky 'the Swiss Watchmaker', wrote an opera set in a clock shop?
5. Which country-rock singer was run out of Britain in 1958 for having married his thirteen-year-old cousin?
6. With his music for 'Dear Lord and Father of Mankind', who became the only British Prime Minister to be represented in the *English Hymnal*?

# A

## 60

1. Barry Manilow.
2. Camille Saint-Saëns (*L'Assassinat du Duc de Guise*, 1908).
3. Sir John Barbirolli.
4. *Parsifal.*
5. Tommy Dorsey.
6. A Fox-trot.

## 136

1. Mick Jagger and Keith Richard.
2. *Milk and Honey.*
3. The *Goldberg* Variations.
4. *Dido and Aeneas* (Purcell; 'Dido's Lament').
5. Vincent Youmans.
6. It has only one string.

## 212

1. The Three Degrees.
2. Double bass and saxophone.
3. Sir Malcolm Sargent.
4. Maurice Ravel (*L'Heure Espagnole*).
5. Jerry Lee Lewis.
6. W. E. Gladstone.

# 61

1. Whose wife were the Everly Brothers singing about in their 1958 hit 'Claudette'?
2. Who played the crooner in *The Godfather*?
3. What was Smetana's first name?
4. Before writing the libretto for William Walton's *Troilus and Cressida*, with which composer had Christopher Hassall collaborated?
5. Who was known as 'the Swooner Crooner'?
6. Which singer first sold a million records?

# 137

1. Before the Band-Aid single, which UK single sold most?
2. Which song did Mel Brooks and Anne Bancroft sing in Polish in *To Be Or Not To Be*?
3. A visit to which of Queen Victoria's palaces inspired Mendelssohn's *Scottish* Symphony?
4. Which Victorian singer during a vocal crisis was forbidden to speak – let alone sing – for an entire year?
5. Who is 'the Rhinestone Rubinstein'?
6. How many entries are there in *The New Grove Dictionary of Music and Musicians* (± 5000)?

# 213

1. Who in 1972 wanted to get on 'The Cover of the *Rolling Stone*' – and did?
2. In which film version of a Gilbert and Sullivan opera did Frankie Howerd star in 1962?
3. Whose *Marcia Pontificale* is the Vatican's anthem?
4. To which Britten opera did E. M. Forster contribute?
5. Who sang 'I Want to Be Loved By You' – 'boop-boop-a-doop' – thirty years before Marilyn Monroe did?
6. What was Wendy Carlos before she 'Switched-On Bach'?

# 61

1. Roy Orbison's (he wrote it).
2. Al Martino.
3. Bedřich.
4. Ivor Novello.
5. Frank Sinatra.
6. Enrico Caruso ('On With the Motley').

# 137

1. 'Mull of Kintyre' (Wings).
2. 'Sweet Georgia Brown'.
3. Holyrood.
4. Jenny Lind.
5. Wladziu Valentino Liberace.
6. 32,000.

# 213

1. Dr Hook.
2. *Cool Mikado*.
3. Charles Gounod's.
4. *Billy Budd*.
5. Helen Kane.
6. A man (Walter Carlos).

## 62

1. Who had a hit with a Bob Dylan song before he ever did?
2. Which song is playing, faultily, in the gramophone shop in *Penny Serenade* when Cary Grant meets Irene Dunn?
3. Which composer's piano teacher was called Mrs Tinkler?
4. Which Bulgarian Salome, even in a Salvador Dali production, insisted on wearing her own gown?
5. Which classical composer unwittingly gave Frank Sinatra his 1946 hit 'Full Moon and Empty Arms'?
6. Who brought about the 'Renaissance of the Celtic Harp'?

## 138

1. Who in 1962 sang 'The Theme From Dr Kildare'?
2. Which 1976 Martin Ritt film opens with 1950s newsreel footage and Sinatra singing 'Young at Heart'?
3. Which work is often referred to as 'Verdi's finest opera'?
4. Whose advice to Clara Butt, on repertoire for an Australian tour, was 'Sing 'em muck'?
5. Better known as 'The Rockin' Chair Lady', who was also one half of 'Mr and Mrs Swing'?
6. What is a 'Kaffir Piano'?

## 214

1. Who was Derek in Derek and the Dominos?
2. Faye Dunaway and Steve McQueen courted each other to which song in *The Thomas Crown Affair*?
3. Who was the composer of *Stars and Stripes* and author of memoirs entitled *Marching Along*?
4. In which French romantic opera is the heroine deep-fried?
5. Which music-hall star, adored by Oscar Wilde, Rodin and Cocteau, at seventy decided to retire when she forgot the words of her motto song, 'Mon Homme'?
6. Which song did Franklin D. Roosevelt adopt for his presidential campaign in 1932?

## 62

1. Peter, Paul and Mary ('Blowin' in the Wind').
2. 'You Were Meant For Me'.
3. Michael Tippett's.
4. Ljuba Welitsch.
5. Sergei Rachmaninov (Second Piano Concerto).
6. Alan Stivell.

## 138

1. Richard Chamberlain
2. *The Front.*
3. His *Requiem.*
4. Dame Nellie Melba's.
5. Mildred Bailey.
6. A marimba.

## 214

1. Eric Clapton.
2. 'Windmills Of Your Mind'.
3. John Philip Sousa.
4. *La Juive* (Halévy).
5. Mistinguette.
6. 'Happy Days Are Here Again'.

## 63

1. Which Muswell hillbillies were members of the Village Green Preservation Society?
2. Charlie Chaplin and Claire Bloom had a hit with the title theme from which 1953 movie?
3. Who is the audience in *Master Peter's Puppet Show*?
4. What was Janáček's 'Cunning Little Vixen's' name?
5. Which suave bandleader used to greet his ladyfriends with four kisses – 'one for each cheek'?
6. Which Jimmy McHugh song does Sally Bowles sing in Isherwood's novel *Goodbye to Berlin*?

## 139

1. Who had a 1974 hit with 'I Get a Kick Out Of You'?
2. In which musical does Lee Marvin sing?
3. The 1921 one-act ballet *The Newly-Weds of the Eiffel Tower* was written by how many French composers?
4. Of the five principals in Strauss's *Elektra*, how many survive the final, bloody scene?
5. Which jazz original was the subject of Dorothy Baker's novel *Young Man With a Horn*?
6. How many copies must an album sell to go titanium?

## 215

1. Who was the gravedigger enlisted by Rat Scabies after hearing him sing 'I Love the Dead' at his sister's funeral?
2. Which English novelist wrote the lyrics for the Jerome Kern hit shows *Oh, Boy!* and *Oh, Lady, Lady!*?
3. Which composer first wrote 'novelettes'?
4. Whose Newfoundland dog was Robber?
5. 'Kansas City style, with four heavy beats to the bar, and no cheatin' was which band leader's recipe for success?
6. In which country are single notes used therapeutically to treat organs of the body?

## 63

1. The Kinks.
2. *Limelight.*
3. Don Quixote (Falla).
4. Sharpears.
5. Duke Ellington.
6. 'Exactly Like You'.

## 139

1. Gary Shearston.
2. *Paint Your Wagon* ('Wandering Star').
3. Five (Auric, Honegger, Milhaud, Poulenc, Tailleferre).
4. Two (Chrysothemis on stage, Orestes off stage).
5. Bix Beiderbecke.
6. Three million.

## 215

1. Dave Vanian.
2. Pelham Grenville Wodehouse.
3. Robert Schumann (*Noveletten*).
4. Richard Wagner's.
5. Count Basie's.
6. China.

## 64

1. On which band's 1975 album *Commoner's Crown* did Peter Sellers play ukelele?
2. In which 1938 movie did Dick Powell sing to Olivia de Havilland, 'You Must Have Been a Beautiful Baby'?
3. Which Nordic saga inspired many of Sibelius's works?
4. Who inspired a recipe for 'Chicken "La Stupenda"'?
5. What did 'My Very Good Friend the Milkman' suggest?
6. Which folk tune was forbidden air-play during WWII as it was to be the D-Day signal to the French Resistance?

## 140

1. What was the title of the Monotones' doo wop classic derived from a Pepsodent toothpaste commercial?
2. What advice was given to the eponymous heroine of *Gypsy* by Miss Mazeppa, Tessie Tura and Electra?
3. What was the title of the first music book to be printed in England?
4. With which mystical opera was Massenet thought by the critics to be 'taking the road to Bayreuth'?
5. Who was 'His Highness of Hi-de-Ho'?
6. In a conventional orchestra, which instrument is capable of playing its highest note ($G^{v}$ or 7272 cycles)?

## 216

1. '. . .and nobody was gettin' fat 'cept' – who?
2. In which disastrous, one-performance adaptation of the *Odyssey* did Yul Brynner star?
3. What is an obstinate bass?
4. Which Spanish painter inspired an opera by Granados?
5. In which US city would you have found Andy Kirk's Twelve Clouds of Joy and Walter Page's Blue Devils?
6. Who were the sea-songstresses who charmed sailors to their corpse-littered island?

## 64

1. Steeleye Span's.
2. *Hard to Get.*
3. The *Kalevala.*
4. Joan Sutherland.
5. 'That you should marry me'.
6. 'Sur le Pont d'Avignon'.

## 140

1. 'Book of Love'.
2. 'You Gotta Get a Gimmick'.
3. *Parthenia* (maidenhood).
4. *Esclarmonde.*
5. Cab Calloway.
6. A handbell.

## 216

1. Mama Cass.
2. *Home, Sweet Homer.*
3. A repeated bass melody or rhythm.
4. Goya (*Goyescas*).
5. Kansas City.
6. The Sirens.

# Q

## 65

1. What does USA stand for in USA for Africa?
2. The show *Curley McDimple* spoofed whose career?
3. Which piano work depicts paintings of *A Polish Farm Cart, Unhatched Chickens* and *A Hut on Fowl's Legs*?
4. Which contemporary of Puccini also wrote a *La Bohème*?
5. Who were Slim and Slam, perpetrators of the 'Flat Foot Floogie'?
6. In what musical activity does one use a hammer, anvil and stirrup?

## 141

1. What do the Dutch band Focus, Frank Ifield and Slim Whitman have in common?
2. Who was the drummer on the soundtrack of the 1959 film *The Gene Krupa Story*?
3. In which of his works did William Walton use the tune, 'Oh, I Do Like to Be Beside the Seaside'?
4. As what is 'Ombra mai fu' in *Serse* better known?
5. Which Billy Strayhorn composition was based on a painting of London by Whistler?
6. When did the LP first become available?

## 217

1. Who says, 'We are Ninja (Not Geisha)'?
2. Which hit musical was almost called *My Lady Liza*?
3. Which symphony carries the subtitle, 'A Soviet Artist's Practical Creative Reply to Just Criticism'?
4. In what opera does *The Flight of the Bumble Bee* depict an insect-prince stinging his treacherous relatives?
5. What was unusual about Bix Beiderbecke's 1927 recording of 'In a Mist'?
6. Which animal, making a sound as loud as a four-engined jet a mile away, remains inaudible to humans?

## 65

1. United Support of Artists.
2. Shirley Temple's.
3. *Pictures at an Exhibition* (Mussorgsky).
4. Ruggiero Leoncavallo.
5. Slim Gaillard and Slam Stewart.
6. Listening (they are bones in the ear).

## 141

1. Yodelling.
2. Gene Krupa.
3. *Façade*.
4. Handel's *Largo*.
5. 'Chelsea Bridge'.
6. 1948.

## 217

1. Frank Chickens.
2. *My Fair Lady*.
3. Shostakovich's Fifth.
4. *The Tale of the Tsar Sultan* (Rimsky-Korsakov).
5. It was a piano solo.
6. A bat.

## 66

1. Who says he formed the band Modern Lovers 'because he was lonely'?
2. Which musical did Marvin Hamlisch and an ex-girlfriend write about themselves?
3. Which plainsong melody did Rachmaninov make use of in his *Rhapsody on a Theme of Paganini*?
4. Which Mozart opera was presented in Victorian times as *Les Mystères d'Isis*?
5. Which bandleader wrote a 'Concerto to end all Concertos'?
6. What is the earliest documented English song?

## 142

1. Which pop star in 1972 attended his own burial in the River Thames?
2. What was the unsuccessful sequel to *No, No, Nanette*?
3. Which Elgar work derived from a story by Algernon Blackwood and had in its scoring a wind machine?
4. Which singer, after a certain Dr Cazzaroti claimed that a diet of 'psychological macaroni' had aided her weight loss, sued the Pantanella pasta factory?
5. Which ragtime piano player, a hundred years old in 1983, attributed his longevity to never drinking water?
6. How many grooves does an average LP have?

## 218

1. Which country in 1958 banned rock and roll because it thought 'extreme gyrations' injurious to the hips?
2. When Adele retired, Fred Astaire went solo in *Gay Divorce* singing which Cole Porter hit?
3. One of whose works was written after he said to his publisher, 'I'd give my best quartet for a new razor'?
4. What was Verdi's other comic opera besides *Falstaff*?
5. In whose band were 'Bubber' and 'Tricky Sam'?
6. What was 'flicker music'?

## 66

1. Jonathan Richman.
2. *They're Playing Our Song* (Carole Bayer Sager).
3. The *Dies Irae.*
4. *Die Zauberflöte.*
5. Stan Kenton.
6. 'Sumer Is Icumen In'.

## 142

1. Gary Glitter.
2. *Yes, Yes, Yvette.*
3. *The Starlight Express.*
4. Maria Callas.
5. Eubie Blake.
6. Two (one on each side).

## 218

1. Iran.
2. 'Night and Day'.
3. Joseph Haydn's (*Razor* Quartet).
4. *Un Giorno di Regno.*
5. Duke Ellington's (Bubber Miley; Joe Nanton).
6. Music for silent films.

## 67

1. Which Radio One DJ refused to play 'Relax (Don't Do It)' and then did the voice-over for a TV ad for the album?
2. Who was 'The minx in mink with a yen for men'?
3. Mendelssohn's *Wedding March* comes from which work?
4. What is the name of Siegfried's sword?
5. Which female pianist had hits with 'Let's Have a Party', 'Let's Have Another Party' and 'Let's Have a Ding-Dong'?
6. Who wrote the theme music for *The Onedin Line*?

## 143

1. What was the title of Cliff Richard's first (1958) hit?
2. For which 1962 movie did Henry Mancini write 'The Walk of the Baby Elephants'?
3. For which melody is Johann Aegidius Schwartzendorf (a.k.a. Giovanni Martini) solely remembered today?
4. How many women did Don Giovanni seduce?
5. Which British jazz band leader's hit, 'In a Golden Coach', celebrated Queen Elizabeth II's coronation?
6. Who wrote, 'Music has charms to soothe a savage breast,/ To soften rocks, or bend a knotted oak'?

## 219

1. Whose 1972 album *Garden in the City* had a 'scratch 'n' sniff' sleeve?
2. Which rock 'n' roll singer-drummer once played the Artful Dodger in a production of *Oliver Twist*?
3. Which virtuoso was refused a Christian burial?
4. To whom is Norma's 'Casta Diva' addressed?
5. Who were the 'Gentlemen rankers out on a spree', whose lyrics were inspired by Rudyard Kipling?
6. Which major nineteenth-century novelist wrote a biography of a major nineteenth-century composer?

## 67

1. Mike Read.
2. Ginger Rogers.
3. *A Midsummer Night's Dream.*
4. Nothung.
5. Winifred Atwell.
6. Aram Khachaturian.

## 143

1. 'Move It'.
2. *Hatari!*
3. *Plaisir d'Amour.*
4. 2065.
5. Billy Cotton's.
6. William Congreve (*The Mourning Bride*).

## 219

1. Melanie's.
2. Phil Collins.
3. Niccolò Paganini.
4. The moon.
5. The Whiffenpoofs.
6. Stendhal (Rossini).

# 68

1. What did Carl and the Passions change their name to?
2. What is the title of the *M*A*S*H** theme tune?
3. In whose household did Haydn find that 'There was no one near to confuse me, so I was forced to become original'?
4. Which famous Marschallin, interviewed on *Desert Island Discs*, chose to be cast away with eight of her own records?
5. Whose fame grew on 'The Biggest Aspidistra in the World'?
6. What kind of singer was an *evirato*?

# 144

1. Who sang 'God Save the Queen' but were 'Pretty Vacant'?
2. In which 1933 movie did Fred and Ginger dance 'The Carioca' on seven white grand pianos?
3. What did the organists Cabezón, Bach, Handel and Widor have in common?
4. Whose 'elderly, ugly daughter' could 'pass for forty-five in the dusk with the light behind her'?
5. Who was 'The Fat Man' of the 1949 hit song?
6. Which of the Muses presides over the art of love songs – and a French record label?

# 220

1. What is a 'Jefferson airplane'?
2. Where in the land of Oz will your 'troubles melt like lemon drops away above the chimney tops'?
3. In which ballet is there a giant with green fingers who turns wayfarers into stone?
4. What is the sub-title of Mozart's *Il Dissoluto Punito*?
5. Whose 1930 hit was ''Fonso My Hot Spanish (K)Night'?
6. What was the Christian name of the 'Rose of Tralee'?

## 68

1. The Beach Boys.
2. 'Suicide is Painless'.
3. Prince Nikolaus Esterhazy's.
4. Elisabeth Schwarzkopf.
5. Gracie Fields's.
6. A castrato.

## 144

1. The Sex Pistols.
2. *Flying Down to Rio.*
3. They were, or went, blind.
4. The rich attorney's (in *Trial By Jury*).
5. Fats Domino.
6. Erato.

## 220

1. A split matchstick for holding a marijuana cigarette.
2. 'Somewhere Over the Rainbow'.
3. *The Firebird* (Stravinsky).
4. *Don Giovanni.*
5. Gracie Fields's.
6. Mary.

## 69

1. Which punk-rock star in 1977 sang 'Looking After No. 1' and at Christmas 1984 was looking after millions?
2. Which musical soundtrack holds the record for most weeks in both the UK and US album charts?
3. Which critic wrote, 'There are some sacrifices which should not be demanded twice of any man, and one of them is listening to Brahms's *Requiem*'?
4. Which great Italian Violetta once said, 'Nobody really sings in opera. They just make loud noises'?
5. Which blues singer, named after an African one-stringed guitar, played a square guitar?
6. What replaced 'Waltzing Matilda' as Australia's anthem?

## 145

1. Whose 1960 hit was 'Itsy Bitsy Teeny Weeny Yellow Polka Dot Bikini'?
2. Who played the piano in the film *Moonlight Sonata*?
3. What, in sixteenth-century music, were maggots?
4. Under what title is the opera *The Bat* better known?
5. With how many fingers of his left hand did Django Reinhardt play the guitar?
6. What is an erotikon?

## 221

1. Who played harmonica on Millie Small's 'My Boy Lollipop', and in 1979 asked 'Da Ya Think I'm Sexy'?
2. In which 1957 musical was Rita Hayworth 'Bewitched, Bothered and Bewildered'?
3. Who was Mendelssohn's philosopher grandfather?
4. Which Haydn opera waited 150 years for its première?
5. Who had the 'Wasted Life', the 'Empty Bed' and the 'Dirty No-Gooder's Blues'?
6. Which Italian instrument's name means 'little goose'?

## 69

1. Bob Geldof (Band Aid).
2. *The Sound of Music*.
3. George Bernard Shaw.
4. Amelita Galli-Curci.
5. Bo Diddley.
6. 'Advance, Australia Fair'.

## 145

1. Brian Hyland's.
2. Jan Paderewski.
3. Instrumental dances.
4. *Die Fledermaus*.
5. Three.
6. A love song.

## 221

1. Rod Stewart.
2. *Pal Joey*.
3. Moses Mendelssohn.
4. *Orfeo ed Euridice*.
5. Bessie Smith.
6. The ocarina.

# 70

1. What was Elvis Presley's twin brother called?
2. Beach Boy Dennis Wilson starred with James Taylor in which 1972 film?
3. Who in 1919 composed for Diaghilev a ballet based on pieces referred to by Rossini as his 'sins of old age'?
4. Which Puccini opera is based on Dante?
5. Which singer began life as Norma Deloris Egstrom?
6. Where in Dorset is found the phenomenon of 'musical sand', which at certain times 'sings' or 'moans'?

# 146

1. Who played a plastic saxophone with his group David Jones and the Lower Third?
2. Whose 'Tears Flowed Like Wine' in *The Big Sleep*?
3. Which orchestra was once the Goldsbrough Orchestra?
4. In Wolf-Ferrari's opera, what is *Susanna's Secret*?
5. 'The Blue of the Night' was whose motto song?
6. Which musical types did Sir Thomas Beecham describe as 'drooling, drivelling, doleful, depressing, dropsical drips'?

# 222

1. On which unusual instrument is Dusty Springfield a noted performer?
2. In which film did Dooley Wilson relive 'As Time Goes By'?
3. From which composer did George Bernard Shaw say he 'learnt to say important things in a conversational way'?
4. How many Covent Garden theatres have there been on its present site?
5. Who was the British child prodigy billed as 'Kid Krupa' who guested with the Glenn Miller band in 1942?
6. To which Arthur Sullivan tune did Tom Lehrer sing the entire table of chemical elements?

## 70

1. Jesse.
2. *Two Lane Blacktop.*
3. Ottorino Respighi (*La Boutique Fantasque*).
4. *Gianni Schicci.*
5. Peggy Lee.
6. Studland Bay.

## 146

1. David Bowie.
2. Lauren Bacall's.
3. The English Chamber Orchestra.
4. She smokes.
5. Bing Crosby's.
6. Critics.

## 222

1. The spoons ('but only Woolworth spoons').
2. *Play It Again, Sam.*
3. Mozart.
4. Three.
5. Victor Feldman.
6. 'The Modern Major-General'.

## 71

1. Whose song was Eric Clapton's 'I Shot the Sheriff'?
2. Which impressionist painter made it to Broadway?
3. Which symphony did Sir Thomas Beecham describe as 'the musical equivalent of St Pancras Station'?
4. Who first based an opera on *The Barber of Seville*?
5. Which West Indian country's national dance did Cole Porter appropriate in 'Begin the Beguine'?
6. In which Wilde play does someone say, 'Musical people . . . always want one to be perfectly dumb at the very moment when one is longing to be absolutely deaf'?

## 147

1. Which cartoon characters had a No. 1 hit in 1969?
2. The World Wide Wickets Co. featured in which 60s musical?
3. Who in 1911 wrote a suffragette battle-hymn and conducted it with a toothbrush in Holloway Prison?
4. In which opera is the best-known aria based on the Irish ballad 'The Groves of Blarney'?
5. Whose band featured a latrinophone – a toilet seat strung with catgut – and an octave of flitguns tuned to E♭?
6. Which Harlem dance-hall was also known as 'The Home of the Happy Feet' and 'The Track'?

## 223

1. Who in 1976 immortalized the wreck of the *Edmund Fitzgerald* which sank in Lake Superior?
2. Which Italian opera featured in the 1984 film *Diva*?
3. Which virtuoso violinist confounded the critics by attributing to other composers his own compositions?
4. Whose mechanical 'daughter' does Hoffmann love?
5. Who was 'the Empress of the Blues'?
6. What is the Italian song 'Funiculì, funiculà' about?

# 71

1. Bob Marley's.
2. Seurat (*Sunday in the Park With George*).
3. Elgar's Symphony No. 1 in A♭.
4. Giovanni Paisiello (1782).
5. Martinique's.
6. *An Ideal Husband*.

# 147

1. The Archies ('Sugar, Sugar').
2. *How to Suceed in Business Without Really Trying*.
3. Ethel Smyth.
4. *Martha* (von Flotow; 'The Last Rose of Summer').
5. Spike Jones's.
6. The Savoy Ballroom.

# 223

1. Gordon Lightfoot.
2. *La Wally* (Catalani).
3. Fritz Kreisler.
4. Dr Spalanzani's (*Tales of Hoffmann*).
5. Bessie Smith.
6. A funicular railway (in Naples).

## 72

1. On which day in 1980 was John Lennon murdered?
2. The film *2001* opened with which Richard Strauss work?
3. Which composer's cousin Constanze did Mozart marry?
4. What were the names of the 'three little maids who all unwary come from a ladies' seminary'?
5. Who jazzed up *Peer Gynt*?
6. Which beautiful singer of German legend lured sailors to their death on the rocks by the sound of her voice?

## 148

1. Who does 'P.' from the band E.L.P. now play for?
2. Which song by Womble-turned-producer/songwriter was used in the 1979 film *Watership Down*?
3. Berlioz's *Symphonie Fantastique* describes his passion for which Irish actress?
4. What was Bellini's version of *Romeo and Juliet*?
5. Which instrument was introduced into the saxophone section to create the 'Glenn Miller sound'?
6. Where in Britain are gongs, bells and sirens illegal?

## 224

1. For which publisher does Pete Townsend work?
2. Who whistles 'Isn't It Romantic' to Marlene Dietrich in *A Foreign Affair*?
3. Which Austrian conductor did Thomas Beecham once describe as 'a kind of musical Malcolm Sargent'?
4. About which sculptor did Berlioz write an opera?
5. Who once described rock 'n' roll as 'sung, played and written by cretinous goons . . . the martial music of every side-burned delinquent on the face of the earth?
6. Which song was *Dad's Army*'s signature tune?

## 72

1. 8 December.
2. *Also Sprach Zarathustra*.
3. Carl Maria von Weber's.
4. Yum-Yum, Pitti-Sing and Peep-Bo (*The Mikado*).
5. Duke Ellington.
6. The Lorelei.

## 148

1. Asia (Carl Palmer).
2. 'Bright Eyes' (Mike Batt).
3. Harriet Smithson.
4. *I Capuletti ed i Montecchi* (*The Capulets and the Montagues*).
5. The clarinet.
6. On motor vehicles.

## 224

1. Faber & Faber.
2. John Lund.
3. Herbert von Karajan.
4. Benvenuto Cellini.
5. Frank Sinatra.
6. 'Who Do You Think You Are Kidding, Mr Hitler'.

# 73

1. Which punk band made a single entitled, 'The Strange Circumstances Which Led to Vladimir and Olga Requesting Rehabilitation in a Siberian Health Resort as a Result of Stress in Furthering the People's Policies'?
2. Who sang 'Blue Moon' in *Grease*?
3. To which king did J. S. Bach make a *Musical Offering*?
4. Which composer's name translates as 'Joe Green'?
5. What was the *Billy Cotton Bandshow* signature tune?
6. What did Sir Thomas Beecham dismiss as 'that chicken-coop down by the river'?

# 149

1. Who sent Ronald Reagan, Margaret Thatcher and Leonid Brezhnev a copy of his single 'Happy Talk'?
2. During which song in *A Star is Born* did Humphrey Bogart (off screen) keep interrupting Judy Garland, saying 'Sing, melancholy baby'?
3. Which British conductor was known as 'Old Timber'?
4. In which Italian opera are a mother and child burned to death, a young woman poisoned and a brother beheaded?
5. Who was the original 'Laughing Policeman'?
6. How many instruments comprise a 'chest of viols'?

# 225

1. Who was 'The Prettiest Star' who on 22 January 1972 announced that he was gay, and later said he wasn't?
2. Which Bill Forsyth film has a score by Mark Knopfler?
3. Which choral anthem has been performed at the coronation of every British monarch since 1727?
4. What did eighteenth-century opera audiences customarily do during an *aria di sorbetto*?
5. Which Great War song was Ivor Novello's first hit?
6. In which key does Big Ben sound the hour – F, A or C?

## 73

1. The Stranglers.
2. Sha Na Na.
3. Frederick the Great.
4. Giuseppe Verdi.
5. 'Somebody Stole My Girl'.
6. The Royal Festival Hall.

## 149

1. Captain Sensible.
2. 'Born in a Trunk'.
3. Sir Henry Wood.
4. *Il Trovatore* (Verdi).
5. Charles Penrose.
6. Six.

## 225

1. David Bowie.
2. *Local Hero*.
3. *Zadok the Priest* (Handel).
4. They bought ice-cream.
5. 'Keep the Home Fires Burning'.
6. F.

## 74

1. Which ex-King Crimson singer believed in Father Christmas in 1975?
2. Who composed the film scores for *Missing*, *The Bounty* and *Chariots of Fire*?
3. Who was 'Corno di Bassetto'?
4. After which greedy composer is a steak named?
5. Which brand of cigarette sponsored Benny Goodman's 1930s radio shows?
6. Which producer went from The Goons to The Beatles?

## 150

1. Which band teamed Gerry Rafferty with Billy Connolly?
2. Which Sondheim–Rodgers show was based upon a film, *Midsummer Madness*, of the Arthur Laurents play *Time of the Cuckoo*?
3. From whom did Beethoven withdraw the dedication of his Third Symphony?
4. In which opera did Holst parody Wagner?
5. Which jazz pianist was nicknamed 'Smack'?
6. Which commercial product inspired the New Seekers to 'Want to Teach the World to Sing'?

## 226

1. Why did the Small Faces go to 'Itchycoo Park'?
2. What were the classical sources of *The Golden Apple*?
3. If in Cage's composition *4′ 33″* the performer is silent for four and a half minutes, what happens in *0′ 0″*?
4. In which opera is an emperor turned into stone?
5. Who made wearing horn-rimmed glasses, a goatee beard and a beret the height of hipster fashion?
6. By international agreement, concert pitch is the note A sounding at 400, 414 or 440 vibrations per second?

# A

## 74

1. Greg Lake.
2. Vangelis (Papathanassiou).
3. George Bernard Shaw (as music critic).
4. Gioacchino Rossini.
5. Camel.
6. George Martin.

## 150

1. The Humblebums.
2. *Do I Hear a Waltz?*
3. Napoleon Bonaparte.
4. *The Perfect Fool.*
5. James Fletcher Henderson.
6. Coca-Cola.

## 226

1. 'To get high'.
2. Homer's *Iliad* and *Odyssey*.
3. Anything the performer chooses.
4. *Die Frau Ohne Schatten* (Richard Strauss).
5. Dizzy Gillespie.
6. 440.

# 75

1. Who was 'the Lizard King's' 'Queen of the Highway'?
2. Who was the 'divinely decadent' heroine of *Cabaret*?
3. What was the other profession of the music critic 'Monsieur Croche, antidilettante'?
4. Which operetta based on Greek mythology ends with a riotous can-can?
5. With which composition did James P. Johnson launch a world-wide dance craze in 1922?
6. Who was 'Mary, Mary, Quite Contrary'?

# 151

1. Of which song-writing duo was Nanker Phelge a pseudonym?
2. Which 1977 musical was set on board a train?
3. Which French composer wrote *Three Pear-Shaped Pieces* and *Limp Preludes For a Dog*?
4. On which island is *The Gondoliers* set?
5. Whose daddy wouldn't buy her a bow-wow?
6. Which musician discovered where Richard the Lionheart was imprisoned by the Duke of Austria?

# 227

1. Which Sixties rock band derived its name, via Aldous Huxley, from a poem by William Blake?
2. The 'Harry Lime' theme in the 1949 film *The Third Man* was played on which instrument?
3. Which composer called one of his symphonies 'Pathetic'?
4. The composer of the opera *Le Devin du Village* was better known as an 'Enlightened' philosopher. Who was he?
5. What did the Ink Spots love besides coffee and tea?
6. What do the initials EMI stand for?

## 75

1. Pamela (wife of The Doors's Jim Morrison).
2. Sally Bowles.
3. Composer (he was Claude Debussy).
4. *Orpheus in the Underworld* (Offenbach).
5. 'The Charleston'.
6. Mary, Queen of Scots.

## 151

1. Mick Jagger and Keith Richard.
2. *On the Twentieth Century*.
3. Erik Satie.
4. Barataria.
5. Vesta Victoria's.
6. Blondel.

## 227

1. The Doors (of perception).
2. A zither.
3. Pyotr Tchaikovsky. (No. 6).
4. Jean-Jacques Rousseau.
5. The java-java.
6. Electrical and Musical Industries.

# 76

1. Of which album was The Mothers of Invention's 1967 *We're Only In It For the Money* a parody?
2. A quartet of ocarinas featured in which 1930 show?
3. When Wagner married Hans von Bülow's ex-wife he became whose son-in-law?
4. What do *Cav.* and *Pag.* refer to?
5. Who was the 'Nimble-Fingered Gentleman'?
6. Which instrument gave its name to a breed of dog?

# 152

1. Which singer took a philosophy degree at Reading and later set his hair on fire on *Top of the Pops*?
2. Louis Malle's first film, *Lift to the Scaffold*, featured the improvised music of which jazz trumpeter?
3. Which composer's cook was named Waltz?
4. Which singer said of Joan Sutherland, 'She will have a big career if she can keep it up, but only we know how much greater I am'?
5. Which Irish singer was once fired as a drummer for blowing his nose during a tango?
6. What would a French musician understand by a *tampon*?

# 228

1. Who, when asked by The Beatles what key she would like to sing in, replied, 'It can be a Yale key for all I care'?
2. Rodgers and Hammerstein's only film score was written for which 1945 movie?
3. Which French composer of 'Perpetual Songs' died after crashing his bicycle into a wall?
4. The ancestors of which family come to life from their portraits in *Ruddigore*?
5. What do B. B. King's initials stand for?
6. Where in the USA is Charleston?

# 76

1. *Sergeant Pepper's Lonely Hearts Club Band.*
2. *Girl Crazy.*
3. Franz Liszt's.
4. The operas *Cavalleria Rusticana* and *I Pagliacci.*
5. Billy Mayall.
6. The basset horn.

# 152

1. Arthur Brown.
2. Miles Davis.
3. George Frideric Handel's.
4. Maria Callas.
5. Val Doonican.
6. A drumstick.

# 228

1. Cilla Black.
2. *State Fair.*
3. Ernest Chausson.
4. The Murgatroyds.
5. ('The Beale Street) Blues Boy'.
6. South Carolina.

# Part 5
# The Politics Quiz

## Edited by Michael Morrogh

with
Bruce Alexander
Lizzy Buchan
Andrew Kennedy

# Introduction to The Politics Quiz

It is commonly supposed that a successful politician needs most of all a set of elastic opinions, the loyalty of his constituency, a modest supply of babies to be kissed and an iron constitution to withstand late nights at Westminster. Such things are important, certainly, but not absolutely essential. More than anything else, the genuine politician has to have a deep reservoir of trivial knowledge.

No person can pretend to familiarity with the political world who does not know which MP is called 'The Beast of Bolsover' (Mr Skinner); whose battle cry has been 'Save Ulster from Sodomy' (The Rev. Ian Paisley); and the unusual claim Jean-Marie Loret has to make about Hitler (that the latter was his father). Possession of these profoundly significant facts can make the most ignorant of men sound like a pundit correcting Sir Robin Day. Dropped at the right moment (in the right company) they will impress and entertain – and ease the way to political advancement. Who could ask for more?

Everyone can have fun with this section testing their knowledge of political events, past and present. And it is not all plain politics. Many of the questions deal with historical episodes and institutions. Here is the chance to test your know-all friends; find out the real politician in the family; expose the ignorance of that irritating person who claims to be soaked in the details of British history. Take £5 off the uncle who thinks he knows every Prime Minister since Waterloo. Memorize the answers and astound Magnus Magnusson. The possibilities are endless.

We have considerately divided the questions into six loose categories:

1. **British Politics Since 1945**
2. **International Events**
3. **Political Institutions**
4. **British Political History**
5. **World Rulers**
6. **General Scandal** – politico flagrante, and bizarre or unclassifiable facts.

Every quiz contains a question from each category. Some of the questions are ones many people will know, though not so easy as to deprive one of that glow of self-satisfaction after answering correctly. Others are ones most people *should* know; on receiving the answer to these, the usual response will be an inarticulate noise as of an animal in pain, followed by 'but of course!' Finally some questions might not be generally known but are there to make an interesting (or indeed political) point. If you disagree with these particular answers, then the only course is to compile your own book.

Michael Morrogh

## 1

1. Who 'gave up politics when I discovered that I would rather be a poet than a Prime Minister'?
2. Which emperor's dismissal of his chief minister earned the *Punch* cartoon 'dropping the pilot'?
3. What does Caudillo mean?
4. Which son of a Spanish father, born in New York, became Ireland's longest serving Prime Minister?
5. What was the title of the rulers of Hyderabad?
6. 'King's Moll Renoed in Wolsey's Home Town'. Who?

## 77

1. Who defended her father on his becoming PM in 1963: 'He is used to dealing with estate workers. I cannot see how anyone can say he is out of touch'?
2. What sovereign republic is surrounded by Italy?
3. Who is the only man since Jesus and not a saint to have colleges named after him at both Oxford and Cambridge?
4. Edmund Burke denied he was a delegate of Bristol citizens as their MP, but instead a . . . what?
5. Who was the only leader of a major western country not to attend Mr Chernenko's funeral?
6. What modern political party is named after Irish thieves?

## 153

1. Which government minister is known as Tarzan?
2. Toussaint L'Ouverture led which rebel colony?
3. What is the eastern equivalent of NATO?
4. Who was Trollope's Irish politician on the make in London?
5. Who was the first invading sovereign to enter Paris since Henry V of England?
6. Who was the fattest ex-king on the Riviera in the 1950s?

# 1

1. John Pardoe.
2. Wilhelm II retiring Bismarck.
3. Leader (Spanish); Franco's self-awarded title.
4. Eamon De Valera.
5. The Nizam.
6. Mrs Simpson, divorced at Ipswich before her marriage to the future Duke of Windsor.

# 77

1. Lady Caroline Douglas-Home.
2. San Marino.
3. Lord Wolfson.
4. Representative – and thus free to use his own judgement on issues.
5. President Reagan.
6. The Tories.

# 153

1. Michael Heseltine.
2. Haiti.
3. Warsaw Pact.
4. Phineas Finn.
5. Tsar Alexander I of Russia in 1814.
6. Farouk of Egypt.

## 2

1. Who is the present Father of the House?
2. What is the 'Second World'?
3. According to Tony Benn, what is 'the British Outer Mongolia for retired politicians'?
4. In 1837, the Salic Law prevented Queen Victoria's accession to what state?
5. Who repeatedly said '[expletive deleted]'?
6. What phrase did Mandy Rice-Davies coin in the Profumo scandal?

## 78

1. Which modern politician has an ancestor who opposed Charles I?
2. Which small African country is in the eye of the beholder?
3. Name the six counties of Northern Ireland. All of them.
4. What was Lord Mansfield's famous judgement in 1772?
5. Which Middle Eastern ruler is invariably described as the 'Sandhurst-trained King'?
6. What did Lady Churchill do with the portrait presented to Sir Winston by Parliament?

## 154

1. Why did Churchill recommend Macmillan and not Butler to succeed Eden in 1957?
2. What event caused St Augustine to write *The City of God*?
3. Which film star drawled, 'From what I hear about Communism I don't like it because it isn't on the level'?
4. Who first used the phrase 'Glittering prizes'?
5. What country did King Zog I rule over in the 1930s?
6. Whose name has become the eponym for the puppet leader of a foreign-imposed regime?

# 2

1. James Callaghan.
2. The Eastern bloc.
3. The House of Lords.
4. Hanover.
5. President Nixon.
6. 'Well he would, wouldn't he?' (on being told her allegations had been strenuously denied).

# 78

1. Francis Pym.
2. Djibouti.
3. Armagh, Antrim, Londonderry, Tyrone, Fermanagh and Down.
4. That slavery was illegal in England.
5. King Hussein of Jordan.
6. Destroyed it.

# 154

1. Because Butler had supported Chamberlain's appeasement policy in the late 1930s.
2. The sack of Rome in AD 410.
3. Gary Cooper, bless him.
4. F. E. Smith, Lord Birkenhead.
5. Albania.
6. Vidkun Quisling.

## 3

1. Who first called the Tory moderates 'Wets'?
2. Who parachuted into Scotland on a solo peace mission in 1941?
3. What is the Conservative backbenchers' lobby called?
4. What minister was known for his pies during the war?
5. Charles the Bald, Charles the Fat and Charles the Simple were all Kings of what country?
6. With whom did the Duke and Duchess of Windsor have tea in 1937, upsetting many back in England?

## 79

1. What was the result of the government's attempt to conceal an intelligence officer under the name of Colonel B in court in 1977?
2. Which Middle Eastern leader has the mysterious power of keeping a continuous three-day beard?
3. What is the assembly of Cardinals to elect a new Pope called?
4. Which territory was Lord Lundy sent out to govern?
5. Who was deported from a Mediterranean island to an Indian Ocean island for one year in 1956?
6. What was the family name of Pope Alexander VI?

## 155

1. Who invented the 'swingometer', seen on television at elections?
2. Which eastern European countries allied themselves to Germany in the Second World War?
3. Does the House of Lords have more or less representatives than the Commons?
4. Which country invaded Afghanistan in 1839?
5. Which ruling family had a prominent lower lip?
6. What was the game shot by Lord Whitelaw in 1984?

# 3

1. The Monday Club (of course).
2. Rudolf Hess.
3. The 1922 Committee.
4. Lord Woolton.
5. France.
6. Hitler.

# 79

1. That Colonel Hugh Johnstone temporarily became the most famous officer in the British army.
2. Yasser Arafat.
3. The Conclave.
4. New South Wales.
5. Archbishop Makarios.
6. Borgia.

# 155

1. Robert McKenzie.
2. Hungary, Romania and Bulgaria.
3. More (1188 to 650).
4. Britain.
5. The Habsburgs.
6. Beaters.

## 4

1. Which politician described himself as 'a turn-up in a million'?
2. Who demonstrated his footwear to the UN?
3. Which Cambridge college is associated with the New Right?
4. Whom did Balfour call 'a Tory in all but essentials'?
5. Which future South African Prime Minister was interned during the war for his pro-fascist views?
6. Name the five Kings of England with reputed homosexual inclinations.

## 80

1. What is the name of Tam Dalyell's house?
2. Which ancient capital city was described by a Stoppard character as the Reykjavik of the south?
3. What financial reform suggested by Trollope's Plantagenet Palliser was adopted in Britain in 1971?
4. Which English king was described as 'a tall black man two yards high'?
5. Which ruler has the best pair of teeth in south-east Asia?
6. Who is Speaking out nowadays more than he should?

## 156

1. Hugh Gaitskell, Richard Crossman and Douglas Jay were the products of which school?
2. What sort of thing is *Rude Pravo*?
3. Which parliamentary candidate in the twentieth century has received the least number of votes?
4. What is *1066*'s version of 'Honi soit qui mal y pense'?
5. Who is the current dictator of Paraguay?
6. What reform did Lord Grey say in 1857 would induce a high rate of brain disease if adopted?

# 4

1. Ernest Bevin.
2. Khrushchev.
3. Peterhouse.
4. Gladstone.
5. Hendrik Verwoerd.
6. William II, Richard I, Edward II, James I and William III.

# 80

1. The Binns.
2. Edinburgh.
3. Decimal coinage.
4. Charles II, on the parliamentary 'wanted' notices in 1651.
5. President Zia of Pakistan.
6. Ex-Speaker George Thomas, Lord Tonypandy, whose memoirs have been embarrassing MPs.

# 156

1. Winchester.
2. Czech party newspaper.
3. Lt. Cdr. Bill Boakes, who got five in 1981.
4. 'Honey, your silk stocking's hanging down.'
5. Alfredo Stroessner.
6. Exams for army officers; it had already happened in France, he said.

# 5

1. Which politician flourished a pair of handcuffs above her head at a Tory conference?
2. Who are the Broederbond?
3. What are Green Papers?
4. Who was the incendiary king?
5. Who was Cambodia's leader when it achieved independence from France in 1953?
6. Which South American churchman recently said, 'When I give food to the poor they call me a saint. When I ask why the poor have no food, they call me a communist'?

# 81

1. Claret and chips distinguish which political party?
2. What doctrine bans European involvement in the Americas?
3. What form of voting can be found in every European democracy except Britain?
4. At what age did Gladstone retire from politics?
5. Which American Presidents are known by initials?
6. Whom did Marcus Lipton name as the 'Third Man' in 1955?

# 157

1. Who is known as 'The Beast of Bolsover'?
2. Who are the indigenous inhabitants of New Caledonia?
3. In what decade was the first British Parliament with members from Scotland and Ireland?
4. What colour shirts did Ireland's fascist party wear?
5. Which Saxon king minted gold coins with Arabic inscriptions?
6. What campaigner against 'filth in the media' has a girlie magazine named in her honour?

# 5

1. Edwina Currie.
2. Members of an Afrikaaner secret society anxious to keep the old ways going.
3. Interim documents for consultative purposes before the final White Paper.
4. King Alfred.
5. Prince Sihanouk.
6. The Archbishop of Recife.

# 81

1. The SDP.
2. The Monroe Doctrine.
3. Proportional representation.
4. Eighty-five.
5. FDR, JFK and LBJ.
6. Kim Philby.

# 157

1. Dennis Skinner MP.
2. The Kanuks.
3. The 1650s.
4. Blue.
5. Offa of Mercia.
6. Mrs Whitehouse.

## 6

1. Which Labour politician is the son of an ex-priest?
2. Which American Founding Father had an enormous signature?
3. What does the UDA stand for in Ireland?
4. Cecil Rhodes said, 'Remember you are (what?) and therefore have won first prize in the lottery of life.'
5. Which south-east Asian communist leader formerly worked as a pastry cook at the Carlton Hotel in London?
6. Why do children like President Theodore Roosevelt?

## 82

1. Who used to refer to Mrs Thatcher as 'The Blessed Margaret'?
2. Why do the French hate the word Fashoda?
3. What is the ruling body of the USSR?
4. Which Foreign Minister ordered the blockade of Athens on behalf of the British subject Don Pacifico?
5. Which monarch was the indirect cause of Descartes's death?
6. John Bloom forced the price of what to fall in the 1960s?

## 158

1. Who was the youngest English Foreign Secretary since William Pitt the Younger?
2. What country does South Africa prefer to call South-West Africa?
3. Before 1832 what were boroughs called which still returned MPs but no longer existed as habitable places?
4. Which Indian viceroy was 'a most superior person'?
5. Over what unhappy country did Enver Hoxha rule?
6. The mild and apparently harmless drug Distaval caused a scandal in the sixties. By what name is it better known?

## 6

1. Roy Hattersley.
2. John Hancock.
3. Ulster Defence Association.
4. An Englishman.
5. Ho Chi Minh.
6. Because his bulk inspired Teddy Bears.

## 82

1. Norman St John-Stevas.
2. It reminds them of a humiliating episode when the British forced them to withdraw from the Sudan in 1898.
3. The Politburo.
4. Palmerston.
5. Queen Christina of Sweden – he had to get up so early to teach her that he caught a chill.
6. Washing machines.

## 158

1. David Owen.
2. Namibia.
3. Rotten boroughs.
4. Lord Curzon.
5. Albania.
6. Thalidomide.

## 7

1. Which lady was not for turning in 1980?
2. What are the Benelux countries?
3. What is a fellow-traveller?
4. What was the name of the ship in which Ian Smith and Harold Wilson held their talks after the Rhodesian UDI?
5. Who complained, 'How can anyone govern a nation that has 240 different kinds of cheese'?
6. Which British politician was the victor of a Great Drinking Contest when a young man in India?

## 83

1. Who is the oldest member of Parliament?
2. Which city is known for two infamous defenestrations?
3. What is the name for the unfair manipulation of electoral divisions?
4. Name the lady politician whose last words were 'Am I dying or is this my birthday?'
5. Were there really Saxon kings called Egbert?
6. Who was Shirley Catlin's mother?

## 159

1. Which 'fragrant hackette' is a tireless worker against the CND?
2. It is said that when Lord Halifax first met him in 1937 he thought him to be the footman and handed him his hat. Who?
3. What group was formed to oppose Mrs Gandhi in 1977?
4. What did William Pitt ask for on his deathbed?
5. Who participated in the international conference at London in 1931 dressed in a loincloth?
6. What animal epithet was invariably applied to the Whigs by Samuel Johnson?

## 7

1. Mrs Thatcher.
2. Belgium, Netherlands and Luxembourg.
3. A sympathizer, though not member, of the Communist Party.
4. HMS *Tiger*.
5. Charles de Gaulle.
6. James Prior.

## 83

1. Lord Shinwell at 100.
2. Prague – in 1618 and 1948.
3. Gerrymandering.
4. Lady Astor.
5. Yes, several.
6. Vera Brittain.

## 159

1. Lady Olga Maitland.
2. Hitler.
3. Janata.
4. One of Bellamy's veal pies.
5. Mahatma Gandhi.
6. Dogs.

## 8

1. About what did Mrs Thatcher only 'make one speech'?
2. Who murdered whom in the Sicilian Vespers?
3. What was the Russian Parliament called in the 1900s?
4. Which seventeenth-century religious leader did Macaulay consider 'too much disordered for liberty'?
5. Which queen shouted, 'Off with his head'?
6. How did Bernadette Devlin demonstrate her feelings for the Home Secretary in 1972?

## 84

1. According to Bevan, how would the Foreign Secretary of a non-nuclear Britain attend conferences?
2. Which American announced, 'Ich bin ein Berliner'?
3. Who ensures that MPs attend important divisions?
4. The Gordon riots of 1780 were directed against a Relief Act for which particular group?
5. Who built those extraordinary late-nineteenth-century castles in Bavaria?
6. From whom did the British seek information about French radicals, in exile after the 1871 Paris Commune?

## 160

1. Which famous foreign correspondent died early in 1985?
2. What military-ruled country has long been part of NATO?
3. In Russia the central organization of the work camps had what acronym?
4. Who was the leader of Britain's Blackshirts in the 1930s?
5. What happened to Prime Minister Holt of Australia in 1967?
6. How did Francis Bacon die?

## 8

1. Entering the Common Market.
2. The Sicilians the occupying French.
3. The Duma.
4. George Fox (founder of the Quakers).
5. The Queen of Hearts in *Alice in Wonderland*.
6. She slapped his face.

## 84

1. Naked.
2. President Kennedy.
3. The Whips.
4. Catholics.
5. King Ludwig II.
6. Karl Marx (who compiled a detailed report).

## 160

1. James Cameron.
2. Turkey.
3. GULAG.
4. Sir Oswald Mosley.
5. He was drowned.
6. By catching cold after an experiment in refrigerating a chicken.

## 9

1. The Catholic Church and the Brigade of Guards were two of the three forces Macmillan said no prudent person would wish to meet. The third?
2. Who climbed over the shipyard walls at Gdansk?
3. What is the CAP?
4. Which Prime Minister lost the North American colonies?
5. Who was the tutor of Alexander the Great?
6. What was the journalists' nickname for Mrs Thatcher's PPS, Ian Gow?

## 85

1. Who is the bouncy commissioner for the Falklands?
2. By what name do some African nationalists prefer to call South Africa?
3. Where did King Charles I hold his government after leaving London?
4. What gentleman thief had the same name as the founder of British Singapore?
5. What was Madame Mao Tse Tung's original profession?
6. Whose royal cronies were said to 'Get on. Get honour. Get honest'?

## 161

1. Does MI5 catch spies or spy itself?
2. Who cried in front of the television cameras and lost the chance of the US presidency?
3. What is the Welsh name of the Welsh Nationalist Party?
4. Who was described as 'the rising hopes of those stern and unbending Tories'?
5. Who is the aptly named leader of Philippines' Catholics?
6. Which Foreign Secretary fought a duel in 1809?

# 9

1. The NUM. (This saying is also attributed to Stanley Baldwin.)
2. Lech Walesa.
3. The Common Agricultural Policy of the EEC, which causes such joy for food exporters (like France) and woe for importers (like Britain).
4. Lord North.
5. Aristotle.
6. Supergrass.

# 85

1. Sir Rex Hunt.
2. Azania.
3. Oxford.
4. Raffles.
5. An actress.
6. Edward VII's.

# 161

1. It attempts the former; MI6 does the spying abroad.
2. Edmund Muskie.
3. Plaid Cymru.
4. Gladstone (by Macaulay).
5. Cardinal Sin.
6. George Canning, with Castlereagh.

# 10

1. Who or what is known as Little Gum Gum?
2. Who adopted the cross of Lorraine during the Second World War?
3. Is the John Birch Society left wing?
4. In which war were sections of the British army unfortunately supplied with left boots only?
5. Which African ruler's forenames are Apollo Milton?
6. Which antipodean Prime Minister has lost eight stone in the last few years?

# 86

1. What Irish political party's name, translated, means 'The Warriors of Destiny'?
2. Is Walid Jumblatt and the Druzes a heavy metal group?
3. Which democracy has the highest proportion of women legislators?
4. Chamberlain called where 'a faraway country' in 1938?
5. Which one of Alexander the Great's generals founded a dynasty in Egypt?
6. According to Addison, how many Frenchmen could one Englishman beat?

# 162

1. Who was the Chancellor who presided over the property boom in the early 1970s?
2. What city was called Tsaritsyn and then Stalingrad?
3. When was the Church of Ireland disestablished?
4. What did Pride's Purge of 1648 leave behind?
5. What was so controversial about the Australian Governor-General's action in 1975?
6. About what did Byron say, 'I'm damned sorry for it'?

## 10

1. John Selwyn Gummer.
2. The Gaullists.
3. Decidedly not.
4. The Crimean war.
5. President Obote of Uganda.
6. Robert Lange of New Zealand.

## 86

1. Fianna Fáil.
2. No, Walid Jumblatt is the leader of the Druze Islamic minority in Lebanon.
3. Finland – with 30.5 per cent compared to Britain's 4.3 per cent.
4. Czechoslovakia.
5. Ptolemy.
6. Three.

## 162

1. Anthony Barber.
2. The present Volgograd.
3. 1869.
4. The Rump Parliament.
5. His removal of Prime Minister Whitlam.
6. Napoleon's defeat at Waterloo.

# 11

1. Who said, 'Politics is the art of the possible'?
2. Which country was Kissinger talking about when he remarked in 1970, 'I don't see why we need to stand by and watch a country go communist due to the irresponsibility of its own people'?
3. When was the Church of England disestablished?
4. Who published the works of the Left Book Club in the 1930s?
5. Who were the two Cardinals who dominated France in the mid-seventeenth century?
6. Which MP is said to be so boring that you fall asleep half-way through his name?

# 87

1. Which politician saw the River Tiber foaming with much blood in 1968?
2. Who said, 'The only thing we have to fear is fear itself'?
3. Does the South African Parliament sit in Cape Town or Pretoria?
4. Of what did Cromwell die?
5. Who is the world's heaviest monarch?
6. Whose battle-cry has been 'Save Ulster from Sodomy'?

# 163

1. Who owned and sailed *Morning Cloud*?
2. What party does Jean-Marie Le Pen lead in France?
3. How many weeks does the Commons sit each year?
4. Of which politician was it said, 'He always played the game and he always lost it'?
5. Which High King of Ireland beat the Danes in 1014?
6. Which political theorist is stuffed in University College, London?

## 11

1. R. A. Butler.
2. Allende's Chile.
3. We are still waiting for this.
4. Victor Gollancz.
5. Richelieu and Mazarin.
6. Robin Maxwell-Hyslop.

## 87

1. Enoch Powell.
2. F. D. Roosevelt.
3. Both: six months in each.
4. Malaria.
5. The King of Tonga.
6. The Rev. Ian Paisley.

## 163

1. Edward Heath.
2. The National Front.
3. Thirty-two.
4. Austen Chamberlain.
5. Brian Boru.
6. Jeremy Bentham.

## 12

1. Which veteran Labour MP walks his dog, Dizzy, on Hampstead Heath?
2. Who were the participants in the 'Cod War' of the early 1970s?
3. What does *Enosis* stand for?
4. Who was the last ruling Stuart monarch?
5. Which Prime Minister cried on television in 1984?
6. Which American President has been recreated as a speaking robot in Disneyland, Los Angeles?

## 88

1. Who is the only English Prime Minister to have played first-class cricket?
2. Which famous composer is a Greek Communist MP?
3. What are psephologists?
4. Who was largely responsible for obtaining the rights of Catholics to sit in Parliament?
5. Why might J. F. Kennedy have disliked pigs?
6. What was William Pitt's self-confessed 'atrocious crime'?

## 164

1. Does a government minister ever 'leak' an official secret?
2. What did Mussolini invade in 1935?
3. The Oireachtas is the parliament of which country?
4. What was the original name of the Mountbatten branch of the Royal Family?
5. Which ruler first welcomed the Jews into England after their expulsion in the thirteenth century?
6. Which nineteenth-century Irish politician's career was ruined by being named in an adultery suit?

## 12

1. Michael Foot.
2. Iceland and Britain – which subsequently adopted the Icelandic position regarding sea boundaries.
3. The union of Cyprus and Greece.
4. Queen Anne.
5. Bob Hawke of Australia.
6. Abraham Lincoln.

## 88

1. Alec Douglas-Home.
2. Mikis Theodorakis.
3. Investigators of voting patterns.
4. Daniel O'Connell.
5. Because of the US-sponsored Cuban exiles' attempt to overthrow Castro, which was defeated at the Bay of Pigs in 1961.
6. That of being a young man.

## 164

1. No, he 'briefs' a favoured journalist.
2. Ethiopia.
3. Ireland.
4. Battenberg.
5. Oliver Cromwell.
6. Charles Stewart Parnell.

# 13

1. Which foreign President said of Mrs Thatcher, 'She has the eyes of Caligula and a mouth like Monroe'?
2. Which Nicaraguans has President Reagan recently hailed as the modern Founding Fathers?
3. What was the Anschluss?
4. Who was the original Jethro Tull?
5. Who was originally named Frahm and became Chancellor of West Germany?
6. Whose slushy activities bruised the House of Orange?

# 89

1. Which Labour MP has been a stern opponent of the Royal Family?
2. Jean-Marie Loret has an unusual claim to make about Hitler. What?
3. Which American institution has more than twelve tons of waste paper daily?
4. His father split the party, his brother wore a monocle, he himself had a wing collar. Who?
5. Which African ruler habitually carried a fly whisk?
6. Which is higher, Marquis or Viscount?

# 165

1. Which royal Greek became a British national in 1947?
2. Who said, 'You cannot step twice into the same river'?
3. What is the oldest legislative body in Europe?
4. Who was executed 'pour encourager les autres'?
5. At what town did the Holy Roman Emperor submit himself to the Pope in 1077?
6. Which MP emerged from the waves, reborn in Australia?

# 13

1. Mitterrand.
2. The American-backed Contra guerrillas.
3. The annexation of Austria by Germany in 1938.
4. An eighteenth-century agricultural improver.
5. Willy Brandt.
6. Prince Bernhard of the Netherlands for accepting 'slush money' from the Lockheed corporation.

# 89

1. Willie Hamilton.
2. That Hitler was his father.
3. The Pentagon.
4. Neville Chamberlain.
5. Jomo Kenyatta.
6. Marquis.

# 165

1. Prince Philip.
2. Heraclitus.
3. The Althing of Iceland.
4. Admiral Byng.
5. Canossa.
6. John Stonehouse.

## 14

1. What phrase uttered in early 1985 by Health Minister Kenneth Clarke managed to upset many people?
2. Hubert Who?
3. How many women MPs were elected in 1983?
4. What did King George III address as the King of Prussia?
5. Which African leader is commemorated by a university in Moscow?
6. Whom did Burke impeach 'in the name of the people of India'?

## 90

1. Which London leader loves pond life?
2. Who were the Dixiecrats?
3. Where is the headquarters of the Open University?
4. What dawned on the Prince of Wales 'with ghastly inexorability'?
5. Who left Morocco for Spain in 1936 and was the major cause of the loss of three quarters of a million lives at the end of three years?
6. The scandal of the Norwich Insurance Society occurred because their Arab clients made them do what?

## 166

1. Who was the first grammar-school boy to become Prime Minister?
2. What is Charter 77?
3. What capital city rhymes with 'ruder pest', used in *My Fair Lady*?
4. What letter was probably forged to discredit the Labour Party in 1924?
5. Who is the oldest man to become President of the USA?
6. Who first created baronets?

## 14

1. Bongo-bongo land.
2. Humphrey.
3. Twenty-three.
4. A tree in Hyde Park.
5. Patrice Lumumba.
6. Warren Hastings.

## 90

1. Ken Livingstone.
2. American Democrats who believed in racial segregation.
3. Milton Keynes.
4. The fact that some day he would be king.
5. General Franco.
6. Sack Lord Mancroft for being a Jew.

## 166

1. Harold Wilson.
2. Czech dissident group monitoring abuses of human rights.
3. Budapest.
4. The Zinoviev letter.
5. Ronald Reagan.
6. James I, who sold them at an average £400.

## 15

1. Blue Streak, Black Arrow, Black Knight were all rockets which did what in the creation of Britain's defences?
2. Who regarded Hitler as an avatar-messiah and himself as the reincarnation of Henry the Lion, a king of Saxony?
3. What is sometimes called the Fourth Estate?
4. Which political party has had the largest-ever majority?
5. What officer was the effective ruler of Japan for much of its history?
6. Who lied about his relationship with Christine Keeler?

## 91

1. Who promised a 'white-hot technological revolution'?
2. Which Scandinavian country allied itself to Nazi Germany in the Second World War?
3. What part of Canada was a British colony until 1949?
4. Who were the English supporters recognizing King Henry IX?
5. Carol has been the name of two kings of which European country?
6. Who was 'Kharshoggied' a few years ago?

## 167

1. Who was Britain's Prime Minister during the Suez crisis?
2. Which power ruled Crete from the thirteenth to the seventeenth century?
3. What is Joshua Nkomo's party in Zimbabwe?
4. It was said the men of Kent had tails as punishment for what crime?
5. Whose Year was it for Living Dangerously in 1965?
6. Who got sacked because of his tasteless remarks on rape?

# 15

1. Fail.
2. Himmler.
3. The Press (usually a self-awarded title).
4. The Liberals in 1832, with 67 per cent of the vote.
5. The Shogun.
6. John Profumo.

# 91

1. Harold Wilson in 1964.
2. Finland.
3. Newfoundland.
4. Jacobites.
5. Romania.
6. Winston Churchill MP.

# 167

1. Anthony Eden.
2. Venice.
3. ZAPU.
4. The killing of Thomas à Becket.
5. President Sukarno of Indonesia.
6. Nicholas Fairbairn, former Solicitor-General for Scotland.

## 16

1. Which noble lord, whose name was on the map of Rhodesia, vigorously opposed all sanctions against the Rhodesian regime of Ian Smith?
2. What is the RAF in Germany?
3. The Storting is the Parliament of which country?
4. Which two English kings had a stammer?
5. Who ascended the throne to rule jointly with her ten-year-old brother and husband in 51 BC?
6. In what part of Christ's anatomy did Oliver Cromwell beseech his audience?

## 92

1. Who defected to Britain and back again to Moscow in 1984?
2. What country ruled Finland from the seventeenth to the nineteenth century?
3. Rosa Luxemburg led what political party?
4. What politician metamorphosed from Mr Hyde to . . . ?
5. What was the title of the independent ruler of Tunis?
6. Which of the Services' expanding bureaucracy provoked Parkinson's famous law?

## 168

1. Which profession is best represented among Conservative MPs?
2. Who were the Huguenots?
3. By custom in Parliament, those referred to as 'honourable and gallant' members are who?
4. Who set up a model factory at New Lanark in the 1800s?
5. Who was Israel's first Prime Minister in 1948?
6. What name did Sheridan give when found drunk and challenged by the watch?

# 16

1. The Marquess of Salisbury.
2. The terrorist organization, Red Army Faction.
3. Norway.
4. Charles I and George VI.
5. Cleopatra.
6. The bowels.

# 92

1. Oleg Bitov.
2. Sweden.
3. The Spartacists.
4. The Earl of Clarendon.
5. Bey (monarch).
6. The Navy.

# 168

1. Barristers.
2. French Protestants in the sixteenth and seventeenth centuries.
3. Commissioned officers of the three Services.
4. Robert Owen.
5. David Ben-Gurion.
6. 'Wilberforce' (the pious reformer).

## 17

1. To what was Sir Hartley Shawcross referring when he claimed 'we are the masters' in 1946?
2. What was the ruling family in Milan during the Renaissance?
3. In 1858 Baron Rothschild was the first MP to swear on the Old Testament. Why?
4. Who was supposed to have organized Elizabeth I's intelligence service?
5. The President of France and the Bishop of Seo de Urgel are the joint Heads of State of what country?
6. What did Aristotle regard as appropriate for men aged thirty-seven and women aged eighteen?

## 93

1. Who is the dancing MP?
2. The Sublime Porte was the loose name for the government of what empire?
3. What does the Speaker do to a persistently disruptive MP?
4. Who complained, 'It is a miserable thing to be a constitutional queen and be unable to do what is right'?
5. Where was Nehru educated?
6. Who were the Tonton Macoute?

## 169

1. Which Prime Minister arranged for Sir Roger Casement's bones to be returned to Ireland?
2. Which western European powers invaded Russia in 1918–19 to aid the anti-Bolshevik forces?
3. What was Gdansk called before 1945?
4. On 11 November 1920 what was unveiled in Whitehall?
5. Who were the White Rajahs?
6. Which Prime Minister-to-be wrote the novel *Savrola*?

## 17

1. Labour's overwhelming majority in Parliament.
2. The Sforzas.
3. A Jew.
4. Sir Francis Walsingham.
5. Andorra.
6. Marriage.

## 93

1. Geoffrey Dickens.
2. Ottoman.
3. He names him.
4. Victoria.
5. Harrow and Cambridge.
6. 'Papa Doc' Duvalier's security forces in Haiti.

## 169

1. Harold Wilson.
2. Britain, France and America.
3. Danzig.
4. The Cenotaph.
5. The Brooke family who ruled Sarawak.
6. Sir Winston Churchill.

## 18

1. What scored about 800 for and 255 against in 1982?
2. What were the Adenauer years in West Germany?
3. Who painted Westminster burning in 1834?
4. After whom in the Oxford Movement was a college named?
5. What did Dorothy Parker say about President Coolidge's death?
6. What were authenticated by Lord Dacre, printed in the *Sunday Times* and exposed as forgeries within days?

## 94

1. What is Peter Bruinvels' claim to fame?
2. Who are the Falashas?
3. In Charles Humana's guide to World Human Rights, three countries come highest: Denmark, Finland and . . . ?
4. What was significant about the election of Dadabhai Naorogi as MP for Finsbury in 1892?
5. What Russian leader said, 'If people don't like Marxism, they should blame the British Museum'?
6. Which French king had three sisters as his mistresses?

## 170

1. Sir Anthony Duff heads which organization?
2. Who said, 'Show my head to the people. It's worth it'?
3. Clause 4 of the Labour Party's constitution recommends. . .?
4. Name the Dublin man who led the Ulster Unionists' campaign in the 1910s.
5. Whose last words were allegedly, 'What an artist the world is losing'?
6. America's total casualties in the First World War were less than which Commonwealth country's?

# 18

1. The Falklands War.
2. The 1950s (1949–63).
3. J. M. Turner.
4. John Keble.
5. 'How could they tell?'
6. The Hitler diaries.

# 94

1. He offered to act as hangman should capital punishment be reinstated.
2. Ethiopian Jews recently airlifted to Israel.
3. New Zealand.
4. He was the first Asian in Parliament.
5. Mikhail Gorbachev.
6. Louis XV.

# 170

1. MI5.
2. Danton.
3. Widespread nationalization: 'common ownership of the means of production, distribution and exchange'.
4. Edward Carson.
5. Nero.
6. Australia's.

## 19

1. Who said, 'Whichever party is in office, the Treasury is in power'?
2. In Central America what two countries do not bridge the Atlantic and Pacific?
3. What is the ANZUS pact?
4. Who was generally expected to lead the Conservative Party in 1923 instead of Stanley Baldwin?
5. Who was held to ransom for a room filled with gold?
6. In the Watergate scandal, who was Woodward's inside leaker?

## 95

1. Who said, 'When you've spent half your political life dealing with humdrum issues like the environment . . . it's exciting having a real crisis on your hands'?
2. What did Cato stress about a north African city?
3. Who said, 'The US Presidency is a Tudor monarchy plus telephones'?
4. Which husband and wife socialist team founded the LSE?
5. What American President took his country into the First World War?
6. What exposed Profumo and his affair with Keeler?

## 171

1. Who assured us in 1967, 'Communists have taken over in England, though nobody knows it'?
2. Who repeatedly said, 'It is indeed a great wall'?
3. What is the ultimate court of appeal?
4. Who spoke to Queen Victoria as if she were a public meeting?
5. Which American President built a house where he could leap out of bed straight into his study.
6. What do they tell about the Guards?

## 19

1. Harold Wilson.
2. Belize and El Salvador.
3. Defensive alliance between Australia, New Zealand and the US.
4. Lord Curzon.
5. The Inca Emperor, Atahualpa.
6. Deep Throat.

## 95

1. Mrs Thatcher on the Falklands war.
2. Carthage must be destroyed.
3. Anthony Burgess.
4. The Webbs.
5. Woodrow Wilson.
6. The letter he wrote beginning 'Darling'.

## 171

1. Sir Wilfred Hughes.
2. President Nixon when visiting the Great Wall of China.
3. The House of Lords.
4. Gladstone.
5. Thomas Jefferson; the house was called Monticello.
6 'You can always tell a Guards officer, but you can't tell him much.'

## 20

1. Who was the first Prime Minister to rise up through the unions?
2. What is the state claimed by both India and Pakistan?
3. Which city in Northern Ireland acts as a shibboleth according to the form preferred?
4. The principal feature of the British pavilion in the 1937 World Exhibition was a picture of which Prime Minister fishing?
5. Who was the short-ruling President of Cyprus in 1974?
6. Complete Belloc's line: 'We had intended you to be . . .'

## 96

1. Which Tory MP, son of a famous diarist, lost his Bournemouth seat after criticizing Eden's Suez escapade?
2. What does France like to call its nuclear striking force?
3. The Commissioner for Local Administration is otherwise known as what?
4. Who was on the throne of England at the end of the fifteenth century?
5. Which ally irritated Churchill and enraged Roosevelt and yet was helped by both to achieve his aim?
6. Who set fire to the Reichstag in 1933?

## 172

1. Which Minister said, 'You don't need brains to be Minister of Transport because the civil servants have them'?
2. What used to be Salisbury?
3. How many archbishops and bishops sit in the Lords?
4. Which Governor-General of India is said to have worn his decorations on his nightshirt?
5. Who said, 'Only an anti-semite is a true anti-communist'?
6. Why was Evelyn Waugh's Agatha Runcible miffed?

## 20

1. James Callaghan.
2. Kashmir.
3. Londonderry (for Unionists); Derry (for Republicans and residents).
4. Neville Chamberlain.
5. Nicos Sampson.
6. '. . . the next Prime Minister but three.'

## 96

1. Nigel Nicolson.
2. Force de frappe.
3. Ombudsman.
4. Henry VII.
5. Charles de Gaulle.
6. Probably van der Lubbe and not the Nazis as commonly supposed; though the latter certainly made political capital from the incident.

## 172

1. Ernest Marples.
2. Harare, capital of Zimbabwe.
3. Twenty-six.
4. Lord Wellesley.
5. Adolf Hitler.
6. Because she had heard somebody mention the Parliamentary Labour Party and was furious she hadn't been asked.

# 21

1. What event in 1956 created the New Left?
2. Under what coalition did Begin become Israel's Prime Minister in 1977?
3. What is the youth section of the Communist Party in the USSR?
4. Who were the Cat, the Rat and the Hog in the fifteenth century?
5. Who was the leader of the Khmer Rouge when they controlled Cambodia after 1975?
6. Why did Pepys think Major-General Harrison was as cheerful as any man could be in that condition?

# 97

1. The burning of the oil slick from the *Torrey Canyon* shook the British public. Why?
2. When did Ceylon become Sri Lanka?
3. What is known as Foggy Bottom in the USA?
4. How did Balfour acquire his sobriquet of Bloody Balfour?
5. The King of Thailand has as one of his titles 'Possessor of the Four and Twenty . . .' what?
6. Who ran Katanga with the backing of whites and mercenaries from 1960–62?

# 173

1. Where was Harold Wilson's holiday bungalow?
2. What was Willy Brandt's Ostpolitik?
3. Is the Western Sahara recognized by the UN?
4. Which monarch on first seeing his bride whispered, 'Harris, I am not well; pray get me a glass of brandy'?
5. Who was the Soviet leader between Stalin and Khrushchev?
6. Eichmann said, 'A hundred dead is a catastrophe. Five million dead is a . . .' what?

# 21

1. The Russian invasion of Hungary.
2. Likud.
3. Komsomol.
4. Catesby, Radcliffe and Richard III.
5. Pol Pot.
6. He was being hung, drawn and quartered at the time.

# 97

1. It revealed that the RAF had napalm.
2. May 1972.
3. The State Department.
4. From his harsh coercive policies when Secretary for Ireland.
5. Umbrellas.
6. Moise Tshombe.

# 173

1. In the Scilly Isles.
2. Recognition of East Germany and general détente with the eastern bloc.
3. Yes – to Morocco's annoyance.
4. George IV, when Regent.
5. Malenkov.
6. Statistic.

## 22

1. Who became Minister of Technology in 1966?
2. How did Gary Powers arrive in the USSR in 1962?
3. What is the Government side of the Lords known as?
4. If a pub is called the White Swan, to which of Henry VIII's wives does it refer?
5. Who has had the shortest run as Prime Minister this century?
6. Which of Elizabeth I's favourites is said to have arranged the murder of his wife?

## 98

1. What was special about P. Piratin's election to the Commons in 1945?
2. In 1937 Franco made an unusual Christian figure one of his Field Marshals. Who?
3. Name the original six EEC countries.
4. George I derived his claim to the throne from which English king's daughter?
5. In whose office did the buck stop?
6. Which Chancellor of the Exchequer died of syphilis?

## 174

1. How many of Latvian descent are in the present cabinet?
2. 'I have said many times in private conversation that the real danger in Europe is Germany.' Who was the speaker?
3. Which maritime country has the shortest coastline in the world?
4. Which Duke of Lancaster was excessively thin?
5. Which future Prime Minister failed to obtain a seat in England and became MP for Dundee instead?
6. Which of Charles II's mistresses is said to have put a laxative in a rival's food?

## 22

1. Anthony Wedgwood Benn, as he was then.
2. His U2 spy plane was shot down.
3. The Spiritual Side.
4. Anne of Cleves.
5. Bonar Law (seven months).
6. Robert Dudley, Earl of Leicester.

## 98

1. He was the last Communist Party MP.
2. The Blessed Virgin Mary.
3. France, Germany, Italy, the Netherlands, Belgium, and Luxembourg.
4. James I.
5. President Truman's.
6. Lord Randolph Churchill.

## 174

1. Two: Leon Brittan and Lord Young.
2. Lord Montgomery in 1966.
3. Monaco.
4. John of Gaunt.
5. Winston Churchill.
6. Nell Gwyn.

## 23

1. Where would you find the *Penguin News*?
2. Sir Frederick Bennett MP has written of China justifiably reclaiming its territory in 1950, otherwise known as . . . what?
3. What does an MP do when filibustering?
4. What were King Charles I's words when he saw the five members had fled from Parliament in 1642?
5. Jinnah was the founder of which state in 1947?
6. The British bobby was sent to force Anguilla to re-submit to whose rule?

## 99

1. When was Margaret Thatcher first elected to Parliament?
2. Who were kicked out of Jordan in September 1970?
3. What does a barrister do when he 'takes silk'?
4. Who was the first English monarch to become King of Ireland?
5. Who was the third member of the triumvirate along with Antony and Augustus?
6. Who was the only Commonwealth Prime Minister to have been an amateur heavyweight boxing champion?

## 175

1. Deakin, Holmes and Le Mesurier joined whom in the dock in 1979?
2. What number of republics is the current Republic of France?
3. When was the SDP formed?
4. Which Prime Minister lost his own seat in 1906?
5. What type of tree belonging to his father was George Washington supposed to have destroyed when a boy?
6. What was unusual about Lord de Clifford's trial in 1935?

# 23

1. It is the Falklands newspaper.
2. The invasion of Tibet.
3. Engage in deliberate time-wasting and obstructionist procedures.
4. 'I see the birds have flown.'
5. Pakistan.
6. St Kitts'.

# 99

1. 1959.
2. The PLO.
3. Becomes a QC.
4. Henry VIII (previous monarchs were Lords of Ireland).
5. Lepidus.
6. Sir Roy Welensky.

# 175

1. Jeremy Thorpe.
2. The fifth republic, established in 1958.
3. 25 January 1981.
4. A. J. Balfour.
5. A cherry tree.
6. He was the last lord to be tried by his peers in the House of Lords.

# Q

## 24

1. Which is by far the largest government department?
2. Which country withdrew from NATO in 1966?
3. What are the two chambers of the US Congress?
4. Who was the historian who dissected eighteenth-century Parliaments and Parliamentarians?
5. Which famous Bolshevik died in 1924?
6. In 1971, who was selling Spongecake Fascist Empire, Spaghetti Blackshirt and Beefsteak Benito in a café?

## 100

1. Who was in charge of the Falklands Task Force?
2. In 1914 there were only two republics in Europe, not including Switzerland which was a federation. Which two?
3. About how many (nearest hundred) people have a vote in Parliament by virtue of birth alone?
4. If the Roundheads were Right but Repulsive, what were the Cavaliers?
5. Which Moghul Emperor concluded a treaty with Queen Elizabeth I?
6. Who was the last Etonian Prime Minister?

## 176

1. Whom did Nye Bevan consider to be 'lower than vermin'?
2. Where did the fourth crusade end up?
3. What is the quorum for the House of Lords?
4. Who were the Ditchers in the first few decades of the twentieth century?
5. General Lon Nol controlled which country before the Khmer Rouge took over in 1975?
6. Whose body was found in a boot near Rome in 1978?

# 24

1. The Ministry of Defence.
2. France.
3. The Senate and the House of Representatives.
4. Sir Lewis Namier.
5. Lenin.
6. Mussolini's wife.

# 100

1. Rear Admiral John Woodward.
2. France and Portugal.
3. 800.
4. Wrong but Wromantic (from *1066 And All That*).
5. Akbar the Great.
6. Sir Alec Douglas-Home.

# 176

1. The Tories.
2. Storming Constantinople.
3. Three peers.
4. Tory ultras who swore to die in the last ditch rather than allow reform.
5. Cambodia.
6. Aldo Moro.

## 25

1. Harold Wilson, Nye Bevan and (who?) resigned from Attlee's government in 1951.
2. What was the German Republic called in 1919–33?
3. The British National Party and the League of Empire Loyalists were among those who formed what?
4. Which British Prime Minister was so short-sighted that he failed to recognize a member of his own cabinet?
5. What religion is Richard Nixon?
6. Who ended his days in a botanical garden in Peking?

## 101

1. Who said, 'We are not at war with Egypt. We are in an armed conflict'?
2. Who was known as 'Stupor Mundi'?
3. What is the judicial capital of South Africa?
4. What article of attire so offended Wellington on his inspection of the first reformed Parliament?
5. Which 1970s European leader was nicknamed the 'Lip'?
6. In what newspaper did the headline 'Gotcha!' appear after the sinking of the *Belgrano*?

## 177

1. Who grandiloquently announced in 1980 that 'the defence of democracy knows no bounds'?
2. What is the South African-backed rebel force in Angola?
3. German East Africa, South-West Africa and two other colonies were lost by Germany after 1918. Which ones?
4. Why is Britain traditionally called Great Britain?
5. John of Leyden, one of the Anabaptist élite, declared himself as what ruler?
6. What former premier was convicted of accepting Lockheed bribes and sentenced to four years' imprisonment?

# 25

1. John Freeman.
2. Weimar.
3. The National Front.
4. Lord Salisbury.
5. Quaker.
6. The last Emperor of China, who died in 1967.

# 101

1. Sir Anthony Eden in 1956.
2. Emperor Frederick II.
3. Bloemfontein.
4. Hats.
5. Helmut Schmidt.
6. The *Sun*.

# 177

1. Francis Pym, after the Russian invasion of Afghanistan – a country not noted for its democratic tradition.
2. UNITA.
3. The Cameroons and Togo.
4. To distinguish it from Brittany.
5. King of the world.
6. Mr Tanaka of Japan.

## 26

1. Dalton did not become Foreign Secretary in 1945. Why?
2. Who told Alexander the Great to get out of his sunlight?
3. What was Dubrovnik in Yugoslavia formerly called?
4. What did Strafford say on hearing that King Charles had assented to his execution?
5. Who is the current ruler of Zaire?
6. To whom did Edmund Backhouse give advice about homosexual relationships with Prime Ministers?

## 102

1. Who is opposition spokesman on Trade and Industry?
2. What is the main ethnic group comprising Hungary?
3. Are there senators in the Republic of Ireland?
4. Before Sir Oswald Mosley began the New Party, he belonged to which British political party?
5. Who held the Vice-Presidency and Presidency of America without being elected to either office?
6. Which Caribbean leader once acted as an extra in an Esther Williams movie?

## 178

1. Whose recent report on MI5 revealed that all authorized warrants to tap telephones had been authorized warrants?
2. What was the Second Reich?
3. On what day is there no Question Time in Parliament?
4. Which British politician might have been Prime Minister, it was said, had he been half a head taller and his speeches half an hour shorter?
5. Daniel Ortega is President of which Central American country?
6. Who was supposed to have written out Harold Wilson's last Honours List on lavender notepaper?

# 26

1. King George VI loathed him and made his feelings known to Attlee.
2. Diogenes.
3. Ragusa.
4. 'Put not your trust in Princes.'
5. General Mobutu – a great friend to the West.
6. Lord Rosebery.

# 102

1. Peter Shore.
2. Magyars.
3. Yes.
4. Labour.
5. Gerald Ford.
6. Fidel Castro.

# 178

1. Lord Bridges, for which information much thanks.
2. The German Empire from 1887 to 1918.
3. Friday.
4. Leo Amery.
5. Nicaragua.
6. Marcia Falkender.

## 27

1. Who lost his head while swimming around a Soviet warship in Portsmouth?
2. Which French politician gave his name to populist, small-business conservatism in 1950s France?
3. Hawthorn near Bath is the official site of what?
4. This famous London street is named after Oliver Cromwell's representative to The Hague. His name?
5. Which Swedish king was 'The Madman of the North'?
6. Professor Alan Ross first divided the British into what in a Finnish periodical in 1954?

## 103

1. How many VCs were won in the Falklands campaign?
2. Who devised the German U-boat 'Wolf-Pack' attacks?
3. Who was the first woman MP to take her seat?
4. Who was Lawrence, then Ross, then Shaw?
5. Why did Emperor Pedro II of Brazil delight Alexander Graham Bell?
6. Which family, supported by the US until President Carter came to office, ruled Nicaragua for fifty years?

## 179

1. Who stood for the Democratic Monarchist Public Safety White Regionalist Party for North Devon in 1979?
2. Which parallel divides Korea?
3. The rules that a speech in Parliament should not be out of order, irrelevant or repetitive give us what radio game?
4. Who did Jocelyn Hambro brand as the worst Prime Minister since Lord North?
5. Which Italian freedom fighter recalls a biscuit?
6. Who instructed his mistress not to wash too much before he came home from the sea?

## 27

1. Commander Crabbe – a strange choice as spy since he exhibited a number of curious habits, one of which was to sleep in his wet-suit in bed.
2. M. Poujade, from which Poujadism.
3. Central Government War HQ.
4. George Downing.
5. Charles XII.
6. U and non-U.

## 103

1. Two.
2. Admiral Doenitz.
3. Nancy Astor in 1919.
4. T. E. Lawrence of Arabia.
5. He was the intrepid first monarch to use the telephone.
6. Somoza.

## 179

1. Commander Bill Boakes.
2. The thirty-eighth parallel.
3. 'Just a Minute'.
4. Harold Wilson (Lord North presided over the loss of America).
5. Garibaldi.
6. Nelson (to Lady Hamilton).

# 28

1. Who were the Big Three at Yalta in 1945?
2. Which two leading European countries were cultural units long before being united politically?
3. What is the parliament of West Germany called?
4. He wrote about a marooned man in 1719 and had been a spy off and on for seventeen years. Who was he?
5. Why was Anne Boleyn sometimes thought of as a witch?
6. De Madariaga said, '. . . the Anglo-Saxon conscience does not prevent the Anglo-Saxon from sinning. It merely prevents him from . . .' what?

# 104

1. Who seized the Speaker's symbol of office and twirled it about his head?
2. What period did Gibbon regard as most congenial?
3. In Parliament, who signs the 'Test Roll'?
4. Who has been the shortest-serving Prime Minister?
5. Which Roman Emperor arrived, examined and won?
6. Norman St John-Stevas described what as 'partial, inadequate and propaganda'?

# 180

1. What was the policy supported by Harold Wilson in 1960 but rejected by him as Prime Minister?
2. Which statesman said, 'The French are wiser than they seem, and the Spaniards seem wiser than they are'?
3. How does an MP resign his seat during a Parliament?
4. Who said that for two centuries Ireland had been as badly governed as Sicily?
5. Who has been the youngest head of state in France since Louis Napoleon in 1848?
6. How did Charles VI of France manifest his madness?

## 28

1. Churchill, Stalin and Roosevelt.
2. Italy and Germany.
3. Bundestag.
4. Daniel Defoe.
5. She had a rudimentary sixth finger on one hand.
6. Enjoying it.

## 104

1. Michael Heseltine.
2. The years between the death of Domitian and Constantine.
3. A new member.
4. George Canning in 1827.
5. Julius Caesar.
6. The Papal encyclical, Humanae Vitae.

## 180

1. Unilateral nuclear disarmament.
2. Francis Bacon.
3. Apply for stewardship of the Chiltern Hundreds.
4. Stendhal in the early 1800s.
5. Giscard d'Estaing.
6. He thought he was made of glass and would break if moved.

## 29

1. What did Edward Heath buy with the proceeds of the Charlemagne Prize for his work for Europe?
2. Who was the Sea-green Incorruptible?
3. What did the ILP stand for?
4. Who pretended to be a butterfly collector to spy in the Balkans and ended up wearing shorts?
5. According to Unity Mitford, which European leader wanted Edward VIII to remain King?
6. Which Prime Minister this century was illegitimate?

## 105

1. Who 'got on his bike and looked for work'?
2. What is France's largest colony?
3. SMERSH was a genuine acronym of an arm of the KGB. What did it mean?
4. What was the greatest petition presented to Parliament?
5. Whom did Nixon run against in the 1968 Presidential election?
6. Which current Tory MP had a brother who fought for Nazi Germany and was executed by the British in 1945?

## 181

1. Who was 'on holiday at the time' in 1984?
2. Which dynasty replaced the Ming dynasty in China in 1644?
3. What is the IRSP, known as the Irps in Ireland?
4. Which two Victorian Prime Ministers were related by marriage?
5. What was the ruling family in the Netherlands for most of the seventeenth century?
6. For which department did the spy William Vassall work?

# 29

1. A grand piano.
2. Robespierre.
3. Independent Labour Party.
4. Baden-Powell.
5. Hitler.
6. Ramsay MacDonald.

# 105

1. Mr Tebbit's father.
2. New Caledonia.
3. Death to spies.
4. The Chartist petition of 1848 (even excluding false entries).
5. Hubert Humphrey.
6. Julian Amery.

# 181

1. Mrs Thatcher – and so unable to order the prosecution of Mr Ponting.
2. The Manchu dynasty.
3. The Irish Republican Socialist Party.
4. Melbourne and Palmerston.
5. The House of Orange.
6. Admiralty.

## 30

1. Who first defined 'the unacceptable face of capitalism'?
2. In which country did the 'Know-nothings' operate as a political party in the 1850s?
3. Who said, 'My love for an institution is in proportion to my desire to reform it'?
4. Shaw regarded whom as the saint of the nineteenth century?
5. Which Roman Emperor's favourite expression was 'as quick as boiled asparagus'?
6. What links the names of Gorky, Trotsky, Litvinov, Lenin, Zinoviev, Stalin, Molotov and Tito?

## 106

1. What was operation 'Corporate' in 1982?
2. What territory regards itself as 'Nationalist China'?
3. What units make up the Swiss Confederation?
4. To what was Lord Randolph Churchill referring, when Chancellor of the Exchequer, as 'those damned spots'?
5. Who has been the President of Malawi since 1966?
6. Which eighteenth-century king played the flute?

## 182

1. Who was appointed in charge of the British Secret Service's anti-communist section in 1945?
2. What was 'the wrong war, at the wrong place, at the wrong time and with the wrong enemy'?
3. What pleased Lord Melbourne by having 'no damned merit?
4. Who ruled England at the end of the twelfth century?
5. Which Roman Emperor's name meant Little Boots?
6. Which aristocrat sent clippings of her pubic hair to her poet lover?

## 30

1. Edward Heath.
2. The USA (they opposed Catholic immigration and supported slavery).
3. J. S. Mill.
4. William Morris.
5. Augustus.
6. They were all pseudonyms.

## 106

1. The recovery of the Falklands.
2. Taiwan (Formosa).
3. Cantons.
4. Decimal points.
5. Dr Hastings Banda.
6. Frederick the Great of Prussia.

## 182

1. The Russian spy, Kim Philby.
2. General Bradley's view of the proposal to extend the Korean war against mainland China.
3. The Order of the Garter.
4. King John.
5. Caligula.
6. Lady Caroline Lamb to Byron.

## 31

1. 13 July 1962 was for seven ministers Macmillan's what?
2. What was the name of the Gold Coast after independence?
3. How often do Labour constituencies reselect their members?
4. According to Harold Nicolson, who called out, 'You speak for Britain,' to Arthur Greenwood on 2 September 1939?
5. To which island did the Emperor Tiberius retire?
6. Who has ten children and is a fierce opponent of contraception for girls under sixteen?

## 107

1. Which Chancellor of the Exchequer called in the IMF?
2. What was known as 'Seward's folly' until the Klondike Gold Rush?
3. Room 40 stood for what in the First World War?
4. What did Sir John Harrington install for Elizabeth I in Richmond Palace?
5. How were Mrs Gandhi and the Mahatma related?
6. The would-be murderer, Newton, who featured in the Thorpe trial, killed only what in 1975?

## 183

1. Which Conservative MP has referred to the Prime Minister as the great she-elephant?
2. President Nixon's internal White House police unit was collectively known as the what?
3. Where did the House of Commons sit from 1941 to 1950?
4. Why was Charles Bradlaugh, an elected MP from 1880, excluded from sitting in the House until 1886?
5. Which Russian Tsar occasionally practised as a shipwright, barber and dentist?
6. How many suits for civil libel has Sir James Goldsmith had against *Private Eye* (to date)?

## 31

1. 'Night of the Long Knives'.
2. Ghana.
3. Every two years.
4. Bob Boothby (not Leo Amery).
5. Capri.
6. Victoria Gillick.

## 107

1. Denis Healey.
2. The American Secretary of State's purchase of Alaska from Russia in 1867.
3. Naval Intelligence.
4. A water-flushed lavatory.
5. None.
6. A dog.

## 183

1. Julian Critchley.
2. The plumbers.
3. In the House of Lords while their own chamber was being rebuilt.
4. He was an atheist.
5. Peter the Great.
6. Sixty-four.

## 32

1. Who mislaid his trousers on the train?
2. How did Socrates die?
3. What was the Roman name for what is now France?
4. For how long did Lady Jane Grey reign as Queen?
5. Which American President came from Abilene?
6. Of what part of his anatomy did King James I, in a fearful rage, promise a view for his English subjects?

## 108

1. Which film on the effects of nuclear war in Britain has been consistently banned from TV by the government?
2. Who said, 'I would rather be a pineapple grower in Alaska than candidate for the Chancellorship' (of West Germany)'?
3. Which city did Canberra succeed as capital of Australia?
4. Why did Ireland's fascists give up the ritual hailing of their leader in the 1930s?
5. Which Russian Tsars killed their sons?
6. The head of MI6 is always referred to by what initial after its founder?

## 184

1. Constantine Sergio Davidoff went to South Georgia to do what?
2. What was the name of the Nazi laws against Jews?
3. What are the initials of the Basque separatist movement?
4. According to Kipling, what weapon did patriotic Englishmen use against the Boer leader, Paul Kruger?
5. What was Cleopatra's first child called?
6. In *Private Eye* during 1978, who was known as the 'Ditto Man'?

## 32

1. Sir Geoffrey Howe.
2. He was condemned to drink hemlock.
3. Gaul.
4. Nine days.
5. Eisenhower.
6. His arse.

## 108

1. *The War Game.*
2. Franz-Joseph Strauss – who soon after these words put forward his name.
3. Melbourne.
4. Because 'Hail O'Duffy' was less euphonious than 'Heil Hitler'.
5. Ivan the Terrible and Peter the Great.
6. 'C' – doubtless for reasons of national security.

## 184

1. Collect scrap iron.
2. The Nuremberg Laws of 1935.
3. ETA.
4. Their mouths.
5. Caesarion.
6. Jeremy Thorpe, who would first say 'no comment' and then 'ditto' to subsequent questions.

## 33

1. From where did Commander-in-Chief Admiral Fieldhouse run the Falklands war?
2. What was the medieval name for China?
3. Who wrote, 'A politician is a man who can be verbose in fewer words than anyone else'?
4. What was the Pale in medieval Ireland?
5. How many rulers have there been of the Soviet Union before Gorbachev?
6. What kind of doctor was Stephen Ward, the linkman in the Profumo scandal?

## 109

1. Who has the most prominent eyebrows: Denis Healey, Eric Heffer or Ian Mikardo?
2. Who were the Tupamaros?
3. A change of sandal style indicated what in ancient Rome?
4. Which English king had most legitimate children?
5. Who was known as the sick man of Europe in the late nineteenth century?
6. Did Sara Keays ever dare to disturb Cecil Parkinson's Brylcreemed hair?

## 185

1. 'Is he one of us?' Who he? Who us? Who speaking?
2. What nineteenth-century anarchist was also a prince?
3. What was the capital of India from 1772 to 1912?
4. Which English king had most illegitimate children?
5. Who was the President of the southern states during the American civil war?
6. Which Liberal MP and future Regius Professor of History at Cambridge was banned from attending the university as a student?

# 33

1. Navy Operations Headquarters, Northwood, London.
2. Cathay.
3. Peter de Vries.
4. The small area around Dublin controlled by the Crown.
5. Seven.
6. An osteopath.

# 109

1. Healey, by a short hair.
2. An urban guerrilla movement in Uruguay, crushed in the 1970s.
3. A man had become a senator.
4. Edward I.
5. The Turkish Sultan.
6. Alas, we will never know.

# 185

1. A senior civil servant being considered for promotion; current Conservative thinkers; Mrs Thatcher.
2. Prince Kropotkin.
3. Calcutta.
4. Henry I.
5. Jefferson Davis.
6. Lord Acton, who as a Catholic was banned by the Religious Tests.

## 34

1. What is otherwise known as MI6?
2. What is the Spanish hero, Rodrigo Diaz, better known as?
3. What was the conference called which established the post Second World War financial system?
4. Who was astonished at his own moderation?
5. What connected Napoleon to a palindrome?
6. What battle in 1827 was described by a British politician as an 'untoward incident'?

## 110

1. What did the Home Secretary do to Philip Agee after the ABC trial?
2. Which senior member of the Politburo bears the same name as Russia's reigning family until 1917?
3. Katherine Graham owned what American 'institution'?
4. For six months from September 1944 Britain was visited by 1,150 of these. What were they?
5. Who was the Swedish king who won a series of victories in the Thirty Years War?
6. What was Christine Keeler on trial for?

## 186

1. Who has been only the second Conservative PM to be re-elected after a full term?
2. Which country is the 'cockpit of Europe'?
3. In 1949, Canada, the USA and members from western Europe signed what?
4. Which Henry was shocked by a low-necked gown?
5. Who was known as Barbarossa; and how was 'Barbarossa' used as a codename in the Second World War?
6. What seasonal decoration did Prince Albert introduce into England?

## 34

1. SIS (Secret Intelligence Service).
2. El Cid.
3. Bretton Woods.
4. Robert Clive.
5. Elba (Able was I ere I saw Elba).
6. Navarino; the British, French and Russian fleets utterly destroyed a Turkish fleet without any declaration of war.

## 110

1. Deport him.
2. Grigory Romanov.
3. The *Washington Post*.
4. V2s.
5. Gustavus Adolphus.
6. Perjury.

## 186

1. Mrs Thatcher; the first was Lord Salisbury in 1900.
2. Belgium – the place is full of battlefields.
3. The NATO treaty.
4. Henry VI.
5. Emperor Frederick I; for Hitler's invasion of Russia.
6. The Christmas tree.

## 35

1. Which prominent left-winger surprisingly supported Labour's pro-nuclear-weapons resolution in 1957?
2. How do the Russians refer to the Second World War?
3. The UN still recognizes East Timor, now occupied by what country?
4. When was England's first Commonwealth?
5. Which foreign prince was killed fighting with the British army in the Zulu war of 1879?
6. The Japanese Purple and the German Enigma were opposed by what?

## 111

1. In the Falklands the Paras called marching with packs 'tabbing' but the Marines called it what?
2. What is the derivation of the devil's name 'Old Nick'?
3. How many universities are there in Britain?
4. Which English king reigned the longest, uninterrupted?
5. What was the French King Charles the Beloved's other epithet?
6. Which President was taped solemnly saying, 'No, it is wrong – that's for sure'?

## 187

1. Kim Philby, Guy Burgess, Donald Maclean and Anthony Blunt went to which university?
2. Which country controlled Norway from the fourteenth to the nineteenth century?
3. What is the Dail?
4. The theory of modern anti-semitism largely derives from the writings of which Englishman?
5. On which day was Charlemagne crowned Emperor?
6. Which one of Wilson's peers went to jail for fraud?

## 35

1. Aneurin Bevan.
2. The Great Patriotic War (of 1941–5).
3. Indonesia.
4. From 1649–53.
5. The Prince Imperial, son of Napoleon III.
6. Ultra.

## 111

1. Yomping.
2. From Niccolò Machiavelli.
3. Forty-five.
4. George III, 1760–1820.
5. Charles the Mad.
6. Nixon.

## 187

1. Cambridge.
2. Denmark.
3. The Irish Assembly or lower house of Parliament.
4. Houston Chamberlain.
5. Christmas Day.
6. Lord Kagan.

## 36

1. Denis Healey has said he wants to be the Labour Party's . . . (what seemingly indestructible Soviet politician?)
2. The Pathet Lao were communist forces from where?
3. Local Education Authorities have a legal duty to educate children from what age?
4. Which Liberal leader delighted in saying, 'Wait and see'?
5. Which dancer bewitched King Ludwig of Bavaria?
6. What recent operation on English soil needed more soldiers than it took to capture Port Stanley?

## 112

1. Which politician's name has shrunk over the years?
2. What is the Republic in the Soviet Union where people live to an extraordinary age?
3. What two airlines made up British Airways?
4. How many English queens have ruled in their own right?
5. What was Tsar Alexander II's fate in 1881?
6. Apart from *Lady Chatterley's Lover*, two other novels were prosecuted for obscenity in the 1960s. What were they?

## 188

1. Who asked, 'Would you buy a second-hand scooter from [John Selwyn Gummer]'?
2. Whom did General Custer attempt to discipline with 264 men at Little Big Horn?
3. The House of Commons cheered when what were abolished in 1952?
4. Who led the Peasants' Revolt in 1381?
5. Who fled from France to Edinburgh and back three times between 1789 and 1830?
6. John Morley said, 'Politics is a field where the choice lies constantly between two . . .' what?

# 36

1. Andrei Gromyko.
2. Laos.
3. Five.
4. Asquith.
5. Lola Montez (born Eliza Gilbert).
6. Removing the protesters at Molesworth in February 1985.

# 112

1. The present demotic Tony Benn.
2. Georgia.
3. BOAC and BEA.
4. Five.
5. He was blown up by a bomb.
6. *Fanny Hill* and *Last Exit to Brooklyn*.

# 188

1. Denis Healey.
2. The Sioux.
3. Wartime identity cards.
4. Wat Tyler.
5. The Bourbon, King Charles X.
6. Blunders.

## 37

1. Which government minister supervised the campaign to remove Molesworth protesters in February 1985?
2. What was the Risorgimento?
3. What office is bestowed on a cabinet minister without portfolio?
4. The Duke of Windsor spent the Second World War how?
5. Philip the Arab was on the throne of what in AD 244?
6. Who stood against Jeremy Thorpe for the Dog Lovers Party in 1979?

## 113

1. In the autumn of 1970 Mr Heath released a terrorist in an exchange for hostages. Who was she?
2. Which country ruled the Dodecanese islands in the Aegean from 1912 to 1945?
3. Who wrote in 1981, 'For two decades the state has been taking liberties, and these liberties were once ours'?
4. Where did the Scots come from?
5. Two bloodthirsty Presidents of Afghanistan and Uganda shared the same name in the 1970s. What was it?
6. The Japanese government apparently consulted what book over major decisions before the First World War?

## 189

1. Who talked about 'the wind of change' in 1960?
2. What were Spartan serfs called?
3. Who wrote, 'Who controls the past controls the future?'?
4. The Albemarle pippin was which monarch's favourite apple?
5. Who was Portugal's dictator from 1932 to 1968?
6. Why did Kaiser Wilhelm II travel with a barber?

## 37

1. Michael Heseltine.
2. Italian unification in the nineteenth century.
3. Chancellor of the Duchy of Lancaster.
4. As Governor of the Bahamas.
5. The Roman Empire.
6. Auberon Waugh.

## 113

1. Leila Khaled.
2. Italy.
3. E. P. Thompson.
4. Ireland.
5. Amin.
6. The I Ching.

## 189

1. Harold Macmillan.
2. Helots.
3. George Orwell in *1984*.
4. Queen Victoria's.
5. Antonio Salazar.
6. To make sure the ends of his moustache always curled up.

## 38

1. Which Liberal MP called Mrs Thatcher 'Attila the Hen'?
2. What was the old name for Ho Chi Minh city?
3. Which American right-winger tells us, 'Conservatism is the politics of reality'?
4. Who was the Speaker of the House of Commons in the Long Parliament?
5. Who engineered Khrushchev's downfall in 1964?
6. Which Prime Minister was shot dead in the lobby of the Commons?

## 114

1. Richard Needham MP had a very high-ranking fag when at Eton. Who?
2. Who were the self-styled Prisoners in the Vatican?
3. Before 1832 what were parliamentary seats regarded as the property of landowners called?
4. How many children did Queen Victoria have?
5. Who married Napoleon's jilted fiancée and went on to greater things?
6. What went from A to 15 recently?

## 190

1. Dr Bob Jones of Dr Bob Jones University, America, awarded another doctorate to which holy man and loud-voiced politician?
2. 'J'accuse!' Who on behalf of whom?
3. The Parliamentary Labour Party is the correct term for the Party at Westminster; what is it for the Tories?
4. Who was the GOM?
5. Who wasn't Lenin *then*?
6. Arriving by helicopter on Exmoor, the Archbishop of Canterbury blessed a monument to which MP's first wife?

## 38

1. Clement Freud.
2. Saigon.
3. William F. Buckley – writing in *Playboy* (1970).
4. William Lenthall.
5. Leonid Brezhnev.
6. Spencer Perceval, in 1812.

## 114

1. The King of Nepal.
2. Successive Popes from 1870 until 1929.
3. Pocket boroughs.
4. Nine.
5. Jean-Baptiste Bernadotte, elected heir to the King of Sweden in 1810.
6. The film classifications.

## 190

1. Ian Paisley.
2. Zola for Dreyfus.
3. The Conservative Party.
4. Gladstone (Grand Old Man).
5. Vladimir Ilyich Ulyanov.
6. Jeremy Thorpe's.

## 39

1. Which bishop announced in March 1985 that the government's economic strategy was 'threateningly divisive'?
2. What two European dictatorships fell in 1974?
3. What is the correct term for the Conservative Party outside Parliament?
4. Which English title was in abeyance between 1572 and 1623?
5. Ben Bella was which country's first President?
6. What were George V's attributed last words?

## 115

1. Mr Heath's pledge to sacrifice 'lame ducks' was ruined by intervention in two firms. Name one.
2. When did Spain and the Soviet Union resume diplomatic relations after 1939?
3. What was a Polish Diet?
4. A British thriller writer worked in wartime intelligence under the code name '17F'. Who was he?
5. What happened when the authorities opened Tsar Alexander I's coffin in 1865 to allay reports that he had fled to become a hermit?
6. What were George V's actual last words?

## 191

1. What did the British government give back to the Falklanders that it had taken away before?
2. What caused the Great Schism in the fourteenth century?
3. What was the capital of unoccupied France in alliance with Germany during the Second World War?
4. What was the Roman wall north of Hadrian's Wall?
5. Tibet was ruled before the Chinese invasion by a reincarnation of Buddha called what?
6. Who was described as 'a fat gentleman in a passion'?

## 39

1. Durham.
2. Greece and Portugal.
3. The National Union of Conservative and Unionist Associations.
4. Dukes.
5. Algeria.
6. 'How is the Empire?'

## 115

1. Rolls-Royce and Upper Clyde Shipbuilders.
2. 1977.
3. Poland's Parliament or Assembly in the seventeenth and eighteenth centuries.
4. Ian Fleming.
5. The coffin was found to be empty.
6. 'Bugger Bognor.'

## 191

1. Full British citizenship.
2. Rival Popes at Avignon and Rome.
3. Vichy.
4. The Antonine Wall.
5. The Dalai Lama.
6. Charles James Fox.

# 40

1. Who are the Mebyon Kernow in Britain?
2. The Chinese named them 'Heavenly Harmony Fists' but to the British in 1900 they were what?
3. What institution did King Charles II consider better than a play?
4. Who was the oldest English king to start his reign?
5. What future major statesman was largely responsible for the Allies' defeat at Gallipoli?
6. In 1977 what was wrong with the *Daily Mail*'s campaign on bribery and corruption at British Leyland?

# 116

1. Did Hugh Gaitskell support or oppose Britain's proposed entry into the Common Market in the early 1960s?
2. What is the official name for America's 'Star Wars' project?
3. What is the Opposition side of the House of Lords called?
4. Jacob Winstanley led which radical sect in the 1650s?
5. How many emperors were involved in the First World War?
6. What is the diminutive of President Jean-Claude Duvalier of Haiti, son of the infamous 'Papa Doc'?

# 192

1. Who kept on confessing in drunken moments that he was a Russian spy, only to find no one believed him?
2. What was bogus about Mussolini's 'March on Rome' in 1922?
3. What does the word Utopia mean?
4. Sir John Oldcastle was the historical original for which Shakespearean character?
5. Which Roman Emperor died at York?
6. Which right-wing journal can be said to be 'Then'?

## 40

1. Sons of Cornwall wanting a separate Cornish state.
2. 'The Boxers' – xenophobic young Chinese who attacked foreign legations.
3. The House of Lords' debates.
4. William IV, aged sixty-four in 1830.
5. Kemal Ataturk, General of the Turkish forces.
6. It was based on a forged letter.

## 116

1. He carefully examined the economic considerations and sensibly opposed the move.
2. Strategic Defence Initiative.
3. The Temporal Side.
4. The Diggers.
5. Five: Indian (GB), Russian, German, Austrian and Ottoman.
6. 'Baby Doc'.

## 192

1. Guy Burgess.
2. The fact that he came to Rome by express train.
3. Nowhere (from the Greek).
4. Falstaff.
5. Severus.
6. Sir James Goldsmith's defunct *Now!*

# 41

1. Which British politician has Peter Jenkins described as 'Keeper of the Cloth Cap'?
2. What was the name of Crete when a Venetian colony?
3. Who is or was the longest-serving MP of all time?
4. Who made the Balfour Declaration in 1917?
5. How many emperors survived the First World War?
6. Who was sacked after Edward Heath had replied 'damned lies' to those asking if the reports of the sacking were true?

# 117

1. Which two founding members of the SDP lost their seats in the 1983 election?
2. Against which country was 'jingoism' first coined?
3. The bundle of papers for business in Parliament are coloured: white for current, blue for what?
4. What did Lord Derby say to Disraeli when he demurred at becoming Chancellor of the Exchequer?
5. Who ended up with an ice-pick in the back of his skull?
6. The Pencourt file finally did whom in?

# 193

1. Tony Benn could do this only after a bill was passed in 1963. What?
2. What city was Polish until 1795, Austrian until 1815, independent until 1846, Austrian until 1919, and then Polish again?
3. With what does Parliament begin its sitting of the day?
4. Who hated all 'Boets and Bainters'?
5. Who was the founder of Moral Re-Armament, aimed at ridding the world of evil and the forces of communism?
6. Who thought the Commons was noisier than anywhere else, 'not excepting Smithfield on a market day'?

## 41

1. Jim Callaghan.
2. Candia.
3. Winston Churchill (1900–64).
4. A. J. Balfour.
5. One: the King of England as Emperor of India.
6. Edward du Cann.

## 117

1. Shirley Williams and Bill Rodgers.
2. Russia in 1878.
3. Future business.
4. 'They give you the figures.'
5. Trotsky.
6. Jeremy Thorpe.

## 193

1. Renounce his peerage.
2. Krakow.
3. Prayers.
4. George I.
5. Frank Buchman.
6. Dickens.

## 42

1. Why is Mrs Thatcher sometimes called Tina?
2. What was the French right-wing political movement in the first half of the twentieth century?
3. What provincial city in Ireland held the seat of government for the Anglo-Irish forces in the 1640s?
4. Who used the British Museum Reading Room under the assumed name of Jacob Richter LI.D.?
5. Which of Napoleon's generals was given Naples?
6. Axel, Count von Fersen, was reputed to have been which French queen's lover?

## 118

1. Of whom was it said, 'He was the last Prime Minister to believe Britain was a great power and the first to confront a crisis which proved she was not'?
2. Who offered a new deal for the American people?
3. Two long bell rings indicate what in Parliament?
4. Which Parliamentarian general never went to war without his coffin and winding sheet?
5. Ex-Prime Minister Ecevit of Turkey was known for what artistic skill?
6. 'Towards the end of '26/They shoved (who?) into politics?

## 194

1. What survived the attack on Pearl Harbor but sank in 1982?
2. Who said 'Non' in January 1963 and again in December?
3. Who disciplines peers in the House of Lords?
4. Who was the radical author of *The Rights of Man*?
5. Who was the 'Winter Queen' in the seventeenth century?
6. What are interviews with the President of Zimbabwe, the Rev. Canaan Banana, never described as?

# 42

1. There Is No Alternative.
2. Action Française.
3. Kilkenny.
4. Lenin.
5. Joachim Murat.
6. Marie-Antoinette.

# 118

1. Anthony Eden.
2. President Roosevelt.
3. A division or count of votes.
4. The Earl of Essex.
5. Poetry.
6. Lord Lundy (from Belloc).

# 194

1. The *General Belgrano*.
2. De Gaulle – to Britain's EEC application.
3. Black Rod.
4. Tom Paine.
5. Elizabeth of Bohemia, daughter of James I.
6. 'Fruitful talks'.

## 43

1. The US spy post called the Berlin Tunnel was betrayed by which Russian agent in 1956?
2. Which country occupied Nicaragua from 1909 to 1938?
3. What is the day of the week for right-wing Tories?
4. Why was the Irish Parliament in the eighteenth century unrepresentative of the great majority of the Irish people?
5. Who was the world's first woman Prime Minister?
6. Lianche-Josiffe was a male model who loved a politician. Who was he better known as?

## 119

1. Which astronomer was a founder of the Democratic Monarchist Public Safety White Regionalist Party?
2. What European territorial question in the 1860s was so difficult only three people were reputed to understand it?
3. What is the London club most associated with the Tory Party?
4. What position did Sir Thomas More hold in Parliament?
5. Which Swedish queen abdicated, went to Rome and became a Catholic?
6. What modern social habit did James I deplore?

## 195

1. What is the link between Hard Rock, Scrum-Half, Square-Leg and Inside Right?
2. What does ASEAN stand for?
3. What was given life, by the American Press magnate Harry Luce, and gained instant popularity in 1936?
4. Who was the first British monarch to set foot in the USA?
5. What discomfort may have distracted Napoleon from his tactics at Waterloo?
6. In America, what did CREEP mean to the electorate?

## 43

1. George Blake.
2. The USA.
3. Monday (Club).
4. Because Catholics could neither sit nor vote.
5. Mrs Bandaranaike of Ceylon in 1960.
6. Norman Scott.

## 119

1. Patrick Moore.
2. The Schleswig-Holstein question.
3. The Carlton Club.
4. Speaker.
5. Queen Christina.
6. Smoking.

## 195

1. They were all recent Civil Defence exercises.
2. Association of South-East Asian Nations.
3. *Life* Magazine.
4. George VI in 1939.
5. Piles.
6. Campaign to re-elect the President (Nixon).

## 44

1. Which Irish political party, once translated, means the tribe (or family) of the Irish?
2. What dynasty did Charlemagne found in France?
3. Which cabinet was a silent film?
4. Who were transported from Dorset in 1834?
5. Who is the President of the Philippines?
6. Southampton University students elected Bruce Reynolds to honorary life membership of their union for what?

## 120

1. Who was the military commander of the British Falklands invasion force?
2. What tiny country lies to the east of Switzerland?
3. What quality national daily paper in Europe appears on the streets in the evening?
4. What playwright and contemporary of Shakespeare was an occasional spy for the government?
5. It was said that Hannibal was corrupted by a winter stay in what Italian coastal city?
6. Why did the Cabinet minister, J. H. Thomas, resign in 1936?

## 196

1. Who was revealed as the Fourth Man in 1979?
2. Which American politician deeply admires Metternich?
3. Until when did the ancient universities elect members to Parliament?
4. Who described Arthur as the 'once and future king'?
5. Gorbachev is how much younger than Mr Reagan?
6. Who complained about the defect in the Constitution which allowed a Liberal government to come to power 'merely on account of the number of votes'?

# 44

1. Fine Gael.
2. Carolingians.
3. *The Cabinet of Dr Caligari.*
4. The Tolpuddle martyrs.
5. Marcos.
6. Organizing the Great Train Robbery.

# 120

1. Major-General Jeremy Moore.
2. Liechtenstein.
3. *Le Monde.*
4. Christopher Marlowe.
5. Capua.
6. He leaked Budget details.

# 196

1. Sir Anthony Blunt.
2. Henry Kissinger.
3. 1948.
4. Sir Thomas Malory.
5. Twenty.
6. Queen Victoria.

# Q

## 45

1. Which Cabinet minister is portrayed by a political cartoonist as Captain Brain-Damage?
2. What was Portugal's colony in India?
3. Who is the only PM to have held all three major offices of state (Chancellor, Home Secretary and Foreign Secretary)?
4. 'Say to the Court it glows/And shines like rotten wood.' Author?
5. 'When [who?] died the little children cried in the streets.'
6. Dr Savundra was convicted of fraud in the 1960s in what line of work?

## 121

1. Which Prime Minister had the 'Kitchen Cabinet'?
2. Which South American country sent Allied troops to Italy in the Second World War?
3. What is the parliament chamber in Israel called?
4. Who first brought back 'peace with honour'?
5. What was the Roman Emperor Julian also known as?
6. Which ruler recognized 350 illegitimate children?

## 197

1. Bettaney is currently serving twenty-three years for what?
2. Name the three Baltic republics independent between the world wars.
3. How many MPs sit in the House of Commons?
4. Which Prime Minister said, 'Damn your principles! Stick to your party'?
5. Which Prime Minister re-wrote *Uncle Tom's Cabin*?
6. What have the British homosexual Russian spies been known as?

## 45

1. Michael Heseltine.
2. Goa.
3. James Callaghan.
4. Sir Walter Ralegh.
5. William the Silent of the Netherlands.
6. Insurance.

## 121

1. Harold Wilson.
2. Brazil.
3. The Knesset.
4. Disraeli in 1878.
5. The Apostate.
6. Elector Frederick I of Saxony.

## 197

1. Attempting to spy for the Russians (who did not accept the offer of his services).
2. Latvia, Lithuania and Estonia.
3. 650.
4. Disraeli.
5. Winston Churchill.
6. The Homintern.

## 46

1. Who won the Crosby by-election in November 1981?
2. 'More mush from the Wimp' was how one newspaper described a speech by which American President?
3. Which former British colony never joined the Commonwealth?
4. What did the British band play at their surrender to the Americans at Yorktown?
5. Bernardo O'Higgins was President of which country in the early nineteenth century?
6. Which African emperor, supported then deposed by the French, bestowed diamonds on the French President?

## 122

1. John Osborne said this was 'the gold filling in a mouth of decay'. What was?
2. Who was the bishop who came to an agreement with Ian Smith in 1978?
3. Who first used the phrase 'the iron curtain'?
4. Which king is said never to have smiled again after his son went down in the White Ship?
5. Hippolyta was the legendary queen of what society?
6. Who lets us know that she drinks Diet-Pepsi?

## 198

1. Alfred Hinds escaped from what prison in Nottingham to try to prove his innocence?
2. What two languages are spoken in Belgium?
3. What was unusual about executions in France until 1939?
4. What is the name Charing Cross a corruption of?
5. What nationality was Stalin?
6. What was the Empress Josephine's chief fault as a beauty?

## 46

1. Shirley Williams for the SDP.
2. Carter.
3. Burma.
4. 'The world turned upside down.'
5. Chile.
6. Bokassa.

## 122

1. The monarchy.
2. Muzorewa.
3. Lady Snowden in 1920 (neither Goebbels nor Churchill).
4. Henry I.
5. The Amazons.
6. Geraldine Ferraro.

## 198

1. Sherwood prison.
2. Flemish and French.
3. They were still held in public – a spectacle abolished by most European countries in the nineteenth century.
4. Chère Reine – after Queen Eleanor's body had rested there before burial at Westminster Abbey.
5. Georgian.
6. Her bad teeth.

## 47

1. When was the highest popular vote for a single political party after the Second World War?
2. Who felt, 'It is a pleasant change to be in a country that isn't ruled by its own people'?
3. How many times can the Lords reject a Bill before it becomes an Act without their approval?
4. Who was known as 'Steenie' to James I?
5. Of whom did Talleyrand say, 'I am amazed that such a great man could be so badly brought up'?
6. What was the forgery which revealed a Jewish-Communist plot to gain global influence?

## 123

1. When is it said the British will leave Gibraltar?
2. Botswana was formerly known as?
3. What financial institution is known as the 'Honkers and Shankers'?
4. Why were the English commanders who captured Jamaica in 1655 thrown into the Tower on their return?
5. Who was the first socialist Prime Minister of France?
6. The last American Presidential car to have these for bodyguards was retired in 1953. What were they?

## 199

1. Who renounced a peerage to become Prime Minister?
2. Name the order of knights which controlled the Baltic territories in the Middle Ages.
3. What went from CHEKA to GPU to OGPU to NKVD to MVD and then to something else in 1954?
4. If Richard III had married Elizabeth of York, as it is said he planned to do, whom would he have married?
5. What family learnt nothing and forgot nothing?
6. Who were John Knox's monstrous regiment of women?

## 47

1. In 1951 for Labour.
2. Prince Philip, visiting Paraguay in 1962.
3. Twice.
4. The Duke of Buckingham.
5. Napoleon.
6. The Protocols of the Elders of Zion.

## 123

1. When the apes leave the Rock.
2. Bechuanaland.
3. The Hong Kong and Shanghai Bank.
4. They were supposed to capture Hispaniola.
5. Leon Blum in 1936.
6. Running-boards.

## 199

1. Sir Alec Douglas-Home.
2. The Teutonic Order.
3. KGB.
4. His niece.
5. The Bourbons.
6. Female rulers at that time: Mary Queen of Scots, Elizabeth I and Catherine de Medici.

## 48

1. What did the councillors of Clay Cross reject in 1973?
2. Which African territory was the personal possession of King Leopold of Belgium?
3. When was the first time the leader of the Conservative Party was elected?
4. When might the House of Lords have been suddenly swelled by an extra 500 peers?
5. Who is still the military leader of the Khmer Rouge, given open support by China and objective support by the West including Britain?
6. A scandalous club had its official name as the Society of St Francis of Wycombe. What was it better known as?

## 121

1. Which Prime Minister once edited the *Church Times*?
2. What does Ernesto Guevara's nickname of 'Che' mean?
3. What action indicates a PM's acceptance by the monarch?
4. Which English monarch was responsible for infecting Europe's royal families with haemophilia?
5. How many presidents of the USA have there been?
6. What was the name of the Emperor Claudius' wife?

## 200

1. According to Beaverbrook, who committed suicide twenty-five years after his death?
2. Which three main ethnic groups comprise Yugoslavia?
3. Where would you find this Article – Everyone has the right to rest and leisure, including reasonable limitation of working hours and periodic holidays with pay?
4. For how many days did the privilege of sanctuary last?
5. Who was known as 'Oom Paul'?
6. Who did Lenin say, was 'a good man fallen among Fabians'?

## 48

1. The raising of council-house rents.
2. The Congo.
3. 1965.
4. During the constitutional crisis of 1911, when the Liberals threatened to ask the King to create 500 Liberal peers to break the Tory majority in the Lords.
5. Pol Pot.
6. The Hellfire Club.

## 124

1. Edward Heath.
2. Chum (in Argentinian argot).
3. Kissing the monarch's hand.
4. Victoria.
5. Ronald Reagan is the fortieth.
6. Messalina.

## 200

1. Field-Marshal Haig.
2. Serbs, Croats and Slovenes.
3. UN Declaration of Human Rights.
4. Forty.
5. The Boer leader, Paul Kruger.
6. G. B. Shaw.

## 49

1. What distinguished an Earl of Leicester's speech in 1972?
2. How many (to the nearest half million) Russians died in German POW camps during the Second World War?
3. Which country has the oldest written constitution?
4. According to the song, how many reigns did the Vicar of Bray serve under?
5. From Stettin in the Baltic to (where?) in the Adriatic, an iron curtain had descended across the continent in 1946.
6. Which member of President Reagan's team is known as 'The Prince of Darkness' for his anti-Russian views?

## 125

1. Britain fought which undeclared war 1970 76?
2. How many points did President Wilson devise in 1918?
3. When is an MP a 'Right Honourable Gentleman'?
4. Who believed that the Garden of Eden was to be found at the bottom of the sea near the Seychelles?
5. By 1974 an estimated twenty-four attempts had been made on the life of which socialist leader?
6. Which Prime Minister had cosmetic dental treatment?

## 201

1. Who got lost in the Sahara and distressed the PM?
2. What is the derivation of the word Pakistan?
3. What was Sir Winston Churchill's method of avoiding the rule against accusing a member of lying in the House?
4. Of whom did Asquith say, 'It is fitting that we should have buried the Unknown Prime Minister by the side of the Unknown Warrior' (in Westminster Abbey)?
5. What was surprising about the 1928 election of Charles King as President of Liberia by a majority of 600,000?
6. When were MPs treated as if they were a ploughed field?

## 49

1. It was the first time for 120 years that anyone of his family had spoken in the Lords.
2. Two and a half million.
3. USA.
4. Five (Charles II to George I).
5. Trieste.
6. Richard Perle, Assistant Secretary of Defence.

## 125

1. A war on behalf of Oman.
2. Fourteen.
3. When they are Privy Councillors.
4. General Gordon (of Khartoum).
5. Fidel Castro.
6. Harold Wilson.

## 201

1. Mark Thatcher.
2. From Punjab, Afghan frontier, Kashmir, BaluchISTAN.
3. Charging him with 'terminological inexactitude'.
4. Andrew Bonar Law.
5. There were only 15,000 registered voters.
6. When Dom Mintoff's daughter threw animal dung at them in 1978.

## 50

1. Whose Devon majority rose by 10,703 in 1974?
2. . . . E. Burger replaced Earl . . . in 1969 as American Chief Justice. What name fills both blanks?
3. When was Canada given full independence?
4. Which queen might have had a palace in Norfolk?
5. Sir Eric Gairy and his 'Mongoose gang' ran which Caribbean island?
6. What was Daniel O'Connell's nickname for Sir Robert Peel when the latter was Chief Secretary in Ireland?

## 126

1. Of which compatriot did Churchill say 'in defeat he is unbeatable, in victory unbearable'?
2. Which poet said of the Second World War 'not even the lowest liar of the BBC has claimed that Hitler started it'?
3. Who prescribed scrutiny as the cure for the House of Lords?
4. Who was on the throne of England in 1099?
5. Who was the Pope who conducted an equivocal policy towards the fascist movements of the 1930s?
6. What do a class of British battleships launched in 1906 and rubber contraceptives have in common?

## 202

1. When did the Argentinians invade the Falklands.
2. What country used to be Northern Rhodesia?
3. What was unusual about the Scotland and Wales Acts of the late 1970s?
4. Who was known as the 'Big Fellow' in Ireland's war of independence against Britain, 1919–21?
5. With 550 of his own men, 250 locals, fifteen horses and ten small cannon, who conquered a nation?
6. What is Queen Anne's fan?

## 50

1. Jeremy Thorpe's.
2. Warren.
3. In February 1982, when the constitution was 'repatriated'.
4. Boadicea of the Iceni.
5. Grenada – before Maurice Bishop replaced him, to the relief of the islanders and annoyance of the USA.
6. Orange Peel.

## 126

1. Field Marshal Montgomery.
2. Ezra Pound.
3. Walter Bagehot.
4. William II.
5. Pius XI.
6. Both are commonly known as Dreadnoughts.

## 202

1. 2 April 1982.
2. Zambia.
3. They were based on referendums.
4. Michael Collins.
5. Cortes conquered Mexico.
6. A gesture – nose to thumb with fingers spread.

# Q

## 51

1. Who now broods in the end seat on the front bench below the gangway on the Government side of the Commons?
2. Which country was responsible for the outrageous clauses in the Versailles Treaty after the First World War?
3. What does the Duke of Westminster get back from the Americans in 2955?
4. The last occasion of what was seen outside Newgate Prison in 1868?
5. Xerxes punished the sea for sinking his pontoon bridge how?
6. Which Victorian Prime Minister had the fullest beard?

## 127

1. Which Labour leader tried to moderate Clause 4 of his party's constitution?
2. Which four Latin American countries make up the present Contadora group?
3. What was the origin of Left and Right wings in politics?
4. What great issue split the Tory Party in the 1840s?
5. Charles V, Holy Roman Emperor, spoke Spanish to God, Italian to women, French to men and (what?) to his horse?
6. Skin clarity was élitist in Spain. Why?

## 203

1. Who is said to be £600 million better off as a result of tax concessions since 1979?
2. In which European country would you find nuclear-shelter places for seven million civilians?
3. How is the French Foreign Department also known?
4. Who shouted out at the end of his maiden speech that the time would come when they would hear him?
5. Who was reputedly destroyed Persepolis when drunk?
6. What did Gary Cooper say when asked if he had discerned any communist influence in the scripts he had been sent?

# 51

1. Edward Heath.
2. France.
3. The American Embassy in Grosvenor Square.
4. A public hanging.
5. Having it whipped.
6. Lord Salisbury.

# 127

1. Hugh Gaitskell in 1959.
2. Colombia, Panama, Mexico and Venezuela.
3. After the French Revolution in 1789, the Assembly sat in a semi-circle with the radicals on the left.
4. The Corn Laws.
5. German.
6. It showed that one was 'blue-blooded', and therefore uncontaminated by Moorish blood.

# 203

1. The Duke of Westminster.
2. Sweden.
3. The Quai d'Orsay.
4. Disraeli in 1837.
5. Alexander the Great (in fact mere legend).
6. That no, he hadn't found any – but then he did most of his reading at night.

## 52

1. Who first hyphenated his names on ennoblement?
2. At the storming of the Bastille in 1789 one prisoner was found who thought he was which Roman hero?
3. Before the Second World War, there were five Secretaries of State: Home, Foreign Affairs, Colonies, War and...?
4. How did the Prime Minister and the Leader of the Opposition confront each other in May 1798?
5. What does Anthony Grey believe the Australian Prime Minister, Harold Holt, was from the 1930s onwards?
6. Who did Mrs Thatcher refer to on the radio some years ago as 'our sworn enemies'?

## 128

1. According to Harold Wilson, who was the 'best Prime Minister we never had'?
2. What was the Polish city of Szczecin before the war?
3. What was the pre-war organization akin to the UN?
4. What did King George VI feel about abroad?
5. Which two Arab rulers have the same surname?
6. What house, made famous by the ITV series *Brideshead Revisited*, was owned by the late chairman of the BBC?

## 204

1. The journalist, Duncan Campbell, featured in what alphabetical trial in the 1970s?
2. The Cameroons have been colonial territories of which three countries?
3. What time does Parliament sit on a normal day?
4. What item of furniture was taken from the Scots in 1296 and is used at every English coronation?
5. Who has provided the Dutch with their first royal heir for a hundred years?
6. What was Nell Gwyn's full Christian name?

## 52

1. Lord George-Brown (followed by Duncan-Sandys and Selwyn-Lloyd).
2. Julius Caesar.
3. India.
4. They fought a duel (both survived unharmed).
5. A communist spy.
6. The Russians (allies in both world wars).

## 128

1. 'Rab' Butler.
2. The German city Stettin.
3. The League of Nations.
4. That it was 'bloody'.
5. Jordan and Iraq (Hussein).
6. Castle Howard.

## 204

1. The ABC trial.
2. Germany, Britain and France.
3. 2.30 pm.
4. The stone of Scone.
5. Queen Beatrix.
6. Eleanor.

## 53

1. Which right-wing historian and *Times* columnist also has a column in the *Sun*?
2. What is generally regarded as the most wretched ambassadorial posting?
3. How do you say 'good-night' to a hereditary knight?
4. Who were the recusancy laws aimed at?
5. What country did the Gemayel brothers rule?
6. Which French politician recently has been accused of torturing suspects when a paratroop officer in Algeria?

## 129

1. Why can Georges Foulkes MP look back upon the Saturday debate on 3 April 1982, on the Argentinian invasion of the Falklands, with some pride?
2. Which American did *The Times* nickname 'the Baboon'?
3. What is the smallest independent country in the world?
4. Who promised the British people Jerusalem as a Christmas present in 1917?
5. Who was India's first Prime Minister?
6. What was said to be the going rate for peerages in 1922?

## 205

1. Who has been described as 'a clever man who, in front of an audience, pretends to be an average man'?
2. When did the heralded Ten become the actual Nine?
3. Who defined the British Empire in India as a system of outdoor relief for the upper classes?
4. Who is regarded as England's first Prime Minister?
5. Who, according to Lyndon Johnson, was 'so dumb that he can't fart and chew gum at the same time'?
6. Who saw political improvements 'as very laughable things'?

## 53

1. Professor John Vincent.
2. Ulan Bator (in Mongolia).
3. Good-night Knight.
4. Catholics.
5. Lebanon.
6. Jean-Marie Le Pen, leader of the National Front.

## 129

1. Unlike the rest of the House – Labour and Tories – he did not sink himself in rage and rhetoric.
2. Abraham Lincoln.
3. Vatican City.
4. General Allenby.
5. Jawaharlal Nehru.
6. £30,000.

## 205

1. Denis Healey.
2. When Norway unexpectedly refused to join the EEC.
3. J. S. Mill.
4. Sir Robert Walpole.
5. President Ford.
6. Samuel Johnson.

## 54

1. Who left the Front Bench and became a Knight of the Garter in 1976?
2. What was the loose name for the political and social structure which prevailed in France before 1789?
3. Did the Conservative percentage of the national vote rise or fall from 1979 to 1983?
4. With what product was Calouste Gulbenkian most associated in British history?
5. Who was the helpful brother of Joseph, Louis, Jerome, Lucien, Elisa, Pauline and Caroline?
6. Which newspaper admiringly saw Hitler as a bulwark against Bolshevism during the 1930s?

## 130

1. How is the Duke of Edinburgh related to Victoria?
2. In which island was the Kingdom of Kandy?
3. What does ANC stand for?
4. Which Cromwell Parliament was named after an MP?
5. Which recent American President was an Earl?
6. Who was the seventeen-stone MP jailed for fraud in 1922?

## 206

1. Nigel Lawson used to edit which weekly journal?
2. Who ruled modern Paraguay through the seventeenth and most of the eighteenth centuries?
3. When does the parliamentary financial year begin?
4. What colour shirts did Mosley's supporters wear?
5. Who was known as the 'Lion of Judea'?
6. What king, deposed in 1952, declared there would soon be only five kings left: the Kings of England, Diamonds, Hearts, Spades and Clubs?

## 54

1. Harold Wilson.
2. The *ancien régime*.
3. It fell by 1.5 per cent.
4. Oil.
5. Napoleon.
6. The *Daily Mail*.

## 130

1. Great-great-grandson (while the Queen is her great-great-granddaughter).
2. Ceylon.
3. African National Congress.
4. (Praise-God) Barebones Parliament.
5. Jimmy Carter (whose second name was Earl).
6. Horatio Bottomley.

## 206

1. *The Spectator*.
2. The Jesuits, who established successful mission states.
3. April the first.
4. Black.
5. Haile Selassie.
6. Farouk.

# 55

1. Of which ex-Labour politician was it said, 'The only thing he ever fought for was a seat in a good restaurant'?
2. When did Russia lose Finland?
3. What was the official office of the Prime Minister before that position was legally recognized in 1917?
4. Who commanded the New Model Army?
5. Which spiritual leader of the Church studied at Carthage and had a son when he was only seventeen years old?
6. Where did Nelson meet his Emma?

# 131

1. Who told us to 'Just rejoice! Rejoice!'?
2. Frelimo was the liberation movement for what country?
3. What Catholic organization, with great influence among businessmen and technocrats, is based in Spain?
4. Who led the first Labour government in 1923?
5. What deposed African ruler has his home in Jeddah, Saudi Arabia?
6. Who has argued a distinction between 'authoritarian' right-wing regimes, which deserve the West's support, and 'totalitarian' left-wing regimes?

# 207

1. Which politician's subsequent title was Lord Avon?
2. What is the river between modern Poland and East Germany?
3. What is the name of the Spanish parliament?
4. According to Sellar and Yeatman, what are the only two memorable dates in English history?
5. Who was known as the Father of Europe?
6. For whose victory was Beethoven's 'Battle' Symphony written?

# 55

1. Roy Jenkins.
2. After the First World War.
3. First Lord of the Treasury.
4. Sir Thomas Fairfax.
5. St Augustine.
6. Naples.

# 131

1. Mrs Thatcher on hearing the news of the recapture of South Georgia in 1982.
2. Mozambique.
3. Opus Dei.
4. Ramsay MacDonald.
5. Idi Amin.
6. Mrs Jeanne Kirkpatrick.

# 207

1. Anthony Eden.
2. Oder.
3. Cortes.
4. 55 BC and 1066.
5. Jean Monnet.
6. Wellington's at Vittoria.

# 56

1. Who is the Conservative Leader of the House?
2. A resident of Corfu was under whose rule 1814–63?
3. Private Members' Bills are introduced on what day in Parliament?
4. Who vowed he would play the Orange card?
5. Who was the main Italian exponent of Eurocommunism?
6. Which British wartime leader was once a prisoner of war?

# 132

1. Which Irish party is mistranslated as 'Ourselves Alone'?
2. What was the old name for the island of Haiti?
3. What did Richard Crossman think was like the *Prisoner of Zenda* but not nearly as smart or as well done as it would be at Hollywood?
4. Who said a decent veil should be drawn over the beginning of states?
5. Whose ego inhabited Colombey-les-Deux-Églises?
6. How were Gordon Lonsdale and Greville Wynne related in 1964?

# 208

1. Macmillan wanted Skybolt but got what instead?
2. Which 'pogroms' were first reported in English newspapers?
3. In front of which building, still standing, was King Charles executed?
4. 'He had acquired, not diligently but with too much ease, the airs of a fox-hunting man who could swear elegantly in Greek.' Whom was George Dangerfield describing?
5. Who nationalized the Suez Canal in 1956?
6. What was Canon Montefiore's suggestion which caused an outcry in 1967?

## 56

1. John Biffen.
2. British.
3. Friday.
4. Lord Randolph Churchill.
5. Enrico Berlinguer.
6. Churchill (under the Boers in 1899).

## 132

1. Sinn Fein (correct translation simply 'Ourselves').
2. Hispaniola.
3. The paraphernalia surrounding the Queen's Speech in the House of Lords.
4. Edmund Burke.
5. Charles de Gaulle's.
6. Russian and English spies exchanged for one another.

## 208

1. Polaris.
2. Russian attacks on Jews in the 1890s and 1900s.
3. The Banqueting House in Whitehall.
4. F. E. Smith.
5. President Nasser.
6. That Jesus Christ may have been a homosexual.

## 57

1. Brian Faulkner was the last of these. What was he?
2. Which country has suffered the most coups?
3. Who said of unwritten laws that they bring 'undeniable shame to the transgressors'?
4. What burst in 1720?
5. Who was the longest-reigning French monarch?
6. Which peer mistook his nanny for his wife and then disappeared?

## 133

1. Which ennobled politician chose the title of Lord Glenamara of Genridding?
2. What did the US call the Korean Police Action?
3. Before 1906 what were so infrequent in the House of Lords that 'when one occurs', a bishop said, 'the peers cackle as if they had laid an egg'?
4. How long was the Republic of Ireland officially Eire?
5. Who contested a South American presidency in 1952, 1958, and 1964, winning in 1970, to be killed by the military in 1973?
6. What did Auden consider to be 'a low dishonest decade'?

## 209

1. Which Parliamentary sketchwriter has worked for the *Sun*, *Daily Telegraph*, *Now!* and *The Times*?
2. With what did the South African security forces celebrate the twenty-fifth anniversary of the Sharpeville massacre?
3. 1872 marked what step forward in the conduct of elections?
4. Who brought down the King's horse on Derby Day 1913?
5. How did Queen Boadicea die?
6. What scandal nearly sank Lloyd George in 1913?

## 57

1. Prime Minister of Northern Ireland.
2. Bolivia has had 189 since independence from Spain.
3. Pericles.
4. The South Sea Bubble.
5. Louis XIV (1643–1715).
6. Lord Lucan.

## 133

1. Ted Short.
2. The Korean War (because the US Congress never declared a state of war).
3. Divisions.
4. For eleven years, 1937–48.
5. Allende.
6. The 1930s.

## 209

1. Frank Johnson.
2. Nineteen more deaths.
3. Voting by secret ballot.
4. The suffragette, Miss Davison, who was killed in the process.
5. She committed suicide.
6. The Marconi scandal.

## 58

1. What rebellion did Harold Wilson believe would be over 'in weeks rather than months'?
2. Who owns the Faroe Islands?
3. What was the old name for Djakarta?
4. Who said, 'What! Do they run already? Then I die happy'?
5. What were Colonel Qadhafi's views on other Arab leaders expressed in March 1985?
6. Where was Archbishop Romero murdered in 1980?

## 134

1. Who accused the Labour Party, during the 1976 Common Market referendum, of 'going around stirring up apathy'?
2. A brave and fearless American general defected to the British, fought America and died in obscurity. Who?
3. What is the quorum for the House of Commons?
4. Lord Leverhulme was raised to the peerage mainly for producing what substance?
5. Who said to eager London photographers, 'Comrades, economize your supplies. That's enough'?
6. Which Prime Minister eventually married his secretary?

## 210

1. What were Operations 'Hurricane', 'Totem', 'Mosaic', 'Buffalo' and 'Antler'?
2. Who was the first man to circumnavigate the world?
3. What was a crime in 1885 but not in 1967?
4. What party did Ramsay MacDonald lead in the 1930s?
5. To which Italian party did the murdered Aldo Moro belong?
6. Who said in 1982, 'We ought to try to overthrow any communist government. I go all the way. I include Yugoslavia . . .'?

# 58

1. The Rhodesian rebellion in 1965.
2. Denmark.
3. Batavia.
4. General Wolfe at Quebec.
5. 'I would behead them one by one.'
6. El Salvador.

# 134

1. William Whitelaw.
2. Benedict Arnold.
3. Forty.
4. Soap.
5. Mikhail Gorbachev.
6. Lloyd George.

# 210

1. Britain's secret nuclear bomb tests in Australia from 1952 to 1957.
2. The Basque, Del Cano, who continued Magellan's expedition after the latter's death in the Philippines.
3. Homosexuality.
4. National Labour.
5. Christian Democrats.
6. Mr Beilenson, a writer whom President Reagan deeply admires.

# Q

## 59

1. When did 'the Argentinian government' suddenly become 'the Argentinian military government' on BBC news?
2. In which country did the Mau Mau rebel?
3. Whom did the Revocation of the Edict of Nantes affect?
4. Which Scottish king died of leprosy?
5. Which Indian ex-Prime Minister enjoyed a daily tipple of his own urine?
6. Who was Princess Margaret most rumoured to marry in the 1950s?

## 135

1. Who is the MP for Brighton (Pavilion and Empire).
2. Hitler said, 'I shall not rest until every German realizes that it is a disgrace to be a . . .' what?
3. 137 Labour MPs have some sort of (what?) sponsorship?
4. 1906 witnessed the Liberals' what?
5. Who was Uncle Joe to the British public?
6. Who headed the inquiry into the Profumo scandal?

## 211

1. Colonel 'Mad Mitch' tried to save these from disappearing in the defence cuts. What were they?
2. Which director of United Technologies Corporation became American Secretary of State in 1981?
3. Who assisted in the design of the Houses of Parliament, contributing the detail and getting most of the credit?
4. Who was the 'fair maid of Kent'?
5. Whose little dog lay whimpering in her skirts after she was executed?
6. Who said, 'Liberty is the right to tell people what they do not want to hear'?

# 59

1. After the invasion of the Falklands in 1982.
2. Kenya.
3. The Huguenots – French Protestants.
4. Robert the Bruce.
5. Morarji Desai.
6. Group-Captain Townshend.

# 135

1. Julian Amery.
2. Lawyer.
3. Union.
4. Greatest ever electoral success.
5. Joseph Stalin – until the truth emerged.
6. Lord Denning.

# 211

1. The Argyll and Sutherland Highlanders.
2. Alexander Haig.
3. A. W. Pugin, assistant to Sir Charles Barry.
4. Joan, wife of the Black Prince.
5. Mary Queen of Scots.
6. George Orwell.

## 60

1. Which economic experts advised Harold Wilson?
2. Who took over in Greece in April 1967?
3. Article 1, section 9, of the American Constitution expressly forbids what, so beloved in Britain?
4. Edward IV belonged to which House?
5. The first Roman triumvirate was made up of Caesar, Pompey and who?
6. The Church Committee in America investigated a scandal concerning what institution in 1975?

## 136

1. Who was the Labour MP, sacked in 1973, who won a by-election as an independent?
2. From where did Gary Powers fly his vulnerable U2?
3. William the Conqueror failed to replace what title with 'Count'?
4. Who was on the English throne in 1599?
5. Madame de Staël asked Napoleon what woman, dead or alive, he thought was the greatest. What did he reply?
6. Who said, 'When the President does it, that means that it is not illegal'?

## 212

1. Who enjoys a high civil-service salary of £107,000?
2. What modern country incorporates Bohemia?
3. What is the name of Spain's fascist party?
4. Who was ordered to paint Oliver Cromwell with 'warts'?
5. Who said, 'I have heard the bullets whistle, and believe me there is something charming in the sound'?
6. Who said, 'A memorandum is written not to inform the reader but to protect the writer'?

## 60

1. Lords Kaldor and Balogh.
2. The Colonels.
3. Inherited titles.
4. York.
5. Crassus.
6. The CIA.

## 136

1. Dick Taverne.
2. Peshawar, Pakistan.
3. The Anglo-Saxon 'Earl'.
4. Elizabeth I.
5. 'The one that has borne the most children.'
6. Nixon (in an interview with David Frost).

## 212

1. Mr Levene, who runs the Ministry of Defence's procurement programme.
2. Czechoslovakia.
3. Falange.
4. Peter Lely.
5. George Washington.
6. Dean Acheson.

## 61

1. What art historian and Fellow of Trinity College, Cambridge, had his knighthood taken away?
2. What country recently experienced a left-wing ruler who was murdered by a military tyrant, in turn supplanted by the nominee of a large foreign invasion force?
3. What was a poll tax?
4. Who referred to Ireland as a fatal disease?
5. Which sergeant was promoted to colonel in 1964 and then promoted himself to head of state in 1971?
6. Who was described as the wisest fool in Christendom?

## 137

1. Which statesman boasted of bricklaying as a hobby?
2. When were the occupying forces withdrawn from Austria after the Second World War?
3. Which journal's name recalls left-wing MP's?
4. Who was the 'Old Pretender'?
5. Who was hung from a meat-hook in Milan in 1945?
6. Which Mitford sister shot herself after the outbreak of war between Germany and England?

## 213

1. Which prominent solicitor and peer was known for his arbitrating qualities in the 1970s?
2. When were the occupying forces withdrawn from Germany after the Second World War?
3. What happened to the Department of Economic Affairs headed by George Brown in 1969?
4. Why don't Irishmen call Northern Ireland Ulster?
5. King Cetewayo was king of which people?
6. What happened to Lord Beauchamp, leader of the Liberal Party in the Lords in the 1930s?

# 61

1. Anthony Blunt.
2. Afghanistan or Grenada – take your pick according to political preference.
3. A tax on every head (poll).
4. George Moore.
5. Idi Amin.
6. James I.

# 137

1. Sir Winston Churchill.
2. 1955.
3. *Tribune*.
4. The son of James II.
5. Mussolini.
6. Unity.

# 213

1. Lord Goodman, sometimes known as 'The Blessed Arnold'.
2. They are still there.
3. It was abolished.
4. Because the province contains nine, not just six counties.
5. The Zulus.
6. He retired to the continent after accusations of homosexuality from his brother-in-law, the Duke of Westminster.

## 62

1. Whose face, did James Fenton feel, produced an inevitable impression of superiority and self-regard?
2. Which colonial power was defeated by the Vietnamese in 1954?
3. How many sovereign states comprise the Commonwealth (to the nearest five)?
4. Who coined the term 'the Wars of the Roses'?
5. Which Soviet statesman was known as 'the hammer'?
6. Who wrote, 'Democrats are to the manna born'?

## 138

1. Who was the unctuous, ineffably right-wing, snobbish Conservative MP who kept a diary about social and political events in the 1930s and 1940s?
2. Where do the Tutsis live?
3. What is the world's most populous country with democratic elections?
4. Which mother and two daughters led the struggle before the First World War for women's votes?
5. Who changed his name from Nguyen Tat Thanh?
6. Who was the American ambassador in London who predicted defeat for England in 1940?

## 214

1. What is the largest union in Britain?
2. In 1975 Cambodian gunboats seized this American ship. The subsequent rescue was a disaster. What was its name?
3. What lasted in France from 1946 to 1958?
4. Which English statesman wore a hair-shirt?
5. Which Roman ruler's brother became a gladiator?
6. Rex Barker and the Ricochets made a single after the Thorpe trial called what?

# 62

1. Nigel Lawson's.
2. France.
3. Forty-nine.
4. Sir Walter Scott.
5. Molotov.
6. Ogden Nash.

# 138

1. 'Chips' Channon.
2. In Burundi, central Africa.
3. India.
4. The Pankhursts.
5. Ho Chi Minh.
6. Joseph Kennedy.

# 214

1. The Transport and General Workers Union.
2. *Mayaguez.*
3. The Fourth Republic.
4. Sir Thomas More.
5. Mark Antony's.
6. 'Jerémy is Innocent'.

## 63

1. Vivien Neves was fêted in *The Times*. Why?
2. By 1914 it was thought only two countries in the world had escaped domination by foreigners. Which two?
3. What is the correct name for the building which contains the two Houses of Parliament?
4. Who said on his promotion to the House of Lords, 'I am dead; dead, but in the Elysian fields'?
5. Roxanne was the name of which ancient hero's wife?
6. Who was one of the defence Ministers at the time of the Vassall affair, later to resign as Foreign Secretary?

## 139

1. What has traditionally been known as the Stupid Party?
2. Who is currently the longest-serving Russian minister?
3. What European organization did the British sponsor to rival the EEC in 1959?
4. What was the 'set' based around Lady Astor which met at her house and supported appeasement in the 1930s?
5. Which French king's favourite hobby was locksmithing?
6. Which English king's unattractive mistresses were nicknamed 'the elephant' and 'the pole'?

## 215

1. In the battle for which Falklands settlement did Colonel H. Jones die?
2. Which country colonized Brazil?
3. When did the Dublin Parliament extinguish itself?
4. Egfrith and Wiglaf were both kings of . . . ?
5. Which future European leader once received a report saying, 'He spoils his undoubted talents by his excessive assurance'?
6. Whose ghost is reputed to have run shrieking down the corridor in Hampton Court?

## 63

1. She was the only nude model to appear in it.
2. Thailand and Ethiopia.
3. The Palace of Westminster.
4. Disraeli.
5. Alexander the Great's.
6. Lord Carrington.

## 139

1. The Conservative Party.
2. Andrei Gromyko, Minister of Foreign Affairs since 1957.
3. EFTA.
4. The Cliveden set.
5. Louis XVI's.
6. George I's.

## 215

1. Darwin.
2. Portugal.
3. 1800.
4. Mercia.
5. Charles de Gaulle.
6. Catherine Howard's, wife of Henry VIII.

## 64

1. What did Sir Alec Douglas-Home use in explaining the money supply on television?
2. Which country appears to have used mustard gas in recent warfare?
3. What was the Council of Anglo-Saxon kingdoms?
4. About whom was it said that if he had not been a king, he would have been the best type of sporting publican?
5. Who proclaimed 'Socialism with a Human Face' in 1968?
6. The Royal Commission on Standards of Conduct in Public Life was set up after what scandal in the early 1970s?

## 140

1. What did Mrs Thatcher not expect in her lifetime?
2. Where was Che Guevara born and brought up?
3. How few seats has the Liberal Party held?
4. What was the sobriquet of the seventeenth-century Marquess of Halifax?
5. Who announced in a BBC interview in 1976, 'I consider myself to be the most important figure in the world'?
6. Dean Acheson said in 1962, 'Great Britain has lost an empire and not yet found a . . .' what?

## 216

1. How many ex-Prime Ministers are still living?
2. Who advocated 'brinkmanship' against the Soviet Union?
3. How many governments since 1918 have been formed with more than 50 per cent of the total vote?
4. Who was Stanley Baldwin attacking when he said, 'Power without responsibility is the prerogative of the harlot'?
5. What nationality is the politician Milovan Djilas?
6. What did Churchill retort when Nancy Astor said that if she were his wife she would poison his coffee?

## 64

1. Matchsticks.
2. Iraq.
3. The Witan.
4. Edward VII.
5. Alexander Dubcek in the Prague Spring.
6. The Poulson revelations.

## 140

1. A woman Prime Minister (said in 1972).
2. Argentina.
3. Six.
4. 'The Trimmer'.
5. Idi Amin.
6. Role.

## 216

1. Five – Callaghan, Wilson, Heath, Douglas-Home and Macmillan.
2. J. F. Dulles.
3. Two: 1931 and 1935.
4. The Press Lords, Beaverbrook and Rothermere.
5. Yugoslavian.
6. 'If you were my wife I'd drink it.'

## 65

1. Which author of a thriller set in Northern Ireland now has the chance for a prolonged experience of the province?
2. What Second World War American general was known as 'Old Blood and Guts'?
3. What did the Representation of the People Act do in 1969?
4. Which conspirator in 1605 said a desperate disease required a desperate remedy?
5. Which American President was known as 'Old Hickory'?
6. 'When a nation's young men are (what?) its funeral bell is already rung.'

## 141

1. What football position does Sir Ian Gilmour favour?
2. Who overthrew Mussolini in 1943 and arranged an armistice with the Allies?
3. The American Press magnate Luce wanted to call this magazine 'Power', but called it what instead?
4. Who was the co-founder of the Independent Labour Party?
5. What did Khrushchev say history would do to the West?
6. 'Treason doth never prosper; what the reason?'

## 217

1. Who was Labour's Foreign Secretary for much of the 1960s?
2. Which country has the largest Communist Party outside the communist states?
3. If you are guilty of corrupt and illegal electoral practices, for how many years do you lose the vote?
4. Who said: 'Say what you have to say, don't quote Latin, and sit down'?
5. Where did Lenin's journey across Europe end?
6. Which Italian Freemasons' lodge was exposed in 1981?

# A

## 65

1. The Northern Ireland Secretary, Douglas Hurd.
2. Patton.
3. Lower the voting age to eighteen.
4. Guy Fawkes.
5. Andrew Jackson.
6. Conservative (from Henry Beecher).

## 141

1. *Inside Right*, the title of his book.
2. Marshal Badoglio.
3. *Fortune*.
4. Keir Hardie.
5. Bury it.
6. 'Why if it prosper, none dare call it treason' (Sir John Harrington).

## 217

1. Michael Stewart.
2. Italy.
3. Five.
4. Duke of Wellington.
5. At the Finland Station.
6. P2.

## 66

1. What was Ernest Bevin's foreign-policy aim?
2. Who intoned 'Vive le Québec libre' in 1967?
3. What does the INLA stand for?
4. Why are British forces still in Belize?
5. Who was the Emperor Claudius' nephew?
6. Francis Drake renamed his ship the *Pelican* the . . . ?

## 142

1. Which Chancellor of the Exchequer was known as Geoffrey Who?
2. What book by William Shawcross gives a version about America's involvement in Cambodia markedly different from that offered by Henry Kissinger?
3. What is the ruling party's initials in Zimbabwe?
4. On what occasion did R. H. Tawney write to Ramsay MacDonald asking, 'What harm have I ever done to the Labour Party'?
5. Which religious leader had trouble with his bowels?
6. Who said, 'A revolutionary party is a contradiction in terms'?

## 218

1. Who resigned as Home Secretary in 1972 because of the Poulson investigation?
2. What colour shirts did Garibaldi's followers wear?
3. What is the largest number of seats held by the Liberal Party since 1945?
4. Cartismandua gave up Caractacus to the Romans. She was queen of which people?
5. Who was the victor at Vicksburg who later became President of the USA?
6. Whose report on social insurance was studied by Goebbels?

## 66

1. 'To take a ticket at Victoria station and go anywhere I damn well please.'
2. Charles de Gaulle.
3. The Irish National Liberation Army.
4. To prevent the Guatemalans invading.
5. Caligula.
6. *Golden Hind.*

## 142

1. Sir Geoffrey Howe.
2. *Sideshow.*
3. ZANU.
4. Declining the offer of a peerage.
5. Martin Luther.
6. Richard Crossman.

## 218

1. Reginald Maudling.
2. Red.
3. Fourteen.
4. The Brigantes.
5. Ulysses Grant.
6. William Beveridge's.

## 67

1. Which junior minister in Labour governments crossed the floor until 1981?
2. Madame de Maintenon supplanted Madame de Montespan as whose mistress?
3. What parliamentary division is important enough for MPs to drag themselves out of hospital?
4. When did the House of Hanover change to the House of Saxe-Coburg-Gotha?
5. President Pedro Lascurain of Mexico holds a certain record for a Head of State. What is it?
6. Who in London first heard of the victory at Waterloo?

## 143

1. Which park gave its name to the Heathmen in 1970?
2. Which seventeenth-century painter was also frequently employed as a diplomat for the Spanish authorities?
3. Where are the three lines of a three-line whip?
4. What was the eighteenth-century term for government positions captured through the support of the monarch?
5. Who were the 'Big Two and a Half' at Potsdam in 1945?
6. Who divided the world into two groups: 'The Christian anti-communists, and the others'?

## 219

1. How could you tell when Harold Wilson was lying?
2. Which king, invading Italy, was killed by a tile?
3. Name the small party which won a series of by-elections during the Second World War.
4. How did the Scottish King James IV die?
5. Charlotte Corday murdered whom in his bath?
6. Which recent European Prime Minister has been on trial in the past for arms running?

## 67

1. Reg Prentice.
2. Louis XIV's.
3. A three-line whip.
4. When Edward VII succeeded Victoria.
5. The shortest term of office – one hour on 18 February 1913.
6. Nathan Rothschild.

## 143

1. Selsdon.
2. Rubens.
3. Underlining the particular motion on an MP's order paper.
4. Storming the closet.
5. Stalin, Truman and Attlee.
6. J. F. Dulles.

## 219

1. When his lips were moving (from a TV programme quoted by B. Levin).
2. Pyrrhus.
3. Common Wealth.
4. Fell at the defeat of Flodden, 1513.
5. Jean-Paul Marat.
6. Charles Haughey (acquitted).

## 68

1 Who was the closest challenger to Michael Foot for the Labour Party leadership?
2. What Marshal had a report noting, 'If this officer rises above the rank of major it will be a disaster for France'?
3. What is the Danish Parliament called?
4. Where was the social headquarters of Whiggery in early nineteenth-century London?
5. Nkrumah was the first head of which independent state?
6. For what did Sir Larry Lamb, Sir John Junor and Sir David English receive their knighthoods?

## 144

1. What did Robin Day have to say about the appointment of Lord Harris as chairman of the Parole Board?
2. Which South American country played a prominent role in the search for a solution to the Falklands crisis?
3. Where is the country residence of Prime Ministers?
4. What group was led by John Lilbourne in the late 1640s?
5. Which Byzantine emperor had the good fortune to have two excellent generals, Narses and Belisarius?
6. What American right-wing politician announced that 'extremism in the pursuit of liberty was no crime'?

## 220

1. What maverick politician became a Professor of Greek at Sydney University aged twenty-five?
2. Which American colony most welcomed the Quakers?
3. What event caused deep distress to bibliophiles in 48 BC?
4. Where was Edward II supposed to have been murdered?
5. Who led the 1919 Communist government of Hungary?
6. What was Lord Cochrane's 'secret war plan', revealed forty-eight years after his death?

# 68

1. Denis Healey.
2. Pétain.
3. Riksdag.
4. Holland House.
5. Ghana.
6. Officially 'for services to journalism' – on behalf of the *Sun*, *Sunday Express* and *Daily Mail* respectively.

# 144

1. That it was the last Quango for Harris.
2. Peru.
3. Chequers.
4. Levellers.
5. Justinian.
6. Senator Goldwater.

# 220

1. Enoch Powell.
2. Pennsylvania.
3. The burning of the library at Alexandria.
4. Berkeley Castle; though recent evidence suggests he might have escaped and ended up in Italy.
5. Bela Kun.
6. To overwhelm fleets with sulphur fumes.

# Q

## 69

1. Who is the Chicago monetarist beloved by the present government?
2. The American operation 'Ricebowl' to rescue these in 1979 ended in failure. What were they?
3. What did the GLC replace in 1965?
4. Who was the first and last British poet-peer?
5. Which eastern European ruler usually wears sunglasses?
6. In 1971 the *New York Times* began publication of secret documents stolen by Ellsberg. What were they called?

## 145

1. The 'Dear Bill' of the Denis Thatcher letters is who?
2. The last acquisition of colonial territory by a European power was when?
3. The Parliament Act of 1911 deprived the House of Lords of what power?
4. Who was on the English throne in 1700?
5. The Polish King, Jan Sobieski, is famous for whose defeat outside Vienna in 1683?
6. On Jeremy Thorpe's acquittal, the BBC shredded what?

## 221

1. What old buffer once said, 'The Conservatives do not believe it necessary, and, even if it were, we should oppose it'?
2. Whose life did Pocahontas save in Virginia?
3. 1928 marked the date when women under (what age?) were allowed to vote.
4. What English king was 'the first gentleman in Europe'?
5. What was Louis XVI's diary entry for 14 July 1789?
6. Which woman professor has claimed that if the Nicaraguan government survives 'the whole of Central and Latin America will go communist'?

# 69

1. Milton Friedman.
2. The American hostages held by Iran.
3. The London County Council (LCC).
4. Tennyson.
5. General Jaruzelski.
6. The Pentagon Papers.

# 145

1. William Deedes of the *Daily Telegraph*.
2. Abyssinia by Italy in 1935.
3. The veto of Bills.
4. William III.
5. The Turks'.
6. A two-hour documentary on the case.

# 221

1. Lord Hailsham.
2. Captain John Smith's.
3. Thirty.
4. George IV.
5. 'Nothing.'
6. Jeanne Kirkpatrick.

# 70

1. Which Swiss gentlemen bothered Harold Wilson?
2. According to John Reed, how many days did it take for the Bolshevik revolution to shake the world?
3. Who was the world's second woman Prime Minister?
4. Which king did, Hugh Trevor-Roper, describe as 'an omniscient umpire whom no one consulted'?
5. Which South African Prime Minister explained, 'As far as criticism is concerned, we don't resent that unless it is absolutely biased, as it is in most cases'?
6. Who was the 'Himmler of Russia'?

# 146

1. Which cartoonist gave Macmillan the name of Super-Mac?
2. Which country did Oxenstierna serve as chief minister?
3. Which paper began as the *Daily Universal Register*?
4. Berengaria was whose queen?
5. Which American war hero was sacked by Truman?
6. Who, to Belloc, 'Looked underdone and harassed, And out of place and mean, And horribly embarrassed'?

# 222

1. Of which future Prime Minister did Cyril Connolly say, 'He appeared honourably ineligible for the struggle of life'?
2. Who was the leader of the Chinese Nationalist Party supported by the Americans in the 1940s?
3. All Cabinet ministers, past and present, and some public figures make up what advisory council?
4. Why was 1829 a great year for Catholic politicians?
5. On what throne was the Emperor Maximilian, placed?
6. Can a communist join a darts/tennis/golf, etc., club?

# 70

1. The gnomes of Zurich.
2. Ten.
3. Golda Meir of Israel.
4. James I.
5. John Vorster.
6. Lavrenti Beria.

# 146

1. Vicky.
2. Sweden.
3. *The Times*.
4. Richard I's.
5. Douglas MacArthur.
6. The People in Between (middle classes).

# 222

1. Alec Douglas-Home.
2. Chiang Kai-Shek.
3. The Privy Council.
4. Because at last they could sit in Parliament.
5. Mexico's, in 1864.
6. No, according to the Press, he can only 'infiltrate' it.

# 71

1. What did Denis Healey liken to being attacked in debate by Sir Geoffrey Howe?
2. What did Caesar cross to start the civil war in Rome?
3. The Rev. J. G. MacManaway was not allowed to be elected to Parliament in 1950 because he was what?
4. Who benefited from the 'Peter's Pence' tax?
5. A copywriter once described some toffee as 'rich, dark and brown as the . . .' which ruler?
6. What is the common link between Richard the Lionheart, Attila the Hun and John the Baptist?

# 147

1. Which West Belfast MP decided not to vote Labour in March 1979 and thus caused Callaghan's government to lose the vote of confidence?
2. Who was Louis XIV's chief minister early in his reign?
3. Which country has the longest land frontiers?
4. The original King's Road or 'route de roi' in Hyde Park is now known as what?
5. What ruler of ancient Athens was recognized for the impossibly strict execution of his laws?
6. What is the similarity between these men, noted for their extreme nationalism: Beaverbrook, Hitler and Napoleon?

# 223

1. Which Tory MP said Thatcher was so empty-headed 'she probably thinks that Sinai is the plural of Sinus'?
2. Over whose regime did Castro triumph in Cuba?
3. What did BOSS mean?
4. Which Press Lords formed the New Empire Party in 1930?
5. Which showy king was captured at Pavia in 1525?
6. What did Lloyd George say about Herbert Samuel?

# 71

1. Being 'savaged by a dead sheep'.
2. The Rubicon.
3. An ordained priest.
4. The Pope.
5. Aga Khan.
6. They have the same middle name.

# 147

1. Gerry Fitt.
2. Colbert.
3. China.
4. Rotten Row.
5. Draco (from which draconic).
6. None of them originated from the country in question.

# 223

1. Jonathan Aitken (who has yet to be given a job in the government).
2. Batista's.
3. Bureau of State Security.
4. Lords Rothermere and Beaverbrook.
5. Francis I of France.
6. 'When they circumcized Herbert Samuel they threw away the wrong bit.'

# 72

1. Which Cabinet minister has been variously known as the Mad Monk and the Guru?
2. It was Napoleon III who began the French involvement in this eastern thorn in the side of America. Where?
3. Who are the Third Estate?
4. What did contemporaries call the Black Prince?
5. The Gothic leader, Alaric, sacked which city in AD 410?
6. What was that useful word used by Richard Ziegler, Nixon's Press Secretary, to explain a past lie?

# 148

1. What was the complaint a foreigner made about the Lord Privy Seal, Sir Ian Gilmour?
3. What was the colonial name of Tanzania?
3. When did women over thirty first get the vote?
4. Which king expelled the Jews from England?
5. Dr Malan's period as Prime Minister of South Africa from 1948–54 saw the formal introduction of what system?
6. Where was it that the beautiful Mrs Kharshoggi first set eyes on young Mr Winston Churchill?

# 224

1. Christopher Brocklebank-Fowler was the only Conservative MP to join what before 1983?
2. Did the *Black Hand* ever exist in reality?
3. The Privy Council chamber has what slang name?
4. By the Treaty of Wedmore, King Alfred gave about half of England to whom?
5. Which French ruler was forced to escape to England in 1848, using the name 'Mr Smith'?
6. 'This sort of thing may be tolerated by the French, but we are British – thank God.' Whose comment in 1965?

## 72

1. Sir Keith Joseph.
2. Vietnam.
3. The common people – you and me.
4. Edward of Woodstock (the sobriquet of Black Prince was not in use until the sixteenth century).
5. Rome.
6. That such and such a statement was now 'inoperative'.

## 148

1. That he was neither a lord, a privy, nor a seal.
2. Tanganyika.
3. 1918.
4. Edward I in 1290.
5. Apartheid.
6. In the Central Lobby, Westminster (from her account in the *Daily Star*).

## 224

1. The SDP.
2. It was an actual Serbian secret society in the 1910s.
3. The Cock-pit.
4. The Danes.
5. King Louis-Philippe.
6. Lord Montgomery's.

# 73

1. Which Foreign Secretary had to defend the UK's Suez policy?
2. Which Zimbabwean nationalist movement did Russia support?
3. The UN Maritime Association is the only UN organization in which city?
4. What was the name of Claud Cockburn's cyclostyled sheet that gave 'The news behind the news' in the 1930's?
5. Which Boer general became a British Field-Marshal?
6. Which Foreign Secretary committed suicide?

# 149

1. Which MP, appointed Paymaster-General in 1979 and supposed to supervise the Government's publicity, was known as the 'Mekon', because of his large forehead?
2. In 1931, Japanese troops moved into what country, nominally under the suzerainty of China?
3. The last constituency with two MPs disappeared when?
4. Who was Neville Chamberlain's Parliamentary Private Secretary, later to become a PM himself?
5. Which kingdom did Guy de Lusignan rule (1186-87)?
6. What did Peel do when he caught the Whigs bathing?

# 225

1. When the old LCC had a firm Labour majority, the Government extended its boundaries to the GLC. Now that the GLC has a Labour majority what is to be its fate?
2. Avis was the ruling house of which medieval kingdom?
3. Is the House of Commons bigger or smaller than the House of Representatives in Washington?
4. Who was on the English throne in 1800?
5. What happened to Leonidas, King of Sparta?
6. Bath Spa was founded after what cure was discovered?

# 73

1. Selwyn Lloyd.
2. ZAPU, which lost out to ZANU.
3. London.
4. *The Week*.
5. J. C. Smuts.
6. Lord Castlereagh in 1822.

# 149

1. Angus Maude.
2. Manchuria.
3. 1950.
4. Lord Dunglass (Alec Douglas-Home).
5. Jerusalem.
6. According to Disraeli, never a reliable source, he walked away with their clothes.

# 225

1. Extinction.
2. Portugal.
3. Much smaller.
4. George III.
5. He died defending Thermopylae with his 300 Spartans.
6. That for leprosy.

## 74

1. At whose death did Anthony Barber become Chancellor of the Exchequer in 1970?
2. Who failed in the Munich Putsch of 1923?
3. What was the name of Red Square in Moscow before the 1917 revolution?
4. Who last acquired almost all of England for free?
5. Who was the South American President who made an astounding come-back from 1973 to his death in 1974?
6. Who are the 'Spetsnaz' against whom Operation 'Brave Defender' is being organized for September 1985?

## 150

1. Which spy believed that 'to betray, you must first belong'?
2. What South American state was once called Upper Peru?
3. What are the largest regions within West Germany?
4. An intelligence blunder over the Orkney's clear channel led to the death of which famous leader of men in 1916?
5. Who was the Pope who convened the second Vatican Council in 1959?
6. Which is by far the richest college at Cambridge?

## 226

1. What 'Fundamentalist Right-winger', according to Andrew Roth, has personal traits which make him 'dark, squat, persistent'?
2. Where are St Pierre-et-Miguelon?
3. Where is the Home Office in London?
4. About whom did his steward say, 'A larger soul, I think, hath seldom dwelt in a house of clay than his'?
5. Who was the Menshevik leader in 1917?
6. Which future Irish nationalist leader was sent down from Cambridge in the mid-nineteenth century?

# 74

1. Ian MacLeod's.
2. Hitler.
3. The same: it meant beautiful in Russian.
4. William the Conqueror – after the business of Hastings.
5. Juan Peron of Argentina.
6. Soviet saboteurs, whom defence chiefs apparently believe are the main non-nuclear threat to Britain.

# 150

1. Kim Philby – 'one of us'.
2. Bolivia.
3. Lands.
4. Lord Kitchener.
5. John XXIII.
6. Trinity College (a conservative estimate of its wealth in *1973* was £30 million).

# 226

1. Michael Brotherton MP.
2. Off the Canadian coast (French-owned islands).
3. Queen Anne's Gate, St James's Park.
4. Oliver Cromwell.
5. Alexander Kerensky.
6. C. S. Parnell.

## 75

1. Which retired union leader and ex-Communist has joined the march to the Right?
2. With whom did the British go to war in 1839 over opium?
3. Queen Victoria was promoted to what rank in 1876?
4. Who cared for the sick and wounded at Scutari?
5. Miklos Horthy ran what country in the 1920s and 1930s?
6. Whose advice on the Press was, 'If you can't square them, squash them'?

## 151

1. What pertinent fact about the PM was concealed in 1953?
2. The German and Ottoman lands awarded to the French and British after the First World War were known as . . . ?
3. What was the name for the coalition of French left-wing and centre parties opposed to fascism in the 1930s?
4. There were two naval mutinies in 1797. One was at the Nore, and the other at . . . ?
5. At the Treaty of Versailles, the 'Big Four' were Wilson, Clemenceau, Lloyd George and who of Italy?
6. Who was the publisher of *Lady Chatterley's Lover*, prosecuted in the 1960s?

## 227

1. According to Hailsham, who was 'unflappable'?
2. The Riffs were nationalists of which North African country?
3. In August 1911 what resolution vital for impecunious MPs was passed?
4. George Hudson, an enthusiastic promoter in the 1830s and 1840s, was known as the (what?) King.
5. Whose white war-horse was called Marengo?
6. Which title for a political leader was once misprinted in Hansard as the Teapot?

# 75

1. Frank Chapple.
2. The Chinese.
3. Empress of India.
4. Florence Nightingale.
5. Hungary.
6. Lloyd George's.

# 151

1. That Churchill had suffered a severe stroke; he did not retire until 1955.
2. Mandates.
3. The Popular Front.
4. Spithead.
5. Vittorio Orlando.
6. Penguin.

# 227

1. Macmillan.
2. Morocco.
3. The one instituting salaries for members.
4. Railway.
5. Napoleon's.
6. The Taoiseach (Irish Prime Minister).

## 76

1. How long was a long time in politics for Harold Wilson?
2. What was the ducal title customarily bestowed by French kings on their brothers?
3. After Walpole, who has been the longest-serving Prime Minister without interruption?
4. Three brewers (Allsop, Bass, Guinness) were raised to the peerage and became known as what?
5. Which emperor, still ruling, ceased to be a god in 1946?
6. Which US politician yelled out in 1963, 'Segregation now, segregation tomorrow, and segregation forever!'?

## 152

1. When was the first referendum in England?
2. Jan Palach protested against the Russian invasion of Czechoslovakia by doing what?
3. What is the name for the official report of debates in Parliament?
4. Who was the pacifist leader of the Labour Party 1931–35?
5. England lost its independence twice in the eleventh century. To the Normans and . . .?
6. What was the profession of John Poulson?

## 228

1. Which 1960s Foreign Secretary often 'tired'?
2. What religious order was abolished by the Pope in 1773, only to reappear in 1814?
3. Were there more or fewer MPs before 1832 than today?
4. One English king has died in battle since 1066. Who?
5. According to Ian Smith, what would never happen in his lifetime or in a thousand years?
6. What is the name for that percentage of agricultural produce claimed by the rector of a parish?

## 76

1. A week.
2. Orleans.
3. Earl of Liverpool, 1812–27.
4. The Beerage.
5. Hirohito of Japan.
6. George Wallace.

## 152

1. 1975, on membership of the EEC.
2. Burning himself to death, in Prague, January 1969.
3. Hansard (after the first publisher).
4. George Lansbury.
5. In 1017 to King Canute, who made it part of his Baltic empire.
6. Architect.

## 228

1. George Brown.
2. The Society of Jesus (Jesuits).
3. More (658 to 650).
4. Richard III.
5. Majority rule in Rhodesia.
6. A tithe.

# Part 6
# The Business Quiz

## Edited by Paul Temple

with

John Adams
John Alden
Roy Bromwich
Leslie de Chernatony
Nicola Evans
Anne-Marie Harrison
David Kraithman
Jon Nash
John Philpot
Bob Ryan
Michael Servian
Ian Spurr
Ian Temple
Leigh Thompson

# Introduction to The Business Quiz

Business is back in vogue. The tycoons, wheeler-dealers, and financial whizz-kids who were the *bêtes noires* of public discussion only a decade ago are back with a vengeance. The pin-up is the slick-talking smoothie, even if the portable computer has replaced the umbrella; students who once enrolled on business studies degrees to find out about the 'social conscience' of the corporation now want to find out how to make a million (to be paid, for preference, in whatever currency happens to be 'hot'), as fast as possible. In short, making a profit has once again become shorthand for public beneficence. So if competition is now the name of the game, how about trying the questions in this section which is designed to test exactly how much trivial knowledge you have of the worldwide game called business. If each question contains one item of trivial information, the sum of such trivia might just possibly be the key to success, whether in the bargain basement, the boardroom, or at the pinnacle of achievement, the golf-course.

The questions cover all aspects of business endeavour: from the apparently brutish behaviour of the operators in financial markets (bulls, bears and stags), to the rather more genteel atmosphere of the eighteenth-century aristocracy, who engaged in business only as a last resort (or maybe as a trivial pastime); from the humble ice-cream van to those vertigo-prone 'commanding heights' of the economy.

Questions are arranged into groups of six which together make up a quiz. In each quiz, the number of the question indicates (broadly) what you might expect to find in terms of subject matter. The six categories are:

1. **Products and Promotions.** Questions on all aspects of the business product, from the raw material dug out of the ground, through to production, marketing, advertising, and selling.
2. **British Business.** Firms, industries; take-overs, big deals, little deals; vital facts about the British economy.
3. **International.** Big business overseas; international trade; the Common Market; the world's fastest, longest, etc.
4. **Political Economy.** A rag-bag of policies, politicians;

ideas, economists, management theorists, charlatans; unions and strikes.

5. **Entrepreneurs and Innovations.** Tycoons, tyrants, dynasties, inventions, inventors, pioneers.

6. **Money, Banking and Finance.** Currency, financial markets, speculators, banking, taxation.

These are rough groupings, and business categories overlap in many ways, so be prepared for the joker in the pack! Business is often about the biggest and the best, so answers are subject to change. Although an attempt has been made to exclude questions where such changes are likely, the reference date of 1 March 1985 should be borne in mind. Be fair in accepting or rejecting an answer – a response within 1 or 2 percent of the correct figure often represents a considerable achievement!

Paul Temple

# 1

1. What did Whistler's 'Mother' advertise in 1917?
2. Which British jet airliner failed to come off because of two tragic accidents?
3. In what year did Britain join the EEC?
4. Which London Business School head was knighted?
5. Which celebrated car designer turned his attention in 1984 to the production of fine wines?
6. Why did stockbrokers in Auckland, New Zealand object to their place of work being redesignated as a Regional Stock Exchange?

# 77

1. Why would the marketing of the Nova brand of cars be very difficult in Spain?
2. With which firm is Port Sunlight associated?
3. Which is the largest employers' federation in France?
4. Of which American union was Jimmy Hoffa the scandalous President?
5. What was the name of the world's first atomic submarine launched on 21 January 1954 by Mrs Eisenhower?
6. What is normal market 'backwardation'?

# 153

1. Who sponsors the English National Village Cricket Championship?
2. Why did the Wills and Players form Imperial?
3. How many countries are in COMECON?
4. If the 'terms of trade' are 'improving', which are rising relative to the other: import or export prices?
5. Who invented the safety razor?
6. In which post-war year did the dollar officially cease being convertible into gold at a fixed price?

# A

## 1

1. War bonds (made use of Whistler's portrait on a poster).
2. The Comet (de Havilland's).
3. 1973.
4. Sir Jim Ball.
5. Lamborghini.
6. They thought that the abbreviated form ARSE would demean their standing.

## 77

1. When translated it would become the 'Doesn't Go' car.
2. Unilever.
3. CNPF (Conseil National du Patronat Français).
4. The (International Brotherhood of) Teamsters.
5. *Nautilus.*
6. When the spot price exceeds the future price.

## 153

1. Whitbread.
2. Imperial Tobacco was formed in order to beat off the challenge of the American Tobacco Trust.
3. Ten.
4. Export prices.
5. K. C. Gillette.
6. 1971.

## 2

1. With what product do you associate SU?
2. Which aircraft manufacturer built the Mosquito?
3. What was the name on the label of the earliest Elvis Presley records?
4. What distinction is sometimes made between a 'closed shop' and a 'union shop'?
5. In 1948 a chemist from Sandoz Pharmaceutical Co. cycled home from work at lunchtime. He did not return as he thought he was going insane. What had he discovered?
6. Name two of the four streets surrounding the Bank of England.

## 78

1. What is a POS terminal when applied to computers?
2. What percentage of the Masters of Wine at the beginning of 1985 were women?
3. How long would it take to drink the EEC wine lake (as of spring 1984) at the rate of a 70 cl bottle per day?
4. What is 'Butskellism'?
5. The Baron of Beef in Cambridge staged a fracas between which two entrepreneurs before Christmas 1984?
6. What, in the City, is the 'folded-paper habit'?

## 154

1. Who manufactures the 'ultimate driving machine'?
2. BSA are famous for producing British motorcycles, but what was their original output?
3. Where are the Massey Ferguson headquarters?
4. Which leader of the General, Municipal and Boilermakers Union announced his retirement in 1985?
5. Which head of Renault was sacked in 1985?
6. What is the 'spot price' of a commodity?

# 2

1. Carburettors.
2. De Havilland.
3. Sun (a Sam Phillips label).
4. In the union shop, unlike a closed shop, union membership is required only after a worker is hired.
5. The LSD 'trip' (lysergic acid diethylamide).
6. Threadneedle Street, Princes Street, Lothbury, Bart Lane.

# 78

1. A Point of Sale terminal.
2. About 10 per cent (11 out of 114).
3. Just under 12 million years.
4. A term, originating from H. Gaitskell and R. A. Butler, used to describe the consensus economic policies of the 1950s and 1960s.
5. Sir Clive Sinclair and Chris Curry (Acorn, and a former employee of Sinclair's).
6. Commuters (especially on the Southern Region) fold their *Financial Times* into long thin strips to facilitate reading.

# 154

1. BMW.
2. Guns (Birmingham Small Arms).
3. Canada.
4. David Basnett.
5. Bernard Hanon.
6. The price for immediate delivery.

## 3

1. From what industry come the words 'em' and 'en'?
2. How many women are there in full-time or part-time employment in the UK (March 1985)?
3. Which French car was exported in greater numbers than any other in 1984?
4. In what year was the New Deal launched?
5. Who, by the age of forty, had invented air brakes and electric signalling on the railways?
6. What is the currency unit in Portugal?

## 79

1. President Kennedy stated that the consumer has four basic rights. State two of them.
2. Which city would you call if you lost your Barclaycard?
3. In which country are the headquarters of Nestlé?
4. Who, to *Private Eye*, was Baillie Vass?
5. What use did Charles Green make of coal gas on about 1,400 occasions between 1821 and 1857?
6. How does the word 'coupon' originate?

## 155

1. What is the name given to plain white cotton cloth, originally imported from the East?
2. Which two rivers did the Grand Trunk Canal link?
3. In which leading industrial country do manual engineering workers work most hours per year?
4. Which week day is the Budget usually presented?
5. Whose first business venture was the Great Five Cent Store of Utica, New York?
6. If the cost of acquiring a company is in excess of its net asset value, what is that excess called?

## 3

1. Printing (they are units for measuring the amount of printed matter in a line).
2. 10,200,000.
3. Peugeot 205.
4. 1933.
5. George Westinghouse.
6. The escudo.

## 79

1. The right of safety, the right to be informed, the right to choose, the right to be heard.
2. Northampton.
3. Switzerland.
4. Sir Alec Douglas-Home.
5. Balloon ascents.
6. From the French *couper* – to cut (a coupon is attached to a bond and is cut off when payment is made).

## 155

1. Calico.
2. The Trent and the Mersey.
3. USA.
4. Tuesday.
5. Frank Winfield Woolworth.
6. Goodwill.

## 4

1. Which beer claimed to 'work wonders'?
2. What filled 45 per cent of Metal Box Co's cans in 1937?
3. Which EEC Budget Commissioner was educated at Ampleforth and Caius, Cambridge?
4. When was Mitterand's economic 'u-turn'?
5. 'If you meet a man who has on an India-rubber cap, stock, coat, vest and clothes, with an India-rubber money purse, without a cent of money in it, it is he.' Who?
6. What, on the Stock Exchange, is a 'guinea pig'?

## 80

1. Which two industrial processes involve a stage of 'fining'?
2. Rank the following firms in terms of net profit as percentage of invested capital in 1984: BSR International, Habitat/Mothercare, Ferranti.
3. Which firm sold more than $1 billion diamonds in 1983?
4. Which Archbishop of York (later of Canterbury) advocated government intervention to solve 1930s unemployment?
5. What did Percy Shaw put on the road?
6. What is MO?

## 156

1. What is the name given to a machine in which rotary motion is produced by action on the vanes of a cylinder?
2. What is the newly formed trade association for insurance companies in Britain?
3. Who are America's biggest brewers?
4. Who lives at Gatcombe Park once home of economist David Ricardo?
5. Which was the first British hatchback motor car?
6. Which two Latin American economies had accumulated the largest external debts by 1985?

# 4

1. Double Diamond.
2. Milk and cream.
3. Christopher Tugendhat.
4. 1983.
5. Charles Goodyear.
6. A person who acts as a company director for the sake of the fees.

# 80

1. The clarification of liquid (e.g., in brewing) and the refining of metals (especially the conversion of cast iron into wrought iron).
2. BSR International (26.6 per cent), Ferranti (20.9 per cent), Habitat/Mothercare (20.0 per cent).
3. De Beers.
4. William Temple.
5. Catseyes.
6. A measure of the monetary base of the economy (notes, coins and banks' cash at the Bank of England).

# 156

1. A turbine.
2. The Association of British Insurers.
3. Anheuser-Busch (Budweiser and Michelob beers).
4. Anne and Mark Phillips.
5. The Austin A40.
6. Mexico and Brazil.

## 5

1. What was British 'Car of the Year' in 1985?
2. Which is Britain's biggest unit-linked life assurance company?
3. Which country is Europe's third largest wine producer?
4. Which parson wrote a popular essay on population?
5. Whose story begins: 'It was a Sunday night, April 1 1973. I was arriving in New York City to resign from General Motors Corporation'?
6. What is Gresham's Law?

## 81

1. Which firm pioneered the advertising jingle in 1941?
2. What is the name of the business magazine for women, published for the first time in October 1984?
3. For which tool did the Hughes company make its name?
4. Where did John Maynard Keynes enjoy working?
5. Who pioneered a noise reduction system for stereo cassette players?
6. Which is Germany's biggest commercial bank?

## 157

1. Which clothing company spent $50 million equipping the US Olympic team in Los Angeles?
2. Which corporation took over ICL?
3. How many Beetles were mass produced under Hitler at the huge Volkswagenwerk at Wolfsburg?
4. Who first identified the 'invisible hand'?
5. Where was the first public electric power station in Britain built?
6. What was the venue of the 1944 Conference which shaped the post-war international monetary system?

## 5

1. Vauxhall Astra.
2. Hambro Life.
3. Spain.
4. Thomas Malthus (*An Essay on the Principle of Population 1798*).
5. J. DeLorean (from J. P. Wright, *On a Clear Day You Can See General Motors*).
6. 'Bad money drives out good.'

## 81

1. Pepsi-Cola.
2. *Working Woman.*
3. Drill bits for the oil industry.
4. In bed (during his Bloomsbury days he was often reported to have remained there until twelve o'clock).
5. Dr R. Dolby.
6. Deutsche Bank.

## 157

1. Levi Strauss.
2. STC (Standard Telephone and Cable).
3. None (Wolfsburg only produced war vehicles based on the Beetle on any large-scale basis).
4. Adam Smith.
5. Godalming, Surrey (it was built by the Siemens brothers in 1881).
6. Bretton Woods, USA.

## 6

1. How do 'soap operas' get their name?
2. What do Watney Mann and Truman, Peter Dominic, and Gilbey Ltd have in common?
3. Who or what is GATT?
4. 'Stop-go' was a description of economic policy during the fifties and sixties. If rising unemployment or forthcoming elections indicated 'green', what indicated 'red'?
5. Who became manager of Jimi Hendrix and Slade?
6. By what name is the share-price index on the Hong Kong Stock Exchange known?

## 82

1. What is the relevance of psychographics to advertisers?
2. How big is the market in aluminium foil in Britain?
3. What is the name of Norway's North Sea oil corporation?
4. Who is usually credited with writing the first major economics text-book?
5. Who set up New York's first giant electric advertising sign in 1900 – a forty-foot green pickle?
6. Is housekeeping money paid to a housewife subject to tax?

## 158

1. What are 'white goods'?
2. What is the furthest distance one can get from a railway on the mainland of Great Britain?
3. How far does the UN propose that exclusive fishing rights should extend from the shore?
4. Over the mining of what mineral did Bob Hawke say, 'My heart says no, but my head says yes'?
5. Whose innovation finished the British charcoal industry?
6. How can money become 'hot'?

# 6

1. Day-time radio serials aimed at housewives and sponsored by soap companies became very popular in the US in the 1930s.
2. They are all owned by Grand Metropolitan.
3. The General Agreement on Tariffs and Trade.
4. Balance of payments deficits and/or sterling crises.
5. Chas Chandler.
6. The Hang Seng Index.

# 82

1. Psychographics is the measurement of the life-style of the target market (aiding decisions on the creative approach adopted).
2. £45 million in sales (in 1984).
3. Statoil.
4. John Stuart Mill.
5. Henry J. Heinz.
6. No.

# 158

1. Consumer durables (e.g., washing machines, which provide a service over a period of time).
2. 110 miles by road (in the case of Southead, Mull of Kintyre).
3. 200 miles (the Convention of the Law of the Sea, 1982).
4. Uranium.
5. Henry Cort's (whose puddling and rolling process of 1783 allowed coal to be used in place of charcoal in the production of bar-iron).
6. When it's speculative money which flows into a country to take advantage of high interest rates or an appreciating currency.

## 7

1. What sort of advertisements 'bleed'?
2. What was the most popular national Sunday newspaper in 1983?
3. Which country voted in 1982 to leave the EEC and left in 1985?
4 Why did policemen strike in 1919?
5. What image did John Baird successfully transmit over a distance of a few feet at a demonstration in 1924?
6. What is the FED?

## 83

1. What is the trade of a fellmonger?
2. When did Channel 4 start transmissions?
3. How many members had OPEC at the start of 1985?
4. Which Prime Minister introduced income tax to Britain?
5. Which newspaperman is alleged to have said, 'When I want a peerage I shall buy one like an honest man'?
6. What was the exchange rate between the pound and the dollar between 1949 and 1967?

## 159

1. How did an advertising campaign manage to increase the market share of Lucky Strike cigarettes so dramatically in the US after the First World War?
2. Where do Harland and Wolff build ships?
3. What is the French equivalent of VAT?
4. Who first demonstrated the concept of the 'employment multiplier' in 1930?
5. Which Duke built canals?
6. Who is currently President of the World Bank?

# 7

1. Those which have no margin around the type area.
2. *News of the World* (circulation 4.0 million in 1983).
3. Greenland.
4. The Government refused to allow them to unionize.
5. A Maltese Cross.
6. The USA's central bank.

# 83

1. Stripping, preparing and dealing in sheep's hides.
2. November 1982.
3. Thirteen.
4. Pitt the Younger.
5. Alfred Harmsworth (Lord Northcliffe).
6. £1 = $2.80.

# 159

1. By appealing directly to women (with slogans such as the one suggesting that smoking could ward off double chins).
2. Belfast.
3. TVA (Taxe Valeur Ajoutée).
4. Richard Kahn.
5. The Duke of Bridgewater.
6. Tom Clausen.

## 8

1. How does a 'beta blocker' drug help angina sufferers?
2. Why is Tesco so called?
3. Which was the tenth country to join the EEC?
4. In which month of the year was the 1926 General Strike?
5. In which English city did Jesse Boot establish his first pharmacy?
6. Which country has the schilling as its unit of currency?

## 84

1. Who or what is a YUPPIE?
2. How much does it currently cost to inspect the microfiche records of any British limited company?
3. Where are the headquarters of Levi Strauss?
4. What term does the economist use to designate the cost of something in terms of the benefits foregone?
5. Who is credited with inventing the pneumatic tyre?
6. Which country first used paper money?

## 160

1. What do John Player cigarettes, Courage beer and Ross Foods have in common?
2. Which is the only surviving British tea clipper?
3. In which country did the employees of the entire public sector go on strike during 1984?
4. Which former Chairman of the Manpower Services Commission joined the Thatcher Government?
5. Which British aircraft made history in 1956 as the first plane to exceed 1,000 m.p.h.?
6. Which football club made its USM début in October 1983?

# 8

1. It interferes with nervous stimulation of the heart.
2. Jack Cohen put together the initials of his tea supplier, T. E. Stockwell together with the first two letters of his own name.
3. Greece.
4. May.
5. Nottingham.
6. Austria.

# 84

1. A Young Urban (or sometimes upwardly mobile) Professional Person.
2. £2.50 from the Company Information Bureau.
3. San Francisco, CA.
4. Opportunity cost.
5. John Boyd Dunlop (1888).
6. China (in A.D. 910).

# 160

1. They are all produced by the Imperial Group.
2. The *Cutty Sark* (permanently docked at Greenwich).
3. Iceland.
4. David Young.
5. Fairey Delta II.
6. Tottenham Hotspur.

## 9

1. What is the significance of cyanide to the gold industry?
2. Where in London is the Guinness brewery situated?
3. What is the name of the West German national airline?
4. In 1965 which body was created by the merger of the British Employers' Federation and the British Manufacturers' Association?
5. Which entrepreneur introduced World Series Cricket?
6. In what year did the *FT* Index reach its lowest closing figure of 49.4 on the London Stock Exchange?

## 85

1. Approximately how much potential advertising space exists on a London Routemaster double-decker bus?
2. An agreement at which refinery was generally regarded as beginning the era of 'productivity bargaining' in Britain in 1960?
3. What, in the Russian economy, is a *kalhoz*?
4. Who told us that *Small is Beautiful*?
5. For what contribution to the music industry is Robert Moog famous?
6. What, in banking, is the purpose of the Cooke Committee?

## 161

1. What is copra?
2. In the provision of the UK's telephone services, who are BT's only competitor?
3. Which country is the world's biggest importer of fish?
4. How many Tolpuddle Martyrs were there?
5. What was J. P. Morgan's main line of business?
6. Which famous scientist was once Master of the Mint?

# 9

1. Cyanide acts as a catalyst in refining.
2. Park Royal.
3. Lufthansa.
4. The CBI (Confederation of British Industry).
5. Kerry Packer.
6. 1940 (26 June).

# 85

1. A little more than one hundred square feet.
2. Esso's Fawley refinery.
3. A collective farm.
4. Ernest Schumacher.
5. The synthesizer.
6. It provides guidelines for the supervision by national central banks of foreign subsidiary banks.

# 161

1. Dried kernel of coconut.
2. Mercury.
3. Japan.
4. Six (all were found guilty of taking unlawful oaths in 1834).
5. Banking.
6. Sir Isaac Newton (Master of the Mint from 1699–1727).

# 10

1. Which Police Commissioner argued that a particular tyre was 'a major contribution to road safety'?
2. Which London peninsula has a 482-acre Enterprise Zone?
3. About what business did Chuck Berry complain in a song?
4. Which city institutions helped local authorities beat spending curbs by 'pre-funding'?
5. What is South Africa's debt to John Macarthur and the Forrests?
6. What is the base year for the *FT* Ordinary Share Index?

# 86

1. On the socio-economic scale, what letter is assigned to middle-class people?
2. Of which book did the prosecution ask the jury: 'Is it a book that you would wish your wife or your servants to read?'
3. What does BASF stand for?
4. What did the 1720 Bubble Act prohibit?
5. Who was caught by means of Marconi's new invention?
6. What determines the colour of an auditor's ball-point?

# 162

1. Who painted the 'Bubbles' used by Pears soap?
2. How many standard UK economic regions are there?
3. In whose Presidential term did the first post-war devaluation of the dollar occur?
4. Who is economics editor of *The Times*?
5. Who initiated the 'scientific management' movement?
6. What proportion of a company's share capital must be owned by another before it becomes an associated company'?

# 10

1. Sir Robert Mark (Goodyear Grand Prix S).
2. The Isle of Dogs.
3. (Too Much) Monkey Business.
4. The merchant banks (pre-funding allows councils to spend receipts from sales of council houses).
5. The Macarthur–Forrest process for extracting gold from ore with a low gold content (1887).
6. 1935.

# 86

1. B.
2. *Lady Chatterley's Lover*.
3. Badische Anilin und Soda-Fabrik.
4. The formation of joint stock companies (except under special dispensation from Parliament).
5. Dr Crippen.
6. The year.

# 162

1. Sir John Millais.
2. Eleven (Scotland, North, North-West, Wales, Yorkshire and Humberside, South-West, East Anglia, East Midlands, West Midlands, South-East and Northern Ireland).
3. Richard Nixon.
4. Sarah Hogg.
5. Frederick Winslow Taylor.
6. 20 per cent.

# 11

1. Which market research company provides the BBC with the record charts?
2. Which hamburger chain completely owns its UK outlets?
3. Which coin was named after a French emperor?
4. What is the classical title of George Pompidou's book on the post-war French economy?
5. What was Wedgwood's pioneering pottery called?
6. Which bank houses the gold reserves of over seventy nations?

# 87

1. What is the 'Hodden Grey' in a Burns poem?
2. A billiard hall was often above which chain store?
3. If goods are sold in a foreign country at below cost they are said to be —?
4. Which Chancellor of the Exchequer once fired Auberon Waugh?
5. Who owns Virgin Records?
6. How many edges has a 20p piece?

# 163

1. What 'is strong enough to take your breath away'?
2. Which firm of chartered accountants become known as 'Poodle Slaughterhouse' in 1984, and why?
3. Who are the Japanese rivals to IBM in mainframe computers?
4. During the Second World War which politician acted as Britain's 'dictator of labour'?
5. Which Hungarian transformed writing?
6. During which war was income tax 'temporarily' introduced in Britain?

# 11

1. Gallup.
2. McDonalds.
3. The Napoleon.
4. *Le Noeud Gordiea* (*The Gordian Knot*).
5. Etruria.
6. The Federal Reserve Bank of New York.

# 87

1. A coarse woollen fabric made from the wool of the Blackface.
2. Burton's (the tailor).
3. Dumped.
4. Nigel Lawson.
5. Richard Branson.
6. Seven.

# 163

1. Listerine mouthwash.
2. Price Waterhouse, who acted as sequestrators during the 1984 miners' strike.
3. Hitachi and Fujitsu.
4. Ernest Bevin.
5. Biro.
6. The Napoleonic War.

## 12

1. Which British Prime Minister was instrumental in promoting Gannex raincoats?
2. What is Roger Dean's connection with the music business?
3. Rank the following countries according to life expectancy at birth: Tunisia, Greece, Chile, Syria.
4. What phrase was coined by George Brown in 1964, when referring to the anonymous but powerful Swiss Bankers?
5. Who designed Princess Di's wedding dress?
6. What Russian coin is one hundredth of a rouble?

## 88

1. What does net weight mean?
2. Which brewer owns the Thresher chain of off-licences?
3. With which industry have the fortunes of Widnes, Ludwigshafen and Leverkusen been associated?
4. Who claimed that: 'It is not from the benevolence of the butcher, brewer or baker that we expect our dinner, but from their regard to their own interest'?
5. In what century did James Watt develop a steam engine with rotary movement?
6. Who was called the 'Little Scotch Pirate' on Wall Street?

## 164

1. Who described the *Confessions of an Advertising Man*?
2. How many Stock Exchanges operate in the British Isles?
3. Which of the following is not a member of COMECON: Bulgaria, Hungary, Yugoslavia, Outer Mongolia?
4. What does RPI stand for?
5. What was the decisive contribution that made Watt's steam engine superior to Newcomen's?
6. Which former clearing bank used to operate under the sign of the grasshopper at 68 Lombard Street?

## 12

1. (Sir) Harold Wilson.
2. He is an artist for album covers.
3. Greece (74 years), Chile (70), Syria (66), Tunisia (61) (World Bank figures, 1982).
4. 'The faceless gnomes of Zurich'.
5. Elizabeth and David Emmanuel.
6. The kopek.

## 88

1. The weight of goods without the packaging.
2. Whitbread.
3. Chemicals.
4. Adam Smith (*The Wealth of Nations*).
5. Eighteenth (1782).
6. Andrew Carnegie.

## 164

1. David Ogilvy.
2. Eight.
3. Yugoslavia (but it has observer status).
4. The Retail Price Index.
5. Incorporation of a separate condenser (this prevented the need to reheat the cylinder after every stroke).
6. Martins Bank.

## 13

1. Which computer firm produces the VAX computer?
2. In 1935 Allen Lane was having a hard time selling his first series of ten paper-covered reprints until which big retailer ventured a large order?
3. How many albums have to be sold in the US in order to earn a Gold Record?
4. What was Morton's Fork?
5. Which entrepreneur controls the *Daily Mirror*?
6. What is Israel's unit of currency?

## 89

1. Which organization is responsible for ensuring misleading advertisements are not broadcast?
2. What proportion of cars imported into the US in 1959 were British?
3. Why was 1933 such a bad year for the soft drinks trade in the US?
4. Was the setting up of Industrial Training Boards a Conservative or Labour initiative?
5. Who introduced Skytrain?
6. According to the *Washington Post* which bank occupies 'the precise center, geographical as well as metaphysical, of financial America, and even of the financial world'?

## 165

1. In which year did the Renault 5 make its début?
2. Who are the 'big two' in detergent manufacture?
3. When does Britain's lease on Hong Kong expire?
4. Which organization was set up to fight the Corn Laws?
5. What invention came from 'two pocket handkerchiefs, some pink ribbon and thread'?
6. Which US bank has caused headaches for the Midland?

# 13

1. DEC (Digital Equipment Corporation).
2. Woolworth.
3. 500,000.
4. The view of Bishop Morton during the reign of Henry VII that the rich can well afford to pay taxes, and the poor must have saved enough to do so.
5. Robert Maxwell.
6. The shekel.

# 89

1. The Independent Broadcasting Authority (IBA).
2. Nearly one half.
3. The repeal of prohibition.
4. Conservative (1963).
5. Sir Freddie Laker.
6. Morgan Guaranty Trust.

# 165

1. 1972.
2. Unilever, and Procter and Gamble.
3. 1997.
4. The Anti-Corn-Law League.
5. The bra.
6. Crocker National.

# Q

## 14

1. What was the name of Katie's husband in the long-running Oxo TV commercial?
2. According to official figures from the CSO, what was the contribution of housewives to the national output in 1984?
3. What figure was on the price tag on RCA's first black and white television in 1946?
4. Which American economist was once appointed Ambassador to India?
5. What nationality was Alfred Nobel?
6. What is New York's equivalent to the *Financial Times*?

## 90

1. What was Alfred Leete's great contribution to the First World War effort in Britain?
2. Which is the only UK coalfield to produce anthracite?
3. Which are the only two countries from the southern hemisphere to export significant quantities of wheat?
4. Of which political economist and philosopher could it accurately be said: 'He's dead but he won't lie down'?
5. Which new technology was introduced in 1984 to help Visa and Access combat fraud?
6. The most comprehensive Stock Index on Wall Street is the Standard and Poor's 500. What is Standard and Poor's?

## 166

1. Which beer 'refreshes the parts that other beers cannot reach'?
2. From which company did Robert Maxwell purchase Mirror Group Newspapers?
3. Which American body vets new drugs?
4. What is a cartel?
5. What was Frank Whittle's rank in the RAF in 1939?
6. What is the name of Saudi Arabia's unit of currency?

# 14

1. Philip.
2. None (only paid employment is included).
3. $375.
4. J. K. Galbraith.
5. Swedish.
6. The *Wall Street Journal*.

# 90

1. He painted the Kitchener poster: 'Your Country Needs YOU!'
2. South Wales.
3. Australia and Argentina.
4. Jeremy Bentham (who made provision that his bones should not be 'laid to rest' but should be set in the Hall of University College, London).
5. The hologram.
6. A stock research firm.

# 166

1. Heineken.
2. Reed International.
3. The US Food and Drug Administration (FDA).
4. A formal collusion among a small group of firms.
5. Air Commodore.
6. The riyal.

## 15

1. When is a boat 'clinker built'?
2. Whose marriage began the English affection for claret?
3. A business woman arrives at a hotel with JFK, LAX and LHR labels on her baggage. Which cities has she been in?
4. Nigel Lawson announced his first Budget in which month?
5. Who was 'Mr Five Per Cent'?
6. What is a 'paper profit'?

## 91

1. Which American company became a household name without advertising between 1900 and 1970?
2. Besides Sinclair Research which British firm was intending in 1984 to market an electric car?
3. Which atmospheric gas is the world's biggest earner?
4. By what percentage did NHS prescription charges rise between 1979 and 1985?
5. Which company launched the first pre-recorded tape cassette?
6. What do 'Accepting Houses' accept?

## 167

1. What does *caveat emptor* mean?
2. Who or what is NEDDY?
3. Which firm is currently Japan's second biggest car manufacturer?
4. Which politicians held the post of Chancellor of the Exchequer between 1852 and 1868?
5. Which firm first managed to get a jet aeroplane operational?
6. In the jargon of the City, what is a 'stag'?

## 15

1. When it is built so that its timbers overlap below.
2. Henry Plantagenet (to be Henry II) and Eleanor of Aquitaine (in 1152 giving England lands in the Bordeaux region).
3. New York (J. F. Kennedy airport), Los Angeles (L.A. International airport) and London (Heathrow).
4. March.
5. Calouste Gulbenkian (because of his efforts to bring about a *rapprochement* between Shell and the Deutsche Bank in 1914, each company gave him a 2½ per cent stake in the settlement).
6. A profit arising from a rise in the price of an asset which, being unsold, is unrealized.

## 91

1. Hershey (the Hershey candy bar).
2. HIL Electric.
3. Oxygen.
4. 900 per cent (from 20p to £2.00).
5. Philips.
6. Bills of Exchange.

## 167

1. Let the buyer beware.
2. The National Economic Development Council.
3. Nissan.
4. William Gladstone and Benjamin Disraeli.
5. Messerschmitt (1944).
6. A speculator in new firms.

# 16

1. What product left Henry Cooper smelling 'great'?
2. During the fifteenth century which three English towns had a printing press?
3. In its time as an airline, TWA has stood for two different things. What are they?
4. Why did Nigel Lawson's first Budget please the wine tipplers?
5. Whose name does the RSO record label represent?
6. Which top ten US bank nearly failed in May 1984?

# 92

1. What is DERV fuel?
2. Early British experiments in nuclear power favoured gas-cooled reactors. What was the gas?
3. In what year was OPEC established?
4. Where did Karl Marx write most of *Das Kapital*?
5. Why was Lord Northcliffe particularly concerned to prevent the monopolization of the soap industry?
6. What name was given to the December 1971 agreement which was the last to attempt worldwide fixing of exchange rates?

# 168

1. Why are 'underwriters' so-called?
2. What site did the Roskill Commission recommend as the best for the proposed third London airport?
3. Which city has the world's largest taxi fleet?
4. Which British Prime Minister was largely responsible for the repeal of the Corn Laws in 1846?
5. Who was the 'miners' friend'?
6. When was Selective Employment Tax introduced?

## 16

1. Brut.
2. London, Oxford, St Albans.
3. Transcontinental and Western became Trans World Airlines (after the Second World War).
4. An 18p reduction in the duty on a bottle of wine.
5. Robert Stigwood (Organization).
6. Continental Illinois.

## 92

1. Fuel for Diesel Engine Road Vehicles.
2. Carbon dioxide.
3. 1960.
4. In the Reading Room at the British Museum, London.
5. He feared it might reduce the large amount of soap advertising in his publications.
6. The Smithsonian Agreement (Washington).

## 168

1. Because they write their name on the bottom of an insurance policy and so take a portion of the risk.
2. Cublington.
3. Mexico City (over 30,000 in 1984).
4. Robert Peel.
5. Sir Humphrey Davey.
6. 1966.

## 17

1. What is DADA?
2. In what year could you make your first purchase of a stereo record in Britain?
3. Which of the two applicants to the EEC in 1985 is not a member of EFTA?
4. What was the 'Treasury View' of 1929 on the efficacy of public works programmes as a means for alleviating unemployment?
5. Which entrepreneur explained *What They Don't Teach You at the Harvard Business School*?
6. What is a bond?

## 93

1. Which famous chef appeared on TV to endorse which supermarket chain?
2. What building houses Lloyd's underwriters?
3. Which Silicon Valley firm rose from nothing in 1977 to over $1 billion in sales in 1983?
4. Which was the only American union to support Ronald Reagan in the 1980 presidential campaign?
5. Which firm introduced FM Radio?
6. What was the partly paid price at which British Telecom shares were offered to the public before legal trading began?

## 169

1. Which firm makes Buicks and Oldsmobiles?
2. Which Cathedral city was chosen in 1981 to test the Government's faith in competition?
3. Who replaced John Opel as IBM's Chief Executive?
4. What was 'Mr Cube' originally up in arms about?
5. What firm did Colin Chapman head?
6. What does USM stand for?

# 17

1. The Design and Art Directors' Association.
2. 1958.
3. Spain.
4. That such programmes could do nothing to help, and would only reduce private spending.
5. Mark McCormack (the title of his recent book).
6. A fixed-interest security.

# 93

1. Robert Carrier for Tesco.
2. The Royal Exchange.
3. Apple.
4. The International Brotherhood of Teamsters.
5. Telefunken, Germany (1902).
6. 50p.

# 169

1. General Motors.
2. Hereford (where competition in bus services was introduced).
3. John Akers.
4. The threatened nationalization of the sugar industry.
5. Lotus.
6. Unlisted Securities Market.

## 18

1. What is the name given by Fine Fare to their generic range of products?
2. Which engine powered the Spitfire?
3. Why did Hooker Chemical sell Love Canal for only $1?
4. Which is Britain's largest trade union?
5. Which eccentric 'stole' a Lockheed Constellation from his own airline in order to practise landings in the Bahamas?
6. Who signs a company's balance sheet?

## 94

1. Which famous advertising slogan for Guinness would probably not be permitted today?
2. At what venue was the Great Exhibition of 1851?
3. What was bought with the 1854 Gadsden Purchase?
4. Which well-known politician resigned from his Treasury post along with Chancellor Thorneycroft in 1958?
5. Who was Elvis Presley's manager?
6. Who issues Treasury Bills?

## 170

1. Which car manufacturer spent the most money advertising in Britain during 1982?
2. Which is Britain's only helicopter manufacturer?
3. Which former Chancellor of the Exchequer became President of the EEC?
4. At what general election were the electorate first told that they had 'never had it so good'?
5. In what year did the first Model T roll off a conveyor belt?
6. What name is given to the City line on the London Underground?

# 18

1. Yellow Labels.
2. The Rolls-Royce Merlin.
3. Because it was a chemical waste dump and the deed absolved them from liability for future mishap. (Years later hundreds of families were evacuated when toxic chemicals started to bubble up through basements.)
4. The TGWU (Transport and General Workers Union).
5. Howard Hughes.
6. The Directors.

# 94

1. 'Guinness is Good for You.'
2. Hyde Park, London.
3. Parts of Arizona and New Mexico.
4. Enoch Powell.
5. 'Colonel' Tom Parker.
6. The Bank of England.

# 170

1. Austin Rover (at £15.4 million).
2. Westland.
3. Roy Jenkins.
4. 1959 (Harold Macmillan's famous phrase).
5. 1910 (earlier models were not mass produced by assembly line techniques).
6. The drain.

## 19

1. Who told advertisers that 'the consumer is not a moron, she is your wife'?
2. Which body advises the Queen before a charter is given to a professional or academic organization?
3. What is the world's largest landowner?
4. What is 'Petty's Law'?
5. Did barbed wire first have a peaceful or warlike use?
6. Which Italian city gave its name to a British coin?

## 95

1. What, in marketing, is USP?
2. What was the basic pay of an airman, on joining the RAF, in 1958?
3. Outside the Soviet Union which eastern European nation produces the most oil?
4. What international body is the ILO?
5. Who invented the jet engine?
6. Where are the headquarters of the Bank for International Settlements?

## 171

1. Which Italian dairy-produce company sponsors Niki Lauda?
2. What was the principal purpose of the horn used on mail coach's and depicted on countless Christmas cards?
3. What did the Treaty of Rome establish?
4. On what day did the 1984–5 miners' strike begin?
5. Which firm introduced Terylene?
6. In which post-war year was the pound first permitted to float?

# 19

1. David Ogilvy.
2. The Privy Council.
3. United States Government (769,863,000 acres).
4. The proposition that, as economic development occurs, a higher proportion of the working population will be engaged in service industries (after Sir William Petty 1623–87).
5. Peaceful (in agriculture).
6. Florence (the florin).

# 95

1. A Unique Selling Proposition.
2. £4 10s. per week (all found).
3. Rumania.
4. The International Labour Office.
5. Sir Frank Whittle.
6. Basle, Switzerland.

# 171

1. Parmalat.
2. To ensure that toll gates should open before the coach arrived.
3. The EEC.
4. 12 March 1984.
5. ICI.
6. 1972.

## 20

1. What is the name of *The Times*'s alternative to bingo?
2. In what city was a celebrated decomposing snail found in a bottle of ginger beer?
3. What is the world's largest mineral water firm?
4. Under the auspices of which business school were the 'Hawthorne experiments' conducted?
5. What are the first names of the Al Fayed brothers?
6. What is the difference between a firm which is 'zero rated' and one which is 'exempt' for VAT purposes?

## 96

1. In the drugs industry what is a 'magic bullet'?
2. Which British railway company lost the 'battle of the gauges' at the end of the nineteenth century?
3. What do the initials OPEC stand for?
4. To an economist what are a) cheaper train fares for students b) cover charges at restaurants and c) dumping all examples of?
5. Which brothers established a famous name in European banking in the early nineteenth century?
6. What is the name of the quarterly journal published by the Bank of England?

## 172

1. What does Goodyear do with Enterprise, America, Columbia, Europa?
2. Why are ASDA stores so called?
3. Which is the biggest Indian corporation?
4. Who was the only post-war Prime Minister to have a formal training in economics?
5. What were the first steam pumps used for?
6. What is a gilt-edged security?

# A

## 20

1. Portfolio.
2. Glasgow (the case that followed, Donoghue *v.* Stephenson, established the modern law of negligence).
3. Source Perrier, Nîmes.
4. The Harvard Business School.
5. Mohamed and Ali.
6. Only the former is entitled to a VAT rebate on its purchases. Neither have to charge VAT on sales.

## 96

1. A drug which attacks only diseased cells and not healthy ones.
2. The Great Western Railway (abandoned its 7ft-wide gauge).
3. Organization of Petroleum Exporting Countries.
4. Price discrimination (the charging of different prices to different consumers for the same goods in order to increase profit).
5. The Rothschilds.
6. *Bank of England Quarterly Bulletin.*

## 172

1. It flies them (they are all airships used for promotional purposes).
2. From Associated Dairies.
3. The Tata Group (1982 assets $2.4 billion).
4. Harold Wilson.
5. Pumping water out of mines.
6. A British Government security (yielding a fixed rate of interest).

## 21

1. What was the first mark registered under the Trade Marks Registration Act?
2. Why would an eighteenth-century Englishman want crap in his pocket?
3. Which tyre company was forced to recall 10 million steel-belted radials for safety reasons in 1978?
4. What was the year of the Jarrow hunger march?
5. Who masterminded the *Great Rock and Roll Swindle*?
6. How large were the debts of the world's biggest bankrupt?

## 97

1. What do retailers call losses of goods due to shoplifting, staff pilfering or mistakes?
2. In 1984 what percentage of engineers were women?
3. Which country is the leading supplier of orange juice?
4. Which Soviet biologist was responsible for carrying out 'The Great Stalin Transformation of Nature'?
5. What distance did Marconi achieve when he demonstrated radio on Salisbury Plain in 1896?
6. Who said of the typical accountant that 'they have eyes like a cod-fish' and that 'happily they never reproduce and all of them finally go to hell'?

## 173

1. What is the strongest (highest tar and nicotine level) cigarette available in the United Kingdom?
2. To the nearest 5 per cent what percentage of the adult population in the UK reads a daily newspaper?
3. What do the first two letters of Toshiba stand for?
4. Which animal depicts the TUC in Low's cartoons?
5. Which Astor emigrated to England in 1899?
6. What is the name of the Paris Stock Exchange?

# 21

1. The Bass Red Triangle (1876).
2. Crap was a slang expression for money.
3. Firestone.
4. 1936.
5. Malcolm Maclaren (title of the film concerning his exploits with the Sex Pistols rock band).
6. £100 million (William Stern, a property dealer, 1978).

# 97

1. Shrinkage.
2. 1 per cent (survey carried out by WES).
3. Brazil.
4. T. D. Lysenko (reference is to a scheme which intended to transform climate through the planting of trees).
5. 1¾ miles.
6. Elbert Hubbard.

# 173

1. Capstan Full Strength (25/2.4 mg per cigarette).
2. 75 per cent (1983).
3. Tokyo.
4. A cart-horse.
5. William Waldorf Astor.
6. The Bourse.

## 22

1. What was the nàme of the HMV white fox terrier?
2. Which national daily has the highest proportion of its readers aged between fifteen and twenty-four?
3. Which is the biggest jute manufacturing city?
4. Who is currently economics editor of the *Sunday Times*?
5. What school is Rosemary Hume at?
6. What was the British currency D-Day?

## 98

1. Which politician was featured in the promotional video of Tracey Ullman's 'My Guy'?
2. What class of steam locomotive broke the world speed record with a recorded speed of 126 m.p.h. on 3 July 1938?
3. Which of the oil exporting countries has the highest per capita national income?
4. Which is Elton Mayo's school of industrial relations?
5. Who first demonstrated the existence of radio waves?
6. On the back of which bank note is Sir Christopher Wren?

## 174

1. What does it mean when a good is delivered CKD?
2. Which government-sponsored project cost some £190 million, but finished as scrap worth £53,000?
3. Which plane was produced about 13,000 times and under various names such as the Dakota or PS-84?
4. A peer became a centenarian in 1984; what post did he hold in the 1945 Labour Government?
5. The work of William Shockley at Bell Telephone Company led to a Nobel Prize. What did he invent?
6. Why was 1 March 1946 of significance at the Bank of England?

## 22

1. Nipper.
2. The *Sun* (1983).
3. Calcutta.
4. David Lipsey.
5. The Cordon Bleu School in London.
6. The conversion to decimal currency.

## 98

1. Neil Kinnock.
2. The Pacific (LNER's 'Mallard').
3. The United Arab Emirates ($23,770 in 1982).
4. The Human Relations School.
5. Heinrich Hertz (Hertzian waves).
6. The £50 note.

## 174

1. Completely Knocked Down (a method of transporting goods flat and unassembled).
2. The TSR 2 (the Tactical Strike and Reconnaisance bomber scrapped in 1965).
3. The Douglas DC-3.
4. Minister of Fuel and Power (Lord E. Shinwell).
5. The first useable transistor.
6. The Bank was nationalized.

# 23

1. Where and when did the 'Grand Cru' classification of Bordeaux wines originate?
2. In which year did BBC2 begin broadcasts?
3. In which Northern European country are the middle-aged (35–54) most prone to an early death?
4. By what other name are the French group who called themselves '*les economistes*' commonly known?
5. Which novelist wrote begging letters to Andrew Carnegie?
6. What event caused champagne corks to pop at the Stock Exchange on 18 January 1985?

# 99

1. Where is genuine Harris Tweed spun, dyed and woven?
2. In what year did HM the Queen start the flow of oil from BP's Forties Field?
3. Which was the first foreign company to penetrate extensively the hinterland of China?
4. What is an oligopoly?
5. Which film pioneered sulphur drugs in medicine?
6. Which was the first British company to buy back its own shares after the lifting of the ban on such transactions?

# 175

1. In former times what product would you expect to find below the 'Sign of the Civet Cat'?
2. Which brewer owns one sixth of all Britain's pubs?
3. In Rwanda in 1981 what percentage of the relevant age group were receiving secondary education?
4. What was Britain's 'Oilgate' scandal?
5. Who brought in Tiny Rowland to revitalize Lonrho?
6. Which particular issue of government stock had the largest nominal value, and a large patriotic response?

## 23

1. At the 1855 Paris World Exhibition.
2. 1964.
3. Finland (in 1975 mortality rates were about 15,000 per million or about double the figure for Holland).
4. The Physiocrats.
5. Mark Twain.
6. The *FT* Index passed 1,000 for the first time.

## 99

1. The Outer Hebrides.
2. 1975.
3. British American Tobacco (until the Japanese invasion).
4. A market in which there is competition between only a few firms.
5. I. G. Farben (Germany, during the 1930s).
6. GEC.

## 175

1. Perfume (the civet cat provided a substance often used in making perfume, as well as providing a symbol for its sale).
2. Allied Brewers.
3. 2 per cent.
4. The defiance of oil sanctions against Rhodesia by BP.
5. Angus Ogilvy.
6. War Loan (£1,909 million in 1917).

## 24

1. Which industry spends the most money on advertising?
2. What was the name of the Beatles' company?
3. Which country is the biggest exporter of fish?
4. A tax on salt was the inspiration of which French Minister of Finance?
5. Who was at the controls on 27 July 1949 when a jet airliner left the ground for the first time?
6. What was the official price of gold throughout the 1960s?

## 100

1. Which metal was the first to be used for general practical purposes?
2. In what year did ERNIE start picking the winners?
3. Which firm claims to supply two thirds of the schools in the US with computers?
4. Which politician was a business partner of Jim Slater?
5. What was 'Drake's Folly'?
6. Which is the biggest of the London merchant banks?

## 176

1. What is the minimum speed required to get a modern telecommunications satellite successfully into orbit?
2. Which of the nine 'Clarendon Schools' charged the highest fees in 1981?
3. For what event in the oil industry was Dr Mossadeq famous?
4. What is the highest rung on the ladder in the Civil Service?
5. Who owned a yacht called *Christina* on which the goings on became the focus of much press gossip?
6. What is the name given to the board at the Bank of England?

## 24

1. Retailing (1983).
2. Apple.
3. Canada ($1.6 billion in 1983).
4. J. B. Colbert.
5. John Cunningham (flying the de Havilland Comet).
6. $35 per ounce.

## 100

1. Copper.
2. 1956.
3. Apple (1984).
4. Peter Walker.
5. The name given by locals (of Titusville, Pennsylvania) to the very first oil derrick created by 'Colonel' Edwin Drake in 1859.
6. Morgan Grenfell.

## 176

1. 25,000 m.p.h.
2. Charterhouse (£4,380 p.a.).
3. The nationalization of Iranian oil in 1951.
4. Permanent Secretary.
5. Aristotle Onassis.
6. The Court.

## 25

1. What is delicately woven cotton fabric called?
2. According to the General Household Survey (1981) in which female socio-economic group were female cigarette smokers most likely to be found?
3. Which is the bigger market in the US, baby or pet food?
4. What is the balance of trade?
5. Which Getty lives as a recluse in London?
6. Values under current cost accounting are calculated on the same basis as losses for insurance claims. What is the name of the current cost valuation basis?

## 101

1. Where are the 'gondolas' in supermarkets?
2. The Bridgewater Canal connects which cities?
3. Which country is the world's largest producer of cheese?
4. 'Supply creates its own demand' – whose law?
5. The names of two capital cities formed the name of a new synthetic fibre. What was the fibre?
6. By 1984 which US bank had made the largest loans to Brazil?

## 177

1. Maxim, Sweetheart, Baron Solemacher and Tonto are varieties of what?
2. What was the original name of Lonrho?
3. When Alexander Graham Bell was buried in 1922 how many telephones were silenced in the US?
4. Who were the unions' left-wing 'terrible twins' elected to run the two biggest unions in 1967–8?
5. Who was 'The Commodore'?
6. Which religious society on the Board of Barclays has never stopped South African investments?

# 25

1. Muslin (after the town of Mosul in Mesopotamia).
2. Skilled Manual (43 per cent).
3. Pet food.
4. The difference between exports and imports of goods.
5. Paul Getty II.
6. Deprival value.

# 101

1. The shelving which carries displays of goods with aisles on either side.
2. Liverpool and Manchester.
3. USA (some 2,165,000 tons in 1980).
4. J. B. Say's (the French economist).
5. Nylon (from New York and London).
6. Citicorp (some $4,600 million by 1984).

# 177

1. Strawberry.
2. London and Rhodesia Mining and Land.
3. Thirteen million.
4. Jack Jones and Hugh Scanlon.
5. Cornelius Vanderbilt.
6. The Quakers.

## 26

1. Who makes tennis rackets for John McEnroe?
2. Who are Britain's two biggest bakers?
3. Which American steel producer has a biblical connection?
4. Who first showed that specialization between countries on the basis of comparative advantage can lead to gains through international trade?
5. Which technology should make it possible to dial a symphony after dinner?
6. What is the unit of currency in Iceland?

## 102

1. What did Tom Wolfe describe as the 'one hand magazines'?
2. Which independent TV company serves the most households?
3. Which US president de-regulated domestic air routes?
4. Which economist became Greek Prime Minister?
5. When (approximately) was the safety pin invented?
6. What could no longer be removed when women became members of the London Stock Exchange?

## 178

1. What was 'Mammoth Powder' used for last century?
2. What was the record label on the early Beatles' hits?
3. The 'Red Line Agreement' split up what industry?
4. Which Chancellor of the Exchequer once claimed that he wanted 'to do for forecasters what the Boston Strangler did for door-to-door salesmen'?
5. Which ex-Ambassador to Washington became a Chairman of London Weekend Television?
6. Which bank has the tallest office block in the City?

# 26

1. Dunlop.
2. Allied Bakers (Associated British Foods) and British Bakeries (Rank Hovis McDougall).
3. Bethlehem Steel.
4. David Ricardo.
5. Fibre optics.
6. The krona.

# 102

1. 'Girlie' magazines (such as *Playboy*).
2. Thames/London Weekend Television.
3. President Carter (1978).
4. Andreas Papandreou.
5. 500 B.C.
6. The trousers of new members.

# 178

1. Blasting (an invention of Lammot du Pont).
2. Parlophone.
3. Oil (Gulbenkian drew a line in red on a map of the Middle East and so divided up the consortia seeking concessions).
4. Denis Healey.
5. John Freeman.
6. The National Westminster (the Nat West Tower).

## 27

1. What size of paper has exactly twice the area of A4?
2. Where is the Lutine Bell?
3. What is the French acronym for the EEC?
4. Who urged the expansion of higher education in 1963?
5. Which entrepreneur was reportedly 'the first American economist to invent an industry and make a fortune out of it'?
6. How does Lombard Street get its name?

## 103

1. What name is given to the mark made on precious metals after an assay test?
2. Poles still measure area in which agricultural sector?
3. What was the world's poorest economy in 1982?
4. Which philosopher and political economist had learnt ancient Greek by the age of seven?
5. Which firm introduced the Wankel motor?
6. What post did Jacques de Larosière hold during 1984?

## 179

1. What is the jumping toy resembling a stilt?
2. Which firm topped *The Times*'s '1,000 Largest UK Industrial Companies' in 1984?
3. In which of the following foodstuffs was the EEC not self-sufficient in 1978–9: wheat, sugar, fresh fruit, oats?
4. Who introduced 'monetary targets' as a means of controlling public expenditure and inflation?
5. Which two nephews of Lord Northcliffe became Fleet Street barons in their own right?
6. Which bank still uses a quill pen for lunch guests to sign their names in the visitors' book?

# 27

1. A3.
2. At Lloyd's of London.
3. CEE (Communauté Economique Européenne).
4. Lord Robbins's.
5. Otto Eckstein (computerized economic forecasts – Data Resource Incorporated).
6. From the Italian moneylender of that name who settled there.

# 103

1. A hallmark.
2. Private allotments.
3. Chad (per capita income $80 in 1982).
4. John Stuart Mill (who was educated according to the rigorous theories of his father, James).
5. NSU (Germany).
6. Managing Director of the IMF.

# 179

1. A pogo stick.
2. BP.
3. Fresh fruit (production fell short of consumption).
4. Denis Healey.
5. Cecil King and Lord Rothermere.
6. Coutts & Co.

# 28

1. What are the first names of the Saatchi brothers?
2. Which chain introduced a five-shilling price limit in 1928?
3. Which OPEC member had the largest oil reserves in 1985?
4. What was 'required reading' for economic advisers in the Civil Service in 1979?
5. What drug was developed by the Americans to counter the supposed Nazi use of adrenal gland extract?
6. How many shares are included in the *FT* Ordinary Index?

# 104

1. What is CAD in computing circles?
2. Which two merchant banks act as financial advisers to most quoted companies?
3. In the non-communist world which country has the largest proven reserves of 'low-cost' uranium?
4. Which Marxist economist invented the concept of the 'kinky' or 'kinked' demand curve?
5. Who invented Coca-Cola?
6. What would your income tax code number be if your allowances totalled £2,420?

# 180

1. In a famous First World War poster what did a little girl sitting on her father's knee ask?
2. What nitrogenous fertilizer was used in Britain in the 1850s?
3. Where had Geigy, Sandoz, CIBA and Hoffman La Roche dyestuff works by 1900?
4. Whose amendment to the 1977 Finance Bill raised income allowances automatically in line with inflation?
5. Who was once sacked by Henry Ford, wrote a best-selling autobiography and is a favourite with the Democrats?
6. Where was Robin Leigh-Pemberton educated?

## 28

1. Charles and Maurice.
2. Marks and Spencer.
3. Saudi Arabia (some 169 billion barrels).
4. *The Wealth of Nations* (Adam Smith).
5. Cortisone.
6. Thirty.

## 104

1. Computer Aided Design.
2. Hill Samuel and S. G. Warburg (end 1983).
3. Australia (some 474,000 tonnes).
4. Paul Sweezy.
5. John Styth Pemberton.
6. 242 (plus L, H, P or V, depending upon your circumstances).

## 180

1. 'Daddy, what did YOU do in the Great War?'
2. Guano.
3. Basle.
4. Jeff Rooker and Audrey Wise.
5. Lee Iacocca.
6. Eton and Oxford.

# 29

1. Where are a newspaper's 'ears'?
2. When were Old Age Pensions introduced in the UK?
3. Which US President offered a New Deal?
4. What is MITI which has coordinated Japan's economic success?
5. What were K. C. Gillotte's christian names?
6. What is an 'ad valorem' tax?

# 105

1. What is measured by the truss?
2. What is the most popular women's magazine in Britain?
3. Who was President of the EEC Commission 1981–4?
4. Who said the capitalist motto was 'Accumulate, accumulate! That is Moses and the Prophets'?
5. How did the laser get its name?
6. Which US President has been frequently blamed for causing the American financial panic of 1837?

# 181

1. According to Defoe, when were there posters 'quacking and tampering with Physick'?
2. The fact that Trust House hotels were founded by Quakers made for what attractive feature at the hotel bar?
3. Between which three cities is Europe's 'golden triangle'?
4. Who did Anthony Sampson call the 'tireless zoologist' who dominated Whitehall science during the 1960s?
5. Which Lord Mayor of York had such a large railway empire in the nineteenth century that it was claimed that York City Council was a mere subsidiary of the York and North Midland Railway?
6. Which seven metals are traded on the London Metal Exchange?

# A



## 29

1. The advertising space on the top left or right of a newspaper's front page.
2. 1909.
3. Franklin D. Roosevelt.
4. Ministry of International Trade and Industry.
5. King Camp.
6. A tax (like VAT) which is a proportion of the value of the commodity.

## 105

1. Hay or straw.
2. *Woman's Own* (0.59 million circulation in 1982).
3. Gaston Thorn (Luxembourg).
4. Karl Marx.
5. From Light Amplification by Stimulated Emission of Radiation.
6. Andrew Jackson.

## 181

1. 1665 (from Defoe's *Journal of the Plague Year*).
2. Lower prices (Quakers refused to take a profit from alcohol sales).
3. London, Hamburg and Milan.
4. Sir (later Lord) Solly Zuckerman.
5. George Hudson.
6. Copper, tin, lead, zinc, silver, aluminium, nickel.

## 30

1. Which school of design adopted the principle 'Function equals beauty'?
2. Who bought Sealink in 1984?
3. Where is three fifths of the free world's gold produced?
4. Which President of the Board of Trade was killed by a locomotive at the opening of the first-ever railway service?
5. What consumer product did RCA introduce in 1953?
6. Are premium bond winnings subject to taxation?

## 106

1. Which grocery chain was founded in Oakland, California and had 2,507 stores in USA and Europe by 1983?
2. Which company was the first British industrial company to announce pre-tax profits greater than £1 billion?
3. What are Sacilor and Usinor?
4. Which daughter of a Chief Economic Adviser to the Government was an economics editor of the *Guardian*?
5. Who first introduced cash-point machines?
6. On what day does the tax year start in Britain?

## 182

1. Which hair product did Denis Compton sport?
2. Which ship laid the cable establishing links across the Atlantic and between Suez and Bombay?
3. The enthronement of which young Japanese Emperor in the nineteenth century is generally regarded as dating the beginning of industrial Japan?
4. What happened when the Labour Government tried in 1976 to 'manage' a devaluation of sterling?
5. Whose purchase of five DC10s in 1980 led to financial disaster?
6. Which London Exchange has a potato futures market?

# 30

1. The Bauhaus.
2. Sea Containers.
3. South Africa.
4. W. Huskisson.
5. Colour television.
6. No.

# 106

1. Safeway Stores.
2. ICI (1985).
3. France's state-owned steel companies.
4. Frances Cairncross.
5. Barclays.
6. 6 April.

# 182

1. Brylcreem.
2. The Great Eastern.
3. Meiji (1868).
4. The pound crashed out of control.
5. Sir Freddie Laker.
6. The Baltic Exchange.

# 31

1. For what does DB stand in Aston Martin sports cars?
2. Which UK company is the largest manufacturer of glass?
3. Which company was broken up by a historic 1911 US Supreme Court decision?
4. What is Keynesian fiscal policy?
5. Which meat business family is notorious for tax avoidance?
6. Why, according to legend, is Wall Street so named?

# 107

1. Which lord is supposed to have said that he knew half of what he spent on advertising was wasted, but he did not know which half?
2. Which accounting firm was sued by the UK Government over DeLorean Cars 'irregularities'?
3. Under whose Presidency was the Space Shuttle programme launched?
4. How many constituents did David Ricardo MP represent in Portarlington in 1819?
5. Who is responsible for the hologram on Access cards?
6. Who or what is LIFFE?

# 183

1. What is a *spritze*?
2. The British consumption of which spirit trebled 1710–50?
3. Which NATO country was the last to invite women to join the armed forces?
4. Which Governor of the Bank of England did Churchill regard as bamboozling him into his 'biggest blunder'?
5. Whose anti-Semitic views were published in his own newspaper, the *Dearborn Independent*?
6. What is a 'greenback'?

# 31

1. David Brown.
2. Pilkington.
3. Standard Oil (which was broken up into thirty-four different companies).
4. The use by Government of its expenditure and tax revenues to influence aggregate demand in the economy.
5. The Vesteys.
6. From the wall guarding the Dutch from the Indians.

# 107

1. The First Viscount Leverhulme.
2. Arthur Anderson and Company.
3. Richard Nixon's.
4. Twelve.
5. The American Bank Note Company.
6. The London International Financial Futures Exchange.

# 183

1. A mineral water and white wine mixed half and half.
2. Gin.
3. West Germany.
4. (Lord) Montagu Norman (the quote comes from Lord Moran and refers to the return to gold).
5. Henry Ford (he later apologized).
6. An American dollar bill (so called because of the green ink used on the back).

## 32

1. In relation to what product did Ian Botham create a stir by ordering three?
2. How many AA stars has the Waldorf Hotel, London WC2?
3. In what American state would you find Oil City, centre of the first oil boom?
4. Which well-known politician argued in 1963 that Britain was 'suffering from galloping obsolescence'?
5. Of what company did Jean Denton become a managing director?
6. Name one of Japan's two biggest banks.

## 108

1. What is Airbus Industries' 150-seat airliner called?
2. Unlike CAP, the British Farm Price Review did not result in food surpluses. Why not?
3. Which economy of the original EEC six achieved the fastest rate of output growth between 1970 and 1982?
4. What were Lord Keynes's christian names?
5. Who brought what *Back from the Brink*?
6. Who is Britain's 'lender of last resort'?

## 184

1. Which automobile make has a 924 944 and 928 series?
2. What was the IRC?
3. For what is COCOM an acronym?
4. Which ministry, now defunct, was responsible for carrying out the National Plan?
5. Which billion dollar oilman is owner of 20th Century Fox?
6. What was the first move towards the decimalization of the British currency?

## 32

1. Shredded Wheat.
2. Four.
3. Pennsylvania.
4. Tony Benn.
5. Heron Drive (the car-fleet and finance company).
6. Fuji and Dai-Ichi Kangyo.

## 108

1. The A-320.
2. Because prices agreed at the Review were made up by a subsidy.
3. France (the average annual growth of gross domestic product was 3.2 per cent according to the World Bank).
4. John Maynard.
5. Sir Michael Edwardes, BL (title of the book describing his experiences at BL).
6. The Bank of England.

## 184

1. Porsche.
2. The Industrial Reorganization Corporation (set up in 1966 to promote mergers in British industry and disbanded in 1971).
3. The Coordinating Committee for Multilateral Export Controls.
4. The Department of Economic Affairs.
5. Marvin Davis.
6. The introduction of the florin (1849).

## 33

1. What, in publishing circles, is JICNARS?
2. In which industry do male employees enjoy (or suffer) the longest continuous employment within the same firm?
3. Which is the largest non-union employing firm?
4. What is ASLEF?
5. Who first used electricity to talk to someone else?
6. What is New York's equivalent to the *FT* Index?

## 109

1. Wayne Richmond (Indiana) produced a popular hearse with a reversible floor which doubled as what?
2. Whose head offices were at Michael House, 82 Baker Street, from 1913 to 1958?
3. Who was US President at the time of the Wall Street crash?
4. What was the title of Giscard d'Estaing's survey of French society and economy, written in 1976?
5. Which company was first to market a 1600 ASA film?
6. Which High Street bank announced their intention to reintroduce Saturday opening in September 1984?

## 185

1. What does 'Supérieure' mean on a bottle of claret?
2. Which famous novelist has a familial connection with a Suffolk brewery?
3. Which country became the biggest exporter of oil during the Second World War?
4. Who is First Lord of the Treasury?
5. Which entrepreneur failed to buy up the Savoy in 1981?
6. By the end of 1983 which group of 'institutional investors' had investments totalling some £89 billion?

# 33

1. Joint Industry Committee for National Readership Surveys.
2. Insurance, banking and finance (average job duration was calculated by Mean in *Economica*, 1982 at twenty-eight years).
3. IBM.
4. Associated Society of Locomotive Engineers and Firemen.
5. Alexander Bell.
6. The Dow Jones Industrial Average.

# 109

1. An ambulance.
2. Marks and Spencer.
3. Herbert Hoover.
4. *French Democracy* (*La Démocratie Française*).
5. Fuji.
6. National Westminster.

# 185

1. A higher alcohol content.
2. Graham Greene (Greene King).
3. Venezuela.
4. The Prime Minister.
5. Charles Forte.
6. The Pension Funds.

## 34

1. In the computer industry what does MIPS measure?
2. Which project was originally expected to cost £150 millon, then in 1964 £275 million, in 1966 £400 million, in 1968 £570 million, in 1970 £825 million and in 1972 £970 million?
3. Which company paid $13.5 billion for Gulf Oil in 1984?
4. Who did Heathcoat-Amory replace as Chancellor of the Exchequer in 1958?
5. How did Andrew Carnegie finance his first share purchase?
6. Which monarch established the Bank of England?

## 110

1. Which company has registered Father William as a trademark?
2. Name the Committee that reported in 1971 on the role of small firms in the British Economy.
3. Which company is known in France as *la Régie*?
4. In what year were the Corn Laws repealed?
5. Who runs Channel 9, Australia?
6. Can a profitable company still go into liquidation?

## 186

1. Which Beach Boys' hit does British Caledonian use?
2. The keel of which important British ship was laid at Portsmouth on 2 October 1905?
3. By what name is the Visa card known in France?
4. What was the annual salary, at appointment in 1985, of Peter Levene, head of the Defence Procurement Office?
5. Whose affordable luxury in carpets ended in ruin?
6. Through which stockbroking firm does the Government control the supply of its stock to the market?

# 34

1. Computer processing speed (MIPS are millions of instructions per second).
2. Concorde.
3. Chevron.
4. Peter Thorneycroft.
5. He mortgaged his mother's house.
6. William III.

# 110

1. William Younger (brewers).
2. The Bolton Committee.
3. Renault.
4. 1846.
5. Kerry Packer.
6. Yes (if it runs out of cash).

# 186

1. 'California Girls'.
2. HMS *Dreadnought*.
3. *Carte Bleue*.
4. £95,000.
5. Cyril Lord.
6. Mullens & Co.

## 35

1. What is a Merolite pack?
2. Which accounting professor became a British Telecom watch-dog?
3. Which country has the highest per capita consumption of coffee?
4. What is the National Debt?
5. Who first discovered the beneficial aspects of penicillin?
6. What tax replaced estate duty?

## 111

1. What quality does the octane number of petrol represent?
2. What was Sir Terence Beckett's position at the CBI during 1984?
3. Which European nation had the highest per capita national income in 1982?
4. For what did Disraeli pay the Khedive of Egypt £4 million in 1875?
5. Name the 'Famous Five' who launched TVAM?
6. What is the difference between a stockbroker and a stockjobber?

## 187

1. What product is described as 'liquid engineering'?
2. How much did a businessman pay for his copy of the *FT* on the day after the 1985 Budget?
3. Which US firm was allowed to build plants in the Soviet Union in return for importing Stolichnaya vodka?
4. Rank the following unions in descending order of their membership in 1981: ASTMS, AUEW, NUPE.
5. Which publisher created the highly successful Left Book Club between the wars?
6. What is the rate of betting tax in the UK?

## 35

1. A flexible plastic film pouch, reinforced with a paper sleeve.
2. Professor Bryan Carsberg.
3. Finland.
4. Outstanding government debts.
5. Alexander Fleming (1928).
6. Capital Transfer Tax.

## 111

1. It's anti-knocking quality.
2. Director General.
3. Switzerland.
4. Shares in the Suez Canal.
5. Michael Parkinson, Angela Rippon, Anna Ford, Peter Jay and David Frost.
6. The latter does not deal directly with the public, but functions more like a wholesaler.

## 187

1. Castrol GTX.
2. 35p.
3. Pepsi-Cola.
4. AUEW (1,100,000), NUPE (699,000), ASTMS (491,000).
5. Victor Gollancz.
6. 10 per cent.

## 36

1. Which product gets exposure at both the darts and snooker World Championships?
2. Which firm owns Waitrose?
3. Which city is the centre of the French aeroplane industry?
4. The slush fund of which American firm paid out $845,000 to foreign politicians between 1970 and 1975?
5. Who opened the Kinetoscope Parlor on Broadway, New York, in 1894?
6. On which French banknote is Debussy portrayed?

## 112

1. What is the difference between cast and wrought iron?
2. Which contraceptive was licensed in Britain in 1985?
3. Which is Europe's biggest electrical/electronics group?
4. George Bernard Shaw learnt in 1935 about which book 'on economic theory which will largely revolutionize . . . the way the world thinks about economic theory'?
5. Who joined ICL four months before it was taken over, and left when it was?
6. To an American banker what is a 'non-performing asset'?

## 188

1. In what market are Sindy and Barbie deadly rivals?
2. About which London casino was it revealed that one punter had bounced 138 cheques totalling £2.7 million?
3. What do the rates of output growth in Zaire, Chad and Uganda, between 1970 and 1982, have in common?
4. What is the name of Nigel Lawson's wife?
5. Who first demonstrated electro-magnetic induction to the Royal Society in 1831?
6. When was (long-term) Capital Gains Tax introduced?

## 36

1. Embassy cigarettes.
2. The John Lewis Partnership.
3. Toulouse.
4. Goodyear.
5. Thomas Edison (possibly the first cinema).
6. The twenty franc note.

## 112

1. The carbon content (wrought iron has a much smaller carbon content and is consequently more malleable and less brittle).
2. Depo-Provera.
3. Philips.
4. *The General Theory of Employment, Interest and Money* (J. M. Keynes).
5. Sir Michael Edwardes.
6. A loan on which interest is not being paid.

## 188

1. Toy dolls.
2. The Playboy Club.
3. They were all negative.
4. Thérèse.
5. Michael Faraday.
6. 1965.

## 37

1. Which company makes Hartley's jams and Chivers jellies?
2. What use would a business make of the ECGD?
3. What was the mainstay of the economy of Zanzibar in the early nineteenth century?
4. In October/November 1982 the Government found a way of reducing the official unemployment figures. How?
5. Which former President of the CBI was also Dunlop Chairman from 1978 to 1983?
6. In 1985 which country became a net debtor to the rest of the world for the first time in six decades?

## 113

1. What does GT stand for in motor car designation?
2. Which British industry has been subject to continuous regulation of prices since the Second World War, but has achieved one of the best records for productivity growth?
3. Which company owns 25 per cent of Mazda Motor?
4. A management theorist distinguished between 'hygiene' factors which cause job dissatisfaction, and 'motivation' factors which cause job satisfaction. Who was he?
5. Who was the inspiration for Auric Goldfinger?
6. How does a bear speculator make a profit?

## 189

1. Which is the 'Number One Name' in expectorants?
2. How late can one order dinner at the Savoy?
3. On what did India place an export ban in 1984?
4. Where did Nigel Lawson get his secondary education?
5. Who intended to put a Rolls in every kitchen?
6. How many cheques were cleared by the London Clearing House in 1982?

# 37

1. Cadbury Schweppes.
2. It would use it to insure itself against the risks of default when exporting (the Export Credits Guarantee Department).
3. An entrepôt for the slave trade.
4. It changed the method of count to exclude those looking for work but not entitled to benefit.
5. Sir Campbell Fraser.
6. USA.

# 113

1. Grand Tourer/Grand Tourisme/Gran Turismo.
2. Agriculture.
3. Ford.
4. Frederick Herzberg.
5. Charles Engelhard (a close friend of Ian Fleming).
6. By selling forward on a falling market, and buying at a lower price when delivery is due.

# 189

1. Benylin.
2. 11.15 p.m.
3. Tea.
4. Westminster.
5. John Bloom.
6. 1,565 million.

## 38

1. Why does Woolworth use the brand name Winfield?
2. Toad Lane, Rochdale, was the birthplace of which organization?
3. To which US airport does Virgin Atlantic fly?
4. A strike at which railway company gave rise to a significant House of Lords decision in 1901?
5. Which firm introduced xerography?
6. Which two of the High Street banks were prevented from merging by the Monopolies Commission in 1967?

## 114

1. Marketing managers talk about classifying people according to their ACORN category. What is it?
2. Which national daily newspaper has the highest proportion of women amongst its readership?
3. Which country is the biggest producer of natural rubber?
4. Which is the longest 'strike' in British history?
5. Who produced the first 'device for generating power and transmitting it to a machine performing the work desired'?
6. In the City what are 'Blue Chips'?

## 190

1. Which brand of coffee uses the slogan 'When coffee tastes this good, who needs caffeine?'
2. What is the Alvey Project supposed to achieve for Britain?
3. In which country can you order a 'Fix' in the bar?
4. Who represents a connection between *Blue Peter* and *The Money Programme*?
5. Whose often screened signature wasn't really his own?
6. Which City institution acts as a residual purchaser of Treasury Bills?

## 38

1. It was the middle name of the founder, Frank W. Woolworth.
2. The Co-op.
3. Newark, N. J.
4. The Taff Vale Railway (the decision made unions liable for damages inflicted by its officials).
5. Haloid Corporation, USA.
6. Lloyds and Barclays.

## 114

1. A Classification of Residential Neighbourhoods.
2. The *Daily Telegraph* (1983).
3. Malaysia.
4. The strike by Norfolk schoolchildren at Burston school (a 'strike school' was set up which lasted twenty-five years).
5. Thomas Newcomen (who produced the first-time steam engine in 1705, and which dominated the early market in prime movers).
6. First-class shares with low risk.

## 190

1. Café Hag.
2. 'Fifth-generation' computing technology.
3. Greece.
4. Valerie Singleton.
5. Walt Disney (apparently some genuine signatures were thrown away by autograph hunters who thought they were fake).
6. The Discount Houses (tender for the entire supply of Treasury Bills).

## 39

1. What was the wealth in Golconda?
2. What was Clive Ponting's annual salary in 1984?
3. What do the initials OECD stand for?
4. Who advocated public works programmes as a cure for unemployment in the General Election of 1929?
5. Which firm produced the first electric car?
6. Which part of the UK uses a plastic pound note?

## 115

1. Which two atmospheric gases freeze vegetables?
2. Britain's 'canal mania' is associated with which decade?
3. How was the computer in the movies *2001* and *2010* related to the largest computer firm in the world?
4. What was the voluntary incomes policy of the mid-1970s?
5. During Congressional hearings in 1974 which family were found to have investments of at least $1 billion?
6. In 1984 what was the maximum amount of loan for which mortgage tax relief could be claimed?

## 191

1. What is the name of Nepal's only brand of cigarette?
2. Which was the first nuclear power station to feed electricity on to the grid in Britain?
3. The humorous Soviet journal *Krokodil* once published a cartoon showing a nail factory which had just produced a single gigantic nail. What absurdity did the cartoon reveal?
4. Who became Chief Economic Adviser in 1980?
5. What did John Harrison invent in 1713?
6. If you were walking down Lothbury into Throgmorton Street, on which side of the street would you find the London Stock Exchange?

# 39

1. Diamonds (Golconda is the former name of Hyderabad, famous for its diamond mines).
2. £23,000.
3. Organization for Economic Cooperation and Development.
4. D. Lloyd George.
5. Acme and Immisch (Britain, 1895).
6. The Isle of Man.

# 115

1. Carbon dioxide and nitrogen.
2. The 1790s.
3. HAL's initials precede IBM's by one in the alphabet.
4. The Social Contract.
5. The Rockefellers.
6. £30,000.

# 191

1. YAK.
2. Calder Hall.
3. Success indicators based on physical production targets (such as weight).
4. Terry Burns.
5. The chronometer.
6. On the right.

# 40

1. In computing terminology, what is RAM?
2. What advantage has the person possessing Jaguar's 'Ultimate Businessman's Car'?
3. What does cartoonist Steve Bell call the dollar in the 'If' strip whenever the pound plummets?
4. Which Chancellor of the Exchequer returned the pound sterling to the Gold Standard?
5. Who created The Body Shop?
6. What does 'funding' the National Debt mean?

# 116

1. Which drug occurs in the bark of a willow tree?
2. With which Japanese firm has ICL been collaborating in computer mainframe design?
3. Which is the largest free trade area in the world?
4. Where did Alfred Marshall become a professor?
5. Whose son was killed going for the world air speed record over the Thames estuary on 27 September 1946?
6. What is an SDR?

# 192

1. What is the British equivalent of kerosene in the US?
2. By 1939 how many telephones were there in Britain per thousand of population?
3. Which non-communist airline flew the most passenger kilometres on international routes in 1983?
4. In what year were the functions of the Department of Economic Affairs taken over by the Treasury?
5. What is significant about the nationality of Sir James Goldsmith?
6. Why should crooked financiers fear 'FIG'?

# 40

1. Random Access Memory, i.e. memory whose content can be changed by the user.
2. An office, complete with computer, replaces the passenger section.
3. The turd.
4. Winston Churchill.
5. Anita Roddick.
6. The conversion of government borrowing from a short-term to a long-term basis.

# 116

1. Aspirin.
2. Fujitsu.
3. The EEC and EFTA combined (which formed a free trade area from January 1984 and has the biggest value of trade for any free trade area).
4. Cambridge.
5. Sir Geoffrey de Havilland's (his son Geoffrey was flying a DH108).
6. Special Drawing Right (from the IMF).

# 192

1. Paraffin.
2. Sixty-five.
3. Pan-American (34.45 billion passenger kilometres in 1983).
4. 1969.
5. He is both French and British.
6. It is the DPP's Fraud Investigation Group.

# 41

1. According to the Advertising Standards Authority every ad should be legal, decent, honest and what?
2. To what refinery does the oil from the Forties Field flow?
3. Which firm achieved notoriety on Monday 3 December 1984?
4. What is the acronym for the Pit Deputies' union?
5. What are Inderal and Tenormin, and which company pioneered their development?
6. Who is currently Chairman of the Stock Exchange?

# 117

1. Which slippery product was once likened, in the seventeenth century, to the 'frogs of Egypt'?
2. How many professional accounting bodies in the UK are designated 'chartered'?
3. Off which coast did Shell Oil abandon exploration after spending $250 million?
4. Who is barred by a 'barrier to entry"?
5. Who was the real-life model for Citizen Kane?
6. Of what is 'Sterling M3' a measure?

# 193

1. Which breakfast cereal goes 'snap, crackle and pop'?
2. What do Holme Moss, Kirk O'Shott's and Wenvoe have in common?
3. With what stream do you associate the last gold-rush of the nineteenth century?
4. Who were the Council of Four, Paris, 1919?
5. Who resigned as Chairman of Minet after an offshore reinsurance scandal?
6. In what post-war year did the Bank of England stop having to enforce an exchange control policy?

## 41

1. Truthful.
2. Grangemouth.
3. Union Carbide (a poisonous cloud released from the plant in Bhopal, India, killing thousands).
4. Nacods.
5. They are both heart drugs pioneered by ICI.
6. Sir Nicholas Goodison.

## 117

1. Soap.
2. Three.
3. The US Atlantic coast.
4. Potential competitors (barred from an industry or market).
5. William Randolph Hearst (newspaper baron).
6. The money supply.

## 193

1. Rice Krispies.
2. They were all sites for early television transmitters.
3. The Klondike (1896, a tributary of the Yukon river, and originally called Thron-diuck).
4. Wilson, Lloyd George, Clemenceau and Orlando.
5. John Wallrock.
6. 1979.

## 42

1. Before coal which material was usually used in the smelting of iron?
2. What percentage of British adults read the *FT*?
3. Which typewriter firm began in Turin in 1908?
4. What is GNP?
5. Did ascertaining latitude or longitude present the bigger problem for early navigators?
6. Which are the 'Big Four' clearing banks?

## 118

1. What is the name given to the document supplying details of goods shipped?
2. What is the major difference between the 1929–33 recession and the 1979–83 recession in the UK?
3. What do the initials UNCTAD stand for?
4. Between 1980 and 1984 what was the fastest growing component of US Government expenditure?
5. Which came first: Marconi's first celebrated wireless message or the Wright brothers' first flight?
6. What is a 'bullionist'?

## 194

1. What is a quota sample?
2. What was the former name of Sellafield?
3. Which New York store is on eleven floors and covers an entire city block on 34th Street at Herald Square?
4. Who was Chairman of the *FT* and the Conservative Party?
5. How many telephones did Alexander Graham Bell keep in his study?
6. Which building society announced its willingness to grant mortgages for nuclear shelters in 1981?

## 42

1. Charcoal.
2. 2 per cent (1983, GB).
3. Olivetti.
4. Gross National Product (a measure of the income earned from productive activity by the residents of a country).
5. Longitude (eventually solved in theory by Newton).
6. Barclays, Lloyds, National Westminster, Midland.

## 118

1. A Bill of Lading.
2. In the earlier recession both retail and wholesale prices fell.
3. The United Nations Conference on Trade and Development.
4. Interest payments on a rapidly expanding National Debt.
5. Marconi (1901), Wright brothers (1905).
6. One who advocates a metallic currency.

## 194

1. A sample where interviewers find fixed numbers of respondents with predetermined characteristics.
2. Windscale.
3. Macy's.
4. Lord Poole.
5. None (he couldn't stand being interrupted).
6. The Woolwich.

## 43

1. In the electronics industry what is an ASIC?
2. How many times is the Lutine Bell rung for bad news?
3. What is c.i.f. in international trade?
4. Which economist was also Madame de Pompadour's physician?
5. Who invented the Spinning Jenny?
6. What was replaced by Minimum Lending Rate?

## 119

1. Which particular brand of cigarettes were you once advised to smoke 'for your throat's sake'?
2. Into which industry did Sir Reay Geddes inquire in the 1960s?
3. Which EEC Commissioner was also a Director of the London School of Economics?
4. Whose theory of the business cycle was based on sunspots?
5. For what invention is Chester F. Carlson remembered?
6. What was the unit of currency in West Germany before the Deutschmark?

## 195

1. With what product do you associate the Gay-Lussac process?
2. What is the significance of Prince Consort Road, Kensington, for the mining industry?
3. In the US what did the Sherman Acts outlaw?
4. To what feature on Britain's roads did the Minister of Transport from 1931 to 1937 give his name?
5. Was the hovercraft invented before or after the Suez Crisis?
6. What kind of institution is Gerrard and National?

# 43

1. An Application Specific Integrated Circuit.
2. Once.
3. Cost, insurance, freight (a means of valuation that includes insurance and carriage as well as the price of the good).
4. François Quesnay (famous for his *Tableau Economique*).
5. J. Hargreaves.
6. Bank Rate.

# 119

1. Craven A.
2. Shipbuilding (Geddes Report, 1966).
3. Ralph Dahrendorf.
4. W. S. Jevons.
5. The xerographic copying process.
6. The Reichsmark (the D-mark replaced it at a ratio of 1 to 10 in 1948).

# 195

1. Sulphuric acid.
2. It contains The Royal School of Mines.
3. Monopolies.
4. The Belisha Beacon (after Leslie Belisha).
5. After (1958).
6. A Discount House.

# Q

## 44

1. What deadly poison was released at Seveso?
2. In 1900 the entire output of the British steel industry was exceeded by a single firm. What was the firm?
3. In the textile industry to what does MFA refer?
4. What discipline uses statistical techniques to estimate the parameters of an economic model?
5. Whose Anglo-American dynasty was based on landownership in a rapidly expanding New York?
6. What, exactly, was a groat?

## 120

1. What is computer 'down time'?
2. Which post-war British aircraft flop was to have sleeping berths, promenade decks and a dining-room?
3. Which country was the second biggest cereal crop producer in the EEC in 1984?
4. Where does the word 'budget' come from?
5. Close to death, who was told by a secretary that he had given away $324, 657, 399 (or 90 per cent of his wealth)?
6. To what does SEC refer on Wall Street?

## 196

1. In 1962 why did Courtauld's say 'Courtauld's alone can make the most of man-made fibres'?
2. In what year did registered unemployment in tho UK (including school leavers) reach three million?
3. By 1985 whose sexual favours cost $1 million a time?
4. Which Prime Minister said, 'Whichever party is in office, the Treasury is in power'?
5. 'I have fifty-two and Prime Minister Gladstone only seventeen'? To what was Andrew Carnegie referring?
6. What functions from the Old Corn Exchange Building?

# 44

1. Dioxin.
2. Carnegie Steel.
3. The Multi-Fibre Agreement.
4. Econometrics.
5. The Astors.
6. A coin, used in various European countries, and equal in England to four pence.

# 120

1. The time during which a system is inoperative.
2. The Bristol Brabazon.
3. Britain.
4. From the French *bougette* (a wallet).
5. Andrew Carnegie.
6. The Securities and Exchange Commission.

# 196

1. To ward off a takeover attempt by ICI.
2. 1982 (January, non-seasonally adjusted).
3. Northern Dancer's ('the most valuable racehorse stallion of all time').
4. Harold Wilson.
5. The number of times that he had been granted freedom of the city.
6. The London Commodity Exchange.

## 45

1. What was the first musical paper to publish a singles' chart in Britain?
2. In which county were Fremlin's beers and pubs a feature before acquisition by Whitbread in 1968?
3. Which Californian company 'controls every important area of policy and growth in California . . . energy, land, transportation, urban development and environment'?
4. What is CBA in economic appraisal?
5. For the movement of what product was the first English canal sponsored in 1761?
6. What does the FDIC do for American Banking?

## 121

1. Why are brand names so called?
2. The 1895 edition of Mrs Beeton's *Book of Household Management* talks of 'an important trade that has sprung up in the last quarter of a century'. Which trade?
3. What is the Lomé Convention?
4. In which publication would you find 'Lombard'?
5. Who was manager of the Beatles and the Rolling Stones?
6. Which building society ceased trading in 1984?

## 197

1. Whose 1985 advertising poster consists of a lot of dots, 91 per cent of which are black, and the rest red?
2. Where in London did the Covent Garden market move?
3. What began at Sutter's Mill near the junction of the American and Sacramento rivers in 1848?
4. Which is France's largest trade union?
5. With which industry is Ludwig Mond associated?
6. What is bimetallism?

# 45

1. *New Musical Express* (*NME*).
2. Kent.
3. Southern Pacific.
4. Cost Benefit Analysis.
5. Coal (the Duke of Bridgewater's Canal).
6. It insures all deposits of up to $100,000 against bank failure.

# 121

1. It was once the practice to brand packing-cases with hot irons.
2. Tinned foods.
3. An agreement on trade and aid between the EEC and (sixty-five) countries of African, Caribbean and Pacific group.
4. The *Financial Times*.
5. Allen Klein.
6. The New Cross Building Society.

# 197

1. British Rail (black dots indicate trains that ran on time in 1984).
2. Nine Elms.
3. The Californian Gold Rush.
4. The CGT (Confédération Générale du Travail).
5. Chemicals.
6. The system of allowing two metals to function as currency at a fixed rate of exchange between them.

## 46

1. What advertising space was denied to advertisers by an Act of Parliament from 1 January 1962?
2. What name is often given to Britain's fixed social capital in such things as roads, railways and electricity?
3. What French post did Michael Rocard hold in 1984?
4. Whose 'law' says that the proportion of household income spent on food will tend to decline as income increases?
5. With what invention do you associate the names of Sir Ambrose Fleming and Lee de Forest?
6. What is a 'rights issue'?

## 122

1. What is a 'loss leader'?
2. How much did a pop single cost in 1964?
3. Which city contains the world's most expensive land?
4. Who presented the Budget in 1952?
5. What plane did Amy Johnson use for her flight to Australia?
6. By what other name is the International Bank for Reconstruction and Development better known?

## 198

1. What do catalytic converters do on automobiles?
2. During which war was BST introduced?
3. Which is the only state in the US not served by Greyhound buses?
4. In Britain which Ministry has been used to try to curb local authority spending?
5. Who was Professor of Mining at Birmingham University, petroleum adviser to the Colonial Office and Chairman of BP at different stages of his career?
6. What is 'specie'?

## 46

1. The sky (it became illegal to 'emit' or 'display' any advertisement from an aircraft).
2. The infrastructure of the economy.
3. Minister of Agriculture.
4. Ernst Engel.
5. The valve (Fleming: the diode, 1904; de Forest: the triode, 1906).
6. An offer of new shares to the existing shareholders in a company.

## 122

1. A product sold at a loss in order to attract customers towards other goods.
2. 6s. 8d.
3. Hong Kong.
4. R. A. Butler.
5. The Gypsy Moth.
6. The World Bank.

## 198

1. They enable them to run on unleaded petrol.
2. The First World War (British Summer Time was introduced in 1916).
3. Hawaii.
4. Environment.
5. Sir John (later Lord) Cadman.
6. Money in the form of minted pieces of metal.

## 47

1. What is ALGOL?
2. Which tea clipper recorded the fastest passage from Hong Kong to London?
3. Which computer giant lost in the 'Jap Scam'?
4. What ministry did Cecil Parkinson hold in 1983?
5. Which business dynasty was started by 'flimfamming the Iroquois Indians and by selling patent medicines'?
6. Why did the *FT* Index fall by 24 points on 1 March 1974?

## 123

1. 'One day you're going to be too old for it' – which drink ad.?
2. Out of whose merger was British Airways born?
3. Which country's currency had the value in 1946 of 1/150 million pence?
4. Which King of England sold the same 'exclusive trading rights' to different companies?
5. In which new radio station has Richard Branson a share?
6. Where is the world's oldest Stock Exchange?

## 199

1. What is VLSI in the construction of computer chips?
2. Where did Shawn Conter queue for 302 hours, 40 minutes from 16 to 29 December 1982, to be first at the sales?
3. What does IBM stand for?
4. In which country has the 'Flick Affair' created a scandal?
5. Which banker said, 'I must atone for my wealth,' and became a major patron of the arts in America?
6. Have Stock Exchange jobber numbers been rising or falling?

## 47

1. A computer programming language (Algorithmic Orientated Language).
2. The *Hallowe'en* (eighty-nine days).
3. Hitachi (accused of stealing IBM product secrets).
4. Secretary of State for Trade and Industry.
5. The Rockefellers (the story relates to William Avery Rockefeller).
6. Realization of a Labour Government.

## 123

1. Santiago rum.
2. BOAC and BEA (British Overseas Airways Corporation and British European Airways).
3. Hungary (the pengö).
4. Charles I (had two East India Companies operating at the same time).
5. Radio Mercury.
6. Amsterdam (founded 1602).

## 199

1. Very Large Scale Integration.
2. Selfridges, Oxford Street.
3. International Business Machines.
4. West Germany (refers to 'political donations' by the Flick Corporation).
5. Otto H. Kahn.
6. Falling (in the last decade).

## 48

1. Which alloy is made from tin and lead?
2. What do William Hill and Mappin & Webb have in common?
3. Who is the biggest manufacturer of lead-crystal glass?
4. Who was the founding father of industrial psychology?
5. That sex was good clean fun for the decent pipe-smoking bachelor was turned into a 'philosophy' by whom?
6. In the event of a company liquidation, who takes preference: debenture holders or preference share holders?

## 124

1. What is the name given to the code used on labels and read by a wand?
2. What percentage of Royal Dutch Shell is British?
3. The function of 'marker crude' for OPEC prices is served by which oil?
4. What is the full name of the economic forecasting quango known as the 'National Institute'?
5. The first commercial internal combustion engine was fuelled by what?
6. What does PAYE stand for?

## 200

1. What is a 'sampling frame'?
2. When did the East India Company's charter expire?
3. Who produces both tyres and guide books?
4. Which British Prime Minister moralized about 'the unacceptable face of capitalism'?
5. 'The five-dollar day' is synonymous with which new production technique?
6. What do the initials CTT stand for?

# 48

1. Pewter.
2. The same parent (Sears Holdings).
3. Waterford Glass (Ireland, 1983).
4. Hugo Munsterberg.
5. Hugh M. Hefner (the *Playboy* 'philosophy').
6. Debenture holders (preference shares take precedence only over ordinary shareholders).

# 124

1. A bar code.
2. 40 per cent.
3. Arabian Light.
4. The National Institute of Economic and Social Research.
5. Gas (the 'Otto Silent' was first produced in 1876 by N. A. Otto).
6. Pay as you earn.

# 200

1. The possible members of the population from which the sample is to be selected.
2. 1834.
3. Michelin.
4. Edward Heath.
5. The assembly line.
6. Capital Transfer Tax.

## 49

1. Cooper, Ionic, Times are examples of what?
2. What was British Rail's former name?
3. According to the EEC's Common Fisheries Policy what is the minimum limit for exclusive national fishing rights?
4. Who promised the transformation of Britain by a 'white-hot technical revolution'?
5. Where in London were experiments carried out in 1876 to see whether rubber could be a plantation crop?
6. What are 'amortization funds'?

## 125

1. What does a marketing person understand by FMCG?
2. By what name is the 1963 Report outlining proposals for 'the reshaping of British Railways' better known?
3. For how many hours work per week were German metal workers pressing by striking in 1984?
4. How did the Fabian Society get its name?
5. Who invented the 'Archimedes screw'?
6. Which Zola novel dealt with the workings of the Paris Stock Exchange?

## 201

1. In what year did a thumb bar replace the ring on the steering wheel as a means of operating the horn on a VW Beetle?
2. Which shoe manufacturer is based at Street, Somerset?
3. Which are the three biggest jet engine builders for the world's airlines?
4. For what body is Sir John Hoskins currently the Chairman?
5. Who has been the scourge of the NGA at Messenger Group Newspapers?
6. When is a stock or share 'above par'?

## 49

1. Type-faces.
2. British Railways.
3. Six.
4. Harold Wilson.
5. Kew Gardens (early plantations were in Singapore).
6. Funds built up for the purpose of repaying a debt.

## 125

1. Fast-moving consumer goods.
2. The Beeching Report.
3. Thirty-five.
4. After Quintus Fabius Maximus (the Roman General who defeated Hannibal by means of delaying tactics and the avoidance of a head-on battle; hence Fabians do not endorse revolutionary tactics).
5. Archimedes.
6. *Money* (*L'Argent*).

## 201

1. 1964.
2. Clark's.
3. Pratt Whitney, General Electric, Rolls-Royce.
4. The Institute of Directors.
5. Eddie Shah.
6. When its price is higher than its nominal value.

## 50

1. Which company makes Black Magic?
2. On which river would you find the Scott-Lithgow shipyards?
3. For what is COMECON an acronym?
4. What was Kenneth Baker's role when he was at the Department of Industry?
5. Who built the first cotton-spinning factory at Cromford, Derbyshire in 1771?
6. What are the 'liabilities' of a commercial bank?

## 126

1. Which is the largest advertising agency in the world?
2. What was 'Imperial Preference'?
3. In which city did local citizens produce an artificial 'sell-out' in order to keep the Minnesota Twins baseball team?
4. Who preceded Roy Jenkins as Chancellor of the Exchequer?
5. Place the following textile innovations in chronological order: the water frame, the spinning jenny, the mule.
6. When must a firm pay its Corporation Tax in advance?

## 202

1. Which computer firm produces the Macintosh?
2. Where does the term 'A1' originate?
3. Which is Europe's largest tyre-making business?
4. For what is Frank B. Gilbreth known?
5. Which French press tycoon controls *Le Figaro*?
6. Who or what was the EEC 'snake'?

## 50

1. Rowntree Mackintosh.
2. The Clyde.
3. The Council for Mutual Economic Aid.
4. The promotion of information technology.
5. Richard Arkwright.
6. Its deposits.

## 126

1. Dentsu (Japan).
2. Preferential tariffs given to members of the British Empire.
3. Minneapolis (the 'warm' body count one day in 1984 was only 9,000, whereas 52,000 tickets were sold).
4. James Callaghan.
5. Jenny (*c.* 1765), water frame (1769), mule (1779).
6. Advanced Corporation Tax is payable whenever a distribution is made.

## 202

1. Apple.
2. From the Lloyd's Register of British and Foreign Shipping which used the term to describe ships of the highest class.
3. Michelin.
4. Time and motion study.
5. Robert Hersant.
6. The direct linking of certain currencies to the D-mark (the system preceding the establishment of the EMS).

# 51

1. Which type of tradesman would use a cambrel?
2. Which stamp dealer dates from 1865?
3. What is the middle name of Saudi Arabia's oil Minister?
4. Who defined economic terms in the following way: 'Recession is when your neighbour is out of a job; depression is when you are out of a job; recovery is when President Carter is out of a job'?
5. Who had the original idea for the Volkswagen Beetle?
6. In the jargon of the City what is a 'bull'?

# 127

1. What is 'unit pricing'?
2. What does ICI stand for?
3. Which American state manufactures over half of America's automobile parts and components, and assembles one third of the country's automobiles?
4. What paradox did Giffen discover?
5. Who invented dynamite?
6. Early banks often originated from what sort of smith?

# 203

1. A chain of restaurants was named after which cartoon character in Popeye?
2. Why is British business under threat from NICs?
3. What is the name of the American car makers' union?
4. Which Labour President of the Board of Trade in the 1960s had pronounced anti-Common-Market views?
5. Who created the Pineapple Dance Studios?
6. The reverse side of the last pound note to be issued depicts whom?

# 51

1. A butcher (it is a kind of hook used for hanging carcasses by the feet).
2. Stanley Gibbons.
3. Zaki (Sheikh Ahmed Zaki Yamani).
4. Ronald Reagan during the 1980 presidential campaign.
5. Ferdinand Porsche.
6. A speculator who expects share prices to rise.

# 127

1. Pricing by volume or weight (to facilitate comparisons).
2. Imperial Chemical Industries.
3. Michigan.
4. That for some goods the demand might increase when prices rose.
5. Sir Alfred Nobel.
6. The goldsmith.

# 203

1. Mr Wimpy.
2. NICs are the newly industrializing countries (such as South Korea).
3. United Auto Workers (UAW).
4. Douglas Jay.
5. Debbie Moore.
6. Sir Isaac Newton.

# 52

1. Which British car was first awarded the design symbol?
2. Which is the oldest company in Great Britain?
3. After General Motors and Ford which company produces the most cars in the world?
4. What is an entrepôt?
5. Who first synthesized indigo?
6. What two things are on the 'tail' of a threepenny piece?

# 128

1. Which famous advertising man was once chef at the Hotel Majestic in Paris?
2. What was the rate of income tax levied in Great Britain between April 1941 and 1946?
3. Which country is the biggest supplier of copper?
4. By what name was the American labour organization, Industrial Workers of the World (formed 1905), better known?
5. What new technology revolutionized glassmaking in the 1970s?
6. How many old pennies in one pound?

# 204

1. Who makes the Sierra and the Fiesta?
2. In 1983 British imports of manufactured goods exceeded, in value, exports of manufacturers. When was the last time that happened?
3. The price of the Model T Ford Runabout was $590 in 1911; what was it in 1926?
4. Who was Thatcher's first Secretary of State for Industry?
5. Who dissolved rubber in naptha for waterproofs?
6. In 1981–2 BAT made £684 million pre-tax profits. How much Corporation Tax did they pay?

## 52

1. Austin Montego.
2. The Royal Mint (first mentioned in AD 287).
3. Toyota (2.49 million in 1984).
4. A centre which receives goods for onward distribution.
5. Adolph Baeyer.
6. Sea thrift or a portcullis.

## 128

1. David Ogilvy.
2. 50 per cent (or 10 shillings in the pound).
3. Chile.
4. The Wobblies.
5. The float-glass technology (Pilkington's).
6. 240.

## 204

1. Ford.
2. The sixteenth century.
3. $290.
4. Sir Keith Joseph.
5. Charles Macintosh.
6. Nil.

## 53

1. What is the American brand name for Esso?
2. Which trade group did Britain leave on entry to the EEC?
3. In 1983 how many persons were there to each car in the USA?
4. Which writer, the author of *The Road to Serfdom*, is much admired by Margaret Thatcher?
5. What was the unpleasant news for the rich in the US Sixteenth Amendment of 1913?
6. What was the last year in which there were (approximately) four dollars to the pound?

## 129

1. Why did Levi Strauss drop the crotch rivet on the 501?
2. In conjunction with which other retail store is Marks and Spencer creating two new superstores?
3. Who met whom at Bretton Woods?
4. What is a rentier?
5. What nationality is Robert Maxwell's wife?
6. Which of the London clearing banks has the largest deposits?

## 205

1. What are 'parachute salesmen'?
2. What is the name of the new company formed by Lucas and Smith's industries?
3. What is the world's largest airline?
4. The largest recorded membership of a trade union at any time was some eight million. Which union?
5. Which entrepreneur for profit kept one of London's tallest buildings devoid of business?
6. What is the name given to the takeover by one company of the responsibility for collecting the debts of another?

## 53

1. Exxon (changed from Esso in 1972).
2. EFTA (European Free Trade Area).
3. 1.9.
4. Friedrich von Hayek.
5. A tax on income.
6. 1949.

## 129

1. The 501 (the original Levis) always had a crotch rivet until the boss, Walter Haas, discovered in 1933 that crouching by the camp fire could be a very painful experience.
2. Tesco.
3. The British, American and Canadian governments met to discuss the post-war international monetary system.
4. A person whose source of income is interest or dividend payments.
5. French.
6. Barclays.

## 205

1. Salesmen who go into a foreign market thinking that they can sell quickly.
2. Lucas Electrical Electronics and Systems.
3. Aeroflot (1,300 aircraft, 620,000 miles of routes, 500,000 employees, 109 million passengers in 1983).
4. Solidarity (1980).
5. Harry Hyams (Centrepoint).
6. Factoring.

## 54

1. What are the 'Four Ps' of the marketing mix?
2. Which peer is Chief Executive of the Marks and Spencer group?
3. Who became President of the EEC Commission in 1984?
4. Who is the author of *The Affluent Society*?
5. 'The most successful Gentile in Hollywood' was a description of which 5' 6" movie magnate?
6. By what name is the report on 'The Working of the Monetary System' (1959) better known?

## 130

1. Which creature is depicted on the Alfa-Romeo badge?
2. Name three of the five Scottish New Towns.
3. Which two European countries consume most spirits per head of population?
4. In what university did Milton Friedman make his name?
5. The post of Minister of Aircraft Production was filled by which newspaper man in 1940?
6. In what year was the Deutsche Bundesbank founded?

## 206

1. What are you without when you have 'No *FT*'?
2. What period do historians regard as the 'Great Depression'?
3. What, in the US, is a 'chop shop'?
4. What is Britain's 'Fourth Estate'?
5. Who insisted that his employees wore dark suits and white shirts, forbade smoking and commissioned a company songbook with many stirring titles?
6. What sort of company is Dow Jones?

## 54

1. Product, Price, Place and Promotion.
2. Lord Rayner (1984).
3. Jacques Delors (France).
4. J. K. Galbraith.
5. Darryl F. Zanuck.
6. The Radcliffe Report.

## 130

1. A serpent.
2. Cumbernauld, East Kilbride, Glenrothes, Irvine and Livingston.
3. Hungary and East Germany (1982).
4. University of Chicago.
5. Lord Beaverbrook.
6. 1957.

## 206

1. Comment (No *FT*, No Comment!).
2. 1873–96 (pre-empting its use for the 1930s).
3. An illegal garage that breaks up stolen cars and sells the parts at a price far greater than the cost of the entire car.
4. The press.
5. Thomas J. Watson (IBM).
6. A publishing house.

## 55

1. 1956 was the year of the Suez crisis and the introduction of a popular new biscuit with a Middle Eastern connection. What was it?
2. Against which industries was SET intended to discriminate?
3. How many standards are there for colour TV sets in the EEC?
4. Which former union leader now fights for pensioners?
5. Which firm's 'Saturn Programme' is intended to revolutionize small car technology?
6. What is the motto of the Stock Exchange?

## 131

1. What did Leonard Rossiter pour over Joan Collins?
2. For what wholesale trade is Mincing Lane, London, famous?
3. Which two EEC countries took the lead in the deregulation of European air routes?
4. Who urged that we should be *Free to Choose*?
5. What invention enabled women to change their position in the 1880s?
6. Who retired as Governor of the Bank of England in 1983?

## 207

1. What is the difference between the warp and the weft?
2. What view of a British company are its accounts meant to show?
3. Which African kingdom submitted an application to join the EEC in 1984?
4. What is an 'invisible' export?
5. In which century was the pressure cooker invented?
6. When would you get a P45?

## 55

1. The Jaffa Cake.
2. Services and construction.
3. Two (the French and German systems).
4. Jack Jones.
5. General Motors.
6. 'My word is my bond.'

## 131

1. Cinzano.
2. Tea.
3. Britain and Holland.
4. Milton and Rose Friedman.
5. The bicycle.
6. Lord Richardson.

## 207

1. The warp are those threads running lengthwise in cloth; the weft threads run across the cloth.
2. 'True and fair'.
3. Morocco.
4. A service, like insurance, provided domestically but paid for by an overseas customer.
5. The seventeenth.
6. When you leave employment.

## 56

1. Which company is the world's biggest advertiser?
2. What does P & O stand for?
3. Which countries joined the EEC at the same time as Britain?
4. Where does the word 'exchequer' come from?
5. What are the initials of Rolls and Royce?
6. What bird was depicted on a farthing?

## 132

1. In which trade would a frisket be used?
2. In which of the inter-war years did Britain a) join and b) leave the gold standard?
3. Who was responsible for the first post-war economic plans in France?
4. What is a duopoly?
5. In what year did the era of the silent movie end with the first full-length talking picture *The Jazz Singer*?
6. What was the 'military guinea'?

## 208

1. Which firm manufactures the BBC Micro?
2. Which company is Britain's largest china maker?
3. What is an MNC?
4. The threatened closure of which pit triggered the 1984–5 miners' strike'?
5. In 1962 Unimation Inc. was the first company to develop and sell a new product. What was the product?
6. Who or what was a Bradbury?

# 56

1. Sears, Roebuck and Co. ($898,800,000 in 1982, excluding its catalogue).
2. The Peninsular and Oriental (Steam Navigation Company).
3. Denmark and Ireland.
4. Refers to a table covered with a cloth divided into squares on which accounts were kept with counters.
5. C. S. Rolls and F. H. Royce.
6. The wren.

# 132

1. Printing (it is a thin iron frame for keeping a sheet of paper in position while printing).
2. 1925 and 1931.
3. Georges Monnet.
4. A market in which power is concentrated in the hands of only two sellers.
5. 1927.
6. A special coin minted specifically to supply Wellington's army in the Pyrenees (1813).

# 208

1. Acorn.
2. Wedgwood (1983).
3. A multinational corporation.
4. Corton Wood.
5. The industrial robot.
6. A £1 or 10-shilling note issued by the Treasury in 1914.

# 57

1. What product is endorsed using a feather and a helicopter?
2. What is the name of the teachers' pay negotiating committee?
3. Which Scandinavian economy had the highest per capita national income in 1982?
4. Who provided a description of the advantages of specialization in a pin factory?
5. Of which company is John Harvey Jones currently Chairman?
6. What is 'money at call'?

# 133

1. Which brand of cassette tape offers the chance 'to break the sound barrier'?
2. Which independent body determines whether certain mergers or monopolies are in the public interest?
3. What is Europe's largest brewery?
4. Where does the Chancellor of the Exchequer reside?
5. To what food process did Louis Pasteur give his name?
6. What are consols?

# 209

1. How does the Bramley cooking apple get its name?
2. By the abolition of what tax did Edward Heath promise to 'cut prices at a stroke'?
3. The citizens of which industrial country pay the highest proportion of national income in tax?
4. In what year was the 'Plan for Coal' signed?
5. In which country was Robert Maxwell born?
6. Are 'gifts' between husband and wife subject to Capital Transfer Tax?

# 57

1. Everest double-glazing (advertisement on TV).
2. The Burnham Committee.
3. Norway ($14,280).
4. Adam Smith (*The Wealth of Nations*).
5. ICI.
6. Money lent by banks for very short periods to the discount market.

# 133

1. Maxell.
2. The Monopolies and Mergers Commission.
3. The Guinness Brewery, Dublin.
4. At No. 11 Downing Street.
5. Pasteurization.
6. Unredeemable government stock.

# 209

1. After an English butcher in Southwell, Nottinghamshire, in whose garden the apple is said to have originated.
2. The Selective Employment Tax (SET).
3. Sweden (in 1983).
4. 1974.
5. Czechoslovakia.
6. No.

## 58

1. Which is the 'listening bank'?
2. Which stockbroker serves more British quoted companies than any other?
3. Which leading French newspaper recently started using photographs in an attempt to combat falling sales?
4. By what name is the 1942 Report on 'Social Insurance and Allied Services' better known?
5. Whose personal motto was 'Pile it high and sell it cheap'?
6. Who is Governor of the Bank of England?

## 134

1. What is fustic?
2. How does the word 'navvy' originate?
3. What meeting was held in Dublin Castle in December 1984?
4. What position does Sir James Cleminson currently hold in the CBI?
5. Who went to San Francisco in 1850 intending to make tents, but perceiving no market used the canvas to make trousers instead?
6. At what time does the London Stock Exchange close?

## 210

1. What is the logo of Apple computers?
2. Who bought the Ealing Studios in 1956?
3. Which company is the world's biggest watchmaker?
4. The blame for unemployment was laid on both workers and management by which politician at Brighton in 1984?
5. What did Tiny Rowland refer to as his 'gilded cage'?
6. What is an ECU?

# 58

1. The Midland.
2. Cazenove (end 1983).
3. *Le Monde* (but it only features pictures on Saturdays).
4. The Beveridge Report.
5. Sir John (Jack) Cohen (Tesco).
6. Robin Leigh-Pemberton.

# 134

1. A yellow dye (obtained from the fustic tree).
2. From navigator, a labourer employed constructing canals or 'navigations'.
3. The EEC Summit.
4. President.
5. Levi Strauss.
6. 3.30 p.m.

# 210

1. A rainbow-coloured apple with a bite-size piece missing.
2. The BBC.
3. Seiko.
4. Nigel Lawson (at the Conservative Party Conference).
5. The *Observer*.
6. A European Currency Unit.

## 59

1. What symbol is used by the British Standards Institution?
2. In what year did the first advertisement appear on British TV?
3. In which American city is the US Treasury situated?
4. What name did Hitler originally give to the Volkswagen?
5. Who is generally regarded as Britain's first 'scientific' roadmaker?
6. How many shareholders does a mutual life assurance company have?

## 135

1. What does ABC mean to an advertiser?
2. Which national daily newspaper had the highest circulation in 1983?
3. What acronym designates the French high-speed train?
4. Which Chancellor of the Exchequer resigned after leaking details of his own Budget to the press?
5. Which company first mass produced nuts and bolts in the early 1900s?
6. What was the cheque guarantee card limit before it was raised to £50?

## 211

1. Who sponsors Arsenal FC?
2. Which was the first English university to award a degree in accounting?
3. What is the *Wirtschaftswunder*?
4. Who wrote the world's bestselling economics textbook?
5. Who built the first 'steam carriage' or locomotive?
6. By what name is the West German central bank known?

# 59

1. The kite-mark.
2. 1955.
3. Philadelphia (Independence Mall).
4. 'The strength through joy car' or KdF-wagen.
5. Thomas Telford (especially noted for the London–Holyhead road).
6. None.

# 135

1. Audit Bureau of Circulation.
2. The *Sun* (4.1 million).
3. TGV (Train Grande Vitesse).
4. Hugh Dalton.
5. Guest, Keen and (later) Nettlefold's (GKN).
6. £30.

# 211

1. JVC.
2. London (LSE).
3. The post-war German 'economic miracle'.
4. Paul Samuelson.
5. Richard Trevithick.
6. The Deutsche Bundesbank.

# 60

1. Which bank uses a black horse as its symbol?
2. The correct spelling of which beer became a condition for a brewing merger?
3. Which computer manufacturer is known as 'Big Blue'?
4. What is a 'father/mother of the chapel'?
5. To which famous banking family did 'Lorenzo the Magnificent' belong?
6. What does VAT stand for?

# 136

1. What is 'knocking copy'?
2. Which American company sold its computer subsidiary to ICL in 1976?
3. What sport was told by the EEC in December 1984 to ease restrictions on the employment of nationals from other EEC countries?
4. Which nineteenth-century French Minister of Finance advised the country 'Enrichissez-vous!' ('Get rich')?
5. Which famous insurance underwriter had a picture collection which forms part of the National Gallery?
6. The cash dispenser of which other 'Big Four' bank can be used by a customer of the Nat West?

# 212

1. Which company used a toucan as its ad. symbol?
2. What were the 'Turnpike Companies'?
3. In which country is the Volkswagen Beetle still produced?
4. Who is *Private Eye's* 'Tarzan'?
5. Which steelmaking innovation came first: the Bessemer or Siemens-Martin process?
6. By what name is Italy's central bank known?

## 60

1. Lloyds.
2. Theakston's Old Peculier.
3. IBM.
4. The equivalent of a shop steward in the printing industry.
5. The Medici family.
6. Value Added Tax.

## 136

1. Advertising which unfairly attacks or discredits other products.
2. Singer (Singer Business Machines).
3. Association Football.
4. Guizot (Minister under Louis-Philippe).
5. John Julius Angerstein (1735–1823).
6. The Midland.

## 212

1. Guinness.
2. Companies granted parliamentary powers to build toll roads.
3. Brazil.
4. Michael Heseltine.
5. Bessemer (1856), Siemens-Martin (1864).
6. Banca d'Italia.

## 61

1. What is the process of heating rubber with sulphur?
2. What percentage of households had a video in 1983?
3. What is the largest South African diamond concern?
4. A politician of which party claimed, and about which industry, 'We are not out to run down an industry but . . . to prevent this enormous waste of your (the taxpayers') money, and help the industry reorganize itself on a sound and viable basis'?
5. What is 'the Whisper'?
6. When was the Bank of England founded?

## 137

1. Which contraceptive is known as 'the Jag'?
2. Where is the *Great Britain* permanently docked after rediscovery in the Falklands?
3. What UN body is known as IFAD?
4. Which financial journalist has a brother in the Cabinet?
5. What did Benjamin Franklin do with a key and a kite?
6. What is 'The Central Bankers' Central Bank'?

## 213

1. Who wrote *Unsafe At Any Speed*?
2. How much foreign exchange were British holidaymakers going abroad allowed to take in 1967?
3. Which nineteenth-century French novel aimed to point out the failings of the then bankruptcy laws?
4. Who is currently the CBI's Director General?
5. Which tycoon asked, 'Who wants to go out and see a bad movie when they can stay at home and see a bad one free on television'?
6. Which is Britain's largest building society?

# A

## 61

1. Vulcanization.
2. 20 per cent.
3. De Beers.
4. Labour Party/aircraft industry (the politician was George Brown speaking about the enormous subsidies to that industry from the previous Conservative administration).
5. A new electric car.
6. 1694.

## 137

1. Depo-Provera.
2. Bristol.
3. International Fund for Agricultural Development.
4. Samuel Brittan.
5. Conduct lightning.
6. The Bank for International Settlements.

## 213

1. Ralph Nader.
2. £50 per person (the travel allowance imposed by the crisis measures of July 1966).
3. *Cesar Birotteau* by H. de Balzac.
4. Sir Terence Beckett.
5. Samuel Goldwyn.
6. The Halifax.

## 62

1. Which bank likes to say 'yes'?
2. To the nearest eighth what proportion of the nation's housing stock is privately owned?
3. Of which company is Lee Iacocca the President?
4. By what name was the mineworkers' union known before it became the NUM in 1944?
5. How did William Randolph Hearst's father, George, make his fortune?
6. Whose picture is on the reverse side of a £10 note?

## 138

1. How many 'bits' make a 'byte'?
2. What is the MSC?
3. Which country was the largest (volume) exporter of tea in 1953?
4. Of which college was J. M. Keynes the bursar?
5. What was David Sarnoff (who went on to found RCA) doing for seventy-two hours non-stop on top of New York's Wanamaker Building in 1912?
6. What is the current rate of Capital Gains Tax?

## 214

1. What became known as the 'Tin Lizzie'?
2. Why was 4 February 1971 a grim day for the British aircraft industry?
3. What commodity is mined at the El Teniente mine, near Santiago, Chile?
4. Which Chancellor established the National Economic Development Office?
5. Which firm introduced Librium?
6. What is a firm's 'gearing'?

# 62

1. The Trustee Savings Bank.
2. One eighth (1983).
3. Chrysler.
4. The Miners' Federation of Great Britain.
5. Mainly in mining.
6. Florence Nightingale.

# 138

1. Eight (a bit is a binary digit, i.e. 1 or 0; bytes are used as a measure of computer memory).
2. The Manpower Services Commission.
3. India.
4. King's College (Cambridge).
5. As a wireless operator for Marconi he was taking down the names of the Titanic's 800 survivors (he got promotion!).
6. 30 per cent.

# 214

1. The Model T Ford.
2. The bankruptcy of Rolls-Royce was announced to Parliament.
3. Copper (it is the largest underground copper mine in the world).
4. Selwyn Lloyd.
5. Roche (Switzerland).
6. The ratio of a firm's fixed interest debt to its total debt.

## 63

1. Which was the first newspaper to award a £1 million pound bingo prize?
2. Where are Land Rovers built?
3. Why did a retired employee reportedly drop a handkerchief into a fermentation vat at an Italian subsidiary of Dow Chemicals?
4. What did Ricardo argue was the cause of high bread prices and high rents at the conclusion of the Napoleonic Wars?
5. With what industry is 'Buck' Duke associated?
6. Which City institution has noticeably few windows?

## 139

1. In which European country is Mechlin lace made?
2. When was Harold Wilson's 'pound in your pocket' speech?
3. Which was the first company to have assets in excess of $1 billion?
4. What is the PSI?
5. In what year were parking meters introduced in the USA?
6. Which street 'begins at Broadway, and runs east, gently downhill to the East River'?

## 215

1. What is the sporting logo of Chemise Lacoste?
2. Which firm took over the Scott-Lithgow shipyard in 1984?
3. What name is given to the association of North German cities which monopolized the Baltic trade from the thirteenth to the seventeenth century?
4. Who advised Reagan and gave his name to a curve describing the relationship between tax rates and tax revenue?
5. What was Sir Clive Sinclair's first home computer?
6. What advantage do 'currency options' offer over ordinary forward foreign exchange contracts?

# 63

1. The *Daily Mirror*.
2. Solihull.
3. Industrial espionage (he obtained bacteria samples for a new anti-TB drug).
4. Diminishing returns in agriculture.
5. Tobacco (he was selling 90 per cent of cigarettes sold in the US by 1900).
6. The Bank of England.

# 139

1. Belgium.
2. After the 1967 devaluation of sterling.
3. United States Steel (formed by merger in 1917 with assets of $1400 million).
4. The Policy Studies Institute (1–2 Castle Lane, London).
5. 1935 (Oklahoma City).
6. Wall Street, New York.

# 215

1. A crocodile.
2. Trafalgar House.
3. The Hanseatic League.
4. Professor Arthur Laffer (who invented the 'Laffer curve').
5. The ZX80.
6. They do not have to be taken up if the exchange rate moves in your favour.

## 64

1. Which brand of soup was depicted by Andy Warhol?
2. What group campaigns against sterilized beer?
3. Which disease destroyed most of the vine-roots in France?
4. What is the difference between a 'customs union' and a 'free trade area'?
5. To whom is the invention of the steam pump accredited?
6. What does the difference between the opening and closing capital account on a balance sheet represent (assuming that no new capital is added during the year)?

## 140

1. In the electronics industry what is a 'silicon foundry'?
2. Where did John Player first establish its tobacco firm?
3. Which western European economy devotes the largest proportion of its output to manufacturing?
4. Which body was set up to safeguard the living standards of workers in the First World War?
5. Which player, famous for an army, was golf's 'first million-dollar man'?
6. What term is used to denote the operation of buying at a low price in one market and selling the same item at a higher price in another?

## 216

1. Who sponsors the Football League Championship?
2. Where were DeLorean cars produced?
3. Which country, apart from Italy, has the lira?
4. Which Prime Minister said, 'All the world over I will back the masses against the classes'?
5. Who invented a method of seed-drilling and gave his name to a rock band?
6. What determines whether an asset or liability is 'current'?

# 64

1. Campbell's.
2. CAMRA (Campaign for Real Ale).
3. Phylloxera.
4. Only the customs union imposes a common external tariff.
5. Thomas Savery (the first pump was applied to a Cornish tin mine in 1702).
6. Profit.

# 140

1. A firm that manufactures silicon chips to a customer's own design.
2. Nottingham.
3. West Germany (35 per cent in 1982).
4. The War Emergency Workers National Committee (representing trades unions, trades councils and co-operative societies).
5. Arnold Palmer.
6. Arbitrage.

# 216

1. Canon.
2. Belfast.
3. Turkey.
4. William Gladstone.
5. Jethro Tull.
6. Whether they can be realized or cleared within one year.

## 65

1. What does AGB Research stand for?
2. When did McDonald's open its first British restaurant?
3. The world's largest what is situated in Great Witchington, Norfolk?
4. What is USDAW?
5. Who converted the Talk of the Town into the Hippodrome?
6. In which city is the West German Stock Exchange?

## 141

1. When did the Trade Descriptions Act become law?
2. Who increased tobacco duty to 4,000 per cent because he found 'in the black stinking fume thereof [it was] nearest resembling the stygian smoke of the pit that is bottomless'?
3. What is the name given to the tax or duty levied in some continental countries on goods entering a town?
4. What forced the ultimate repeal of the Corn Laws?
5. Which Kennedy owned RKO Studios?
6. What is PSL?

## 217

1. Who represents a connection between Domecq sherry and Citizen Kane?
2. What did the 'd' stand for in the old £.s.d.?
3. Name the American lawyer and author who has advanced the cause of consumer protection since the 1960s.
4. Which two Hungarian-born economists acted as advisers to the first Wilson Government and became known as 'Buddha' and 'Pest' in Whitehall circles?
5. For what did William Knox D'Arcy pay £20,000 in cash, £20,000 in shares and 16 per cent of the profits in 1901?
6. What are 'Ways and Means Advances'?

# 65

1. Audits of Great Britain Research.
2. 1974.
3. Turkey farm (Bernard Matthews PLC with some 7,500,000 turkeys).
4. The Union of Shop, Distributive and Allied Workers.
5. Peter Stringfellow.
6. Frankfurt.

# 141

1. 1968.
2. James I.
3. Octroi.
4. The Irish potato famine.
5. Joseph Kennedy (1888–1969).
6. A 'broad' measure of private sector liquidity.

# 217

1. Orson Welles (endorsed Domecq in a TV ad and played Citizen Kane in the movie).
2. From the Latin word *denarius* (a Roman coin).
3. Ralph Nader.
4. Thomas Balogh and Nicholas Kaldor.
5. The exclusive oil concession on 480,000 square miles of Persia.
6. Direct loans from the Bank of England to the Government.

## 66

1. Whose slogan is '*Vorsprung durch Technik*'?
2. Lymeswold is a new British cheese; where is it?
3. Regent Street, London, contains a 'world biggest', with some 300 employees and 45,000 square feet of selling space in 1985. What is it?
4. Which Prime Minister's son failed to become a chartered accountant?
5. Which bank introduced Britain's first nationwide homebanking service in January 1985?
6. From which two banks was the National Westminster formed?

## 142

1. What does TNT stand for?
2. In 1950 the first UK biscuit factory devoted to the mass production of one product was opened. What was it?
3. Where was the 1984 'Economic Summit' of western leaders?
4. Which mining corporation did Allende kick out of Chile?
5. What did Thomas Sullivan of New York invent in 1904?
6. What was the standard rate of income tax in 1960?

## 218

1. Which was the largest selling brand of cigarettes in the UK in 1983?
2. How much income tax would a single person earning £10,000 a year have paid in 1960?
3. What is the world's oldest airline?
4. Where is Karl Marx buried?
5. Which was the first publishing company owned by Robert Maxwell?
6. To a banker who or what is the 'Old Lady'?

# 66

1. Audi cars.
2. It does not exist.
3. The largest toyshop, Hamley's.
4. Margaret Thatcher (son, Mark).
5. The Bank of Scotland.
6. The Westminster and the National Provincial.

# 142

1. Trinitro-Toluene.
2. Penguin.
3. London.
4. Kennecott Corporation.
5. The tea-bag.
6. 7s. 9d. in the pound.

# 218

1. B & H Special filters.
2. £5,350 (and well into the surtax bracket).
3. KLM (established 1919 in Amsterdam).
4. Highgate Cemetery, London.
5. Pergamon Press.
6. The Bank of England.

## 67

1. Which advertising agency is responsible for Margaret Thatcher's public image?
2. Which firm bought up the Government's 76 per cent stake in Inmos in 1984?
3. 'The Schumann Plan' created which European body in 1951?
4. Who presents the TV programme *A Question of Economics*?
5. What first did Howard Aiken of the USA create in 1944?
6. What happened on Wall Street on 16 September 1920?

## 143

1. Which firm runs the History Guild Book Club?
2. What is BNOC?
3. Of the members of OPEC which has the smallest proven oil reserves?
4. Who introduced the concept of 'countervailing power'?
5. Henry Ford is often credited with saying 'History is bunk'; what did he really say?
6. Which merchant bank priced the British Telecom share issue?

## 219

1. During 1982 in which branch of the media (TV, press, cinema, radio) was most advertising money spent?
2. If you were run over by a truck on British roads what is the maximum weight that would bear down on you?
3. In what year did de Gaulle veto Britain's original application to join the EEC?
4. What did Karl Marx regard as the immediate cause of all business slumps?
5. In what year did the Mini first appear on British roads?
6. Which British bank was baled out in September 1984?

## 67

1. Saatchi and Saatchi.
2. Thorn-EMI.
3. The European Iron and Steel Community.
4. Peter Donaldson.
5. The digital computer.
6. An enormous explosion killing forty people and injuring hundreds.

## 143

1. W. H. Smith.
2. The British National Oil Corporation.
3. Gabon.
4. J. K. Galbraith.
5. 'History is more or less bunk' (interview in *Chicago Tribune*, 25 May 1926).
6. Kleinwort Benson.

## 219

1. Press (about 64 per cent of all advertising expenditure).
2. 38 tonnes (but only 11 on any one axle).
3. 1963.
4. A falling rate of profit on capital.
5. 1959.
6. Johnson Matthey Bankers.

## 68

1. When does a salesman make a 'cold call'?
2. In what year did Janet Reger go bankrupt?
3. Where can you stay in the 'Rhett Butler'?
4. Which Government Minister authorized DeLorean's DMC12 project?
5. What was the cost-saving innovation that made the Sinclair ZX81 much cheaper than the ZX80?
6. What, in banking parlance, is the 'back door'?

## 144

1. On which engine did Alcock and Brown depend in their Atlantic crossing?
2. What, during the First World War, was a 'leaving certificate'?
3. Where are casinos legal in the US?
4. What was Sir Robert Hall's post between 1947 and 1961?
5. Who heads Amstrad?
6. How much was a guinea?

## 220

1. What sort of data is alphanumeric?
2. What is the CAA?
3. What is the name of the nationalized American railroad company?
4. Who won the Nobel Prize for Economics in 1984?
5. How did Rupert Murdoch reportedly make a quick $50 million out of Warner Communications shares?
6. In what year did de Gaulle move the decimal point in the French franc?

# 68

1. When it's unsolicited.
2. 1983.
3. At an MGM 'Grand' (one of their casino hotels in Reno or Las Vegas).
4. Roy Mason (1978).
5. Eighteen seperate chips were replaced with a single chip.
6. When the Government Broker eases liquidity problems by buying bills from the discount houses.

# 144

1. The Rolls-Royce Eagle (powering a Vickers Vimy Bomber).
2. The written permission that a worker required before he or she could leave munitions employment.
3. Nevada, and Atlantic City, NJ.
4. Chief Economic Adviser (to the Government).
5. Alan Sugar.
6. Twenty-one shillings (£1.05).

# 220

1. Data which contains alphabetical and numerical information.
2. The Civil Aviation Authority.
3. Amtrak.
4. Professor Richard Stone.
5. He bought 7 per cent of the shares which the management, worried about a takeover, bought back at a higher price.
6. 1959.

## 69

1. What was the disastrous slogan for Strand cigarettes launched by Wills in 1960?
2. Which event gave fire insurance its original fillip in Britain?
3. What is the world's largest restaurant chain?
4. Which miners' leader coined the phrase 'Not a penny off the pay, not a minute on the day'?
5. Who wanted to merge Oxford and Reading?
6. What term is given to Stock Exchange trading on the basis of information not available to the public?

## 145

1. Where is the Robot Chef manufactured?
2. What does an actuary do?
3. In what town did the Philips group begin by manufacturing lightbulbs?
4. Which French Finance Minister implemented the austerity programme under de Gaulle in the early 1960s?
5. Who took Lord Northcliffe on at Liverpool Assizes in 1907 and won £91,000?
6. In relation to exchange rates what does PPP stand for?

## 221

1. What is 'penetration pricing'?
2. Which firm builds ships in Birkenhead?
3. What causes the 'Interstate Drink Prowl' in the US?
4. Which former economics journalist on *The Times* became Ambassador in the US?
5. Until 1977 Ian Macgregor ran which American mining company?
6. What was the most common complaint made by members of the public to the Building Societies' Association?

## 69

1. 'You're never alone with a Strand'.
2. The Fire of London (1666).
3. McDonald's (7,778 restaurants on 1 March 1984).
4. A. J. Cook (of the Miners' Federation of Great Britain).
5. Robert Maxwell (suggested a merger of two football clubs).
6. Insider trading.

## 145

1. Switzerland.
2. Calculates risks and premiums for the purposes of assurance.
3. Eindhoven (Holland).
4. Valéry Giscard d'Estaing.
5. William Lever (First Viscount Leverhume claiming libel damages against the *Daily Mail*).
6. Purchasing Power Parity (that exchange rate which would give each currency equal purchasing power).

## 221

1. The use of lower prices in order to obtain deeper market penetration.
2. Cammel-Laird.
3. Differences in minimum ages for purchases of alcohol between states has helped create a youth drink-driving problem.
4. Peter Jay.
5. AMAX.
6. The insistence by certain societies that borrowers take out insurance with specified companies.

## 70

1. What are Coors, Shlitz and Pabst?
2. Which English city was the home of the lace trade until the Second World War?
3. In September 1984 two nuclear power stations in Florida were forced to shut down by what marine creatures?
4. When did Geoffrey Howe announce his last Budget?
5. Which came first: the modern chain-driven bicycle or telegraphic communications between Europe and USA?
6. Which British bank was the first to make profits in excess of any industrial company?

## 146

1. What is the Midland Bank's advertising symbol?
2. In which year did France and the UK sign the agreement to build Concorde?
3. Who won the airship contract at the 1984 Olympics?
4. Which British Chancellor repealed the Usury Laws and when?
5. Which family attempted to corner the world silver market?
6. In what year was Minimum Lending Rate suspended by the Conservatives?

## 222

1. Which company spent the most money on advertising during 1982 in the UK?
2. Which retailing firm took over Curry's?
3. After what particular event did the post-war German 'Economic Miracle' allegedly begin?
4. What was the real name of 'Red Robbo'?
5. Who invented the hovercraft?
6. Where are the largest commodity futures markets?

# A

## 70

1. American beers.
2. Nottingham.
3. Jellyfish.
4. 1983.
5. The underwater cable (1866).
6. Barclays.

## 146

1. A griffin.
2. 1962.
3. Airship Industries (Britain).
4. William Gladstone in 1854.
5. The Hunts.
6. 1981.

## 222

1. Procter and Gamble (£45.8 million).
2. Dixon's.
3. After the currency reform of 20 June 1948 (production rose by something like 50 per cent in six months).
4. Derek Robinson (the Longbridge convenor sacked by BL).
5. Sir Christopher Cockerell.
6. Chicago.

# 71

1. What is produced by 'etching a silicon wafer with layers of different impurities'?
2. What is the largest life assurance company in the UK?
3. The European Recovery Programme is known by a more familiar name – what?
4. When was the TUC generally regarded as being founded?
5. What is the origin of the word 'robot'?
6. What explains the symbol for the dollar?

# 147

1. Who warned about 'marketing myopia'?
2. Which firm of solicitors were acting as advisers to more British quoted companies than any other by the end of 1983?
3. How high is the rate of income tax on Tristan da Cunha?
4. 'Getting the government off the backs of the people' was one of whose main election pledges?
5. How did Edward Jenner benefit mankind?
6. In what year was decimal currency introduced in Britain?

# 223

1. Which insurance company sponsors Test Match cricket in England?
2. The Post Office 'split' occurred in which year?
3. Currently heroin is most likely to originate from which country?
4. The 'pay pause' was whose creation?
5. Who, at a young age, survived the Nazi massacre of the Jews, and later became virtually an institution at GEC?
6. What name is commonly given to the rate at which CAP prices, agreed in EEC units of account, are converted into sterling?

# 71

1. The silicon chip.
2. Prudential Corporation PLC (amount assured £72,445,300,000 on 1 January 1984).
3. Marshall Aid.
4. 1868 (although no formal organization was then set up, a desire for annual conferences was expressed).
5. From the Czech *robota*, meaning labour or work.
6. It was originally a combination of U and S (US).

# 147

1. Theodore Levitt.
2. Slaughter and May.
3. 0 per cent.
4. Ronald Reagan.
5. He invented vaccination.
6. 1971.

# 223

1. Cornhill.
2. 1981 (it split into British Telecom and the rest).
3. Pakistan.
4. Selwyn Lloyd (incomes policy).
5. Arnold Weinstock.
6. The 'green' pound.

# 72

1. Where does 'Good Food Cost Less'?
2. Why was it common to find houses with blocked-up windows in the early nineteenth century?
3. Name five of Anthony Sampson's 'Seven Sisters' who carved up Middle Eastern oil in the twentieth century?
4. In the medical world who or what is WHO?
5. Who as head of Fire Auto and Marine Insurance left policy holders stranded?
6. Which big American bank recalls the 'Wild West'?

# 148

1. What does an account planner in an ad. agency do?
2. Which company showed the biggest percentage increase in its share value between 1974 and 1983?
3. In 1975 which country in Northern Europe had the lowest number of physicians per head of population and which the highest?
4. Which 'skinhead' is Secretary of Trade and Industry?
5. What was the playground of New York's '400'?
6. What do the initials IMF stand for?

# 224

1. How does Esso get its name?
2. How often has the British steel industry been nationalized?
3. Which country's annual inflation rate reached 1,000 per cent for the first time in 1984?
4. What was the name of Barbara Castle's White Paper on the reform of collective bargaining?
5. Which Kenyan brothers made a million, beginning by selling jeans from a stall on the Portobello Road?
6. Who is reckoned in opinion polls to be the second most powerful person in the US?

# 72

1. Sainsbury's.
2. An increasing rate of window tax.
3. Exxon (Esso), Shell, BP, Gulf, Texaco, Mobil, Standard Oil California (Chevron).
4. The World Health Organization.
5. Emil Savundra.
6. Wells Fargo.

# 148

1. The role is primarily concerned with researching consumers' reactions to advertisements.
2. Polly Peck (+ 26,857 per cent).
3. Great Britain (11 per 10,000) and W. Germany (19.2 per 10,000).
4. Norman Tebbit (*Private Eye's* 'Chingford Skinhead').
5. Newport, Rhode Island (the '400' were the leading society families in New York).
6. The International Monetary Fund.

# 224

1. It is made up from Eastern Seaboard Standard Oil.
2. Twice, in 1951 and 1967.
3. Israel's.
4. *In Place of Strife*.
5. The Pepe brothers.
6. Paul Volcker.

## 73

1. In what colours might you find asbestos 'killer dust'?
2. In what town do Rolls-Royce build aero engines?
3. How many countries are there in the 'Group of Ten'?
4. Which market research companies try to predict election results?
5. Which record producer is famous for his 'Wall of Sound'?
6. What is the 'payback period' of an investment?

## 149

1. What did the Babylonians use as mortar, the Byzantines as Greek fire and the Red Indians as war paint?
2. Which Liberal peer was ennobled for his services to the coal industry?
3. What do the initials CAP stand for?
4. Which founder of 'input-output' economics was made Nobel Laureate in 1973?
5. Who was chastised in *The Times* for touring (and making a profit) with General Tom Thumb?
6. What can cause a member of the Stock Exchange to be 'hammered'?

## 225

1. Describe the logo of Volkswagen.
2. What business are A. C. Nielson in?
3. In which industry is 70 per cent of the world's output of rubber consumed?
4. Which economist presented the TV programme *Whatever Happened to Britain*?
5. Which member of the Rothschilds became Baron and owner of the Lafitte vineyards?
6. When did the Stock Exchange decide to admit women members?

# 73

1. White, blue, brown.
2. Derby.
3. Ten.
4. NOP, Gallup, MORI, Audience Selection.
5. Phil Spector.
6. The period over which the net revenue from an investment pays for its original cost.

# 149

1. Oil.
2. Derek Ezra.
3. The Common Agricultural Policy.
4. Wassily Leontief.
5. Phineas T. Barnum.
6. Bankruptcy.

# 225

1. A circle containing a V sitting upon a W.
2. Market research (particularly retail audit research).
3. The automobile industry.
4. John Eatwell.
5. James.
6. 1972.

## 74

1. What is the end product of the Solvay Process?
2. In 1983 how many persons were there to each car in GB?
3. Who was more enthusiastic over the Concorde during its development – the French public or the British public?
4. Which body held conferences in Portsmouth in 1969, Brighton in 1972 and 1976 and Blackpool in 1983?
5. Which famous family included Eugene, Henry, Alexis and Francis in a big gunpowder business in 1899?
6. What is the unit of currency in both Syria and Jamaica?

## 150

1. What word means both a thick cotton twill and turgid or inflated language?
2. Which company won the RAF 'trainer' contract in 1985?
3. Where are the headquarters of the OECD?
4. Which rock band was sued by Harold Wilson because they featured him in promotion for their single?
5. Who styled the 'New Look' in 1947?
6. What does EMS stand for?

## 226

1. Which cigarette used the campaign 'More doctors smoke X than any other brand' in order to allay health fears?
2. What does BIM stand for?
3. What did neither Henry Ford II nor the British want in March 1948?
4. During what event were train services in London so slow that it was reported: 'We understand that luncheon cars are to be put on trains running between Westminster and Blackfriars'?
5. Who took over the Mothercare company in 1984?
6. Which country has the guilder as its currency?

# 74

1. Ammonia-soda.
2. 3.4.
3. The French (opinion survey conducted by BAC).
4. The TUC.
5. The du Ponts.
6. The pound.

# 150

1. Fustian (originally the cloth of Fostat, near Cairo).
2. Short Brothers (Belfast).
3. Paris.
4. The Move ('Flowers in the Rain').
5. Christian Dior.
6. The European Monetary System.

# 226

1. Camel.
2. British Institute of Management.
3. The Volkswagen factury at Wolfsburg.
4. The General Strike, 1926 (when trains were manned by volunteers).
5. Sir Terence Conran.
6. Holland.

## 75

1. How many football pitches could be laid out on the deck of a 300,000 ton oil tanker?
2. What is the 'Great North Road' now called?
3. Which manufacturer built the plane that dropped the bomb on Hiroshima?
4. President Reagan's notorious 'budget deficit' is the difference between which two totals?
5. Name one of the animals used as the first aerial passengers in the history of the world?
6. What emblem is on the reverse side of the 2p piece?

## 151

1. In an advertising agency what name is given to a sequence of sketches depicting a TV commercial?
2. On which London street would you find Le Gavroche?
3. Which of the leading industrial countries pays the smallest proportion of national income in tax?
4. Which Chancellor of the Exchequer went on a 'dash for growth' in 1964?
5. Which cartoonist gave his name to complicated, ingenious and fantastic devices of machinery?
6. What is the CLCB in the City?

## 227

1. What is the biggest selling brand of spirits in the US?
2. How did Lloyd's of London get its name?
3. Who is currently President Reagan's Treasury Secretary?
4. For how long did Karl Marx live in England?
5. Who took out British patent number 7777?
6. How can an accountant tell if a difference on a balance sheet has been caused by the transposition of two numbers?

# 75

1. Three.
2. A1.
3. Boeing (the B-29 Super fortress).
4. Government expenditure and taxation.
5. A sheep, a cock and a duck (in a wicker basket beneath a balloon released by the Montgolfiers in 1783).
6. The Prince of Wales feathers.

# 151

1. A storyboard.
2. Upper Brook Street, W1.
3. Japan (1983).
4. Reginald Maudling.
5. W. Heath Robinson.
6. The Committee of London Clearing Bankers.

# 227

1. Bacardi (7,673 thousand cases were sold in 1983).
2. From the coffee shop of the same name, where the business began.
3. James Baker.
4. Thirty-four years.
5. Marconi (on a radio tuning device).
6. The difference is exactly divisible by nine.

# 76

1. Where was the first smoke-written aerial ad.?
2. When do wages 'drift' in the British economy?
3. Which is the poorest economy in the Indian sub-continent?
4. Which economist, probably most famous for an educational report, died in 1984?
5. Who designed the Mini motor car?
6 Would speculators on Wall Street have had lunch when panic selling began on Black Thursday, 24 October 1929?

# 152

1. Which is 'the right one'?
2. In what century was the first copper coin in Britain officially issued?
3. Name the G-5 (Group of Five) countries?
4. Out of West Germany, USA, Japan and the UK, which has the highest percentage of the relevant age-group gaining higher education qualifications up to first degree?
5. Which corporation was founded by Charlie Chaplin, Mary Pickford and Douglas Fairbanks?
6. Who is the banker's 'Old Lady'?

# 228

1. What is a 'brand leader'?
2. In the 1870s what was the average annual pay of a textile operative? (Sam Courtauld earned £46,000.)
3. What is the US equivalent of the NUM?
4. Who fought a General Election campaign on the manifesto 'We can conquer unemployment'?
5. On whose decks were chairs first placed?
6. Which chartered accountants are known as Gutter Bros?

# 76

1. Above the Epsom Derby crowds in 1922.
2. When actual wages paid begin to diverge from formally agreed rates.
3. Bangladesh (1982 income per capita was $140).
4. Sir Lionel Robbins.
5. Sir Alex Issigoni.
6. No (in fact the main panic was over by noon. However for those not present, the ticker was running hours behind).

# 152

1. Martini.
2. Seventeenth (1672).
3. America, Japan, Britain, W. Germany, France.
4. Japan (37 per cent in 1979), US (32 per cent in 1981), West Germany (20 per cent in 1979) and UK (18 per cent in 1981).
5. United Artists.
6. The Bank of England.

# 228

1. The brand of product with the largest market share.
2. £15.
3. UMW (United Mine Workers).
4. Lloyd George (1929).
5. The P & O Line.
6. Coopers and Lybrand off Gutter Lane.